W9-COZ-413

ALLE ZEIT WACH
1842

Hans J. Eysenck

The Structure and Measurement of Intelligence

With Contributions by David W. Fulker

With 69 Figures

Springer-Verlag
Berlin Heidelberg New York 1979

Hans J. Eysenck, Ph. D., D. Sc.
David W. Fulker, Ph. D.
University of London, Institute of Psychiatry
De Crespigny Park, Denmark Hill, London, SE5 8AF

ISBN 3-540-09028-2 Springer-Verlag Berlin Heidelberg New York
ISBN 0-387-09028-2 Springer-Verlag New York Heidelberg Berlin

Library of Congress Cataloging in Publication Data. Eysenck, Hans Jürgen, 1916 – The structure and measurement of intelligence. Bibliography: p. Includes index. 1. Intellect. 2. Intelligence tests. 3. Nature and nurture. I. Fulker, David W., 1937 – joint author. II. Title. BF431.E97 153.9 78-10591

Typesetting and bookbinding: G. Appl, Wemding. Printing: aprinta, Wemding.
2126/3140-543210

To the Memory of
Sir Francis Galton
who first sailed upon these uncharted seas

Contents

Introduction

> It is generally and rightly considered a virtue in a teacher to observe accurately the differences in ability among his pupils, and to discover the direction in which the nature of each particularly inclines him. There is an incredible amount of variability in talent, and the forms of minds are no less varied than the forms of bodies
>
> Quintilian (70 A. D.)

There are many good books on Intelligence, such as *Cattell*'s (1971) monumental and original contribution, or *Matarazzo*'s (1972) careful and scholarly analysis, or *Butcher*'s (1968) excellent introduction. Other outstanding contributions are mentioned in the course of this volume. This suggests that an author must have a good reason for venturing to offer another tome where so much is already available to satisfy even the most discriminating customer. There is indeed a powerful reason why the time may be ripe for another book on intelligence. This reason is a very simple one: much has happened in recent years to alter our views on many issues which at one time looked like being closed. Hardly any of these advances have found a place in the books now available, and it seemed desirable to incorporate them in a new text which would be as up-to-date as it is possible to be considering the inevitable delays in writing and publishing a textbook. For example, this is the first book to appear since the so-called "scandal" of Sir Cyril Burt's alleged fraudulence burst upon the scene, and I have tried to rewrite the relevant chapters in the history of the intelligence testing movement without including Burt's now doubtful data. I have no doubt in my own mind that Burt was careless, and may have been fraudulent in his work, but carelessness is sufficient to eliminate the data from serious consideration (*Eysenck*, 1977)[1].

Burt's real or imaginary malfeasance is not actually of great moment scientifically; the genetic argument does not rest entirely or even mainly on his data, and as we shall see, omitting them completely makes no difference to the conclusions to be drawn from what is a very large and respectable body of evidence. Nevertheless, several writers (e. g. *Jensen*, 1974; *Kamin*, 1974; *Mcaskie* and *Clarke*, 1976) have gone over the whole material, or portions of it, with a very critical eye, and have unearthed a number of anomalies and faults which must be taken into account in any proper evaluation of this mass of empirical work. Clearly some of these critics (e. g. *Kamin*) have taken their criticism too far, and in turn committed serious errors of statistical calculation and genetic estimation, as *Fulker* (1975) for instance has pointed out, in a very thorough re-analysis of

1 Appendix A gives a short account of the facts of the Burt affair.

the data criticized by *Kamin* (1974). All these recent studies have been taken carefully into account in this book, and I have asked Dr. Fulker to join me in the authorship of those chapters which deal directly with his major area of expertise, i. e. the genetic analysis of intelligence (Chaps. 5, 6, and 7).

It is not only a reconsideration of older work that makes the present time so exciting; there is a certain amount of new work coming out which is on an altogether larger scale, as well as being technically superior, to that which was done in past decades. One may refer here to the well-planned and executed studies of Behrman, Taubman and others in the Department of Economics of the University of Philadelphia, dealing with the genetics of socio-economic status, income and schooling (*Taubman*, 1976), or to the work of *Jensen* (1972) on his theory of level 1 and level 2 of intelligence, and its implications for educational practices. Other examples are *Munsinger's* (1975) study of the resemblance of children to their adoptive and biological parents with respect to intelligence; *Bashi's* (1977) work on the effects of inbreeding on the intelligence of the offspring of Israeli Arab children; and the interesting discovery by *Sanderson* et al. (1975) of a marked relationship between intelligence and the shape of the jaw bone, suggesting certain genetic links (pleiotropy). As far as possible I have tried to introduce new work into this book, sometimes with recalculation of certain genetic and other parameters where the original calculations seemed to be lacking in one way or another. This is not necessarily a criticism of these previous analyses; one can look at data from different points of view, or with different aims in mind, and methods of analysis appropriate to one may not be appropriate to another. The construction of the new British Intelligence Scale (*Elliott* et al., 1976) is another important new development which must have an impact on the measurement of intelligence, seeing that here for the first time we find an attempt to use the Rasch model in the practical construction of a scale for measuring IQ.

Most important of all, however, has been a rather different line of development, namely the great improvement in the analysis of genetic data which has taken place in recent years, pioneered by *Mather* and *Jinks* (1971) of the Birmingham University Department of Genetics. For many years we have seen psychologists analyse twin data using a formula originally proposed in the twenties, and having little or no genetic meaning at all; the most it could do was to tell us whether identical (MZ) twins were significantly more alike than fraternal (DZ) twins or not. This is no doubt an important bit of knowledge, but it does not enable us to calculate the heritability of whatever trait or ability has been measured, and the easy assumption that heritabilities could be so calculated gave rise to much justified criticism. *Mather* and *Jinks*, like *Cattell* (1960) before them, started out on the basis of *Sir Ronald Fisher's* famous 1918 paper in which he applied the principles of Mendelian genetics to polygenic inheritance; they succeeded in working out methods by means of which we can test the applicability of certain genetic models to empirical sets of data. In this way we can look, not only at simple heritability, but also at assortative mating, dominance, within-family and between-family environmental influences, interaction and covariance of heredity and environment, and other important constituents of any worth-while genetic model of behaviour.

The first application of these new methods to psychological data (in particular data on intelligence and personality) was made by *Jinks* and *Fulker* (1970) in a paper which immediately reorientated the whole field, and made previous analyses rebarbative. Where previous analyses had vaguely made assumptions about important parameters of the genetic model, Junks and Fulker demonstrated the possibility of putting such assumptions to the test, and making estimates of these parameters which led in fact to the calculation of fiducial limits. This book is the first to base itself entirely on these new methods, and this marks the most important change from previous writings. The old methods are still being used, unfortunately, but there is no doubt that within the next few years a profound reorientation will have taken place towards the use of these newer and much more informative methods. As a consequence we will of course also have to change our research designs; the simple use of MZ and DZ twins is of limited value in this field, and psychologists will have to go to school again to learn more about the intricacies of up-to-date designs in genetical analysis.

On the theoretical side of intelligence measurement too there have been new developments. Guilford's "structure of the intellect" model has been discussed in most recent books on intelligence, but the critical re-analyses of his data, such as those of *Horn* and *Knapp* (1973) and *Undheim* and *Horn* (1977), have not yet been noted. There have been advances in the theory attempting to relate IQ to physiological factors assumed to be causally related to intellectual differences, such as the evoked potential (*Shucard* and *Horn*, 1973; *Perry* et al., 1976; *Eysenck*, 1973 a), which have not yet been assimilated in recent textbooks. Last but not least, attempts have been made to demonstrate that the IQ is not unitary, but, not unlike the atom, can be broken up into constituent parts (*Eysenck*, 1973 a). With these and many other issues which have only recently come to the fore we shall be very much concerned in this book.

It would not be reasonable to list all the new developments which have been taken into account in this book, but a few may be mentioned. *Sternberg* (1977) has gone back to Spearman's original conception of intelligence as being *both* a statistical concept and a psychological one, and has shown how Spearman's psychological analysis of intelligence could be developed into a powerful experimental paradigm. *Resnick* (1976) has assembled a group of psychologists to write on "The Nature of Intelligence", also attempting to put psychology back into the statistical picture. *Stenhouse* (1974) has attempted to look at intelligence from the point of view of evolution, as has *Jerison* (1973), and *Aleksander* (1977) and *Elcock* and *Michie* (1977) have looked at it from the point of view of modern computer science. *Merz* and *Stelzl* (1973) have criticized previous developmental theories of intelligence, and advanced their own; *Franzen* and *Merz* (1976) have shown how verbalization can improve IQ scores, in a most original series of studies. (See also *Merz*, 1969). There is literally no end to the emergence of new and interesting theories and experiments in this field, and while all have been evaluated, not all will be referred to in detail in this book; an attempt had to be made to keep its length within bounds!

The problem of race and intelligence has not been dealt with in this book, because of its complexity, except in passing; interested readers are referred to three outstanding recent books on the topic (*Baker*, 1974; *Hebert*, 1977;

Loehlin et al., 1975.) Three important books have also appeared which deal with environmental factors of various kinds: *Lloyd-Still* (1976) on malnutrition, and *Rutter* and *Madge* (1976) on social factors associated with disadvantage generally. These books contribute important overviews of large bodies of research; their conclusions and arguments have been taken into account in this book, in so far as they are relevant, but usually without specific citation. The third book, *Oliverio* (1977), deals with environmental factors against a genetic background.

One last reason for publishing this new book, and possibly the major one, remains to be mentioned. Modern philosophers of science have pointed out that established sciences have certain paradigms which are universally accepted by practitioners; empirical work is carried out in attempts to improve the paradigm, and to remove anomalies which occur in every scientific discipline (*Kuhn*, 1974). Sometimes these anomalies multiply at an alarming rate, and all efforts to accomodate them within the old paradigm can be seen to be futile and ad hoc; when this occurs there is a likelihood of a scientific revolution occurring, such as the establishment of Einstein's relativity theory in place of Newton's theory of universal gravitation. Psychology has been singled out for not possessing any such paradigms, and to many "hard" scientists this is the hall-mark of a pre-scientific discipline – aspiring to be a science, but not yet having the wherewithall to pay the admission price! In my view this is not a correct assessment of the situation; in several areas of psychology (though admittedly not in all), we already possess paradigms of considerable power, and the field of intelligence is perhaps one of the most impressive areas in which to demonstrate this fact (*Eysenck*, 1973 a.) What is also true, however, is that most presentations of the field fail to present the established paradigm as such; instead, presentation is muddled, uncertain, and constantly sidetracked by considerations irrelevant to the scientific theory, such as practical applications, ideological doubts, and ethical problems. Let us admit straight-away that there may be ideological consequences of scientific findings in this field; that ethical problems may arise from such findings which present us with difficult questions; and that practical applications of our data have often been made which have poor validity, and little scientific evidence to back them up. All this may be true, but it does not affect by one iota the answer to the cricial scientific question: Is there in fact enough information, experimental data, and theoretical agreement to construe the field in terms of a proper scientific paradigm?

In a more highly technical publication I have sought to answer this question, coming to an affirmative answer (*Eysenck*, 1973 a); the reader is referred to this book for a more sustained argument than can be given here. But in essence I have tried to structure this book in such a way that it presents in outline what I believe to be the paradigm which at the moment governs the field. Saying this does not imply that the paradigm could not be mistaken; we know that all scientific theories are likely to be found wanting in the long run, and to be replaced by better ones, nor does it imply that there are not many anomalies to be found; no scientific theory that was ever devised failed to generate such anomalies, and even Newton's hypothesis, which has for centuries been the fundament on which physics and astronomy were based, was full of anomalous findings from the very beginning. And there is certainly no implication that criticisms of the paradigm are not welcome, or are not to be taken seriously. Readers not grown up in the scientific tradition may not realize that the critic is the theoretician's best friend; only by frank and appropriate criticism can one find out the major weakness of one's theories, and try to shore them up, if possible – or to replace them by better theories! Consequently all serious criticisms of the paradigm have been most carefully considered, and if I have come to the conclusion that they are not sufficient to destroy the paradigm, and if I further state that there is no alternative theory which at the moment can take the place of the paradigm here presented, then I should be understood to be speaking strictly of the here-and-now; tomorrow might see revolutionary new advances in theory or experiment which could overthrow the paradigm, and replace it with a new one – incorporating all that was true and worthwhile in the old, but adding vital new components, or rearranging the old ones beyond recognition.

As it happens, however, most of the criticisms to be found in the literature are, not of the paradigm, but of some man of straw erected in its stead, for the express purpose of being shot at and destroyed with ease. It is for this reason that it seemed important to state the case for the paradigm in its strongest form –though of course not without mention of all its many defects. Scientists have to live with the fact that their most cherished theories are far from immortal, and may not even be very longevitous! They should be willing to give up their theories when these are clearly falling down on the job of explaining, unifying and predicting facts. In the field of intelligence testing, the paradigm is far from suffering any of these unseemly fates; it is quite unusually capable of unifying all the known facts, and of predicting new ones. There is no rival on the horizon who could do even one-tenth as well. Under these circumstances, it may be wondered at why the paradigm is not recognized for what it is, and universally celebrated by psychologists everywhere.

Explanations of this odd fact must be extremely speculative, but it is my own opinion that the basic reason is the same that prevented recognition of other paradigms, such as Copernicus' heliocentric model of the stellar system, or Darwin's theory of evolution. There is a strong disinclination to believe what we do not want to believe, however strong the evidence may be. Even now some American states have introduced legislation to make the teaching of the biblical story of genesis a requirement in schools, to be set beside the teaching of biological evolution! To many people, having succumbed to the siren songs of Rousseau and other egalitarians, the very mention of differences in intelligence is anathema, and the offence is made infinitely more heinous by adding that in part these differences are genetically determined (*Eysenck*, 1973b). Dictators, too, have been annoyed by the fact that the paradigm did not concur with their weird theories; thus Stalin banned IQ testing in the USSR for being bourgeois, and Hitler in Germany for being Jewish! Clearly, the theory is judged not on the basis of the empirical evidence, but because the outcome of all this scientific work is liked or disliked, respectively. This is not a good basis to judge a scientific theory on – as was demonstrated to perfection when Lysenko's theories were enthusiastically welcomed and supported by Stalin, for ideological reason, but where in the outcome the adoption of these theories in practice produced famine, and set back Soviet agriculture some twenty years (*Medvedev*, 1969). Medvedev's book should be read by everyone who feels tempted to substitute ideological conviction for scientific, unimpassioned, factual appraisal of the theories discussed in this book; nothing can show more clearly the terrible danger to society of substituting ideological commitments for rational criticism.

However that may be, the main purpose of this book has been to present what to the author appears to be the paradigm towards which the research of the past 80 years converges. For this reason I have not gone into too much detail as far as interesting but somewhat irrelevant issues are concerned. In particular, I have not dealt much with the practical problem of the application of IQ testing in industry, education, military selection, and elsewhere; I believe that this field has been well covered by many other authors, and I also believe that little of what has been done here is of any great scientific interest. The testing of intelligence, as far as practical applications are concerned, was so successful from the beginning that far more time, energy and money was spent on developing this side than on the purely scientific study of the concept of intelligence. I think this is regrettable, but there is little that can be done about it now. I also believe that practical applications could be made much more successfully if practitioners heeded more carefully the results of scientific experiments. It is unlikely that I shall be able to convince these practitioners, particularly as they are unlikely to read this book in the first place; hence I shall not go into these points any further.

The book has a somewhat unorthodox structure, beginning as it does with a consideration of certain general principles of measurement. It is my contention that the scales which have been developed for the measurement of intelligence are in principle exactly analogous to the scales developed in the physical sciences for the measurement of such qualities as heat; in order to make this point more clearly apparent for non-physicists I have drawn the parallel in some detail. Many of those who criticize the view that psychology is (or can be) a science like physics, and that it should take its ways of working and its methods of investigation from the better established sciences, do so on uncertain grounds; they often do not know precisely how the physical sciences in fact proceed, and how close are the parallels between psychology and physics. It seemed opportune to make the analogy a little clearer; indeed, I believe that it is far more than an analogy, more an identity.

This is a book intended for beginners, although I hope that it may also be read by more advanced students. I have tried to make what are in fact complex and difficult ideas understandable, although inevitable this means that some degree of rigour is sacrified in the presentation. This is particularly so when we are dealing with statistical and mathematical models and methods of analysis. These can neither be omitted, as without them the book would be like a performance of Hamlet without the Prince of Denmark, nor can they be properly presented to an audience whose statistical background must be assumed to be limited. I have tried to introduce these methods by appeal to their logical bases, only introducing an absolute minimum of statistical argument to make the general meaning of these methods clearer. I believe that the major importance of these methods for the psychologist lies in their logical ordering of concepts and data; the detailed algorithms are of course important for the specialist, but not every psychologist aims to be a psychometrist, and for him it is more important to understand the underlying logic of the approach then to battle with the mysteries of matrix algebra. An understanding of the purpose and meaning of factor analysis, for instance, is essential to an understanding of modern concepts of intelligence, but the technical details may be taken as read from the point of view of the beginner[2].

The study of intelligence is not the only field of psychology which presents us with at least the beginnings of a proper scientific paradigm; there are others. In my book on The Measurement of Personality (*Eysenck*, 1976) I have argued the case for personality as such an area of study. Here too a paradigm exists, although here too it sometimes seems to be buried under a lot of debris which certainly does not deserve the name of "science". I believe that quite generally psychology would progress more quickly if it adopted the ways of thinking of the older, better established sciences, and did not behave like an unruly adolescent who is out to shock his elders and betters by displays of ungovernable temper directed at the establishment. The structure of scientific theories follows certain rules, as *Suppe's* (1974) book of the same name indicates, and philosophers of science, if not entirely agreed on what these rules are, do nevertheless share enough common ground to feel that psychologists would be well advised to take their view into account. It is in the hope that they may do so in future more than they have perhaps done in the past that I dedicate this book to the man who more than any other was responsible for setting under weigh the flood of investigations, theories, and experiments which form the body of this book – Sir Francis Galton.

---

2 Appendix B sets out the essential equations for the more sophisticated student.

Intelligence: The Development of a Concept

A first-rate theory predicts; a second-rate theory forbids; and a third-rate theory explains after the event

A. I. Kitagorodskii

It has been well said that psychology has a long past, but a short history. People have puzzled over psychological problems for thousands of years, ever since the dawn of recorded history, yet the development of a science of psychology is scarcely a hundred years old. Plato and Arisotle already discussed the notion of "intelligence", but it is only in this century that attempts have been made successfully to measure this important variable. Many misunderstandings have attended this venture, and it will be one of the functions of this book to clarify the points on which these misunderstandings have arisen. However, before doing so it may be useful to trace quite quickly, and without too much detail, the early development of the concept with which this book is essentially concerned. Like most scientific concept, this one arose out of everyday observation. The concept of temperature arose from the different feeling caused in human beings by fire and sunlight, on the one hand, and ice and snow, on the other; in this way were the notions of "cold" and "hot" born, and became the subject matter of science. Similarly, the concept of intelligence arose from observations of people trying to solve problems, to learn difficult and demanding things like mathematics, languages, and history; some seemed to find no difficulty in all this, and succeeded brilliantly, while others were very slow, and often failed altogether. Some countries, like ancient China, used civil service examinations based on such acquired learning to select its governing elite; these examinations were probably early ancestors of our modern scholastic selection techniques.

Plato clearly distinguished between the three major aspects of the mind or soul, which he called intellect, emotion, and will; in a celebrated passage in the *Phaedrus* he gives a picturesque analogy in which he compares the intellect with a charioteer who holds the reins, while emotion and will are compared to the horses that draw the chariot. The former guides and directs, while the latter supply the motive power. Aristotle simplified this three-fold classification; he contrasts the cognitive or intellectual capacities with the "orectic" ones, grouping together emotion and will. Cicero made a lasting contribution by translating the Platonic and Aristotelian concept of cognitive or intellectual ability into *"intelligentia";* thus was born the concept of intelligence.

Other notions which play an important part in our modern discussions were equally familiar to the Greeks. Thus Plato draws a clear distinction between *nature* and *nurture;* he clearly favours the genetic causes in accounting for individual differences in intellect and personality, as is shown in the famous fable of the different metals – perhaps the first clear-cut recognition in print of the importance of individual differences in history! As Plato puts it, "The God who created you has put different metals into your composition – gold into those who are fit to be rulers, silver into those who are to act as their executives, and a mixture of iron and brass into those whose task it will be to cultivate the soil or manufacture goods." He also recognized the fact of genetic regression (the tendency of very intelligent and very dull parents to have children who regress to the mean, i. e. who are less bright, or less dull, than their parents), as when he says: "Yet occasionally a golden parent may beget a silver child, or a silver parent a child of gold; indeed, any kind of parent may at times give birth to any kind of child." And he considered it the most important task of the Republic to allocate tasks and duties according to the innate abilities of the person concerned: "The rulers have therefore received this paramount command from the Gods – that first and foremost they shall scrutinize each child to see what metal has gone to his making, and then allocate or promote him accordingly." The penalty for failure is severe, "for an oracle has predicted that our state will be doomed to disaster as soon as its guardianship falls into the hands of men of baser metal." Modern meritocratic society has come close to fulfilling at least some of Plato's dreams, although of course it would be unwise to consider intelligence by itself the equivalent of his differentiation of the men of gold, or silver, and of iron or brass.

Aristotle made another lasting contribution when he contrasted the actual *observed* activity or behaviour with some hypothetical *underlying* capacity on which it depended; in this way we arrive at the notion of an *ability*. Intelligence is an ability which may or may not be shown in practice, and which has to be deduced from observed behaviour, using certain scientific rules of experimental procedure. How this can be done we shall see in later chapters; here let us merely note the importance of such latent structure concepts as *abilities* (in connection with cognitive task), *traits* (in connection with personality), or *attitudes* (in connection with social views and opinions).

Philosophers throughout the ages were more interested in intellectual matters than in orectic ones, and it is no surprise that in modern times it was a philosopher, Herbert Spencer, who put forward the theory of intelligence which is still widely held. All cognition, he held, involves both an analytic or discriminative and a synthetic or integrative process; its essential function is to enable the organism to adjust itself more effectively to a complex and ever-changing environment. During the evolution of the animal kingdom, and during the growth of the individual child, the fundamental capacity of cognition "progressively differentiates into a hierarchy of more specialized abilities"; we shall encounter these specialized abilities (verbal, numerical, perceptual, etc.) again later on. Here let us merely note that it was Spencer who revived the term "intelligence" to designate the basic characteristic of all cognitive manifestation and differentiation. By his appeal to evolution, and his insistence on observational study of animal intelligence, Spencer added biological factors to the observational generalizations of the ancient Greeks.

A third line of approach was that of the physiologists, where the clinical work of Hughlings Jackson, the experimental investigations of Sherrington, and the microscopic studies of the brain carried out by Campbell, Brodman and others did much to confirm Spencer's theory of a "hierarchy of neural functions", with a basic type of activity developing by fairly definite stages into higher and more specialized forms. Thus in the adult human brain marked differences in the architecture of different areas and of different cell-layers are perceptible under the microscope, specializations which appear and develop progressively during the early months of infant life. The brain, so it was found, always acts as a whole; its activity, as Sherrington pointed out, is "patterned, not indifferently diffuse"; the patterning itself always "involves and implies integration." Lashley contributed, from his massive research activity, the concept of "mass action" of the brain, a mass action theoretically identified with intelligence by several writers.

It is on the basis of such antecedents in observation, biology and physiology that the early psychologists proceded to work out theories of intelligence, and attempts at measurement. They started with a fairly clear-cut, well worked out theory which saw intelligence as *innate, all-round cognitive ability,* based on the anatomical structure and physiological functioning of the cortex; an ability, moreover, which had important social consequences. In addition to this general ability the theory envisaged additional special verbal, numerical, perceptual and other abilities, differentiated from general mental ability through phylogenetic and ontogenetic development. Such a theory requires empirical support, of course; it cannot be assumed that the simple statement of a theory proves the theory to be correct. It may be false, in part or whole; it is also possible that there may be alternative theories which fit the facts better. It is with such issues as these that we shall be concerned in this book.

A few words may be said here about the nature of concepts. We must distinguish clearly between things and concepts. The table I am writing on, the chair I sit on, the room I am working in – these are all "things" which have existence in a sense that concepts like intelligence, gravitation, or temperature have not. Philosophers are likely to dispute even the existence of "things", or at least argue about the meaning of the term, "exist"; they are not likely to dispute that things and concepts are different in a very profound way. Plato of course regarded concepts ("ideas") as really existing, and things as pale copies only of the perfect ideas laid up in heaven; few modern philosophers would follow him in this. The distinction is important because it tells us immediately that there are questions which we cannot ask of concepts which we can quite meaningfully ask of things. We can ask: "Is this a desk?", or "Is there a desk in this room?", and expect a meaningful and truthful answer. All we need is a definition of the term, "desk"; given that we can answer factual questions about desks. But how can we define a concept? In the case of the desk we can appeal to sensible properties of a real object; it has a surface, four legs, drawers. But a concept has no such sensible properties; it is an abstraction! Concepts are invented, not discovered; this is true not only of intelligence, but of all scientific concepts. How then can we define a concept, and how can we answer such questions as: "How do you know that an IQ test really measures intelligence?".

The brief answer, upon which we shall elaborate later on, is that we cannot answer such a question because it is meaningless. It assumes that intelligence is a thing; if it were we could compare our IQ measurement with the real thing, and say whether it was or was not identical with it. There is no such thing as "intelligence" somewhere out there; we have invented the term to classify and co-ordinate a large number of facts, and the concept has no existence outside this large array of facts. We can therefore define our concept in terms of all the facts known about it; this is what science usually does. Or we can use what is called an "operational definition", i. e. we can define the concept in terms of the methods used to measure it, in this case IQ tests. This may seem arbitrary and circular, but it is what is often done in science; the notion of operational definition was first put forward by a physicist (*Bridgman,* 1927). Actually the two methods of defining concepts suggested here come to much the same thing; the operational definition is based on the most representative of all the various facts known about a particular topic or subject, and thus neatly summarizes all the known facts. The selection of a mercury thermometer to measure temperature is the more or less accidental choice from thousands of substances which expand with heat, and contract with cold, any of which could have been chosen. If we define temperature as that which is measured by this thermometer, then we simultaneously identify temperature with thousands of other, similar measurements which could have been made, as well as with a large number of other facts. (Actually different substances have different properties which make them more or less useful for the measurement of temperature; we shall come back to this point.) Similarly, a good IQ test summarizes many different facts about intelligence, and to define intelligence as that which IQ tests measure is not as nonsensical as it may appear at first sight – particularly when we remember that the adjective "good" in connection with an IQ test refers back to a large body of theory and experiment which alone enables us to say which are good and which are bad IQ tests (*Eysenck,* 1973.)

It is often disputed whether we can ever hope to measure something as elusive as intelligence. This is not a reasonable objection; all concepts are elusive and difficult to pin down. Mass, gravitation, temperature are no exceptions. Let us consider gravitation. We have been taught, and hence believe, that when a ball falls to the earth it is attracted by a physical force which pulls it down; if we are very sophisticated we might say that there is a mutual force of attraction between the ball and the earth which is proportional to their masses, and inversely proportional to the square of their distance apart. This force of attraction seems to us so tangible that we tend to reify it, i. e. regard it as a "thing" which exists in the same way as the ball and the earth. But this view is clearly mistaken.

Newton himself was of course well aware of the difficulties in which the notion of such a force, acting as a distance, involved him, and Leibnitz, in his famous letter to Clarke, gave explicit voice to the criticisms which later on Einstein would use as his stepping stones to an alternative theory. As is well known, Newton's theory in fact was found to be in error; it made wrong predictions about such observable events as the precession of the perihelion of the planet Mercury, and it failed to predict other events, such as the bending of light rays coming from distant stars, when they passed the sun. Einstein's theory explained the former, and predicted the latter, but there is no such attractive force as Newton postulated in his theory. Gravity in relativity theory is treated as a warping of space-time, rather as indicated in Fig. 1.1. This type of theory eliminates Newtonian "gravitation" from our armoury of concepts, although of course his mathematical equations still mirror the actual events (falling of apples; motion of planets) as well as ever. We now know that they are only valid in certain special cases, i. e. when the movements involved are rather slow as compared with the speed of light; they represent a special case of a wider, more complex law.

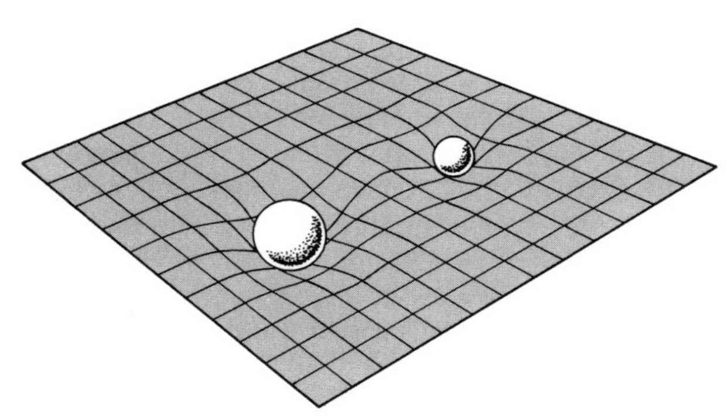

Fig. 1.1. Einstein's theory of attraction between objects in terms of a warping of spacetime

Can we accept Einstein's concepts as more "real" than Newton's? Here again the answer must be no. There is a third view, based on quantum theory; this would treat the interaction of bodies as analogous to the other fundamental forces in nature – the strong nuclear, the weak nuclear, and the electromagnetic force. The origin of these forces is now believed to be related to the exchange of elementary particles; thus a negatively charged electron would repel another electron by exchanging the fundamental quantum of electromagnetism, viz. the photon (as in Fig. 1.2). To account for interactions involving the weak nuclear force, physicists have invented the intermediate W-boson. In a similar way, they try to account for gravity in terms of an elementary (but possibly imaginary) particle, the graviton (Fig. 1.2). If you were to ask a physicist whether any of these concepts possessed real "existence", or if you asked him to give a definition of gravity, other than by simply describing it in terms of some of the elementary facts which caused physicists to invent these theories in the first place, you would get a very dusty answer indeed. The text-book would be likely to fob you off with a definition in terms of a simple measurement process, i. e. it might say that g, the force of gravity, can be found from the measurement of the period T, of a simple pendulum of length *l*; the formula is of course:

$$g = 4 \frac{2}{\pi} x \frac{l}{T} 2$$

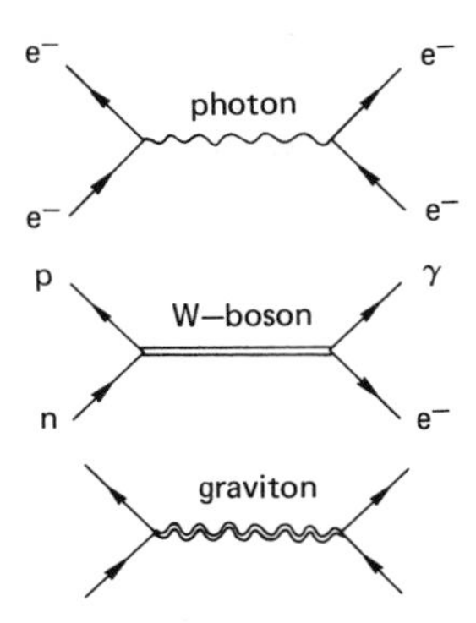

Fig. 1.2. Explanation of the force between objects in terms of particle exchance. Photon exchanges produce the repulsion between electrons; the W-boson probably produces the weak force. Gravity may be produced by "graviton" exchange

We thus see that when we ask for a definition of gravity, we get one of three different answers. (1) We may simply be referred to the actual phenomena which the concept exists to deal with, explain, and predict, i. e. the falling of bodies. (2) We may get a theoretical explanation in terms of concepts like gravitation (Newton), graviton (quantum physicists), or warped space-time lines of force (Einstein). (3) We may be given a formula which tells us how to measure the force involved, i. e. we are told that the concept can be defined in terms of its measurement. When we use this last form of definition, we find that the value of g is in fact different from one place on the earth to another; it is 978.816 in Calcutta and 981.274 in Potsdam! It is easy to see how much ridicule a psychologist would excite were he to say that he could only define "intelligence" by (1) pointing to the actual things that people did to manifest their intelligence, e. g. solve problems, or (2) offer one of several entirely theoretical derivations of the concept, or (3) define the concept in terms of what intelligence tests measure – particularly if he had to admit that scores might differ from one test to another!

But, it might be objected, surely scales of measurement in physics have obvious advantages, such as equal steps and a firm zero point; psychological scales, like those used for the measurement of intelligence, lack these advantages. Also different methods of measuring physical entities, such as temperature, agree, whereas different measures of intelligence, such as different IQ tests, do not. These objections are not in fact justified when examined closely. There are, for instance, several different methods of measuring temperature; there is the mercury-in-glass thermometer, depending on the change in volume of the mercury with increase in heat; the constant-volume gas thermometer, depending on the reactance of the welded junction of two fine wires; resistance thermometers, depending on the relation between resistance and temperature; thermocouples, depending on the setting up of currents by a pair of metals with their junctions at different temperatures; etc. *Nelkon* and *Parker* (1968), in their Advanced Level Physics, point out that temperature scales differ from one another, "that no one of them is any more 'true' than any other, and that our choice of which to adopt is arbitrary, though it may be decided by convenience." (P. 186.) Thus when a mercury-in-glass thermometer reads 300° C, a platinum-resistance thermometer in the same place and at the same time will read 291° C! There is no meaning attached to the question of which of these two values is "correct", and it is clear that the notion that a temperature scale has "equal steps" is a myth.

It is true that the temperature scale has an absolute zero, at −273° C. This value is reached by extrapolation, as shown in Fig. 1.3. According to Charles's Law, if we plot the volume V of a given mass of any gas at constant pressure against its temperature θ, we shall get a straight line graph A as shown in Fig. 1.3. If we produce this line backwards, it will meet the temperature axis at −273° C.; this temperature is called the *absolute zero*. In practice, of course, if a gas is cooled, it liquefies before it reaches this temperature, and Charles's Law no longer holds; we are thus dependent on extrapolation. But this is precisely how we determine the absolute zero on the intelligence scale, as *Thurstone* (1928) has shown. We find that the variance of the mental age measurement increases each year (starting at an age when the child is old enough to be tested); we can extrapolate the regression line backwards, and find that zero is reached a couple of months before birth. This is quite a meaningful result.

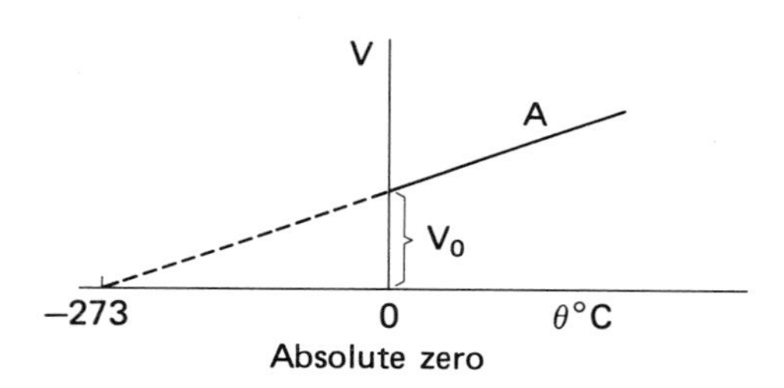

Fig. 1.3. Determination of absolute zero of temperature by extrapolation

Even within a given method of measurement, differences in result arise. To take but one example in the field of liquid-in-glass thermometers, clearly water would not be a good liquid to use because it contracts from the ice point (0° C.) to the temperature of maximum density (4° C), thus giving an illusory decline in temperature when actually the temperature is increasing! In actual fact the liquids most widely used (mercury and alcohol) were chosen in part because they fit in best with the kinetic theory of heat, which predicts that the final temperature reading of a fluid obtained by mixing two similar fluids of masses m_1 and m_2 at the initial temperatures t_1 and t_2 should be:

$$t_f = \frac{m_1 t_1 + m_2 t_2}{m_1 + m_2}$$

The linseed oil thermometer was discarded because measurements made with the instrument did not tally with the predictions made by the kinetic theory;

mercury and alcohol thermometers do tally. Thus the choice of a measuring instrument is in part based on its agreement with theory; the same is true of psychological measurement.

It is sometimes pointed out that intelligence tests are restricted to certain populations; thus they may contain words or symbols unknown to a population other than the one for which the test was constructed. So with thermometers; they too are restricted in their usefulness to certain ranges of temperature. Mercury freezes at −39° C and boils, under atmospheric pressure, at 357° C, although it can be made to serve up to about 550° C by filling the space above the liquid with nitrogen, which is compressed as the mercury expands, and raises its boiling point. Alcohol thermometers can be used at lower temperatures; ethyl alcohol boils at 78° C and freezes at −115° C; it is preferred for carrying out measurements in polar regions. High temperatures are usually measured by observing the radiation from the hot body, and the name *pyrometry* is given to this measurement. Radiation pyrometers are most widely used; they can be either total radiation pyrometers or optical pyrometers. In either case they encompass a range quite different to that covered by other instruments. Thus here too there is an obvious resemblance between measurement in physics and measurement in psychology; we cannot criticize the latter without criticizing the former.

A last point on which we find considerable similarity between the two sciences is in relation to the kind of theory preferred. Thus there are two theories of heat: the thermodynamic and the kinetic. Thermodynamics deals with unimaginable concepts of a purely quantitative kind: temperature, measured on a thermometer; pressure, measured as the force exerted per unit area; and volume, measured by the size of the container. *Nothing is said in the laws of thermodynamics about the nature of heat.* Bernouilli, in his famous treatise on hydraulics, postulated that all "elastic fluids", such as air, consist of small particles which are in constant irregular motion, and which constantly collide with each other and with the walls of the container. This was the foundation stone of the kinetic theory of heat, which results in a picture of events which is eminently visualizable, and which gives to many people a feeling of greater "understanding", of better and more thorough "explanation", than do the laws of thermodynamics. Nevertheless, many phenomena are quite intractable to kinetic interpretations even today, which yield easily to a thermodynamic solution. Similarly we have the psychometric and the experimental-theoretical approaches in intelligence testing, with the former dealing with unimaginable concepts of a purely quantitative kind, such as intelligence, problem difficulty, factors and vectors, n-dimensional space, etc., and the latter with numbers of neurons, synaptic connections, RNA templates, etc., all of them susceptible to empirical study and direct observation (at least in principle.) It would be idle to ask which approach was "better"; both are important, and both must be pursued if we are ever to gain any real insight into the nature of intelligence.

It may seem unusual to begin a book on intelligence with lengthy references to measurement in the physical sciences. The reason for this is a very simple one. It is often said by critics that attempts to measure intelligence are doomed to failure, and even slightly absurd; that science does not deal with intangibles, like mental qualities; and that the intelligence quotient and other psychometric devices used in the endeavour lack the qualities of physical measuring scales. Such criticisms are unfounded, and are likely to be made only be critics lacking in knowledge of what actually goes on in the hard sciences. As we have seen, concepts are equally intangible, whether they relate to intelligence or to gravitation, to personality or to temperature. Defects in the scales used by psychologists exist equally in the scales used by physicists, as in the measurement of temperature. Different types of theory abound in the hard sciences just as much as in psychology, and there is a certain amount of arbitrariness in the selection of measuring devices in the one type of science as in the other. If the measurement of temperature is scientific (and who would doubt that it is?), then so is that of intelligence. This is an important point to make right from the outset.

Why have psychologists so often shown themselves overly self-critical in this respect, ceding point after point in the controversy about the scientific status of intelligence testing when in reality there was no need to? There are two major reasons for this. In the first place, psychology is a young science; psychologists often suffer from feelings of inferiority, and attempt to gain the approval of practitioners in the hard sciences by trying to follow what they conceive to be their example. In doing so they often fall prey to the illusion that physics and chemistry are proceding at a far higher level of accuracy and deductive rigour than is actually the case; elementary textbooks on the history and philosophy of science often increase that erroneous impression. As a consequence of such slavish imitation of what they consider to be the methods of science, these psychologists only too willingly play down the very real achievements of their own science, on the grounds that they fall short of a perfection that is quite alien to science, particularly at an early stage of development.

The second reason is simply that many psychologists, and many educationalists, social workers, psychiatrists and other professionally interested in the work of psychologists, have preconceived notions about what they would like human nature to be like; the results of intelligence testing often contradict these preconceived notions, and as a consequence such people experience a strong temptation to deny the value or the correctness of the results of much psychological research. Stalin, as already noted, rejected and banned intelligence testing as being "bourgeois", and Hitler did the same because it was "Jewish". Ideological motives play a strong part in many of the arguments aroused by the empirical results of intelligence testing, and the temptation is strong to condemn the whole thing as "unscientific" when one does not like the results actually reported! The easiest way of doing this, of course, is to set impossibly high standards for theory-making, measurement, and experimentation; in that way one gains the reputation of being highly critical and rigorous (which is always considered an advantage in a scientist), and of being able to dismiss experimental results not in line with one's preconceived ideas. It is of course not the purpose of this book to persuade readers that they should not aim at the highest standards of rigour in experimental work, or in theorizing, or that they should rest content with shoddy and slipshod work. It is easy to throw out the baby with the bathwater; no science would ever have arisen and become useful in human life if exaggerated standards had been used to stifle discovery and development. The correct stance to take is one which combines a critical appraisal of the available evidence with a proper understanding of the way science works and progresses. It is with the purpose of giving readers a chance to see what standards are adopted in some of the hard sciences that I have taken this slightly roundabout excursion; we shall return once or twice more to comparisons of intelligence testing with the measurement of temperature.

We must now turn to a discussion of what is perhaps the central problem in the development of the concept of intelligence as a scientific theory: the distinction between mental ability and knowledge. Aristotle, as already mentioned, distinguished between observable performance and underlying ability; clearly we can only measure directly the former, and infer the latter from such observations. But is there a reliable distinction between knowledge and intelligence? As *Thorndike* et al. (1928) pointed out, "all scientific measurements of intelligence that we have at present are measures of some product produced by the person or animal in question, or of the way in which some product is produced. A is rated as more intelligent than B because he produces a better product, essay written, answer found, choice made, completion supplied or the like, or produces an equally good product in a better way, more quickly, or by inference rather than by rote memory, or by more ingenious use of the material at hand." Leaving aside for the moment the nature of these tasks, let us note that Thorndike also specifies two major dimensions of intellect, which he calls the *width* and *altitude* of intellect. The former refers to the *number* of tasks of a given difficulty level the person can solve correctly, while the latter refers to the highest level of *difficulty* at which the person can still succeed in solving problems. These two concepts are of course not unrelated; the person who can solve the more difficult problems can probably also solve more of the easier problems. However, as we shall see, the distinction is still an important one, and the two concepts are by no means identical.

Note also the important concept of difficulty level, as applied to the tasks which constitute our measure of intelligence; we may objectively define this by noting the number or percentage of the total population which succeeds in solving the problem, or some mathematical function of this percentage. A problem which can be solved by 95% of the population is easier than one which can be solved by only 55%, and this in turn is easier than one which can be solved by only 15%. Thorndike has drawn several figures to indicate the possible relationship between altitude and area of intellect; these are produced in Fig. 1.4. What is to be noted is that within limits area may be used as a measure of altitude, and vice versa; the relation is not perfect, but it is close enough for certain purposes. Better still of course would be the independent measurement of both variables; this would enable us to demonstrate the precise shape of the resulting figure, here only guessed at (although on the basis of very large-scale experimental work) by Thorndike.

Problems suitable for measurement in the cognitive field are of two sorts, although it must immediately be said that few problems can be assigned with complete accuracy to only one or the other of these categories. In the first place we have problems which call primarily upon aquired knowledge; these may be

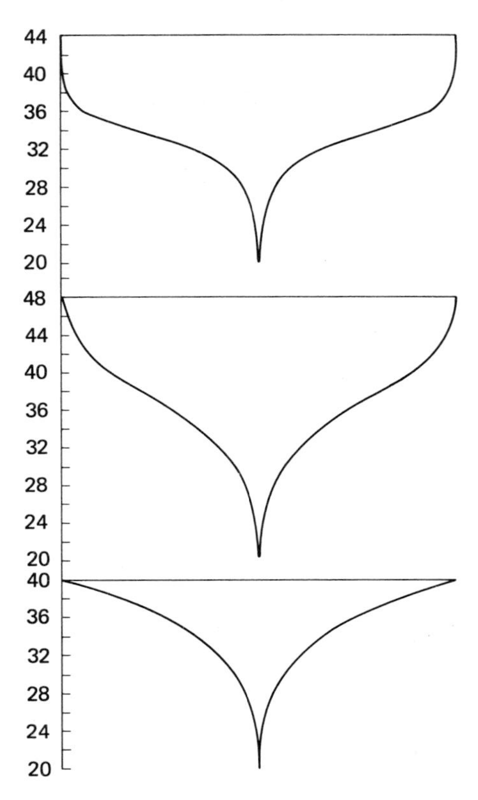

Fig. 1.4. Samples of possible patterns of the increase in the number of different intellectual tasks with increase in intellectual difficulty. Adapted from *Thorndike* et al. (1928)

termed culture-bound problems or tests. Below are given some such problems; in form they resemble orthodox IQ tests, but whether they measure intelligence, or only acquired knowledge, cannot be stated a priori, but depends on empirical fact; the answer may depend on many factors, such as the particular population studied, the age of the people concerned, the educational system of the country in which the testing takes place, and many more.

Culture-bound-Test

1. Odysseus is to Penelope as Menelaus is to:
   Circe – Helen – Nausicaa – Artemis – Eos

2. The Emperor Concerto was written by:
   Beethoven – Mozart – Bach – Brahms – Mahler

3. Charlemagne was crowned in:
600 A. D. – 800 A. D. – 1000 A. D. – 1200 A. D. – 1400 A. D

4. The Mona Lisa was painted by:
Raphael – da Vinci – Michelangelo – Titian – Hals

5. A sari is:
a religious teacher – a Hindu garment – spice – small boat – pageant

6. Paradise Lost was written by:
Sheridan – Shakespeare – Milton – Chaucer – Spencer

7. Carmen is to Bohème as Bizet is to:
Verdi – Puccini – Massenet – Wagner – Strauß

8. Jove is to Zeus as Mars is to:
Ares – Apollo – Hephaestus – Hermes – Poseidon

Note that the answers to most of these questions would be familiar to most educated adults in the Western world. We may assume that in these countries such tests as this might be quite good intelligence tests, seeing that (a) the more intelligent, by and large, continue their education longer than the less intelligent, and thus have more opportunity of learning a larger number of such facts, and (b) regardless of education, the more intelligent are more likely to pick up information, vocabulary, etc. more readily in every-day life than the less intelligent. Whether this assumption is in fact justified is of course a matter of empirical fact; we shall see that it is justified. But note also that educated persons in Oriental countries, as well as in many non-Western countries outside the Orient, would not necessarily be expected to know these facts, and would consequently emerge (erroneously) as lacking in intelligence if submitted to this test. It is for this reason that the test has been labelled "culture-bound"; we would not be justified in comparing scores obtained by members of different cultures. We may not even be able to compare members of different countries within the Western culture; if we substituted the following question for number 6, we might get far fewer right answers in England, but many more in Germany: "Faust was written by: Schiller – Goethe – Heine – Kleist – Uhland." Or in France, if we substituted the following: "Phèdre was written by: Molière – Hugo – Racine – Corneille – Voltaire." Tests of this type can therefore be quite unfair to certain groups, and this unfairness may even exist within a given country; working class boys and girls may be handicapped in answering such questions by virtue of an inferior education, rather than by virtue of an inferior intelligence.

In contrast, consider now the following typical "culture-fair" items; the term "culture-fair" is used to indicate that the influence of knowledge and education has been lessened, and the test made more fair, not that such influences have been completely eradicated.

Culture-fair Test

(1) A C F J O Complete.

(2) 3 8 12 15 17 Complete.

(3) Select the correct figure from the six numbered ones

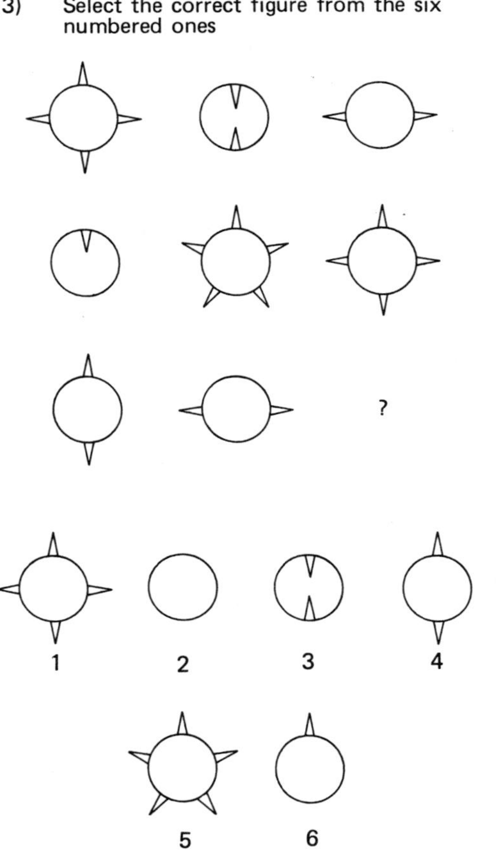

(4) The dog _____ loudly at the stranger. Complete.

(5) 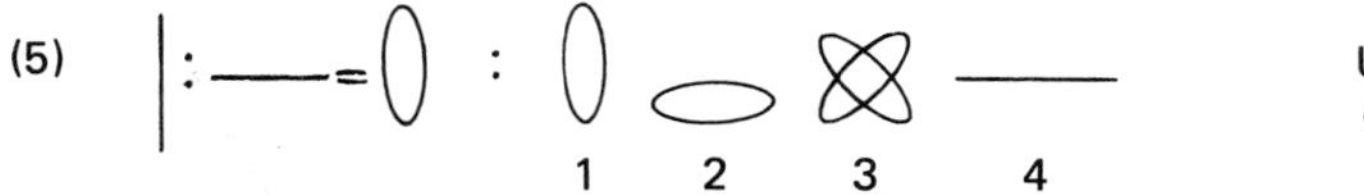

Underline right answer.

(6) 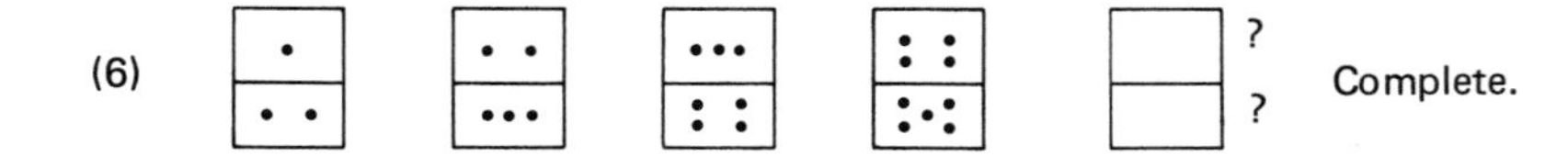

Complete.

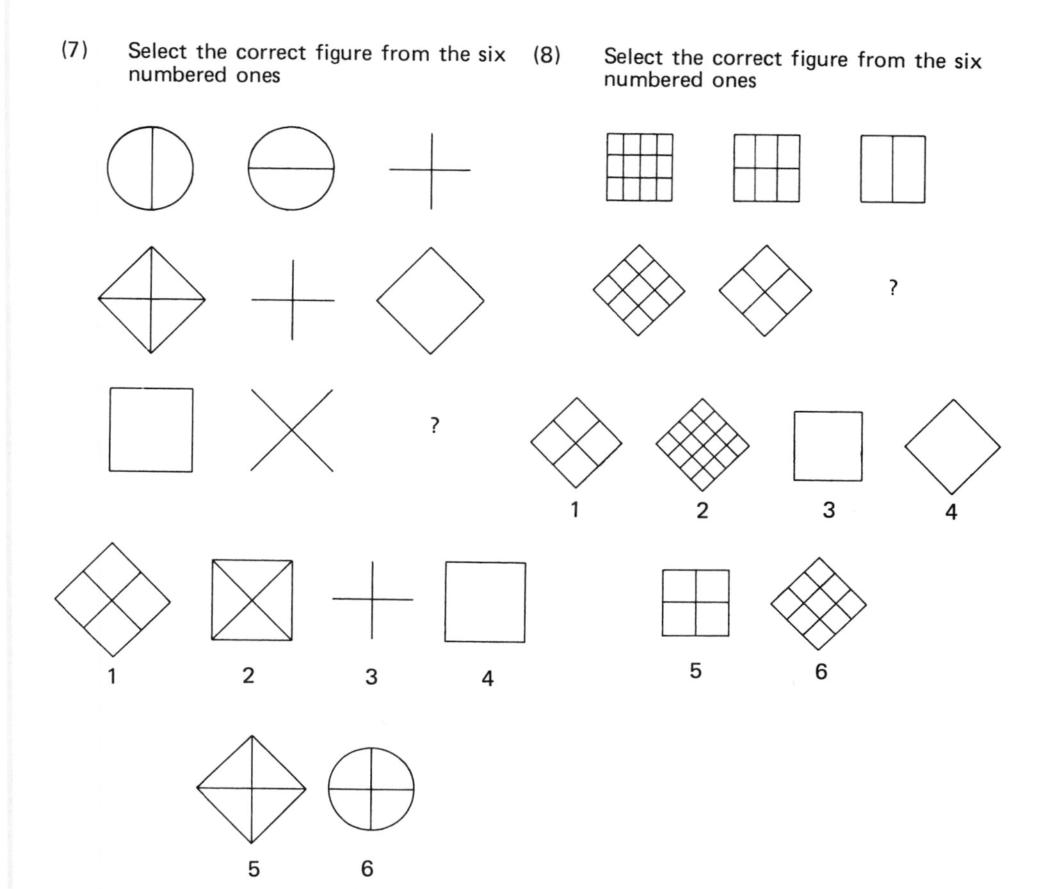
(7) Select the correct figure from the six numbered ones
(8) Select the correct figure from the six numbered ones
?
?
1
2
3
4
1
2
3
4
5
6
5
6

How do these items differ from those in the previous test? The main difference is that the answer is in no case given by simple learning and memory; it has to be worked out from the data given. Hardly any prior knowledge is required, other than that possessed by almost everybody – knowledge of the alphabet; knowledge of the numbers up to twenty, and of simple addition; knowledge of how to read the instructions (but these could be communicated by word of mouth in the case of illiterates); knowledge of how to hold a pencil, and make simple marks on paper; knowledge of how to count the number of lines, and distinguish straight from curved lines. The difficulty of the problems (those here given are of course quite simple) lies in the mental operations which have to be performed; we shall discuss these presently. Many more complex examples of such items have been given in my Pelican books *Know your own IQ* and *Check your own IQ*; the point will be obvious, and does not require much discussion.

As already stated, even these items are not culture-free; a minimum of schooling and acquired knowledge does enter into their solution (or rather into an understanding of the fundaments of which the problem is constituted). We might find savages living in round Kraals unfamiliar with straight lines, or primitive tribes unfamiliar with the alphabet; for these we would have to construct tests taking into account their particular difficulties. Even among highly cultured nations a knowledge of our alphabet cannot be assumed; Russians use the cyrillic alphabet, the Arabs, the Chinese and the Japanese all use scripts fundamentally different from ours. In other words, even culture-fair tests may contain material unfamiliar to certain groups, or less familiar to some groups than to others, and this makes it necessary to consider carefully the composition of tests used for comparisons between groups differing in culture, social background, and education. But this difficulty should not be exaggerated, nor does it provide any reason for assuming that intelligence testing is entirely subjective, or culture-bound. We have already seen that a certain amount of subjectivity enters even into the measurement of temperature, and that different measuring devices are used for different sections of the temperature scale; in this intelligence testing does not differ in principle from temperature measurement. Once these problems and difficulties are known, they can be overcome.

It may be noted that the measurement of temperature had to contend with a difficulty which appears just as daunting. When the first thermoscopes were constructed around the time of Galileo's death, the tops of the tubes containing the fluid whose expansion and contraction indicated the change in temperature were left open; thus the instrument measured both temperature and barometric pressure! This was not recognized until Pascal demonstrated the effect by carrying a thermoscope up the Puy-de-Dôme; he also commented on other difficulties attending the construction of a scientifically valuable thermometer. *Middleton* (1966), in his History of the Thermometer, lists many of these difficulties, the persistent failures, the errors in theory and practice, which attended the measurement of temperature. The book is salutary reading for psychologists. It shows that in spite of sometimes quite absurd vagaries in the process, scientists have never doubted that what they were engaged in was a scientific problem, that the problem was soluble, and that in spite of errors and set-backs they were approaching their aim more and more closely – even though it took them 300 years to get to the present position which still leaves many questions open. Psychology in less than 100 years has made great strides in the measurement of intelligence, yet defeatism characterizes the utterances of many psychologists. This is unrealistic, unless seen against an ideal of perfection quite unacceptable in any empirical science; we have difficulties, and confront awkward problems, but the task is not an impossible one, and improvement has been constant and marked. Given the same amount of time, psychologists will do at least as well with the measurement of intelligence as some of the greatest names in physics have done with the measurement of temperature.

It may seem intuitively obvious that the nationality, the race, and perhaps even the social class of the person constructing the test must influence the outcome of the testing, in such a way that people of similar nationality, race, and class are favoured, and other disfavoured. This argument may hold as far as culturebound types of test are concerned, but they break down as far as culture-fair tests are concerned. As we shall see, there are objective rules which dictate which tests and test-items are "good" and which are "bad" indicators of intelligence; the choice is governed by statistical rules which do not admit of subjectiv-

...it were true that intelligence tests are made by white, middle-class ...ologists to favour white, middle-classe children, then we would expect that ...imo children, who are neither white nor middle-class, and whose education ... severely "deprived" as compared with that of white Canadian children, would do badly on IQ tests; in actual fact they do just as well (*Berry*, 1966; *MacArthur*, 1968; *Vernon*, 1965). Similarly, Japanese children, brought up in a different culture, and having much less money lavished on their education than American children, should do rather badly; in fact, they excel American children by something like 6 points, having a mean IQ of 106, as compared with the American mean of 100! (*Lynn*, 1977) These comparisons do not suggest that white, middle class children are inevitably superior because of the way the tests are constructed; we shall see later that class differences also do not bear out this notion. Working class children do score less well than middle class children, but this may be due to genuine differences in intelligence. It is not admissible to start with the hypothesis that all classes, nations and races are equal in intelligence, and condemn IQ tests when they fail to support this hypothesis; we must look carefully at the possibility that IQ tests are at fault, but we must also look at the possibility that genuine differences may exist.

It may be asked why psychologists use culture-bound tests at all when clearly culture-fair tests have important advantages? The main answer to this query must be that IQ tests are primarily used for practical purposes, such as Officer Selection in the armed forces, pupil and student selection at school and university, and vocational guidance and occupational selection in industry. For these purposes we are often justified in assuming considerable uniformity in cultural background among candidates, and consequently may use culture-bound tests which otherwise would be inadmissible. These tests, in fact, have an important advantage in use: they measure to some extent the candidate's background knowledge and sophistication, and his ability to use his intelligence for the purpose of picking up information, and benefiting from academic and other types of instruction. From the theoretical and scientific points of view this is of course very undesirable; in science we seek to measure one thing at a time, rather than mix up different aspects. But in practice we find that culture-bound tests do in fact give better predictions in these various situations than do culture-fair tests, and consequently educational, military and industrial authorities prefer their use. It seems likely that a better way of dealing with the problem woul... be to use two sets of tests, measuring independently "pure" intelligence, b... means of culture-fair tests, and acquired knowledge, by means of vocabul... and general knowledge tests; the scores could then be combined in some o... mal fashion to give predictions, and the difference between them could gi... additional important information about the candidate. This may sound a co... of perfection, but it could very easily be done, and would not add percep... the cost or the time of examination.

A given IQ test or test-item cannot be classified as being either... bound or culture-fair; test or item must be imagined to lie along a c... from one extreme to the other. Furthermore, its degree of culture-fai... be assessed against the background of the prevailing educational pr... the homogeneity of the group tested. A test which is administered ...

for university admission in Germany, Great Britain or the USA can justifi take for common knowledge certain things which for other populations would be regarded as highly specialized. It is for these reasons that there are many different types of IQ tests; considerable knowledge and expertise are required to select the proper one for a particular purpose. This also means that experiments can often be faulted for using the wrong type of test for the purpose of the experiment. Similarly, criticisms of given experiments and results must always be aware of the precise nature of the test used; criticisms which would be applicable to a culture-bound test might be quite inapplicable to a culture-fair test, and vice versa. Critics who condemn IQ testing on a wholesale basis are often ignorant of these finer distinctions, and merely give vent to their ideological preconceptions.

Technically, the distinction between culture-bound and culture-fair intelligence is often known by another name, introduced by *Cattell* (1971), namely that of fluid ability (culture-fair tests) as opposed to crystallized ability (culture-bound tests). These terms are sometimes symbolized by the letters g_f and g_c; in these expressions, g stands for general mental ability, or intelligence, and f and c respectively for fluid and crystallized ability. The use of letters to denote concepts was introduced by *Spearman* (1927), and his example has been widely followed. Terms in common parlance, like intelligence, carry surplus meaning when used by the scientist, and he may prefer something more neutral; hence Spearman's choice of *g* to denote the general factor which emerges from factor-nalytic studies of correlations between intelligence tests. We shall discuss his thods in the next chapter; here let us merely note that *Cattell* (1971), using lar methods, found strong evidence for the existence of two major factors in tellectual field which he identified with g_f and g_c. What this amounts to, in , is simply that when a large number of tests is given to random samples pulation, people who do particularly well on one test of g_f (i. e. tests shown in our set of culture-fair tests) will also tend to do particularly r tests of g_f; they will tend not to do quite so well on tests of g_c (i. e. e shown in our set of culture-bound tests). Conversely, people who well on one test of g_c will tend to do particularly well on other but not as well on tests of g_f. The two sets of tests are of course anyone tending to do well on g_f tests will also tend to do well on whole, but the relationship between the two sets of tests is not as ithin either set. Put in plain terms, we may say that fluid intelli-ur "raw" innate ability which can be turned to any use what-lized ability refers more go general knowledge acquired on the g_f for the purpose. The concepts involved are in essence 's idea of width of intellect (g_c) and altitude of intellect (g_f). g_c continues to grow longer, and begins to decline much e most bodily skills and sensory abilities, g_f reaches its tween 16 and 20 years) and begins to decline in the l, g_c may continue to grow until the fifties, and may life. We shall return to this point in another chapter. obliquely with the special nature of the problems at precisely is the meaning of "cognitive" as used in relation to the construction of IQ tests? How can we demonstrate that such ideas as we may have in this connection are in fact in line with reality? Few psychologists have given much thought to the former problem, which is in essence a theoretical one; the one outstanding exception has been Charles Spearman of London University, whose extended training at Leipzig University taught him the value of detailed theoretical examination of scientific concepts. Many psychologists (or more accurately, psychometrists) have given thought to the second problem, which also was considered by Spearman who in fact first suggested the correct solution. With this solution we shall be concerned in the next chapter; here let us rather consider Spearman's three laws of neogenesis (*Spearman,* 1927). Neogenesis is the term he coined to denote the origin of novel content in the mind; this, he believed, was the essence of intelligence. He laid down three laws which governed neogenesis. These he labelled the *apprehension of experience*, the *eduction of relations*, and the *eduction of correlates.* The first of these laws he formulated in the following manner: "A person has more or less power to observe what goes on in his own mind. He not only feels, but also knows what he feels; he not only strives, but knows that he strives; he not only knows, but knows that he knows." There are individual differences in awareness of this kind. This may be exemplified by some recent work on individual differences in reaction times. It is well known that simple reaction time measurement has little in common with intelligence; although it was thought at the turn of the century that perhaps the speed of neural conduction might relate to intelligence, and that simple reaction time might measure this speed of conduction, correlations between IQ and reaction time were universally low or zero.

However, complex reaction times tell a different story. In simple reaction time measurement, a signal S is given, and the subject responds by pressing a key; depending on the modality and intensity of the stimulus, reaction times vary around 200 millisec. When the subject is instructed to react only to one of two, or four, or more possible signals (complex reaction time measurement), latencies increase as a linear function of the logarithm of the number of signal choices (i. e. of the "bits" of information offered); the mind takes some time to apprehend the situation before reacting. If Spearman were right in the formulation of his first law of neogenesis, then intelligent subjects should react more quickly to complex stimuli than duller ones, even though both reacted equally quickly in the simple reaction time experiment. This is indeed so (*Roth*, 1964; *Jensen*, personal communication). A rough indication of the results found is given in Fig. 1.5; this shows the linear increase in reaction time with increase in the number of stimuli, and the different slopes of the bright and the dull subjects. Correlations of between 0.4 and 0.6 have been found between this extremely simple experiment and IQ measures, indicating that apprehension of experience can be used to generate testable hypotheses regarding the nature of intelligence.

Spearman's second law, concerning the eduction of relations, states essentially that "when a given person has in mind any two or more ideas (using this word to embrace any items of mental content, whether perceived or thought of), he has more or less power to bring to mind any relations that essentially hold

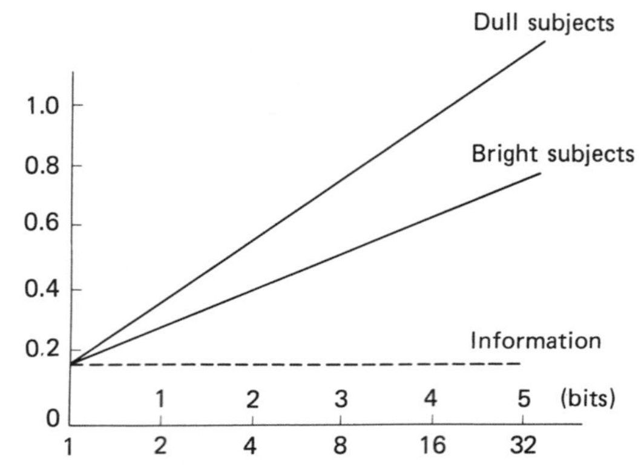

Fig. 1.5. Increase in differentiation between bright and dull subjects in reaction time experiment as the number of alternative signals and responses is increased

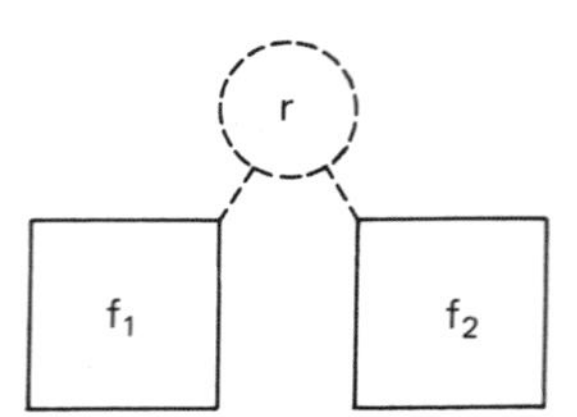

Fig. 1.6. Eduction of relation (r) between two fundaments (f_1 and f_2). Adapted from *Spearman* (1927)

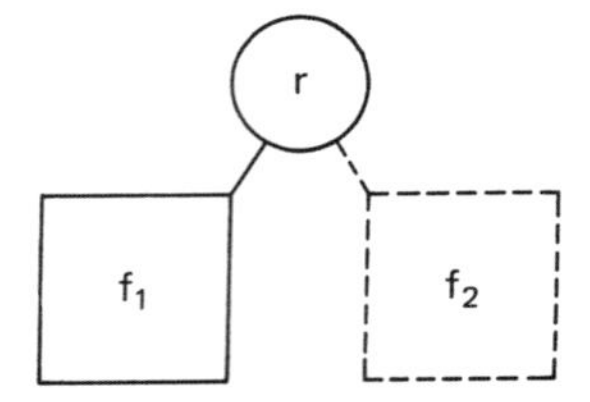

Fig. 1.7. Eduction of correlate (f_2) from fundament (f_1) and relation (r). Adapted from *Spearman* (1927)

between them." Spearman symbolizes this process as in Fig. 1.6, where *r* stands for the relation, whilst f_1 and f_2 denote the "fundaments", as they are termed, etween which the relation is known. The continuous lines represent what is ven originally; the dotted lines represent what is educed by the process.

Spearman's third law, that of the eduction of correlates, states that "when a on has in mind any idea together with a relation, he has more or less power ing into mind the correlative idea." Such educing of correlates may be lized as in Fig. 1.7; where the continuous and the dotted lines have the neaning as before. Spearman discusses at some length the nature of , of which he recognizes ten different kinds, and the way in which they ed to construct intelligence test items; we shall not go into this degree ut will instead look at typical IQ test items to see how well they bear an's analysis.

the following test item, which illustrates what are sometimes called pe tests (Fig. 1.8.) (The term "matrix" denotes a rectangular set of he test item is presented here as 3 × 3 figure containing 8 "fundaempty space the contents of which have to be educed by virtue btaining in the set of "fundaments".)

ng the rows (or along the columns – it makes no difference),

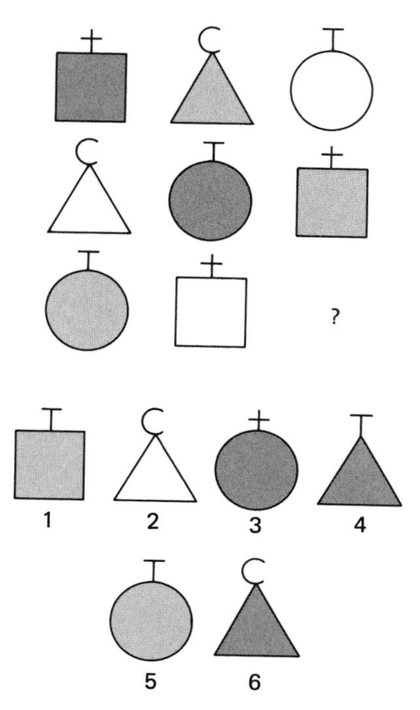
Select the correct figure from the
six numbered ones
?
1
2
3
4
5
6

Fig. 1.8. Eduction of relations and correlates

we find that in each row there are three types of figures; square, triangle, circle. In the last row, there are only a square and a circle, and consequently the missing figure must be a triangle. In each row the figure may be either black, white, or grey; by the same token our missing triangle must be black. Each figure has at the top either a cross, a T, or a C; by the same token the missing black triangle must have a C. It follows that number 6 of the possible solutions at the bottom of the problem must be the correct one. Does this example follow Spearman's rules? We first apprehend the fundaments; next we educe relations between them, such as differences in shape, in shading, and so forth. Last, we educe the necessary correlates in order to determine the shape, shading and top figure in the missing figure. Matrices tests were actually constructed in the first place to put Spearman's theories into a testable form; it was predicted that a test of this kind, embodying in more or less pure form his principles, should be a particularly "good" IQ test; we shall see in the next chapter what is meant by "good" in this context. The outcome was as predicted; Matrices tests have become known as particularly good and powerful intelligence measuring instruments. The same is true of other tests following Spearman's rules; the reader may examine the test items in our list of culture-fair tests to see for himself to what extent they exemplify these rules.

Many psychologists have followed Spearman's lead in using the statistical methods of factor analysis in dealing with the observed correlations between different tests of IQ; comparatively few have followed his pioneering attempts to formulate general psychological laws of "neogenesis", although these laws, and their experimental evaluation, provide an indispensable complement to the purely statistical evaluation along psychometric lines which has been so widely used. The work of *Sternberg* (1977) is particularly impressive in this context; he also summarizes the work of other people who have attempted to take a more theoretical look at the nature of the processes which are involved in "intelligent" activity. Sternberg somewhat extends and particularizes Spearman's three laws. We are here dealing with the fundamental and simplest form of analogy production, i. e. A:B::C:D (A is to B as C is to D, where D is the term to be found. As D differs from the other terms in not geing given, but having to be discovered, it may usefully be written D′ in order to make this distinction.) Sternberg attempts to discover the most fundamental components into which the whole process of problem-solving can be analysed; these are then postulated to act in an additive manner, i. e. the time taken over one process is added to that taken by the others, thus making possible the experimental verification or falsification of particular theories by actual timing of the processes involved.

Sternberg's theory of analogical reasoning contains six information-processing components, five of them mandatory and one optional. The components are of three general types: attribute identification, attribute comparison, and control. *Attribute identification.* There is only one component in this category, namely encoding. "In encoding, the stimulus is translated into an internal representation upon which further mental operations can be performed. The internal representation is stored in working memory, and is available for immediate retrieval. This stage closely resembles Spearman's apprehension of experience. *Attribute comparison.* There are three mandatory attribute-comparison components, and one optional one. (1) *Inference* is the process by which a rule, X, is discovered that relates the A term of the analogy to the B term; the outcome is stored in working memory. (2) *Mapping* is the process by which a higher-order rule, Y, is discovered that maps the domain of the analogy into the range, i. e. what is required is the discovery of a rule that relates A (the first term of the domain) to C (the first term of the range). (Sternberg defines the terms domain and range to refer to the terms A, B and C, D respectively.) Mapping would thus be the discovery of the relation between A and C. (3) *Application* is the process by which a rule, Z, is generated that forms D′ (an image of the correct answer) and evaluates D. The outcome is stored in the working memory. (4) *Justification* is an optional component, denoting the process by which one of several answer options that are nonidentical to D′ is justified as closest to D′. The process is required only in forced-choice analogies, i. e. where one of several imperfect answers has to be chosen. *Control.* There is one control component in the theory. "This component includes the processes by which subjects prepare for solving the analogy, monitor the solution process, and translate the solution into a response. The component, *preparation-response,* contains those operations that were not thought worthy of separate components, but were thought to be suitably represented in combination."

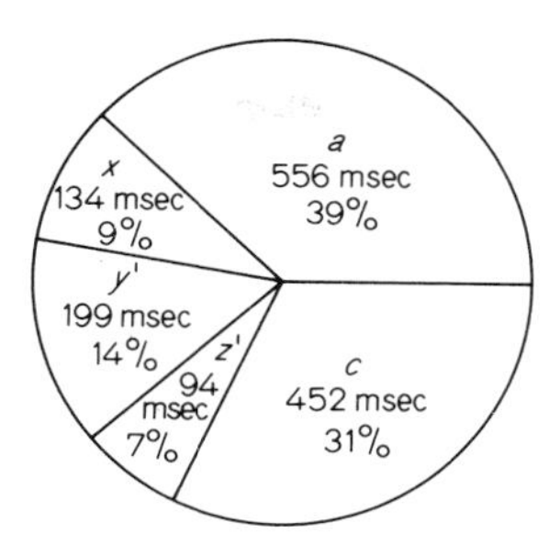

Fig. 1.9. Distribution of component time on a typical People Piece analogy

Sternberg also offers a *combination rule.* "Response time is hypothesized to equal the sum of the amounts of time spent on each component operation. Clearly the testing of such a model as Sternberg's requires (a) experimental manipulation of the presentation of the elements of the analogy, and (b) exact timing of the various processes as they become involved in the presentation. Figure 1.9 shows the results of an experiment designed to put the theory to the test; it presents the percentage of solution time taken up with the various processes postulated. In the figure *a* refers to scanning and encoding time; *c* to constant preparation and response time; *x* to exhaustive inference time; *y'* to self-terminating mapping time; and z' to self-terminating application time. Details of this and other experiments described in Sternberg's (1977) book would not be appropriate here; they demonstrate that the experimental analysis of the laws of noegenesis is feasible, that this application must be adapted closely to the exact nature of the tests used, and that it is possible to assess the relevance of the various processes to the concept of "intelligence" with considerably precision. Sternberg used "reference ability tests", such as the Cattell "culture fair" scales, in order to correlate these with his component scores; in this way he was able to demonstrate the degree to which general intelligence is involved in the various processes which make up his component model.

Sternberg's work has been mentioned, not because his model is the only one which has been constructed on the basis of Spearman's neogenetic rules, nor because it is necessarily the best, but because it illustrates the tremendous value of experimental studies in this field, as long as these are based on sound theoretical reasoning. The isolation of psychometric and factor analytic work from the experimental and theoretical tradition of psychology has had many unfortunate consequences, which were foreseen by Spearman who insisted on the dual basis of the scientific study of intelligence: the psychometric study of individual differences, and the experimental study of the general laws of intellectual functioning. It is unfortunate that his successors embraced wholeheartedly the psychometric method, and disregarded the experimental method. Is is only recently that the process of unification has begun, and our success in gaining a proper understanding of intelligence depends very much on the continuation of this unification.

A slightly different attempt to discover the psychological characteristics of a "good" test of intelligence, as contrasted with a "bad" test of intelligence has been made by *Jensen* (1978). As we shall see in the next chapter, "good" tests, psychometrically speaking, are those which intercorrelate highly with all other tests, while "bad" tests only intercorrelate poorly. Jensen asked the pertinent question: Just what is it that distinguishes "good" from "bad" tests psychologically? He examined the results from hundreds of empirical studies, and discovered that the most important characteristic involved was *cognitive complexity* – good tests were complex, bad ones simple. (This should not be confused with difficulty level of tests – it is difficult to lift a 200-pound weight, or recall a string of 10 digits, but neither is a good *g* test!) The notion of "complexity" is well illustrated by reference to the reaction time experiment already mentioned – simple reaction times do not correlate with intelligence, but the increase in reaction time involved in multiple-choice reactions does.

Jensen, in the same paper, makes the pertinent point that a similar concept of intelligence has arisen independently in the field of zoology, from the comparative study of animal behaviour. Some animals are universally found to be more "intelligent" than others; what are the criteria used? According to Jensen, they are: "The speed of learning and the complexity of what can be learned, the integration of sensory information to achieve a goal, flexibility of behaviour in the face of obstacles, the amount of insightful as contrasted with trial-and-error problem-solving behaviour, transfer of learning from one problem to somewhat different situations, and the acquisition of abstract concepts." There is a definite relationship between ratings of animals' performance along these dimensions and the animals' phylogenetic status. "Behavioural differences among species, like physical differences, are largely a product of evolution. Natural selection, by acting directly upon the behaviour involved in the organism's coping with its environment, indirectly shapes the physical structures underlying adaptive behaviour, of which the nervous system is the most important. There is much evidence for evolutionary continuity in the behaviour of organisms, just as there is in their morphology. The phylogenetic differences in the complexity of behavioural capacities are clearly related to brain size in relation to body size, and to the proportion of the brain tissues not involved in vegetative or autonomic and sensorimotor functions. Development of the cerebral cortex, the association areas, and the frontal lobes phylogenetically parallel behavioural complexity. Also, the higher the animal ranks in the phyletic scale, the more seriously do lesions of the cortex of the brain effect its objectively measured behavioural capacity. Cerebral development, as reflected in cranial capacity, is known to have increased markedly over the five million years of human evolution, almost tripling in size from Australopithecus up to modern man." In humans at the present time, too, there is a highly significant correlation between brain size and intelligence, although the absolute value of this correlation is only about 0.3 (possibly it would be higher if better methods of measuring brain size could be devised.) (*Valen*, 1976)

We must mention one further point. All the test items we have discussed so far are of a kind sometimes referred to as "convergent"; in other words, all the relations among the fundaments converge on a single correct solution. Spearman and his followers also experimented with a rather different type of test under the name of "fluency"; the term refers to the *fluency* with which associations are produced. Thus the test might simply ask for as many different makes of motor car as the subject can think of in 2 minutes, or as many words beginning with the letter B, or as many different things as could be placed on a marked spot in a picture showing a palm tree near a road. It will be clear that here there are no right or wrong answers, or at least no single right answer; the test is "divergent" rather than "convergent". Nowadays such tests are widely used to measure "creativity" or "originality", although whether they succeed in doing so is a moot question. It has even been suggested that such tests measure something quite different from, and by inference more important than, general intelligence. The truth seems to be that "divergent" ability tests correlate quite highly with "convergent" ability tests; that they do seem to measure something slightly different from *g*; and that, as already surmised by *Spearman* (1927), this something may be an attribute of personality, namely extraversion. Tests of divergent ability are of considerable interest, but it would be quite wrong to imagine that they invalidate in any way the importance of more traditional tests, or the known facts regarding intelligence. Divergent as well as convergent tests obey the three neogenetic laws of *Spearman*; in divergent tests the subject is given a fundament and a relation, and instructed to find as many correlates as he can. This is a neogenetic procedure where the relation furnished the subject is open, as much as when it is closed, as in the convergent type of test item. Differences between the two types of tests are of interest to students of personality, and they may also have practical uses in selection and prediction; they do not fundamentally affect the generality of Spearman's laws.

We can now summarize the discussion so far. It is suggested that the measurement of intelligence uses precisely the same sorts of methods, and starts with the same sorts of observations, as do attempts to carry out measurement in the hard sciences. We begin with casual observations, in this case that some people learn cognitive material more quickly, and solve cognitive problems more rapidly, than do others. We attempt to put this observation on a quantitative basis by constructing test items which enable us to observe the success or failure of many subjects in their attempts to solve these problems, and to measure the latency of their attempted solutions. We formulate hypotheses concerning the essential nature of the cognitive processes involved, and try to improve our tests by making them conform to these principles. We discover that certain extraneous factors, such as education, social status, nationality and race may interfere with our measurements, and attempt to eliminate these disturbances or at least reduce their effect, along certain lines, e. g. by constructing culture-fair tests. We are now ready to see how we can use the knowledge gained so far in testing the hypothesis underlying most theories of intelligence from Plato and Aristotle to Spencer and Spearman, namely the generality of intelligence.

2 General Intelligence and Special Aptitudes

> No human investigation can be called real science if it cannot be demonstrated mathematically
>
> Leonardo da Vinci

We have so far acquired some insight into the nature of cognitive tests which might, on theoretical grounds, be considered likely candidates for the measurement of intelligence; we must now turn to a consideration of that part of the theory which asserts that intelligence is the general or all-round cognitive ability which mediates success in such tests *whatever their nature.* Spearman has called this "the indifference of the indicator"; in other words, if a test or test item fulfils the conditions for a "good" test or test item laid down in his laws of neogenesis, then it should not matter much which item or test was chosen for the measurement. This implication of the theory can of course be investigated empirically, and methods for doing this were worked out by members of the London school – Karl Pearson, the great statistician, Charles Spearman himself, and Sir Cyril Burt, who succeeded Spearman in the professorial chair at University College, London. These methods are essentially based on the use of correlation coefficients, and on factor analysis, i. e. the analysis of sets of such coefficients. There are some statistical complexities to analyses of this kind, but these are inevitably outside the scope of this chapter; there are many good books dealing with the technique of factor analysis (*Thomson,* 1939; *Burt,* 1940, and *Thurstone,* 1947, are three classics; among modern texts are *Harman,* 1967, *Pawlik,* 1971 and *Lawley* and *Maxwell,* 1971). It is possible, however, to explain the logical basis of factor analysis with a minimum of mathematics, and this will be our aim here; a basic understanding of what the factor analyst is trying to accomplish, and how he sets about it, will suffice for the purpose of seeing whether the Plato-Spencer-Spearman theory is viable, whether it must be rejected, or whether it has to be supplemented in some way or other.

First let us be clear about the meaning of a correlation coefficient. In the hard sciences we often find laws, written in the form: $a = f(b)$; in other words, a is the dependent variable in an experiment which varies as some function of b, the independent variable. Thus the length of a column of mercury in an enclosed glass tube (a) varies as a function of the prevailing temperature (b). Such relations may be linear or not, but they are usually very clear, in the sense that when we plot them they tend to lie along a line. This is due to the fact that in physics we can usually isolate the variables we wish to study, and thus obtain very simple and elegant laws and relationships. In psychology we are dealing with persons who cannot be cut up into little bits, and thus we can never test hypothetical relationships without the interference of other, extraneous factors. These extraneous factors will muddy the waters, and make the observed relationship much weaker than it would otherwise be. Let us assume that we wish to test Kretschmer's famous hypothesis that mental disease is a function of body-build, in the sense that pyknic persons (squat, stocky, fat) are more liable to develop manic-depressive disorders, asthenic persons (long, lean, thin) schizophrenia. We cannot test this directly very easily because schizophrenia occurs rather early in life (usually in the teens), while manic-depressive illness occurs usually rather late, perhaps after fifty. Thus whatever relation there might be between these two variables, physique and mental disorder, is muddied by the influence of age, hospitalization, differential food intake, and many other, similar factors which are age-dependent. Direct comparisons between manic-depressives and schizophrenics seem to bear out Kretschmer's hypothesis, but when age effects are allowed for the differences vanish!

Instead of having linear or at least simple regression effects, we are thrown back in psychology on correlations, i. e. estimates of the closeness of a relationship which may vary from perfect (r = 1.00, in which r is the symbol used to denote correlation) to non-existent (r = 0.00). Correlations can of course also be negative; thus degree of shortsightedness and ability at ball games are negatively correlated. Correlations can best be understood as indicating a percentage of overlapping elements or factors. It can be shown that if all the elements determining *a* are included within the greater number of elements determining *b*, then r^2 gives us the percentage of determination of *a* by *b*. Thus we might say that a correlation of 0.50 between *a* and *b* tells us that our independent variable (*b*) contains $0.50^2 = 0.25$, i. e. 25% or one-quarter of all the causal factors determining our dependent variable (*a*). A correlation of 0.71 would tell us that the percentage of causal factors measured was 50%; a correlation of 0.95 that 90% of causal factors were being measured, etc. This is the most useful way of looking at correlations in connection with factor analysis.

Let us now look at Spearman's theory (1927) in this light. He postulates in essence that if we take any two tests of cognitive ability, then a person's score on each will be decided by two factors. One is his own ability; the other the degree to which the test measures *g* (general intelligence). Different persons have different degrees of general intelligence; different tests measure general intelligence to a different extent. Let us assume that we had a perfect measure of general intelligence; let us denote this *g*. We could now immediately discover how good a measure of intelligence each of our tests was, by simply administering our battery of tests to a random sample of the population, also administering our perfect test of *g*, and then correlating each test with *g*. This correlation would tell us immediately how good each test was as a measure of *g*; this is sometimes called the *g* saturation or loading of that test. What does each test measure, in addition to *g*? By definition, or rather in terms of the theory, whatever else it measures must be specific to that test, and not in any way in common with any other test; Spearman calls this contribution *s*. (If we had 6 tests in all, then we would have seven factors: *g*, measured to varying extent by all the tests, and s_1, s_2, s_3, s_4, s_5, and s_6.) As we are not interested in these specific contributions of the tests, we may regard them as effectively errors of measurement.

Let us continue our imaginery experiment. We have correlated our 6 tests with our perfect measure of g, and have thus discovered the correlation of each test with g; let us say that test one correlated 0.9 with g, test two correlated 0.8, test three 0.7, test four 0.6, test five 0.5, and test six 0.4; these figures have been entered in Table 2.1 in the last column, headed "Factor Saturation". Can we deduce from this what would be the actual intercorrelations between our sex tests if we decided to correlate them, each with each? The answer is in the affirmative; each correlation would simply be the product of the factor saturations of the two tests. Tests 1 and 2 would correlate 0.72, as shown in the body of the Table, i. e. $0.9 \times 0.8 = 0.72$. Test 5 and test 6 would correlate 0.20, i. e. 0.5×0.4. In this way we could build up the whole table, as shown, with the exception of the values in the diagonal. These have been put in brackets because they are purely notional; they represent the correlations of each test with itself, and here of course we would empirically get a value determined not only by g, but also by s (each test score is made up by $g + s$; correlating each test with itself would thus involve both g and s). The values in brackets thus represent what the correlation of each test with itself would be if we left out of account the test's s element; this clearly cannot be done empirically. If we knew the values in brackets, then we would also know the factor saturations of the tests; these would simply be the square roots of the values in brackets. But we do not know them, and hence this way of discovering the factor saturations is closed to us.

Table 2.1. Hypothetical intercorrelations among six ability tests, illustrating a matrix of rank 1

	1	2	3	4	5	6	Factor saturation
1	(0.81)	0.72	0.63	0.54	0.45	0.36	0.9
2.	0.72	(0.64)	0.56	0.48	0.40	0.32	0.8
3.	0.63	0.56	(0.49)	0.42	0.35	0.28	0.7
4.	0.54	0.48	0.42	(0.36)	(0.30)	0.24	0.6
5.	0.45	0.40	0.35	0.30	(0.25)	0.20	0.5
6.	0.36	0.32	0.28	0.24	0.20	(0.16)	0.4

Now let us retrace our steps. We started out by assuming that we had a perfect test of g, and deduced what should happen as far as the intercorrelations of the actual empirical tests was concerned. Now let us assume that we start out with some actual, observed table or matrix of correlations, such as those in the body of our Table 2.1; can we deduce from these values what the g value, or the factor saturation, of each test is? The answer is again in the affirmative, *provided that our general theory is correct.* Consider how the values in the first column have been formed; we simply multiplied each test's saturation by 0.9. Similarly, each value in the second column was formed by multiplying the saturations by 0.8. Consequently, the pairs of values in these columns are all in the ratio of 0.9/ 0.8. Including for the moment our diagonal values, we thus find six simultaneous equations: 0.81/0.72 = 0.72/0.64 = 0.63/0.56 = 0.54/0.48 = 0.45/0.40 = 0.36/0.32, and all of these = 0.9/0.8. If we now go back and call the two values in the diagonal X and Y (because they are in fact unknown, and not empirically derived), we have several equations which enable us to discover what they are. For instance: X/0.72 = 0.63/0.56, or 0.72/Y = 0.54/0.48. In this way we can easily calculate the values in the diagonals; in fact, the solution is overdetermined, as we have far more equations then unknowns! But as we have already seen, knowing the diagonal values immediately tells us the factor saturations, so that by proceeding in this fashion we can calculate what the factor saturations of our tests actually are – simply from a consideration of the empirical data! If we found a set of six tests the observed correlations between which was as set out in Table 2.1, then the tests would have the correlations with a perfect test of *g* that we have set out in the column headed "Factor Saturations."

How can we tell whether or not the observed correlations do in fact obey the rules of Spearman's theory? Spearman himself devised a mathematical proof, which he named "the vanishing tetrad differences". He showed that if we have four tests, which we may label a, b, p, and q, and calculate the correlations between them, then his rule is satisfied if, and only if,

$$r_{ap}r_{bq} - r_{bp}r_{aq} = 0.$$

If, in our Table, we set a equal to our test 1, b equal to test 2, p equal to test 3, and q equal to test 4, then we get: 0.63 × 0.48 − 0.56 × 0.54 = 0; in other words, our Table passes the test. *Thurstone* (1947) used matrix algebra to express the same idea, and at the same time generalized it; in terms of this particular algorithm, the number of factors corresponds to the rank of a matrix, and in the particular Spearman case that rank is one. There are of course certain complexities; thus empirically observed correlations have certain sampling errors, depending on the number of subjects in the sample tested. But all this is detail; the really important question is: do observed correlation matrices correspond to Spearman's rules? The answer, in brief, is: Yes and No.

In specifying the conditions under which he would expect his rule to be satisfied, Spearman stated that the tests used should not be "too similar"; if they were "too similar", then of course they would contain identical *s* factors, and these would throw out the calculations. This question of similarity is a bothersome one. Suppose test 1 is a vocabulary test, full of items like item 5 in our culture-bound test. Suppose test 2 is also a vocabulary test, full of similar items. Clearly here the *s* of one test would be the same as the *s* of the other; this would be inadmissible according to Spearman. But suppose test 2 was made up of items like this: "Define the word "safari." This is still a vocabulary item, but the problem is put slightly differently; does this still constitute too great similarity? Or take yet another type of item, namely the following;

high : low = mighty : ? (weak – absent – down – flighty – great)

Here the subject has to chose from the five words in brackets the correct one to go in the place of the question mark; knowledge of vocabulary is still being

Table 2.2. Hypothetical intercorrelations among three verbal and three numerical ability tests

	1	2	3	4	5	6	Factor Saturation	
1	(0.04)	0.06	0.10	−0.08	−0.06	−0.10	0.2	
2	0.06	(0.09)	0.15	−0.12	−0.09	−0.15	0.3	V
3	0.10	0.15	(0.25)	−0.20	−0.15	−0.25	0.5	
4	−0.08	−0.12	−0.20	(0.16)	0.12	0.20	−0.4	
5	−0.06	−0.09	−0.15	0.12	(0.09)	0.15	−0.3	N
6	−0.16	−0.15	−0.25	0.20	0.15	(0.25)	−0.5	

tested, but so is the ability to recognize the relation between high and low (opposition), and to select the word which is the best correlate, given the word "mighty" and the relation of opposition. Clearly it is not all that easy to specify the notion of "too great similarity" precisely.

It was here that *L. L. Thurstone* (1938), of Chicago, put forth a quite different theory to that of Spearman, namely that of *primary factors*. Both these men share certain characteristics, primary among which is their background in engineering; Spearman was an engineer in the British Army, while Thurstone was assistant to the famous inventor Edison. Thurstone administered 56 different mental tests to a group of Chicago university students, intercorrelated them, and declared that there was no evidence at all in this gigantic matrix of intercorrelations of a general factor of the Spearman kind. Instead, he argued, there was evidence for a number of special abilities, each independent of the other. Certainly the rank of the matrix was not one, as demanded by Spearman's theory, but between 6 and 12. Before discussing Thurstone's contribution, let us go back to the technique of factor analysis and see how it can deal with the problem of having more than one single, general factor.

Let us assume that of the six tests in our Table 2.1 three are verbal tests, i. e. tests using mainly words and verbal relations, while the other three are numerical, i. e. use numbers and numerical relations. This might give rise, through Spearman's "similarities" or associated s values, to a factor contrasting verbal and numerical tests; this factor would of course be additional to the general factor already mentioned. Table 2.2 shows how such a factor might be constituted; again we may assume that we have a perfect measure of the verbal and numerical abilities of our subjects, and that the factor saturations given in the Table represent the correlations of the tests with this factor. We can now construct a table of observable intercorrelations, very much in the manner of Table 2.1; the values in the body of Table 2.2 constitute the correlations produced by this verbal-numerical factor. They are of course not actually observable because they are additional to the values produced by the general factor; what we would find in actual practice would be a table of correlations in which those in Table 2.2 would have been added to those in Table 2.1 to give the correlations printed in Table 2.3. To put it slightly differently, each of the factors (g and V − N) produces certain correlations between the tests, and these can be added to give

Table 2.3. Combination of correlations in two preceeding tables

	1	2	3	4	5	6	Factor Saturation	
							g	V vs. N
1	(0.85)	0.78	0.73	0.46	0.39	0.26	0.9	0.2
2	0.78	(0.73)	0.71	0.36	0.31	0.17	0.8	0.3
3	0.73	0.71	(0.74)	0.22	0.20	0.03	0.7	0.5
4	0.46	0.36	0.22	(0.52)	0.42	0.44	0.6	−0.4
5	0.39	0.31	0.20	0.42	(0.34)	0.35	0.5	−0.3
6	0.26	0.17	0.03	0.44	0.35	(0.41)	0.4	−0.5

the actual correlations to be expected when the tests are administered and intercorrelated.

Does it make any sense to have negative saturations? Surely all abilities are supposed to correlate positively together; this is demanded by Spearman's theory, and is indeed universally found to be true (the name given by Thurstone to the universally positive tables of correlations between cognitive tests is the "positive manifold".) But note that we have already extracted what is *in common* to the tests, i. e. the general factor; what is left is only that which *distinguishes* them, i. e. the purely verbal and numerical nature of the *s* factors; these are essentially different, and hence may conveniently be represented as + and −. When we add the *g* and the V and N factors, as in Table 2.3, all the correlations will be seen to be positive, as required. The methods used to give us the factor saturations of this second (and any further) factor(s) are a little too technical to be presented here, although in essence they too are quite simple in practice. Factors are extracted one at a time, leaving a residue of residual correlations which cannot be explained by the previous factor(s) extracted; we simply go on extracting factors until the residual correlations are too small to matter. We have several different methods for ascertaining the number of factors to be extracted (the rank of the matrix), but again this is too technical a matter to be discussed here.

What is of much more interest is the way in which we can put in diagrammatic form the results of a factor analysis. Let us take the figures given in Table 2.3 of the factor saturations of our *g* and V–N factors, and plot these saturations along Cartesian coordinates (see Fig. 2.1). If our matrix is of rank two, i. e. can be accurately represented by two factors, then all the intercorrelations between the six tests are accurately shown by the relative positions of the six points which represent the tests. The rule is that the correlation between any two tests is given by their scalar product, i. e. by the cosine of the angle between them multiplied by their distances from the origin. This has been indicated in Fig. 2.1 for the correlation between tests 3 and 6. We take the angle α between the two tests, and multiply this value by the product of the distances from 3 to the origin, and from 6 to the origin, i. e. the lengths of the stippled paths. The cosine of 90° is zero, so that any two tests shown at right angles would have zero correlation. The closer the two tests in the factor space (in this case, the flat, two-dimensional space of the plane of the paper), the higher their correlation. Tests 1 and 2 are clearly closest together in Fig. 2.1 and their correlation is the highest in Table 2.3. Tests 3 and 6 are furthest apart, and their correlation is the smallest.

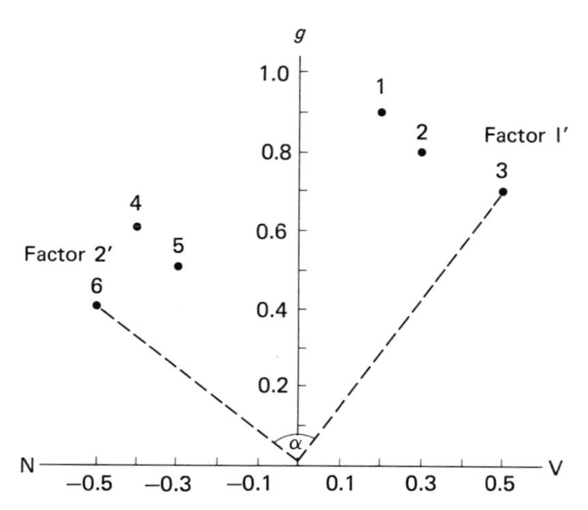

Fig. 2.1. Illustration of factor rotation

Two factors can easily be imagined, or drawn on paper; with three factors we would already have difficulties, although they can be represented in a three-dimensional figure (perhaps analogous to the ribs of an umbrella fully opened.) With four and more factors we enter the realm of n-dimensional geometry where algebra and mathematival symbolism take over, and the imagination cannot follow. In principle, however, there are no special difficulties attending the postulation of any number of independent (orthogonal) factors, which add together to produce the observed matrix of intercorrelations. Instead of pursuing this topic, let us return to Fig. 2.1 and discuss what it is that we have discovered, and what it is that we add in a somewhat arbitrary fashion to the picture. Essentially we have succeeded in showing, by a mathematically acceptable technique, that a table of 36 intercorrelations can be represented by two sets of altogether 12 factor saturations; this is a saving of considerable importance. When we have large numbers of correlations, as in the case of Thurstone's great study of 56 tests, the saving is enormous, and the results are much easier to survey; this is an important advantage. But there is no theoretical, scientific advantage, unless we can give psychological meaning to our factors. There is one difficulty to doing this, and that is the essential *subjectivity* of the position of our factors in the dimensional space defined by our analysis. Let me explain this in relation to Fig. 2.1. In the space defined by our analysis, the position of the 6 tests is invariant; it is given by their intercorrelations, and cannot be changed. But the two lines which represent the factors, and marked *g* and V–N, are somewhat arbitrary; they were useful as a sort of scaffolding in constructing the space in which we have plotted our six tests, but once this has been done their position can be changed without affecting the relations between the tests, or their relative positions! Suppose we were to rotate these two lines, in such a way that the N–V line coincided with that linking test 6 to the origin, and the *g* line in such a way that it coincided with the line linking test 3 to the origin. This would in no way alter anything in the diagram. We would now refer our six tests to these two new "factors", giving them entirely new and different saturations, but nothing material would have been altered. This is the problem of *rotation* in factor analysis; how can we objectively and meaningfully define the position of our factors in n-dimensional factor space? We shall confine our discussion to two-dimensional space, for the sake of simplicity.

Let us first ask ourselves, would the rotated solution, i. e. in terms of factors 1′ and 2′, make any psychological sense? The answer must surely be in the affirmative. Factor 1′ might be regarded as a verbal ability factor, factor 2′ as one of numerical ability. General ability or *g* would disappear completely, very much as it did in Thurstone's research. We might wonder why tests 4 and 5 had saturations for factor 1′, and tests 1 and 2 for factor 2′, but there might be an answer to this. Even numerical tests may call for some verbal ability, i. e. in understanding instructions, or in verbalizing the procedures used in solution. Similarly, verbal tests may require some simple counting, sufficient to "load" them on numerical ability. This alternative position of the factors or "axes" consequently makes psychological sense, just as much as the original position; which is the correct one? As we shall see, this is not a scientifically meaningful question; we shall consider it after looking at some attempts to lay down rules according to which we might be able to rotate factors in a statistically invariant manner. The major rule introduced to achieve this aim is that of "simple structure"; it was first suggested by Thurstone. We can best show how it works by considering an example.

Consider Table 2.4. This sets out twelve personality questions, six concerned with neuroticism, six with extraversion-introversion. The key shows whether a "Yes" answer counts towards the one or the other personality dimension. Table 2.5 shows the matrix of intercorrelations, and the factor saturations for the E and N factors. Fig. 2.2 shows the diagrammatic representation of these saturations; note how closely the six questions defining each factor cluster around the axis in each case, and also that the angle between the axes is 90 °, i. e. that E and N are quite uncorrelated, and absolutely independent. This solution was arrived at by following "simple structure" rules; in brief these state that the preferred solution should have as many zero factor saturations or loadings as possible. (This is not the full requirement of the rule, but it will serve for our purposes. Zero here does not mean exactly zero, but rather includes a band of very low loadings, usually including anything less than 0.10; this is necessary because of sampling errors.) In Fig. 2.2 there are 12 zero loadings in all; this is as many as can possibly reach this value, and consequently no better solution is possible. In addition it makes perfectly good psychological sense, and is in line with prediction from theory (*Eysenck*, 1947). Thurstone's rule apparently works extremely well, in this case at least.

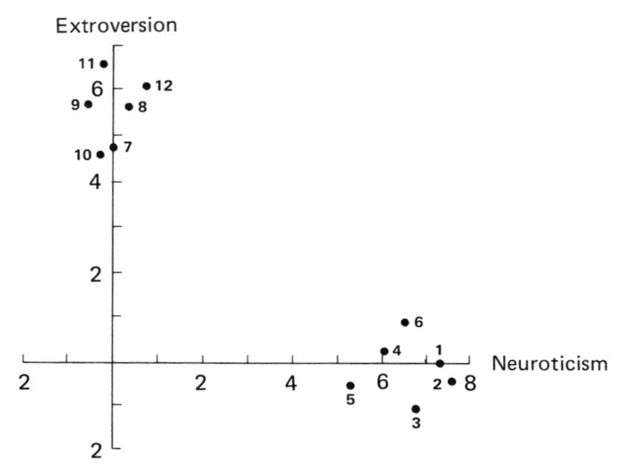

Fig. 2.2. Relative positions in two-dimensional space of six neuroticism and six extraversion questionnaire items

Table 2.4. Personality questionnaire items

	Key
A. Do you sometimes feel happy, sometimes depressed, without any apparent reason?	N
B. Do you have frequent ups and downs in mood, either with or without apparent cause?	N
C. Are you inclined to be moody?	N
D. Does your mind often wander while you are trying to concentrate?	N
E. Are you frequently 'lost in thought' even when supposed to be taking part in a conversation?	N
F. Are you sometimes bubbling over with energy and sometimes very sluggish?	N
G. Do you prefer action to planning for action?	E
H. Are you happiest when you get involved in some project that calls for rapid action?	E
I. Do you usually take the initiative in making new friends?	E
J. Are you inclined to be quick and sure in your actions?	E
K. Would you rate yourself as a lively individual?	E
L. Would you ve very unhappy, if you were prevented from making numerous social contacts?	E

Using this rule of simple structure on his intelligence test data, *Thurstone* (1938) emerged with a number of apparently independent primary factors, or separate abilities; his conclusion that there was no general factor of intelligence seemed to follow from this. However, *Eysenck* (1939) reanalysed Thurstone's data and concluded that an alternative solution was equally possible, resulting in a strong general factor and a number of special ability factors, rather like Thurstone's primary abilities. The two alternatives are very much like those indicated for a two-factor problem in Fig. 2.1. It is now generally agreed that no objective choice can be made between these two solutions; they are of course capable of being converted into each other by a simple mathematical formula, and are therefore mathematically equivalent. However, another criticism may be made

Table 2.5. Factor analyses of twelve personality questions

	Intercorrelations												Factor saturations	
	1	2	3	4	5	6	7	8	9	10	11	12	E	N
1	—	0.65	0.48	0.38	0.29	0.50	−0.04	0.08	−0.04	0.09	−0.07	0.01	0.01	0.75
2	0.65	—	0.60	0.35	0.27	0.46	0.01	0.02	−0.10	−0.11	−0.10	0.05	−0.06	0.74
3	0.48	0.60	—	0.30	0.25	0.45	−0.04	0.02	−0.06	−0.15	−0.15	0.08	−0.09	0.71
4	0.38	0.35	0.30	—	0.50	0.31	0.03	−0.08	−0.04	0.17	−0.04	0.06	0.02	0.58
5	0.29	0.27	0.25	0.50	—	0.32	−0.04	−0.09	−0.14	−0.14	0.17	0.02	−0.06	0.58
6	0.50	0.46	0.45	0.31	0.32	—	0.02	0.12	0.04	−0.02	0.07	0.13	0.09	0.63
7	−0.04	−0.04	0.04	0.03	−0.04	−0.02	—	0.40	0.12	0.17	0.20	0.16	0.48	0.00
8	0.08	0.02	0.02	−0.08	−0.09	0.12	0.40	—	0.19	0.38	0.26	0.21	0.59	0.04
9	−0.04	−0.10	−0.06	−0.04	−0.14	0.04	0.12	0.19	—	0.08	0.44	0.53	0.59	−0.06
10	0.09	0.09	−0.15	0.17	−0.14	−0.02	0.17	0.38	0.08	—	0.42	0.13	0.49	−0.04
11	−0.07	−0.10	−0.15	−0.04	0.17	0.07	0.20	0.26	0.44	0.42	—	0.41	0.68	−0.02
12	0.01	0.05	0.08	0.06	0.02	0.13	0.16	0.21	0.53	0.13	0.41	—	0.64	0.09

of Thurstone's work. He used as subjects highly selected University students, i. e. a group differing only little from each other with respect to general mental ability; hence we would not expect a very powerful general factor to emerge! It is as if we looked for a general factor of height in a sample of London Policemen, who are required to be at least 6 feet tall; variation in height is negligible in this group, and we might only find a very weak factor of height. Thurstone repeated his work on more random samples of school children (*Thurstone* and *Thurstone*, 1941), and was now faced with an interesting dilemma in applying the simple structure rule. This dilemma is illustrated in Fig. 2.3.

Let us assume that we have administered 8 tests of general ability to a group of children; 4 of these tests measure numerical ability (N), and 4 measure spatial ability (S). The position of the eight tests in two-dimensional space is as shown. The solution in terms of *g* and an S − N factor would be that favoured by *Spearman* (1927); the rotated solution in terms of S_1 and N_1 would be reached according to Thurstone's simple structure criterion. But note that there are in fact practically no zero loadings; the two axes come as close as possible to the clusters of tests, but nowhere reach them! This is of course due to the fact that these clusters are too close together; in other words, they are themselves correlated. (Remember that the angle of separation, or rather its cosine, indicates the correlation between two variables or sets of variables.) If we want to have proper "simple structure" we would have to draw our axes as is shown by the stippled lines S_2 and N_2. This would be satisfactory, but now we have two factors which are not independent – the angle between these lines is 60 °, corresponding to a correlation of +0.50! Thurstone was thus forced to make a choice – he could retain simple structure, and abandon orthogonality (independence) between factors, or he could retain independence and abandon simple structure.

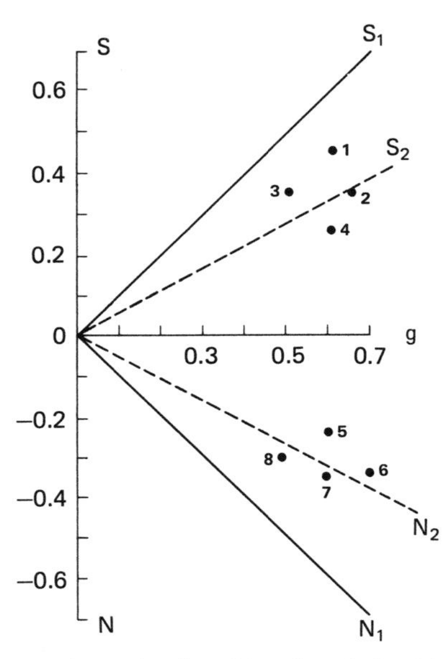

Fig. 2.3. Alternative placements of axes for describing the relationship among eight ability tests

He chose the former; he permitted factors to be correlated, as long as the rules of simple structure were obeyed.

This immediately shows us a way out of our difficulty of having to choose between two apparently equally good solutions, as in the case of Eysenck's reanalysis of Thurstone's original data. We can admit a number of primary abilities, but now note that these are themselves correlated! It is from these correlations that we can derive a general factor, *g*, in the manner of Spearman. In this way we can have our cake and eat it, too. The sort of model we would end up with is a hierarchical one, as indicated in Fig. 2.4. There are a number of correlated primary abilities (verbal, numerical, spatial, etc.); *g* or general intelligence is deduced from the intercorrelations between factors, just as Spearman originally deduced it from intercorrelations between tests. Each of the primary factors, in turn, is based on the intercorrelations between tests (T_1, T_2, T_3 . . . T_4.) The hierarchical model reconciles the apparently antagonistic positions of Spearman and Thurstone, along lines originally suggested by *Burt* (1940). Does this position square with the facts? Table 2.6 gives the intercorrelations between Thurstone's 6 major primary abilities, and the factor saturations deduced from this matrix; it will be seen that the matrix itself is very close to one of rank one, i. e. a matrix which obeys Spearman's rule for the existence and extraction of a general factor, *g*. Furthermore, the primary abilities are arranged in such a manner that the saturations make perfectly good sense on the hypothesis of a general factor of intelligence; thus *reasoning* has a very high saturation of 0.84, while rote memory and spatial ability have quite low saturations. *Thurstone* (Thurstone and Thurstone, 1941) himself agreed that this so-called "second-order factor" (i. e. a factor extracted from the intercorrelations between primary

Table 2.6. Intercorrelations among Thurstone's "primary mental abilities"

	R	W	V	N	M	S	Factor saturation	
R	(0.71)	0.48	0.55	0.54	0.39	0.39	0.84	Reasoning
W	0.48	(0.48)	0.51	0.47	0.39	0.17	0.69	Word fluency
V	0.55	0.51	(0.46)	0.38	0.39	0.17	0.68	Verbal ability
N	0.54	0.47	0.38	(0.36)	0.19	0.22	0.60	Numerical ability
M	0.39	0.39	0.39	0.19	(0.22)	0.15	0.47	Rote memory
S	0.39	0.17	0.17	0.26	0.15	(0.12)	0.34	Spatial ability

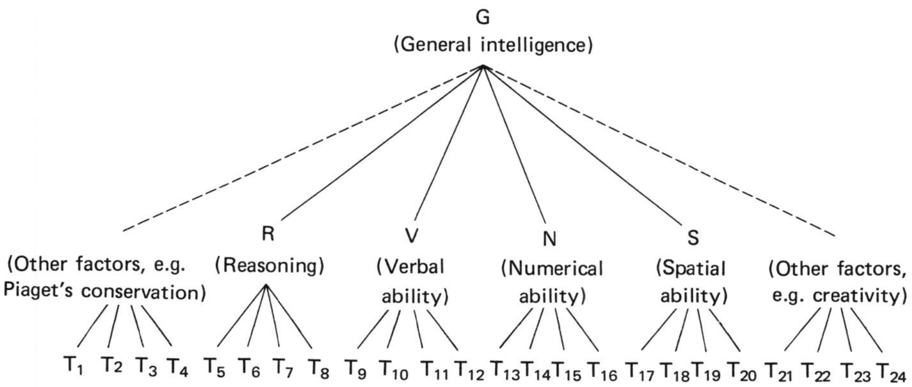

Fig. 2.4. The hierarchical model of human abilities

factors) was in essence quite similar to Spearman's *g*. Provided we permit the extraction and rotation of correlated factors (also sometimes called "oblique" because when diagrammed the axes are oblique, i. e. depart from orthogonality), there is no longer and argument between Spearman and Thurstone, or either of them and Burt.

Thus far we have only dealt with artificial data, and the reader may wonder to what extent these represent reality. Let us therefore next look at some real data, namely intercorrelations between the ten subtests of the Wechsler W. P. P. S. I, i. e. a pre-school battery of tests very widely used. The construction follows that of the adult version, which we shall discuss in some more detail in a later chapter; essentially the test is subdivided into a verbal-educational and a practical-perceptual part, with the latter containing items presented in pictures and blocks, rather than words and numbers. The study, which was carried out in my Department by W. Yule and others administered the test to 76 boys and 74 girls in the age range of 4–6½ years. The sample was randomly divided into two halves, each containing 38 boys and 37 girls, in order to see what extent the factorial analyses of the results of the two samples would compare. The results are shown in Table 2.7, for the two samples separately. The titles of the sub-

Table 2.7. Two different factorial solutions of the Wechsler test subscales intercorrelations, rotated into simple structure, with and without a general factor

	I	II	I	II	III	
			Sample I – Factor Loadings			
1	0.838	0.000	0.697	0.557	0.000	Information
2	0.884	0.000	0.778	0.382	0.000	Vocabulary
3	0.734	0.000	0.742	0.000	0.000	Arithmetic
4	0.609	0.000	0.581	0.000	0.000	Similarities
5	0.720	0.000	0.622	0.347	0.000	Comprehension
6	0.000	0.689	0.689	0.000	0.000	Animal House
7	0.000	0.705	0.663	0.000	0.000	Picture Completion
8	0.000	0.715	0.600	0.000	0.477	Mazes
9	0.000	0.560	0.567	0.000	0.000	Geometric Design
10	0.000	0.863	0.796	0.000	0.370	Block Design
r = 0.760						
			Sample II – Factor Loadings			
1	0.695	0.000	0.576	0.313	0.000	Information
2	0.694	0.000	0.537	0.446	0.000	Vocabulary
3	0.718	0.000	0.733	0.000	0.000	Arithmetic
4	0.592	0.000	0.639	0.000	0.000	Similarities
5	0.799	0.000	0.638	0.694	0.000	Comprehension
6	0.000	0.422	0.429	0.000	0.000	Animal House
7	0.000	0.731	0.708	0.000	0.000	Picture Completion
8	0.000	0.702	0.562	0.000	0.545	Mazes
9	0.000	0.374	0.340	0.000	0.000	Geometric Design
10	0.000	0.784	0.698	0.000	0.320	Block Design
r = 0.717						

tests are given in the Table to give the reader some idea of what these tests are like. The first two columns represent a typical Thurstone-type solution with oblique (correlated) factors; it will be seen that the first factor has loadings only on the verbal-educational tests, while the second factor has loadings only on the practical-perceptual factor. Note particularly that these two factors are highly correlated; r = 0.76 for the first sub-sample, and 0.72 for the second.

The next three columns represent an alternative, Burt-type solution. Here we have a general factor, i. e. all the tests have quite high loadings on this factor; this is followed by two factors, corresponding to the verbal-educational and the practical-perceptual factors respectively. The loadings for these two "primary" factors are now a good deal lower than before because much of the variance has gone to the general factor; in the Thurstone-type solution this general factor is implicit in the high correlation between the two "primaries". At first sight the two solutions look quite different, and seem to have different implications, but

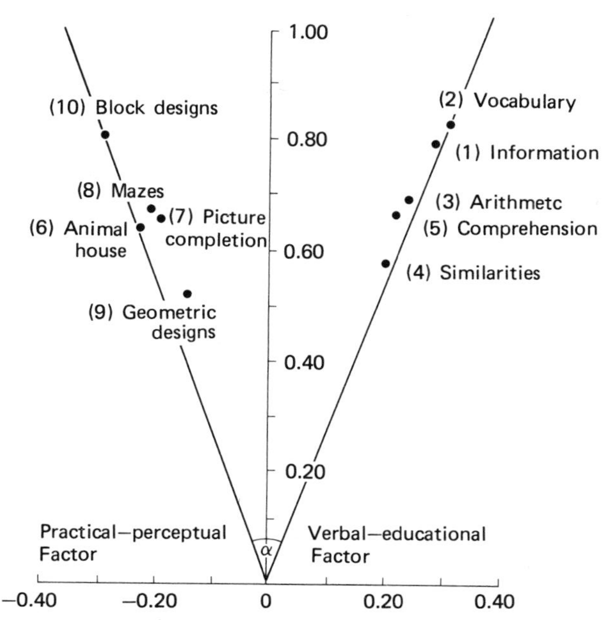

Fig. 2.5. Factorial solution of real-life intercorrelation matrix

they can be mathematically transformed one into the other, and psychologically too they amount to much the same thing. It is easy to be misled into thinking that two apparently different solutions must suggest entirely different psychological mechanism, but this is not so. The two solutions are entirely equivalent for all practical purposes.

Indeed, it is possible to calculate a third solution which is apparently different again, but also amounts to much the same thing. In our second solution we have presented factors 2 and 3 as independent; we would also have presented them on one and the same factor, but with + and – loadings respectively. Such a solution, from the same data, is shown in Fig. 2.5; this should be looked at as analogous to our Fig. 2.3, but with real data. It may seem confusing at first that there are so many mathematically equivalent solutions, all representing the original data equally well; in fact there is an infinite number of such solutions, and thus there is great importance in having rules by which to select the best-fitting and psychologically most meaningful.

Note in Fig. 2.5., that the two sets of verbal-educational and practical-perceptual tests fall into two quite clearly demarcated groups; that all the subtests have high loadings on the general factor; and that the angle between the lines drawn through the centres of the two clusters of subtests is just about 40 °, which gives a correlation of 0.766 (cos 40 ° = 0.766). Thus this agrees perfectly with the first solution given in Table 2.7 which showed a correlation of 0.760, and in which the general factor is hidden in this oblique solution. The solution set out in Fig. 2.5 is perhaps to be preferred to the others because it gives the best and simplest *ad oculos* demonstration of the actual relations obtaining between the tests. It will be quite clear why simple structure and retention of orthogonality between these two factors cannot both be retained, and why Thurstone abandoned orthogonality and preferred the retention of simple structure – the solution shows that if we look at the lines drawn through the clusters (representing Thurstone factors as indicated in the first solution in Table 2.7), there is a maximum number of zero loadings, namely 5 + 5 = 10. With general factor loadings as high as those here found, ranging from a high of 0.83 to a low of 0.52, the sum of the ten subtests clearly gives a good measure of IQ.

How about Spearman's notion of tests so similar that they permitted identical specific factors (*s*) to upset the regularity of the matric of intercorrelations? He might argue that Thurstone's primary factors arose from precisely this cause; that in other words he obtained a verbal factor because his verbal tests all were rather similar in form, and thus produced correlations due to an *s* of "verbality". Looking at the tests typically used by Spearman and Thurstone, it is indeed apparent that Thurstone tolerated tests which were quite similar in many ways, while Spearman insisted on marked differences between them. The argument is largely verbal from here on; fundamentally it matters little whether Thurstone's factors arose because of correlations due to *s* factors or not. What matters is that these factors have important functions in isolating different abilities which determine a person's differential success in verbal, numerical, spatial and other types of school subjects, over and above general intelligence. We might think of *g* as a kind of weighted average of all the primary abilities (weighted by the relative importance, or factor saturations, of each primary ability); the separate abilities can then be indicated on a graph in the form of a personal profile for a given person. Such profiles are much more informative than a simple statement of IQ; they indicate the IQ by the general level of the profile, but also indicate special strengths and weaknesses on the part of the examinee. Some types of tests, such as the culture-fair ones, are almost entirely measures of *g*; they have little by way of loadings on primary mental abilities. This would seem to follow from Spearman's theory of the nature of *g*, and it is satisfying to see the prediction borne out. Other tests, such as vocabulary tests, also have high *g* loadings (as well as a loading on the verbal factor, of course); the difference between these tests rests largely on the differentiation already noted between g_f and g_c, i. e. fluid and crystallized ability.

Reality is perhaps a little less clear-cut than Fig. 2.4 would indicate. Fig. 2.6 illustrates the picture most favoured by English psychologists (*Vernon*, 1965). He notes that *g* is at the top, as in Fig. 2.4; however, he also notes that there is another powerful grouping of the primary factors in two sets, labelled respectively v : ed (verbal-educational) and k:m. A habit has grown up of referring to abilities by letters, just as we refer to general intelligence by the letter *g*; *k* refers to spatial and *m* to motor ability. The letter f refers to fluency; *w* and *v* to verbal-literary and verbal-linguistic ability respectively; *n* to numerical, *p* to perceptual ability, and so forth. As Vernon says: "After removing the general factor . . ., the positive residual correlations always fall into two main groups – the verbal-educational group and the spatial-practical-mechanical group. The v:ed factor usually yields additional minor fluency and divergent thinking abilities-scholastic and n or number subfactors. Likewise the k:m complex includes perceptual, physical, and psychomotor, as well as spatial and mechanical factors, which can be further subdivided by more detailed testing. In addition there seem to be various cross-links: for example clerical tests usually combine verbal ability and perceptual speed, *p*; likewise maths and science depend both on number and spatial abilities, *n* and *k*. Sometimes an inductive reasoning ability (also very relevant to science) can be distinguished, though most of the common variance of reasoning tests is apt to be absorbed into *g*. At a still lower level in the hierarchy come what are usually referred to as specific factors, though of course any specific factor can be turned into an additional narrow group factor by devising additional tests."

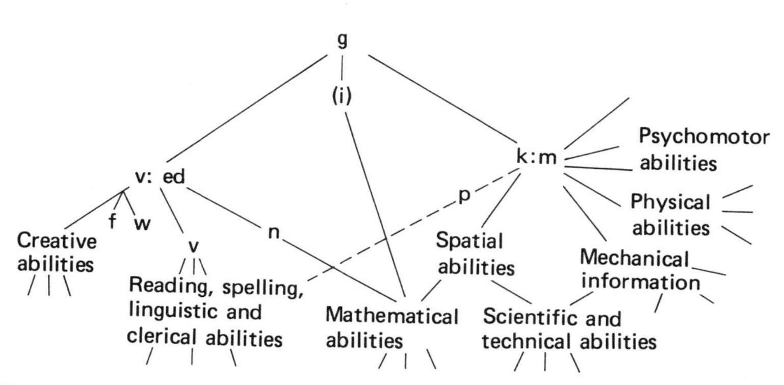

Fig. 2.6. Vernon's model of the main general and group factors underlying tests relevant to educational and vocational achievements

The major division made by Vernon between v:ed and k:m may be related to the differential functioning of the two hemispheres. There is a good deal of evidence partly from split-brain studies (in which the *corpus callosum* and other structures joining the two hemispheres are cut for the relief of intractable epilepsy), to indicate that superiority of speech, calculation and related linguistic or analytic activities are predominantly located in the *left* hemisphere, and configurational, spatial and synthetic activities in the *right* hemisphere (*Bogen* and *Gazzaniga*, 1965; *Levi-Agresti* and *Sperry*, 1968). Thus there seems to be biological support for the major division of cognitive ability, aligning v:ed abilities with the left hemisphere, and k:m abilities with the right hemisphere. We shall later on discuss the biological basis of intelligence, and in particular the relationship between IQ and such physiological measures as EEG evoked potentials; it is interesting that in split-brain work, too, evoked potentials have been linked with the differential roles of the two hemispheres (*Gatt* et al., 1977).

American authors have usually preferred to think largely in terms of primary abilities, possibly by the erroneous analogy with chemical elements, imagining that *g* is built up, like some gigantic molecule, from numerous atoms; English authors tend to follow some such hierarchical model as that of Vernon. Mathematically of course the two schemes are identical, but from the scientific-theoretical and from the practical points of view the British scheme is superior, as has indeed been recognized also by many American writers (e. g. *Humphreys*, 1962; *McNemar*, 1964). The former reasons will be dealt with later on in some detail; they are related to such theoretical predictions as those of Spearman, concerning the nature of high *g* loading types of items, and the fact that biological indices of intelligence, such as the A. E. P. (averaged evoked potential) is correlated with measures of *g* regardless of the particular nature of the primary abilities also measure by each test. The practical advantages in vocational guidance and occupational selection, in school and university work, etc., are simply that the major portion of the predictive burden is always borne by *g*, and after that by v:ed or k:m; other factors make very little addition, except occasionally. We thus save much time and money by concentrating on those factors and measures which make the greatest contribution, rather than on those making the least. This should not lead us to neglect the measurement of primary abilities (even though the word "primary" may suggest a certain superiority for these factors which they do not in fact possess); as scientists it is our duty to obtain as clear and comprehensive a picture of the human intellect as possible.

What are the main primary abilities? In Check Your Own IQ I have given typical examples of the test problem which define each factor. There are many more factors, and those here given are defined by many more different tests than could be reproduced here; the present selection is only given to illustrate the range of problems used by psychologists. The tests illustrated are of course all group tests, i. e. they can be administered to *groups* of children or adults at a time. Many IQ tests require apparatus, and can only be administered to one subject at a time (individual testing). The apparatus concerned might be shapes cut out from wood which have to be fitted together, or blocks of wood, variously coloured, which are to be combined to make certain patterns, or pictures with pieces cut out which have to be inserted, etc. Young children seem to like apparatus tests of this kind (as indeed do some adults) because it gives them something to do with their hands. Individual tests are usually used with psychiatric patients, the reason being that the examiner can detect, and make allowance for, such features as wandering attention, lack of motivation, and even hallucinations which interfere with carrying on with the testing. For most other purposes group tests are preferred, if only because they do not make such great demands on the time of the psychologist; in fact, many such tests can be given by teachers, social workers, nurses and other specially trained for the job. Tests can also be administered by computer; the problems are shown in the form of slides, and responses are made by pressing buttons. Instructions are given in the form of slides also, and the score for each subject can be calculated within a matter of seconds by the computer. The advantage of computer testing, apart from the saving in man-power, is that the test items can be selected for each person in the light of his performance (individualized testing). Thus if we have items ranging in difficulty from 0 to 100, the computer might start with a problem at level 50; if this is passed he goes on to level 75, if failed he goes down to level 25. Depending on whether these new problems are passed or failed, the computer goes up or down the scale of difficulty until he homes on the approximate level of competence of the subject being tested. In this way we save time by omitting lots of items too easy or too difficult for our subject.

The factors most prominent are *Reasoning* (which has since been split up into inductive and deductive reasoning), *Verbal Ability, Numerical Ability, Spatial Ability, Perceptual Speed, Rote Memory,* and *Perceptual Organization.* Most of these factors can in turn be subdivided; we shall come back to this problem in a later chapter, and see that this has given rise to a rather different theory of the "structure of intellect". For the moment, however, we are interested only in demonstrating the variety of tests which have been used in the factorial study of intelligence.

Summarizing the factor-analytic evidence on the validity of the Spearman-Thurstone-Burt theory of intelligence, we find that on the whole there is strong support for the following conclusions: (1) The data are in agreement with the proposition that all cognitive behaviour is determined to varying degree by a general ability underlying all special manifestations; (2) Different persons possess this ability to varying degree; (3) Tests similar in item content (verbal, numerical, etc.) or mental processing requirement (memory, reasoning) may require additional special abilities; (4) A hierarchical model best encompasses these various facts. We shall consider in later chapters possible criticisms of the model, as well as alternative models, such as those suggested by *Guilford, Piaget, Eysenck* and others; for the moment let us merely state that the model as outlined is successful in linking together a large number of divergent facts which are difficult to account for in any other way. Critics who object to the model would have to suggest a different model which would have to deal with the following empirical findings: (1) Correlations between all cognitive tests range themselves in the form of a "positive manifold", i. e. all the correlations are positive. (2) Factor saturations of tests closely follow prediction from Spearman's noegenetic laws, as well as agreeing with common sense (i. e. considering reasoning tests to be more diagnostic of mental ability than rote memory tests). (3) Tests of g_f correlate closely with tests of g_c, suggesting that learned behaviour depends very much on fluid cognitive ability.

All the facts so far considered are statistical in nature, and are therefore susceptible to the charge that they speak with a forked tongue; it is possible, as we shall see later in considering Guilford's "structure-of-intellect" model, to distribute the variance of the general factor over a large number of very small factors, and thus provide a statistically equivalent, although theoretically inferior, model which cannot be disproved by statistical analysis alone. There are fortunately direct experimental ways of answering the question of the psychological meaningfulness of the general factor of intelligence, and although these are rather technical we shall in brief consider two of these. The first deals with the physiological basis of cognitive behaviour, and in particular the measurement of the latency and amplitude of the A. E. P. (averaged evoked potential) on the EEG, i. e. an analysis of the brain waves recorded when visual or auditory stimuli are suddenly presented to the subject. When this occurs, we obtain a result as shown in Fig. 2.7. In this figure the band of small waves at the beginning, enclosed in a stippled rectangle, is the baseline, i. e. the amount of

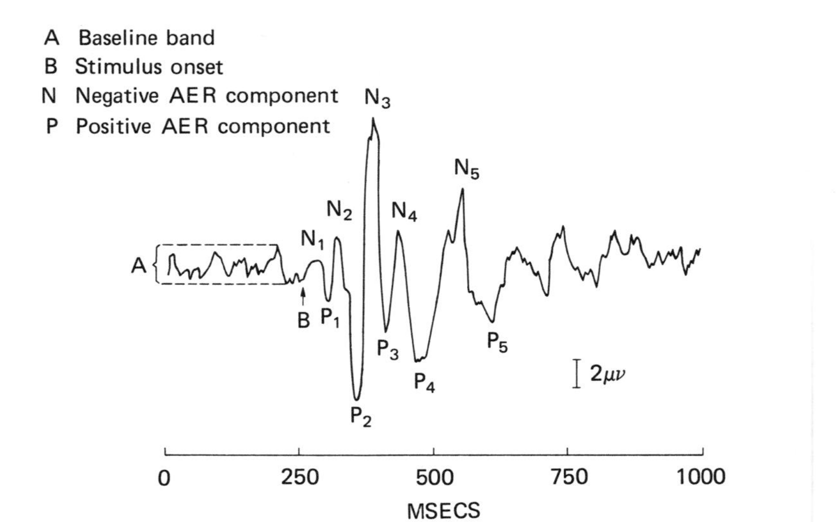

Fig. 2.7. Averaged evoked potential responses, showing record of an actual subject. Adapted from *Shucard and Horn* (1972)

reactivity shown without specific stimulation; this forms the background against which the special effects of stimulation are seen. At point B the stimulus is applied, and the numbered N and P peaks and troughs of the resulting waves are the negative and positive components of the resulting AEPs.

The signal-to-noise ratio is low in this type of work, and hence many time-locked evocations of the response are required to produce an averaged potential which can be measured; fortunately these responses are very similar to each other, and characteristic for a given person, so that averaging is possible. *Ertl* (1968) first looked at these responses with a view to relating them to IQ, and showed that latencies were longer for subjects with low IQs than for subjects with high IQs. This tendency of brighter subjects to produce faster waves is shown in Fig. 2.8; the effect will be quite obvious for these three rather different subjects. These subjects were selected to illustrate the effect; in a later paper *Ertl* and *Schafer* (1969) published a more convincing comparison of ten bright and ten dull subjects (Fig. 2.9) which shows much the same effect.

Ertl's early work suffered from technical and methodological deficiencies, as did many of the later studies, some of which failed to support his early findings; the reported correlations in this early work of Ertl's were too high to be readily acceptable. However, later work of much better technical proficiency (e. g. *Shucard* and *Horn*, 1973) has demonstrated beyond any doubt that quite sizable correlations exist between A. E. P. s and IQ, particularly g_f; the correlations observed depend to some extent on the number of different measures taken, and their combination. (*Street* et al., 1976, have shown the complexity of the evoked response potentials in a factor analysis of correlations between them.) We thus see that it is possible to find a physiological substrate of IQ, and one which is highly heritable; we have found heritabilities of between 80% and 90%

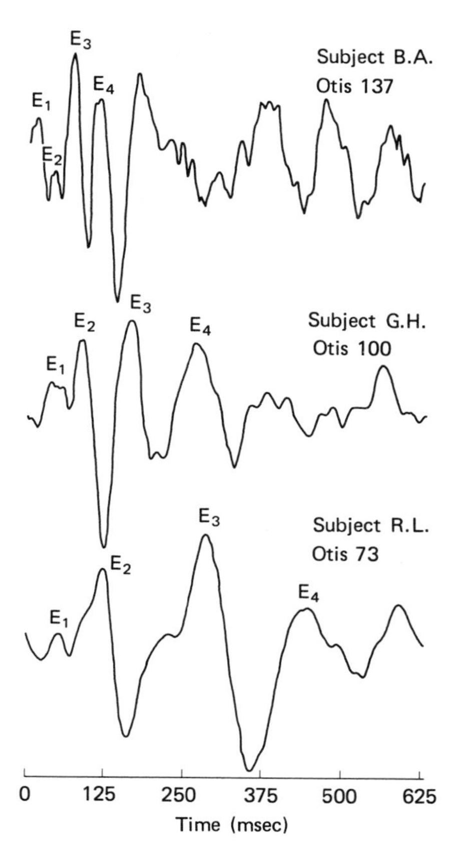

Fig. 2.8. Average evoked potentials from 3 subjects of widely differing psychometric intelligence. Adapted from *Ertl* (1968)

Table 2.8.

Latency:	Verbal	Spatial	Total
P_1	−0.41	−0.39	−0.44
N_1	−0.44	−0.38	−0.45
P_2	−0.48	−0.44	−0.50
N_2	−0.34	−0.35	−0.38
P_3	−0.41	−0.29	−0.38
N_3	−0.29	−0.25	−0.30
Amplitude:			
A3	0.31	0.10	0.22
A4	0.35	0.25	0.37
A5	0.31	0.19	0.27

Correlations between Verbal, Spatial and Total scores on the AH4 test intelligence, and evoked potential latency and amplitude.

Numerical subscripts refer to successive waves; P and N, to positive and negative deviations respectively.

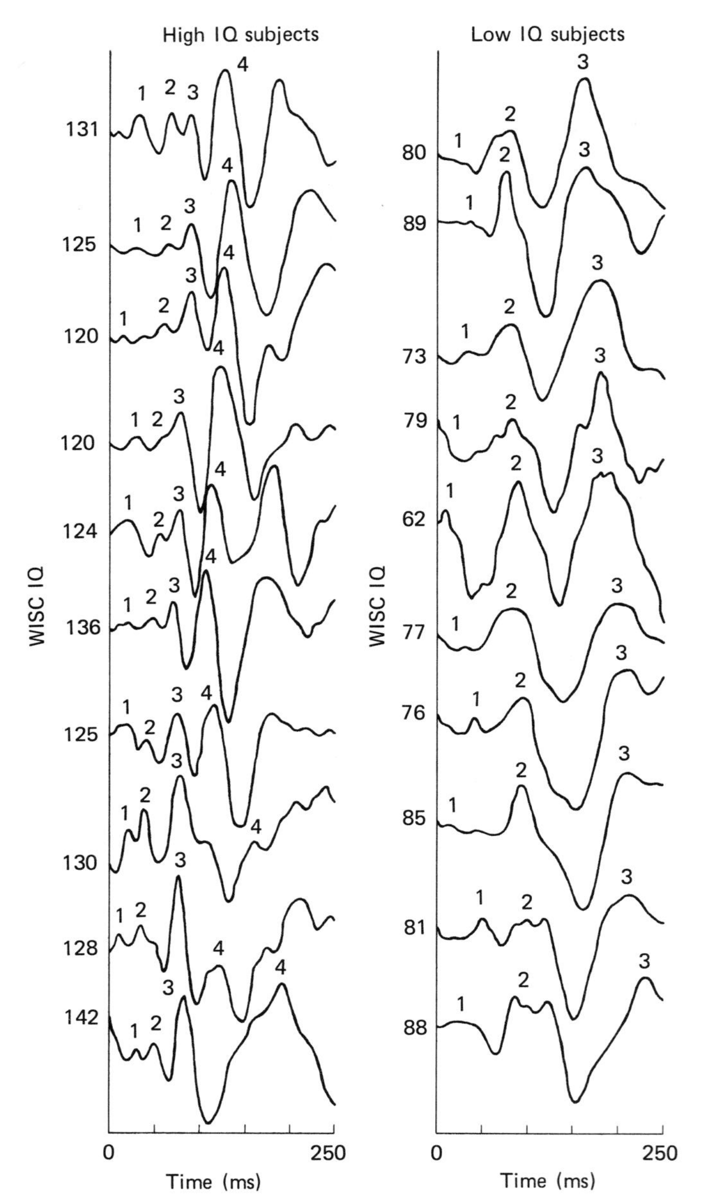

Fig. 2.9. Specimen visual evoked potentials for ten high and ten low IQ subjects. Adapted from *Ertl* and *Schafer* (1969)

in our own work (*Eysenck*, 1973). The question now arises whether this physiological measure is correlated with any particular type of mental test (verbal, memory, spatial, numerical, etc.), or whether it is correlated rather with general intelligence, i. e. relates significantly with all these different types of test. *Shucard* and *Horn* (1972) have found evidence for the latter hypothesis, and this must give strong support for the theory of *g*.

In our own laboratories, E. Hendrickson has found similar support (*Eysenck*, 1973). Using the verbal and spatial parts of the AH4 test of intelligence (a well-known and well-standardized IQ test) she correlated the scores of 93 adult subjects with both amplitude and latency of AEPs, using an auditory stimulus. The observed correlations for the various parts of the resulting waves are shown in Table 2.8; it will be seen that the correlations with verbal and spatial ability are very similar (particularly when we bear in mind the respective reliabilities of the sub-tests), thus demonstrating again that the correlation is with general intelligence, rather than with special primary abilities. Amplitude and latency are not correlated, so that we may add the correlations together via their inverse hyperbolic tangent functions; this shows that the correlation between IQ and AEP is about 0.6; this value is far from unity, of course, but a promising beginning to the physiological study of IQ. The interpretation of AEPs as possibly being related to the processing of information through the cortex would admirably fit into a Spearman-type theory of mental functioning.[3]

An even simpler measure of biological efficiency than the evoked potential is palmar conductance, i. e. the (lack of) resistance to the passage of an electric current offered by the skin of the hand. This is conceived of as a measure of cortical arousal, activated by the reticular formation, and has been found by *Bastendorf* (1960) to be very significantly correlated with IQ as measured by the Wechsler test. Bastendorf used six groups of children, divided into 9 and 12 year olds, and within age groups divided into retarded, normal and superior. The IQs of these three groups were 70, 100 and 132 for the 9 year olds, and 71, 100 and 130 for the 12 year olds. The mean palmar conductance levels, using a rather arbitrary scale, were 34, 48 and 57 for the 9 year olds, and 48, 63 and 75 for the 12 year olds, the values ascending in size with increase of IQ for the two age groups. The results show that palmar conductance increases with increasing age, and it increases with increasing IQ; this suggests that the relationship between mental age and conductance would be even greater than that between conductance and IQ. However that may be, there clearly is a statistically significant relationship between conductance and intelligence ($p < 0.001$), suggesting strongly the existence of some biological substratum for IQ. Bastendorf interpreted his results as falling into line with Wechsler's conclusion that "any practical definition of intelligence must fundamentally be a biological one." (*Wechsler*, 1943).

Quite a different method of attempted proof constitutes our second type of study. As we shall see in a later chapter, intelligence is inherited to a marked

3 Mental retardates have often been compared with normals with respect to the shape of the evoked potential response; as expected, there are large and congruent differences (e. g. *Bignum* et al., 1970).

extent, and apart from the additive genetic factor there are also non-additive ones, such as assortative mating (bright men marrying bright women, and vice versa), and dominance. High IQ is dominant over low IQ, and it may be deduced from this, following traditional genetic theory, that the children of parents who show some degree of consanguinity (such as cousins) would have lower IQs than the children of couples of similar IQ not related to each other. This "inbreeding depression" does in fact exist (*Bashi*, 1977), and is quite marked. *Schull* and *Neel* (1965) have demonstrated the effect on Japanese children, using the Wechsler scale, which consists of 10 separate subtests which span a wide range of different special abilities. (We shall look at this scale in more detail in a later chapter.) The subscales measure general intelligence, but with different success; in other words, their *g* loadings are different, ranging roughly from 0.5 to 0.8. These loadings are almost identical in Japan and America; there seems to be no cultural effect working in the direction of altering the observed structure of the intellect between these two countries.

Jensen (private communication) argued as follows. If there is a genetic-physiological substratum of *g*; if this is measured reasonably accurately by the tests of the Wechsler battery; and if the factor loadings give an accurate picture of the degree to which each test measures this *g*: then it should follow that the degree to which each subtest shows inbreeding depression must be a function of its *g* loading. In other words, tests having high *g* loadings should show the most inbreeding depression, while tests having a low *g* loadings should show the least inbreeding depression. He showed, using the published results of *Schull* and *Neel* (1965) that this was indeed so; the correlation between the two variables (*g* loading and inbreeding depression) was highly significant, in the predicted direction. It is difficult to see how this result could have been obtained unless *g* did indeed have some objective existence; in other words, the result contradicts decisively the notion that *g* is nothing but a statistical artefact.

In conclusion we would emphasize two points which often get submerged in discussions of questions like "Are IQ tests valid measures of intelligence?" The first of these points is concerned with the two meanings in psychology of the term "valid". The term may refer to internal or external validity. Internal validity means essentially that empirical facts correspond more or less closely to theoretical prediction; the facts clearly indicate that cognitive tests give rise to a unitary concept which we may call intelligence or *g*, but which in any case is obviously of considerable interest to psychologists. As far as internal validity is concerned it may be preferable to follow Spearman's example and refer to *g*, leaving it to other types of approach to settle the question of whether *g* corresponds in any reasonable manner to "intelligence" as commonly understood. This quest is a matter for external validity, i. e. the determination of the correlation between *g* and external indicators of intelligence widely accepted as reasonable and representative. Thus if such a measure of *g* failed to correlate positively and reasonably highly with success at school, at university, in life, in one's occupation, and in other types of activity presumed to require intelligence for success, then one would clearly not be justified in equating *g* and intelligence. Conversely, if *g* correlated too highly with such other, practical measures of achievement, we might be doubtful about our success in measuring intelligence;

it is well known, and empirically demonstrable, that success in these various venues is dependent on other qualities as well as on intelligence – qualities such as persistence, emotional stability, strength of character, etc. Too high a correlation between g and outside criteria would suggest that *g* was simply an amalgam of many different, independent qualities, without any great psychological interest – rather like the mixture of temperature and barometric pressure measured by the open thermometer. We shall take up this question of external validity in a later chapter; let us merely note here that the evidence is quite strong in supporting the view that the correlation between *g* and external criteria is markedly positive without being too high for acceptance.

The second point to be made relates to the construction of intelligence tests, and although this will be discussed at some length in the next chapter, it may be useful here to insist on the point that such construction is not dependent on subjective decisions in the choice of tests, but is largely determined by objective facts. (There is of course some element of subjectivity involved, but so there is, as we have seen, in the construction of thermometers!) For the measurement of *g*, we select tests on the basis of (a) high *g* saturations in preliminary testing, and (b) variety of content and mental ability tested. The higher the *g* saturations of the tests, and the greater the variety of content and mental processing involved, the better the final test. It is sometimes objected that IQ tests "are made by white, middle-class psychologists for white, middle-class children". This is simply untrue; tests which have high *g* saturations for white children and adults also have high saturations for Japanese, or black children and adults; tests which have high *g* saturations for middle-class children and adults also have high *g* saturations for working-class children and adults; tests which have high *g* saturations for male children and adults also have high *g* saturations for female children and adults. The choice is therefore objective; having specified the criteria for choice, the social class, colour, or sex of the psychologist putting together the test is largely immaterial. This is a consequence of the "indifference of the indicator" which Spearman proclaimed; as long as the model we have outlined is not displaced by a different and better model, so long will the construction of IQ tests be largely determined by objective factors.

3 The Measurement of IQ

> Everything that exists, exists in some quantity and can therefore be measured
>
> E. L. Thorndike

We have so far considered the *meaning* of intelligence, the kinds of *problems* that are suitable for the measurement of intelligence, and the evidence for the existence of a *global capacity* which might rightly be called intelligence. However, to undertake the actual measurement of this hypothetical construct requires more than the existence of individual problems; we must have a scale having certain psychometric properties. The problem is similar to that of the early workers in the field of temperature measurement who also required to have a proper scale, which they attempted to provide by having a freezing point (0° centigrade) at the bottom, and the boiling point (100° centigrade) at the top, and dividing this range into one hundred equal parts. Something analogous was needed in psychology, and this was first of all provided by the French psychologist Alfred Binet. His work generated eventually the concept of the IQ, but the actual method he used has been given up by modern workers. The scales he constructed are age scales, i. e. they relate a person's performance on a given set of tests to the *average age* at which these tests are successfully completed by children of different ages. As we shall see, age scales are complex to construct, depend on assumptions which are only very partially fulfilled in reality, and lose all meaning once the growth of intelligence with age ceases in late adolescence.

Age scales have been supplanted in most countries, and certainly for adult testing, by point scales, although for the sake of convenience, point scales are usually interpreted in terms of IQ. – in spite of the fact that these scores have nothing to do with quotients of any kind. More recent still, and another important step forward, is the development of measurement models first developed by *Rasch* (1960, 1966) in Copenhagen in the early sixties. This model, which is in many ways superior to either age or point scales, has not yet been widely used for the construction of intelligence tests, but will undoubtedly be so used in the future. In this chapter we shall begin by discussing age scales, and in particular the Binet-Simon scale, then go on to point scales, particularly the Wechsler scales, and end with a consideration of the Rasch-type scales. We will then go on to discuss some general problems of measurement which apply to all these scales.

The intelligence scales that Binet constructed were the result of a number of influences and theories, and of a variety of practical measures and experiments in tests, which created a climate which made possible this new development. Much of this climate is due to Sir Francis Galton, one of those universal geniuses who excel in many different fields. In 1869 *Galton* had published his classic paper on "Classification of men according to their natural gifts", in which he anticipated Spearman's theory of general ability and special abilities; he carried out many practical studies concerning a large number of psychophysiological variables, such as anthropometric measures of hand, arm and body length, reaction time, sensory acuity etc. His work led him to invent the statistical technique of correlation, and he was the first to use the term *mental test*. He and many others tried to use measures of acuity, of reflex activity, and other physiological functions as measures of intelligence, but these efforts failed on the whole. Some writers, including for instance Ebbinghaus, produced tests which would later on be found to be good measures of intelligence, but they had no way of demonstrating this. The first to construct an actual *scale* for the measurement of intelligence were two Frenchmen, Blin and Damaye, some of whose problems were later on taken over by Binet and Simon. They used such questions as: "What colour is this pencil?" "Are you less thirsty when it is hot then when it is cold?" "Is a week longer than a month?" "What do soldiers have on their heads?", and such instructions as: "Put out your tongue." "Put your finger on your left eye." "Go to the wall and come back here." They would also ask such questions as "What is the difference between the Catholic religion and the Protestant religion[4]?"

Binet's interest in the problem of intelligence measurement had begun in 1896, when he published an article together with Henri in which he criticised earlier attempts at mental testing. Binet and Henri believed that the tests commonly used were weighted too heavily in the direction of sensory functioning and the most simple of psychological processes, and they considered that the tests failed to contain a sufficiently varied sample of measures related to the various mental faculties. They suggested the outline of a mental test which they considered more adequate. This test would be designed to sample a variety of psychological functions, using superior or higher mental abilities, and would include tests of such abilities as memory for various materials such as musical notes, digits and words; and tests of imagery, imagination, attention, comprehension, suggestibility, moral attitudes, aesthetic appreciation, judgment and others, making ten faculties in all to be measured.

This programme was brought to fruition when in 1904 the French Minister of Public Instruction formed a committee whose task was to study how mentally defective and severely retarded children could best be taught. One of their recommendations was the inclusion of psychological examinations to determine the child's ability to profit from instruction in the ordinary school, and this recommendation proved a starting point for the development by *Binet* and *Simon* first of a set of tests, published in 1905 and, three years later, of the first Binet-Simon intelligence scales designed for children aged between three and twelve. It was in the 1908 report that *Binet* and *Simon* formally introduced the concept of *mental age* by specifically listing the three to eight items that could be passed by the majority of children at each age level from three through thirteen

4 A good account of the history of the Binet test and its forerunners can be found in *Matarazzo* (1972).

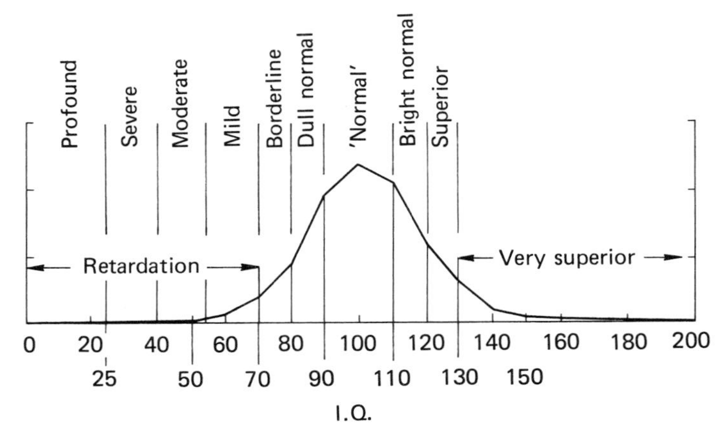

Fig. 3.1. Distribution of IQ test categories, giving rough indication of the meaning of these categories

years. There were fifty–eight such items. The principle underlying the age scale, which had first been suggested and used by *S. E. Chaille* in 1887 and published in the little known *New Orleans Medical and Surgical Journal,* is that children are arranged according to the age at which the tests are normally passed. In other words, we ascertain the average age at which children first pass a given item. We then apply the scale to a given child whose intelligence we wish to estimate, and determine at what level he begins to fail items. His mental age is determined by the age level of the items with which he succeeds. If he succeeds with all the seven year old items, and succeeds with 50% of the eight year old items as well, then his mental age would be seven years and six months. (Provided of course that he fails all the items of the nine year or higher age group.) This mental age is determined quite independently of the child's chronological age; a child with a mental age of eight could be five years old or ten years old, and Binet and Simon determined the relative brightness of a child by looking at the difference between his *chronological* and his *mental* age.

This is not a satisfactory procedure because a difference of one year looms very large in the record of a child who is young, say three or four years old, but makes little difference to a child who is twelve or thirteen. The German psychologist W. Stern suggested the use of a ratio, i. e. the ratio of mental age over chronological age; this is usually multiplied by one hundred to get rid of the decimal point so that formula reads: IQ = 100 (MA/CA). By definition the mean IQ of a given group or population must be 100, and scores above 100 indicate high intelligence, scores below 100 low intelligence. The distribution of IQs in the normal population is of course continuous, but it is customary to label various groups in the manner indicated in Fig. 3.1. This process is meaningful only as long as the relation between score and age is linear, and this is roughly true between the ages of four and twelve, although linearity may hold up a little beyond the age of twelve. Figure 3.2 indicates the development of intelligence as found in a study by N. Bayley in which the same individuals were repeatedly

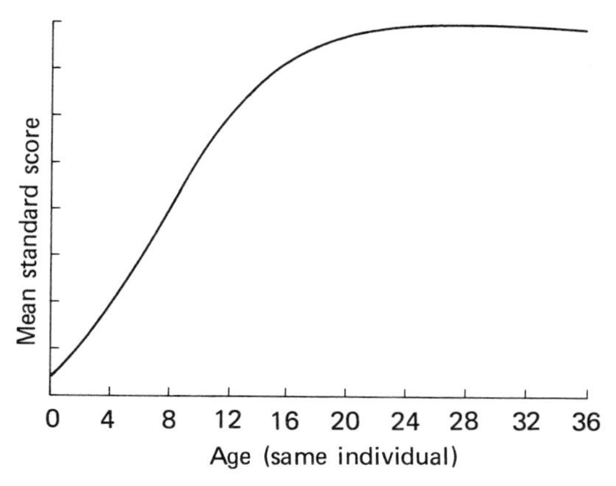

Fig. 3.2. Theoretical curve of growth of intelligence, based on repeated testing of the same individuals. Adapted from N. *Bailey's* Development of mental abilities, 1970

tested. Clearly the concept of IQ as a quotient ceases to have much meaning beyond the age of sixteen, and is certainly useless for adults. Beyond the age of twenty, adults would retain the same mental age but increase their chronological age so that a person who has an IQ of 100 at the age of twenty would have an IQ of 50 at the age of forty! This is clearly nonsense, and point scales were introduced partly in order to obviate this difficulty.

It may be interesting to take a brief look at some of the test items which Binet used in his 1908 scale. At the age of three, a child can point to nose, eyes, or mouth; can repeat sentences of six syllables; can repeat two digits; can enumerate objects in a picture, and give his family name. At the age of four he knows his sex, can name certain familiar objects shown to him such as a key, pocket knife or penny; he can repeat three digits and can indicate which is the longer of two lines five and six centimetres in length respectively.

At the age of five, the child can indicate the heavier of two cubes, one weighing three and the other twelve grams; he can copy a square, using pen and ink; he can construct a rectangle from two pieces of cardboard, having a model to look at; and he can count four pennies. At the age of six, he knows right and left as shown by indicating right hand and left ear; he can repeat sentences of sixteen syllables; he can define familiar objects in terms of their use; he can execute a triple order; he knows his age and he knows morning and afternoon. At the age of seven he can tell what is missing in unfinished pictures; he knows the number of fingers on each hand or both hands without counting them; he can copy a diamond, using pen and ink; he can repeat five digits; he can describe pictures as scenes; he can count thirteen pennies; and he knows the names of four common coins. These are typical of the accomplishments of younger children, and while the facts and broad outline of development were of course known to people interested in children for many years, the exact determination of the mean age at which the child becomes able to carry out these tests was crucial for the construction of Binet's scale.

Binet's whole theory of course is based on the fact that the child's intelligence actually increases with age, at a fairly uniform rate. The facts of this development can be brought home most clearly to adults by looking at the sequence already suggested in what has been said about some of the tests used by Binet. At the age of five for instance a child can copy a square; it is not until the age of seven that he can copy a diamond. This fact has been used at the Gesell Institute of Child Study at Yale University as the basis for a figure copying test. (Fig.3.3) The items are sequentially arranged in order of difficulty, and as the child gets older, he is more able to copy the more difficult items. The child is simply instructed to copy the items on paper, and it is found that young children succeed only with the first one or two items; as they get older, they succeed with more and more difficult items. This is not a function of teaching; it is practically impossible to coach a young child to succeed with an item which is beyond his ability. Even when by dint of hard practice a child is taught to succeed with an item beyond his age, he is found soon to forget his skill after a few days, and to return to his proper stage. This test correlates very well with other tests of intelligence, and is less influenced by cultural and environmental factors than most.

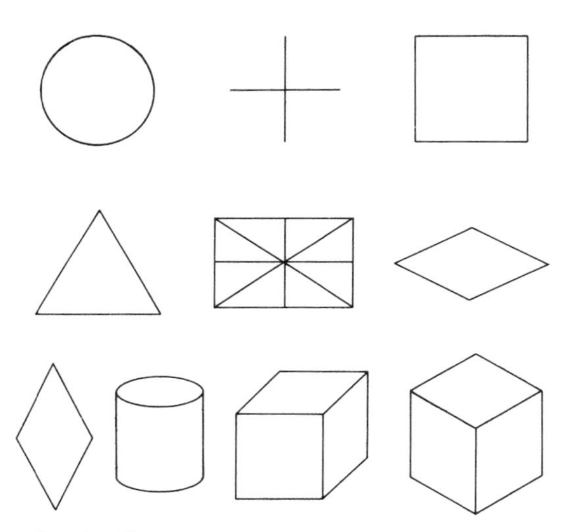

Fig. 3.3. Gesell Figure Copying Test

Binet's test has been widely used, and has profoundly influenced the construction of many other tests. Later revisions have been published by him, and revisions of these revisions in America, England and elsewhere. Binet believed that it was possible to raise intellectual performance by environmental intervention, and developed a series of procedures referred to as "mental orthopaedics". These procedures were designed to increase facility on certain component skills, in the hope that such training would improve overall intellectual functioning. There is no doubt, as we shall see, that this is feasible, although there are apparently fairly strict limitations on the degree to which improvements of this kind can be made.

Binet's views on the nature of intelligence incorporate a clear paradox. His original belief about the nature of intelligence was dominated by the then current views of faculty psychology, i. e. the belief that there were a number of faculties (memory, imagination, reasoning, etc.,) which were independent and which could be located in different parts of the brain; this would lead to the belief that intelligence was defined by a diverse set of independent abilities. Yet the test Binet eventually developed issued in a single index of mental ability, suggesting that intelligence was unitary. Binet never discussed this issue in sufficient detail to make it clear what he really believed, and his theoretical views are now of purely historical interest. Probably *Tuddenham* (1962) was right when he summarized Binet's views by saying that "Regarding intelligence as a product of many abilities, Binet sought in his tests to measure not an entity of single dimension – "general intelligence" – but rather an average level – "intelligence in general" (page 489)." This would also be the view of many American psychologists nowadays, but it does not account for the fact that these many abilities do in fact correlate together, as we have seen, and produce a matrix of rank one – or something very near it. This fact suggests very strongly that to some degree at least intelligence is a meaningful entity.

The principles of the "age"-type test make the concept of the IQ meaningful; it is indeed a quotient. However, as we have seen, this quotient makes nonsense when applied to adults, and the whole method of test construction is clumsy and often leads to odd results – such as different standard deviations in IQ at different ages. (The meaning of S. D. s will be explained presently.) For these and many other reasons, test makers generally prefer the method of the so-called "point" scales, although results are still usually expressed in terms of IQ – this is done for the sake of convenience, and while it may be confusing has become so firmly ingrained in the mental habits of psychologists and test users alike that we shall have to follow suit here.

We have already seen that IQs, when plotted for whole groups of children or adults, tend to fall into a "normal" distribution, i. e. the kind of distribution which is often known affer its discoverer as "Gaussian". Figure 3.4 shows such a distribution of IQs, also indicating the proportion of members of the group expected to lie between certain limits. Thus 25% have IQs between 100 and 110, or between 100 and 90; 2% have IQs between 130 and 140, or between 60 and 70, and so forth. The normal distribution has many statistical properties of great interest; the major one to be noted here is that it is completely described by just two numbers. The first of these is the mean, in this case of course 100. The other describes the variability of the character measured; this is the so-called standard deviation (S. D.) Looking at the curve in Fig. 3.4, we can see that as we descend from the top towards the bottom, the curve bends first one way, then the other. The point where the one bend is transformed into the other locates the S. D. point; in the case of our curve it lies at ± 15, i. e. at 115 and at 85 IQ, respectively. Knowing only that IQ has a mean of 100 and a S. D. of 15 gives us all the information contained in Fig. 3.4, and indeed a great deal more. In actual fact the distribution of IQ is not exactly normal, in this sense; we shall

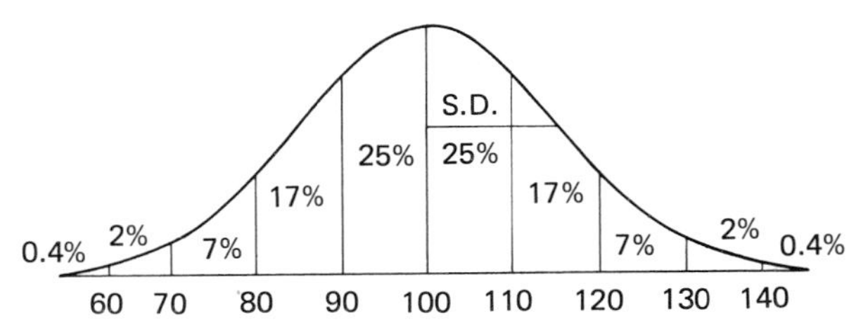

Fig. 3.4. Normal frequency distribution of IQs (Gaussian curve), indicating the percent of cases to be expected at various levels

return to this point presently. However, for all practical purposes we can neglect minor deviations and concentrate on the derivation of point scales, and the determination of their IQ equivalents.

Before doing so, we may just note that the S. D. of the IQ is not precisely known; the figure of 15 is approximate, and will be retained for our further discussion, although different tests, and different populations, give rise to different S. D. s. This makes sense; we would obviously get a larger S. D. if we included mental defectives in institutions in our sample, than we would if we excluded them. Most studies do so exclude mental defectives, and therefore underestimate the S. D. Few studies in fact can be said to test random samples of the population; this is an almost impossible task – certain individuals are almost always excluded (mental defectives, inmates of mental hospitals, prisoners, and down-and-outs.) In addition it can be argued that the purer a test is as a measure of intelligence (i. e. the higher its g saturation), the greater will its S. D. be. Consider a test made up of two types of items, correlating together perhaps 0.60, and suppose that IQs derived from each set separately have a S. D. of 20. The correlation indicates that a child having an extremely high or low score on one set of items will not have such an extreme score on the other otherwise the correlation would be much higher); that means that the curve of distribution of scores will become thinner, i. e. have a lower S. D. In the case mentioned, the S. D. of the combined set of items would be more like 15! *Cattell* (1971) has suggested that tests of g_c are more likely to combine different items in this manner, while tests of g_f are more simple, so that consequently the latter type of test would have a larger S. D. Figure 3.5 shows that this is so; tests of the former type have a S. D. of 16, tests of the latter type one of 24. In comparing IQs, differences in S. D. must always be borne in mind, as otherwise comparisons are meaningless. As we shall see later, S. D. s vary with age, so that comparisons between age groups present a hazard unless we convert results from one group into IQs having a similar S. D.

Let us suppose that we have administered a test consisting of 142 items to a group of adults who are a representative sample of the population, and let us further assume that the mean score of this group was 90, and the S. D. 10. We can immediately translate these figures into IQs by saying, first of all, that the mean score, 90 points, must by definition be equal to an IQ of 100. An IQ of 115 is one S. D. above the mean, and so is a score of 100 points (90+10); consequently a score of 100 is equal to an IQ of 115. Similarly, a score of 80 is

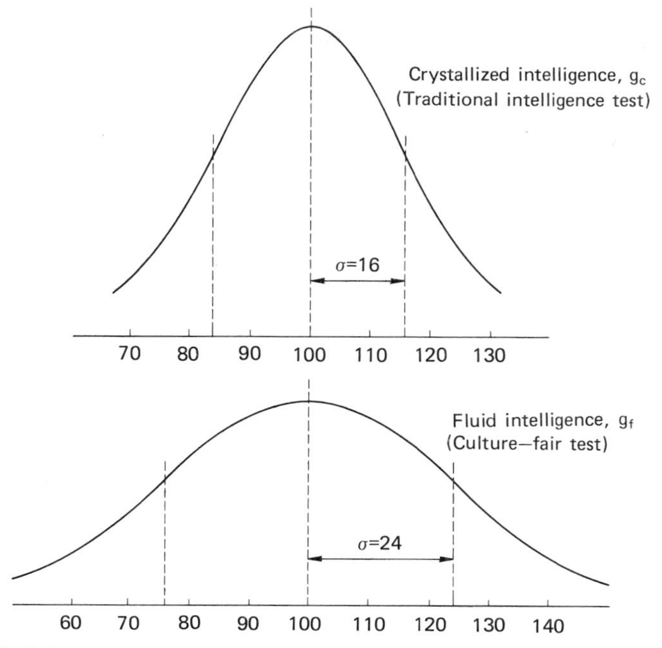

Fig. 3.5. Standard deviations of tests measuring g_c and g_f, Adapted from *Cattell* (1971)

equivalent to an IQ of 85. In this manner we can go on to translate scores into IQs – always remembering that this is just a statistical exercise, and that these artificial IQ are merely equivalents, not real quotients in any sense. In this way we can create a point scale, and score it in terms of IQ, without encountering the difficulties and absurdities of constructing an actual age scale. Note that in the point scale our real unit of measurement is not a quotient (as in IQ measurement proper), nor a simple point score, but rather the S. D.; properly speaking we should score a person as being 1 S. D. above the mean, or $2^1/_2$ S. D. s below the mean, etc. Measurement in terms of the S. D. (also sometimes denoted by the Greek letter *sigma*) is referred to as a *standard measure*; if we now retranslate these standard measures into artificial IQs, as in our example above, we are still in fact dealing with standard measures. This is important because measurement in standard terms liberates us from the restrictions of the particular unit of measurement employed (meter, ounce, pound, IQ), and allows us to compare and correlate characters not sharing the same unit of measurement. It also gives us a scale having interesting and important qualities, such as comparability of units.

We have just stated that the normal curve does not exactly apply to point scale data. There are two major reasons for this, the first trivial, the second of great importance. The trivial reason is that by deviating from proper standards of test construction we can cause the distribution of scores to differ significantly from normal, and indeed become bimodal or U-shaped. Consider an extreme example. Suppose we were to construct a test having only two kinds of items – those easy enough to be solved by anyone above IQ 90, and those so difficult that only those with IQ 110+ could solve them. There would be a large heap of individuals all with high scores, namely those with IQs above 90, who succeeded in solving all the easy items. The distribution would be grossly skewed, and be quite unlike a normal distribution. Similarly, consider a perfectly well constructed IQ test, and suppose that we add a large number of very easy items. These would discriminate between the dull subjects, but not between the bright ones (all of whom would solve practically all the items), and in this way we would get a long tail on the left of the distribution, again causing a marked skew.

Clearly it would be absurd to do these things, but minor errors of this kind do occur, and produce various slight departures from normality in actual distributions found with widely-used tests. The fact that we can influence the observed distribution by choice of items has led some people to argue that the distribution of IQs is arbitrary and subjectively controlled by the test maker, and the we cannot properly speak of the underlying distribution at all. This is not a reasonable conclusion. There are obvious rules of test construction which must be followed in order to obtain a sensible result; e. g. problems of all levels of difficulty must be presented, in reasonable proportions – to arbitrarily include too many easy or difficult problems goes counter to these rules. As we shall see, problem difficulty must be taken into account in constructing proper scales of measurement, and this is done in the more modern types of test. For certain practical purposes we may indeed construct tests having, say, much larger numbers of difficult than easy items; such a test might be used, for example, in selection for advanced education, where our interest is not in the distribution of IQ in the population, but rather in differentiating as efficiently as possible among the brightest 30% of the population, and where therefore we would not be interested in the relatively dull. But such a test, and the distribution of IQs obtained with it, would be irrelevant to the problem of distribution of IQ in the general population.

The other cause of departure from normality is much more serious (*Roberts,* 1952). It is usually found that there are many more cases of very low IQ (below 60 points or so) in the population than there ought to be on the hypothesis of a normal distribution; Fig. 3.6 illustrates this fact (although it exaggerates the hump in the tail for expository purposes.) Why this hump? There are two main reasons. In the first place, some children suffer birth injuries to the brain, with serious consequences for their subsequent mental development. These children furnish us with one group of very low IQ subjects whose low IQ cannot be accounted for in terms of the normal distribution. Secondly there are children suffering from single-gene intellectual defect, i. e. children in whom the defect is produced by very rare genes having the power to interfere with physical, metabolical and anatomical developments essential to the normal development of intelligence. Mongolism (Down's disease), phenylketonuria, and others are examples of such diseases. The existence of such disorders, or of birth injuries, does not invalidate the hypothesis of a normal distribution for intelligence; it merely suggests caution in actually describing existing populations.

While this departure from normality is relatively easy to explain, the fact

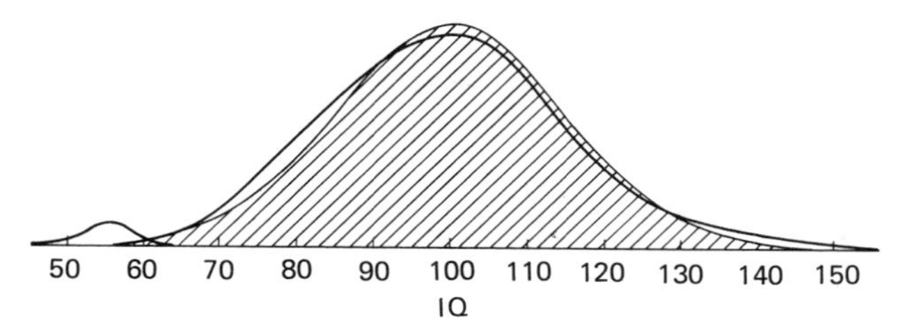

Fig. 3.6. Theoretical "normal" distribution of IQs (shaded curve) and the actual distribution in the population (heavy line), with the lower hump exaggerated for expository purposes. Adapted from *Jensen* (1972)

that at the other extreme of the curve there is a similar excess of cases is more mysterious (*Burt,* 1963). It is usually found that high and very high IQs are found more frequently than should be the case if the distribution were exactly normal. It may be possible to explain this fact by assuming that intelligence is dependent upon the combined effect of large numbers of genes; as we shall see this assumption is in line with empirical evidence. If now all these genes were of equal influence, the resultant distribution would be normal. If however, some of the genes exerted a larger influence than others, we would find a distribution with exaggerated tail effects, i. e. with too large a number of extremely high and extremely low scorers. There is at present no way of testing this hypothesis; it may or it may not be true. It could also be that similarly there were a great many different environmental causes which exerted an influence on IQ; if some exerted a much greater influence than others, again we would find a distribution extendet towards the ends. A decision between environmental and genetic theories must be left until a later chapter.

Nearly all modern IQ tests are point scales, translated (though not always) into IQ equivalents. Perhaps the best known of these tests is the Wechsler Scale, which is available both for use with adults (WAIS) and with children (WISC). The test consists of a number of subtests, some of which are verbal or numerical, others practical (i. e. requiring the manipulation of objects). This allows the tester to derive two separate (but of course quite highly correlated) IQs, namely a verbal and a performance IQ. There are hundreds of other tests, usually group tests, which give rise to some form of IQ; it should however, be borne in mind that because a test is labelled a test of intelligence, and purports to give an IQ score, it is not necessarily a good test of intelligence, or comparable to a Binet or a Wechsler. There are many very bad tests about, and results obtained with these tests are misleading and erroneous at best.

The verbal and performance scales of the Wechsler appear closely analogous to the v:ed and the k:m factors of Vernon which we introduced in Chapter 2. Does factor analysis of the correlations between the subtests of the Wechsler bear out this interpretation? *Berger* et al. (1969) have reported detailed factor analyses of such correlations for four different age groups, and extracted four factors for each group. Only the first two in each case are of much interest; the third and fourth factors have very low loadings and are difficult or impossible to

Table 3.1. Factor saturations of Wechsler subtests

Subtests	Age 18–19 Factors 1	2	Age 25–34 Factors 1	2	Age 45–54 Factors 1	2	Age 60–75 Factors 1	2
Information	57	12	44	08	55	05	66	02
Comprehension	57	02	53	10	51	09	61	02
Arithmetic	52	09	16	10	24	10	55	17
Similarities	58	10	48	04	45	10	43	19
Digit Span	50	05	10	03	08	09	38	07
Vocabulary	68	01	60	−00	60	−06	67	−03
Digit Symbol	42	14	21	21	14	11	19	40
Picture Completion	20	48	21	42	21	30	24	23
Block Design	08	60	03	55	01	55	05	66
Picture Arrangement	14	44	17	32	20	18	21	34
Object Assembly	01	61	−01	59	04	52	−00	57

interpret. Loadings for the first two factors, for all four age groups, are shown, are shown in Table 3.1. It will be seen that the first factor, corresponding to v:ed, loads on information, comprehension, arithmetic, similarities, vocabulary, and (for the youngest and oldest groups only) digit span and digit symbol). The second factor, corresponding to k:m, loads on picture competion, block design, picture arrangement, and object assembly. The names of the tests are self-explanatory (although readers interested in the measurement of intelligence should certainly acquaint themselves with the details of the test by having themselves tested, and by testing others), and the outcome is clearly in support of Vernon's hypothesis.

We have now looked at age and point scales; we next take a brief look at the so-called Rasch scales – named after Georg Rasch, a Danish psychologist. (A good discussion is given by *Gutjahr,* 1974). The look must be brief because the rationale underlying these scales is mathematically complex, and furthermore none but the recently developed British Intelligence Scale has really been designed to take advantage of the improvements made in test construction by this new method of scaling. Rasch begins by taking exception to some of the requirements of age and point scales, particularly their dependence on comparisons of an individual's performance with the performance of others of like age. This is not usual practice in physical measurement, i. e. of length, or of temperature; we measure length and temperature in absolute terms, without having to compare the particular sample we are measuring with other samples. Rasch wants to introduce independent and absolute scaling, and in doing so he more formally than anyone else has introduced the measurement of item difficulty into the measurement process. The requirements for such scaling are four fold: 1. Item difficulties are independent of the abilities of persons attempting them – in other words, if item *a* is more difficult by a certain factor than item *b* for Mr. X, then it must also be that much more difficult for Mr. Y, and Mr. Z, etc. 2. Item difficulties are independent of the difficulties of other items in the test – in other words, if item *a* has a difficulty of 10 on some scale of item difficulty, then the fact that there are other items in the scale of varying difficulty levels must not influence the difficulty level of item *a*. 3. Person abilities are independent of the particular items attempted – in other words, a person has a certain ability which can be given an absolute value along some scale, and this ability does not depend on the particular choice of items used for testing. 4. Person abilities are independent of the abilities of other persons taking the test.

Two simple assumptions are involved in these requirements. The first is that items have a unidimensional difficulty which is independent of the difficulties of other items in the set and of the abilities of subjects who attempt them. This means in essence that all items in the test discriminate along the same ability dimension and no other. The second assumption is that people have a unidimensional ability which alone determines their performance on the test, and this ability is independent of the abilities of other people who take the same test, and of the difficulties of the items which they attempt. In as far as people perform differently on the items of a test (leaving out chance errors for the moment), we may say that a single ability parameter accounts for their performance on each item. Provided the difficulties of all items attempted are known, this ability parameter can be computed and will be the same for the same person, regardless what subset of the available calibrated items is attempted. Both item difficulties and test subjects are characterised by a single measure, and all item difficulties measure the same thing as each other and as the person abilities measure. *Item and person measurements are on the same scale.*

Early work on the British Intelligence Scale suggests that these requirements are fulfilled to a reasonable extent by existing types of intelligence test items. This means that we are able to construct interval scales for intelligence, i. e. scales in which the intervals between successive points are equal in a meaningful way. Temperature measurement in degrees Fahrenheit or Celsius is such an interval scale; we have already seen that there are some difficulties even in that field to obtain proper equality of intervals when different measuring instruments are used, and no doubt similar difficulties will arise in working with the Rasch model. Even more desirable would be a ratio scale, i. e. a scale in which we have an absolute zero. Measurement of quantities such as length in metres or yards possesses such an absolute zero, and indeed so has temperature; we can find a point (by extrapolation) which is meaningfully associated with complete molecular movement, i. e. absolute zero. This point lies at – 273° Celsius, and the temperature scale based on this is named after Lord Kelvin, who discovered this point. Can we hold out the possibility that IQ too could in due course be measured on a ratio scale? *Thurstone* (1928) has attempted to establish such an absolute zero point by extrapolation, based on the finding that in the Binet test, dispersion in ability, measured in sigma units, actually increases with age; if sigma = 1.00 at age 3.5 (i. e. in the three-year old group), then it is 1.792 at the age of 14.5 (i. e. in the year old group). This change in variability was found to have a linear relationship with mean test performance for a number of tests, and by extrapolating this straight line below the ages where tests can be given, until variability vanished, Thurstone found a true zero for ability; this was located just a few weeks before birth. We thus possess scales which in essentials resemble the most powerful physical scales, having a true zero point and equal units. In practice there are of course still many detailed difficulties to overcome, and no doubt we will encounter many more. Nevertheless, it is important to realize that many of the objections made by those critics who have not looked in detail into the psychometric properties of mental testing are untrue and irrelevant in principle. This is a great advance since the days of Binet and Simon.

The Rasch model has been introduced here partly to point out the sort of work psychometrists and statisticians are doing at present in efforts to improve the rationale of mental testing; it was also introduced in anticipation of arguments to be presented in a later chapter concerning the breaking up of the IQ into its constituent parts. The methods used there are based in part on the type of analysis used by Rasch, and a preliminary view, however superficial, of his arguments seemed appropriate. The details of course are inevitably closely wrapped up in statistics, and would not be suitable for presentation here, and the same is true of Thurstone's derivation of a true zero for mental ability.

In summary of this section, we may say that the day of the age scale is definitely finished; it seems most unlikely that anyone will ever again produce a scale such as the Binet. The labour is prohibitive, the disadvantages too great, and the statistical advances which have since been made rule it out as inappropriate. The days of the simple point scale are probably numbered; scales which do not take difficulty levels of items into account in the construction of the test in something more than the usual casual manner do not make proper use of all the information that should be available about items. The future must lie with models such as the Rasch model, although here we are still at a stage of development where much work remains to be done. Measurement proceeds by steps from the most elementary and unsatisfactory to better and better methods; there is no end to this progression. Just as the measurement of temperature started out with quite elementary errors (such as not sealing the top ot the thermoscope, thus mixing up temperature and atmospheric pressure), to the measurement of intelligence started with rather unsatisfactory scales. Just as the measurement of temperature even now is far from completely satisfactory, so obviously the measurement of intelligence is still far from satisfactory. The truth is that measurement is closely tied up with the development of a satisfactory theory about the phenomena in question. Until we have a more satisfactory theory of intelligence, our measurements will be less than perfect.

We must now turn to a consideration of certain problems and criticisms which are often made of mental testing. We have already noted the criticism, often voiced, that IQ tests are made by white, middle class psychologists for white, middle class children, and we have also noted, in our discussion of the construction of test items, that these are selected on an objective, empirical basis, and not through the whim or prejudice of the test constructor. We have in this chapter presented evidence to show that these objectively selected test items are put together into tests along lines which are equally objective and empirical. Results from such, appropriately constructed and used, show that neither colour nor race affects test scores in the direction expected from the criticism. Japanese children and adults, as *Lynn* (1977) has shown, grow up in a society which spends much less money on education, and where that education certainly is not "by whites and for whites"; yet on the Wechsler tests children in all age groups from 5 to 15 were found to score higher than American children (mean score of the Japanese children = 103.1 on the performance scale). This amounts to a difference of 4.6 points, as the American norm for all Americans would be 98.5, for various reasons discussed by Lynn. Later tests gave even greater differences, amounting fo over ten points of IQ (the Japanese IQ mean was 111.7!) After some discussion of possible artefacts, Lynn concludes that "the Japanese mean IQ is significantly higher than that of North American Caucasians by somewhere between approximately three and ten IQ points. If a single figure for the mean Japanese IQ is required the most reasonable procedure is probably to take the average from the three Wechsler standardizations, weighted for the sizes of the samples. This gives an overall Japanese mean IQ of 106.6. It is believed that this is the highest mean IQ ever recordet for a national population." (P.70) Note that this "highest IQ ever recordet" was found for a non-white population significantly less "middle class" than many others with which it can be compared, and who scored significantly lower!

This finding would be difficult to explain in terms of environmental advantages and tester bias. As Lynn explains, "the Japanese have had a considerably lower per capita income than the Americans throughout the whole of the present century and consequently have had less to spend on food, education, health and most of the other environmental variables commonly advanced to explain population differences in mean IQ. For instance, in 1935 (around the time when some of the cohorts tested were born), the Japanese per capita income was approximately one-eighth of the American and, though the Japanese have been catching up fast, even by 1970 their per capita income was well under half that of the United States. Similarly, the calorie consumption of the Japanese has only been about two-thirds that of Americans throughout the period 1935–1970 . . . In education also the Japanese have been at a disadvantage. Before and during the war schooling in Japan was only compulsory from the ages of 6 to 11 and it was only in 1946 that the minimum school leaving age was raised to 14 . . . Thus it seems that the two usual types of explanation advanced by environmentalists to explain low mean population IQs (test bias and impoverished environment) cannot plausibly be invoked to account for the relatively low mean IQ of the Americans as compared with the Japanese." It is interesting that Jensen, who has tested large numbers of underprivileged Orientals in California, has also found them superior to Americans of much higher socio-economic status, taught in much superior schools (personal communication). Such facts do not permit us to accept the criticism of test bias as reasonable. It is of course possible to construct tests which show bias (in any desired direction), but the construction of such tests would violate the rules laid down for the selection of test items and the validation of tests and batteries of tests. These rules are almost entirely objective, and if followed properly should exclude any form of bias.

It is certainly true that American whites and blacks have been found repeatedly over the past 60 years to show differences in IQ of much the same size as those found between white working and middle class groups, i. e. about 15 points (*Shuey,* 1966). A large literature has developed around attempts to explain the causes of this difference (*Eysenck,* 1971); some of the major recent summaries of this work have been referred to in the Introduction. The issue is too complex to discuss here in detail, and no brief examination of the arguments would be adequate. It is important, however, to note that no extension of the finding of differences among American groups to non-American groups (e. g. whites in Europe, blacks in Africa) is permissible. Different groups have different interbreeding patterns, different patterns of immigration and emigration, and different environments requiring different qualities for survival; these differences cut across, and may be more important than, racial differences, assuming these to exist. *Lynn* (1977) has recently shown that the intelligence of Scotsmen is at present something like 4 points lower than that of Englishmen, although a century ago it was at least equal, and possibly higher. He gives strong evidence for the hypothesis that emigration of the more highly gifted Scotsmen is the answer. Thus in a relatively brief period of time quite strongly marked differences may arise between racially similar or identical groups through patterns of emigration and immigration. The discovery of oil in the North Sea, near the Scottish borders, may reverse the trend, and indeed may reverse the direction of the difference. Ethnic, national and local groups and sub-groups are in a constant state of change; this makes impossible or at least very difficult any major generalization affecting racial or other groupings.

Critics sometimes suggest that if certain populations (bushmen in Australia; blacks in Africa) do poorly on typical IQ tests, then perhaps Europeans would do poorly on such "tests" as hunting, throwing the boomerang, or tracking animals. Such activities are largely perceptual and motor tests below the level where they could be regarded as cognitive; these are skills analogous to playing tennis, or skiing. Skills of this kind can be learned, but they fail the first test of a good IQ test item, namely that of correlating with other cognitive items to a high degree. If submitted to the usual rules of test construction, throwing the boomerang or tracking animals through the forest would fail completely. Critics would therefore be better advised to consider the rules of test construction, and the results on which they are based, rather than arbitrarily name activities which have been practised by one group and not the other. If the rules of test construction are faulty, then these faults should be particularized and pointed out in technical detail. If they are not found to be faulty (and while small faults will of course always be present, we are here talking about fundamental faults which would invalidate the whole procedure), then criticism is inappropriate which disregards these rules and concentrates on spectacular but irrelevant comparisons. Whites play football better than aboriginals on the whole; aboriginals throw the boomerang better on the whole. These may be facts, but they are irrelevant to a debate about the construction of IQ tests, or their meaning – neither football nor boomerang throwing correlates to any appreciable extent with intelligence.

Similar criticisms are sometimes made with respect to class differences. It is true, as we shall see, that middle class children do better on IQ tests than do working class children; it does not follow, as is sometimes argued, that this is due to, and in turn demonstrates, that IQ tests are "unfair" to working class children, having been constructed by middle class psychologists. Not all psychologists are in fact middle class, and great efforts have been made to construct tests which would eliminate these differences between the classes; all have failed. Efforts to use slang terms more familiar to working class children to put over the instructions and the contents of the test have equally failed to change the position; even when there is clear bias in favour of the "underprivileged" child of working class origin, nevertheless he fails on the average to come up to the level of the (average) middle class child. (It is necessary to emphasize the "average" nature of these comparisons; there is of course a great deal of overlap in the two distributions, and bright working class children are better at IQ tests than dull or average middle class children.) We may consider with advantage the diagram shown in Fig. 3.7; this gives a schematic picture of the IQ differences between members of different social classes. The picture is only schematic because the terms "working class" and "middle class" are somewhat arbitrary; clearly there is a continuum from the unskilled manual worker through the semi-skilled and skilled, to clerical workers and administrators to the highest forms of professional middle class groups. In making a comparison, therefore, much depends on just where the cut is made. We have assumed a simple manual workers vs. others comparison, which gives a difference in IQ between the groups of about 15 points. Greater or smaller differences could be obtained by defining the classes somewhat differently. More detailed figures for the mean IQ of different occupations and professions will be given in a later chapter. Let us also note that, because of regression to the mean (this too will be discussed later on), the children of working class and middle class parents will show less difference than their parents.

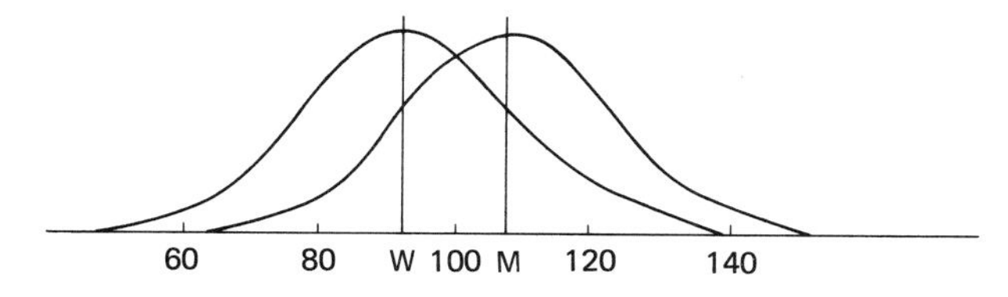

Fig. 3.7. Comparison of working class and middle class IQs, assuming equal numbers in both groups

The figure shows the large amount of overlap between the classes; it is clearly impossible to tell much about a child's IQ from knowing nothing but his social class! Nevertheless, the differences should also not be underestimated; they are particularly noticeable at the extremes. This is a function of the nature of the Gaussian distribution. At an IQ which might be regarded as a required qualification for really successful University completion (say 122.5 points), middle class children are eight times as frequently represented as working class children (16% as compared with 2%). At a point which might be regarded as a normal cut-off point for educational subnormality, requiring special teaching (say IQ 77.5 points), working class children are eight times more frequently represented than middle class children. These differences explain why there are so few working class children at University, and so many in educationally subnormal classes. It may be argued that these differences are due to environmental, not to genetic causes; this argument will be pursued in a later chapter, when we have had a chance of looking at the evidence in the nature-nurture debate. For our present purpose this argument is irrelevant. Whether the observed differences in IQ between classes are due to genetic causes, or to the influence of early environment (or, as seems more likely, to both influences working together in complex and subtle ways), it remains that the tests are fair enough in mirroring the intelligence, here and now, of the children in question, and that their future education and life history will be powerfully influenced by this ability as measured. This discussion is of course only preliminary to a more detailed consideration of the two issues adumbrated here; to what extent is intelligence genetically determined, and to what extent do IQ tests measure what we normally call intelligence? The next chapter will consider the latter question, and the succeeding three chapters will deal with the former.

Before turning to these questions, we must discuss at least in passing the relation of age and sex to measured IQ. Binet's work was of course based on the development of intelligence with age, but the abandonment of age scales leaves open the precise investigation of the nature of this relationship. Broadly speaking of course there is no question that intelligence grows with age, and probably declines with old age, but the precise details need to be investigated, such as the question of whether all types of tests increase pari passu in score with age, or whether there are some types of tests (e. g. measures of g_c) which continue to grow longer than other types of tests (e. g. measures of g_f). Such questions are of considerable importance, not only for the measurement of intelligence, but also for an understanding of its nature. The same is true of differences in ability between the sexes; are we justified in combining scores abtained from males and females, or are there important differences in ability, either general or in relation to specific abilities, which must be taken into account? We shall not go into too much detail here, but just mention the major results obtained.

Figure 3.8 shows the development and decline of the Wechsler IQ with age; the progression is very much as anticipated. IQ grows until the age of 16 to 20 or there abouts; thereafter it declines in a fairly regular fashion. The standard deviations increase with age, from around 16.8 at the age of 10.5 to 24.5 at the age of 55–59. Two things must be said right away about this figure. In the first place the values at different ages are derived from different samples; in other words, the research on which the data are based is cross-sectional, not longitudinal. This is important; we cannot assume that the differences in the cultural environment, or the eating habits, or the teaching between successive generations have not affected their IQ scores, and that we are partly testing hese differences, rather than age effects pure and simple. The other point is that this curve is the average of a number of different tests, and these may show quite marked differences in shape from each other, and from the final average curve. Follow-up data on the whole give results similar to those of cross-sectional studies (*Matarazzo,* 1972), but too few good studies are available to be certain on this point (*Horn* and *Donaldson,* 1976; *Schaie,* 1976). At times, rather divergent results may be found, as is illustrated in Fig. 3.9 (*Schaie* and *Strother,* 1968).

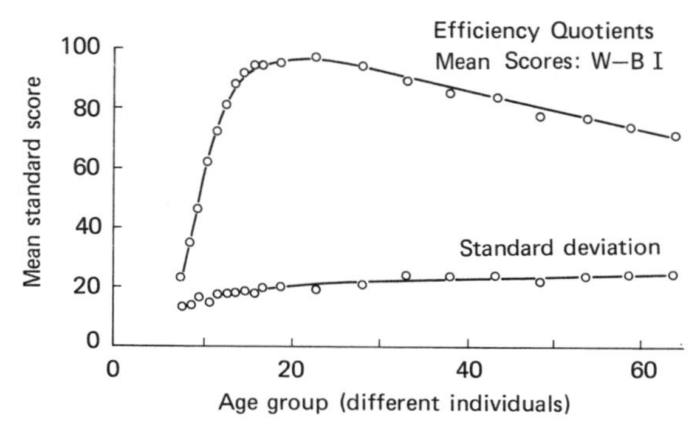

Fig. 3.8. Full-scale Wechsler standard scores, showing growth and decline with age. Adapted from *Matarazzo* (1972)

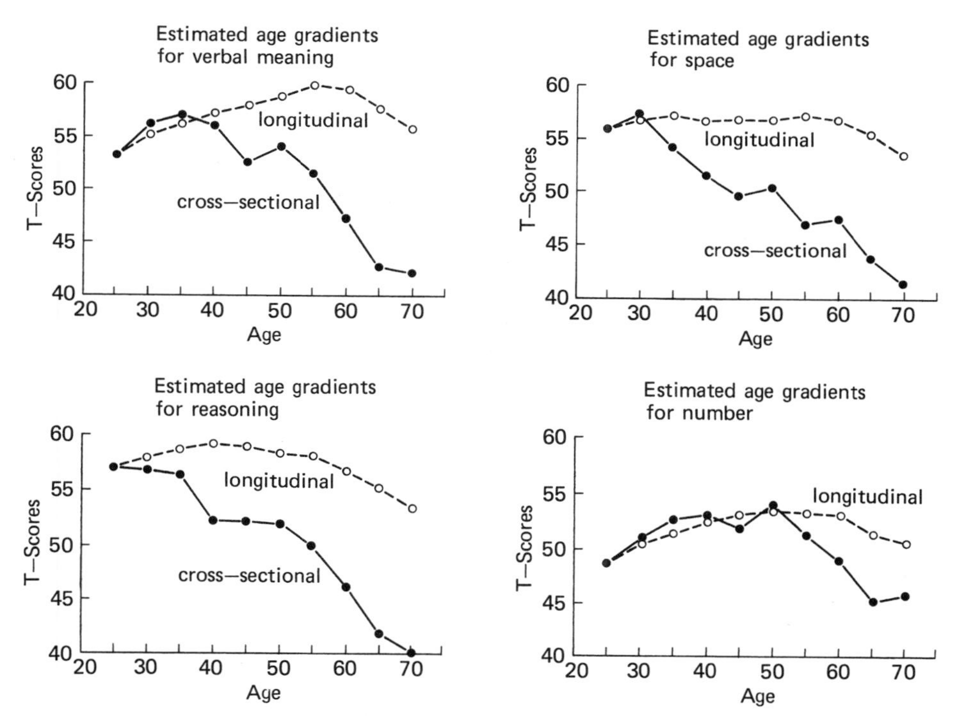

Fig. 3.9. Differences in adult intelligence as assessed by cross-sectional and longitudinal studies respectively. Adapted from *Schaie* and *Strother* (1968)

The shape of the Wechsler curve is certainly not unique; Figure 3.10 gives the combined results of several studies using different types of test – some group, some individual; some culture fair, some not. It will be seen that on the whole there is good agreement between the tests. Figure 3.11 shows that different Wechsler tests have different curves of decline with age; thus in the diagram

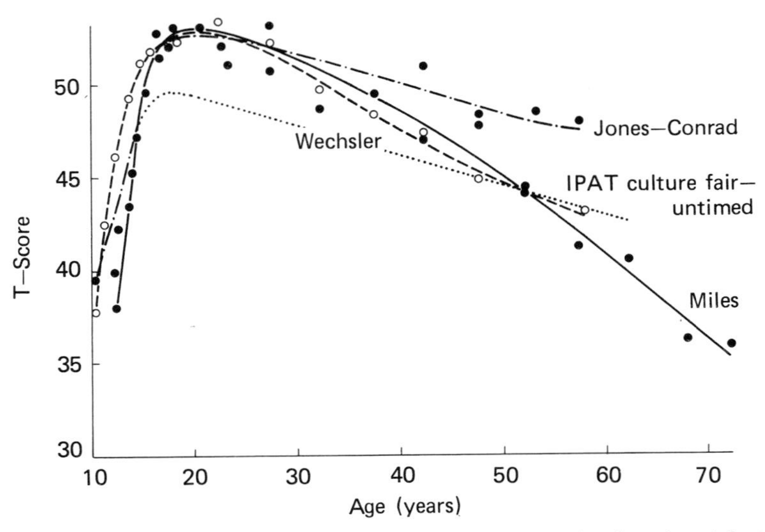

Fig. 3.10. Life-range curves on traditional intelligence tests, cross-sectional testing. Adapted from *Cattell* (1971)

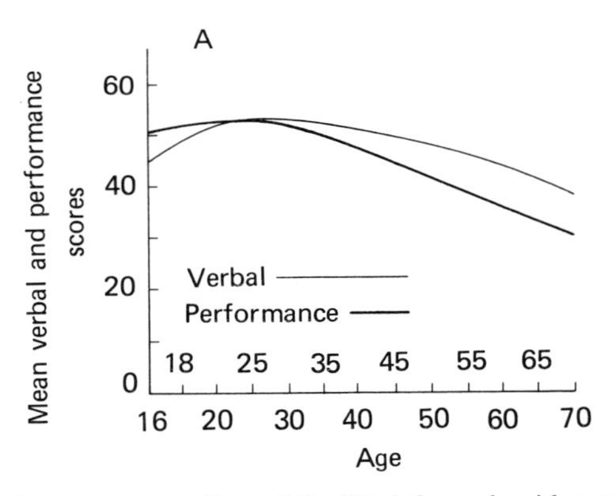

Fig. 3.11. Change in performance on sections of the Wechsler scale with age, showing comparative decline of verbal and performance subtests

verbal scores (perhaps somewhat more g_c than g_f) decline less than do performance test scores (perhaps somewhat more g_f than g_c). Figure 3.12 shows the fate of individual tests; information declines least, block design most. These figures are typical; measures of g_f generally decline much more rapidly than measures of g_c, which decline slowly or not at all.

There is another difference between crystallized and fluid ability, namely the cessation of growth as a function of age and level of ability. Figure 3.13 shows that for g_c there is a tendency for the brighter youths to keep increasing in mean performance longer than the average, and these in turn longer than the dull.

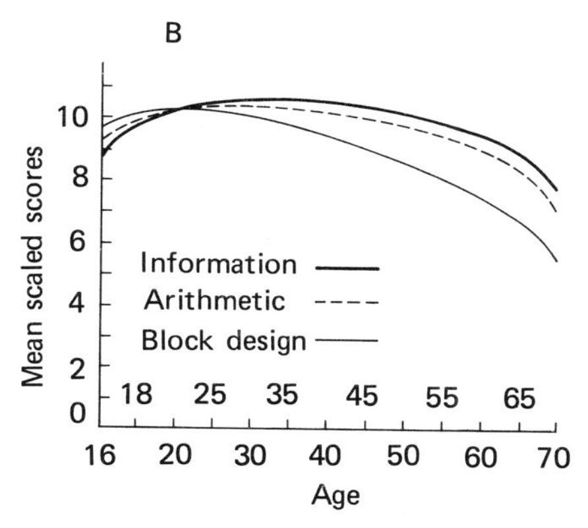

Fig. 3.12. Change in performance on sections of the Wechsler scale with age, showing scores on three subtests

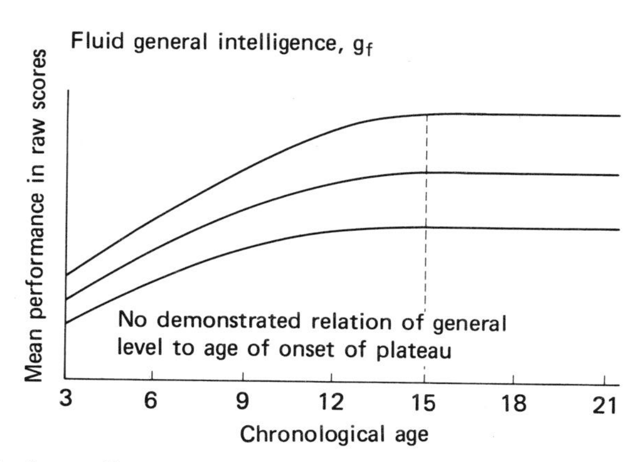

Fig. 3.13. Growth of crystallized ability with age; terminal level is reached later by the more able. Adapted from *Cattell* (1971)

This is not so for g_f, as shown in Figure 3.14. These diagrams are adapted from *Cattell*'s (1971), who discusses in detail the evidence on which the diagram is based.

The growth curve of different abilities is different too, as shown by *Thurstone* (1955). His estimates are shown in Figure 3.15; it will be seen that perceptual speed grows most quickly, word fluency most slowly. The differences are noticeable, but not overwhelming; all abilities follow a rather similar growth curve, with minor variations. In general, *Bloom* (1965) has estimated that 50% of adult IQ is already developed by the age of 4; another 30% accrues from 4–8; and the remaining 20% is consolidated by the time the child reaches the age of 17. These figures are far from accurate, of course, being average estimates subject to all the provisos we have already mentioned, such as the differential

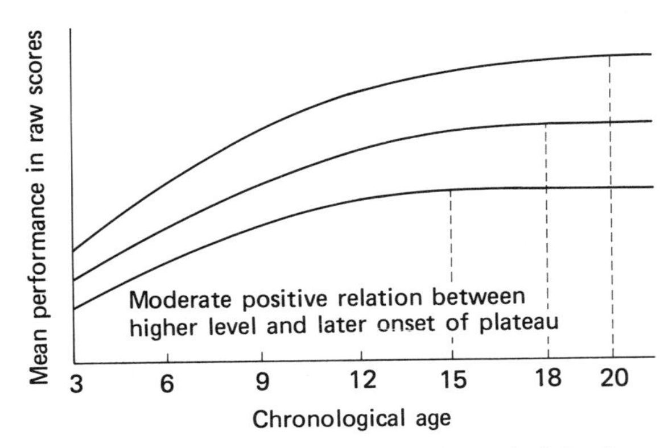

Fig. 3.14. Growth of fluid ability with age; terminal level is reached simultaneously by bright and dull alike. Adapted from *Cattell* (1971)

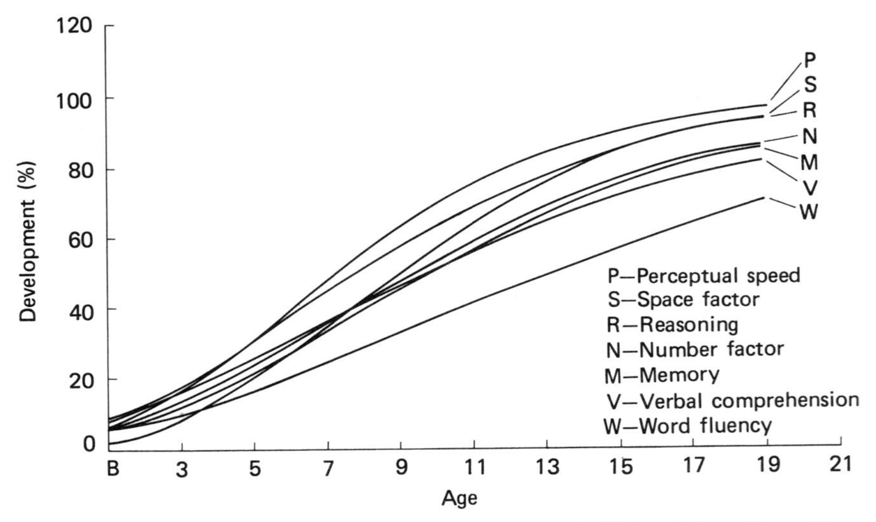

Fig. 3.15. Estimated curves for the development of special mental abilities. Adapted from *Thurstone* (1955)

growth curves, different abilities, and the different growth rates in different people; however, they will do as a general summary of what is known about the increase of intelligence with age.

Sex differences may be said in general to be slight, and not to extend to general mental ability, but rather to various primary mental abilities; *Maccoby* and *Jacklin* (1975) give an excellent review of the evidence. There is some evidence that males have slightly larger standard deviations in IQ, i. e. there are more males with very high and very low IQs respectively, averaging out to the same mean IQ as females. The evidence on this point is doubtful, and in some countries (e. g. Yugoslavia) no differences have been found (*Smiljanic*, personal communication). But men excel in visuo-spatial ability, i. e. the ability to organize, relate and manipulate visual inputs in their spatial context. Animals, such as chimpanzees and rats, show the same sex-related pattern, which does not seem to be affected much by cultural factors. From the point of view of evolution this may be related to the male animal's need to maintain accurate spatial orientation during his foraging, and to detect spatial relationships despite distortions and camouflage. There is evidence both for genetic control of this ability, and also for the suggestion that at least one of the genes controlling it is a recessivel carried on the X-chromosome; in other words, that this ability is to some extent sex-linked. Similarly, there is evidence to show that spatial ability develops under the partial control of the sex hormones.

If men are superior in respect of visuo-spatial ability, women show almost the same degree of superiority with respect to verbal ability. Girls learn to talk earlier, articulate better, and acquire a more extensive vocabulary than do boys, at all ages. They write and spell better; their grammar is better, and they construct sentences better. The earliest beginnings of this differentiation can be located as early as six months. In other species, particularly in those where the individual's affective state is indicated by characteristic vocalizations, females also show pronounced superiority. But this fact should not be generalized too far; females are superior in language usage, or verbal fluency; they are not superior with respect to verbal reasoning, that is the use of intelligence in tasks which are presented verbally. When comprehension and reasoning are taken into account, boys are slightly superior to girls. Allied to the fact that females are superior with respect to those properties of language which can be learned by rote is the fact that women excel in all rote learning tasks. Women seem to be able to hold in their memory store for short periods of time a number of unrelated and personally irrelevant facts, while men are capable of comparable memory feats only if the material is personally relevant and/or coherent. Here too there seems to be present a genetical component, rather than an environmental one.

Boys seem to have a more divergent cognitive style, which may predispose them to be more original and creative; we shall discuss in a later chapter the vexed question of divergent and convergent styles, and the relation of this to originality and creativity. This difference too can be seen already in the play of pre-school children. These brief notes do not exhaust what is a very large area of research, but these are the main facts relevant to our present purpose. We may recapitulate by saying that overall there are no sex differences in intelligence of any size; with respect to particular abilities, women are superior with respect to verbal fluency, and rote memory, men with respect to visuo-spatial ability and probably the k factor (practical and manipulative tests). The old belief in the inequality of the sexes is certainly not supported by these data; as a criterion of intelligence, sex must be disregarded.

4 Does IQ Measure Intelligence?

> If you wish to strive for peace of soul and pleasure, then believe; if you wish to be a devotee of truth, then inquire
>
> Nietzsche

This question is often asked, but it is probably an inadmissible and meaningless question. Does the thermometer measure temperature? If by "temperature" we mean the scientific concept, embodied in a series of laws, then by definition the answer is "Yes"; temperature is almost defined as that which is measured by a thermometer. Similarly if by "intelligence" we mean the concept as worked out by psychologists along the lines indicated in the last three chapters, then obviously IQ tests, properly constructed, measure intelligence; indeed, in a very real sense intelligence may be defined as that which is measured by IQ tests – provided we allow for the presence of chance error, which is attached to all scientific measurement, and provided that the rules of test construction are followed which we have already discussed. But both temperature and intelligence arose as concepts from common, everyday observation – of hot and cold sensations in the one case, of bright and dull people, in the other. Do scientific measurements agree with commonsense observations? This question is not of very great interest if put like this, for several reasons. Nevertheless, the search for "external validity", i. e. for agreement between scientific measurement and criteria external to that measurement, which are agreed to be relevant to the concept in question, is of some importance, and certainly of social relevance in the case of intelligence testing; it will therefore be discussed in this chapter. We will certainly not expect perfect agreement between external criteria and IQ measures; external criteria are affected by many determinants of which IQ is only one. Furthermore, external criteria are often difficult to measure, and this difficulty clouds the exact determination of any relationship. However, some relationship there ought to be, and we would feel disinclined to call something "intelligence" that did not correlate with external criteria such as success at school and university, or in life, or at work.

An example from the measurement of temperature may make it clear why external criteria may be unreliable, and why agreement with them is not perfect, even in the physical sciences. Our perceptions of hot and cold are also affected by irrelevant consideration, e. g. by the humidity of the air, or by our previous practice or exercise; our judgment is therefore not of temperature as such, but of a complex of effects of which temperature is only one. A well known experiment will make this clear. Sit down in front of you three bowls filled with water – hot water in the bowl on the right, cold water in the bowl on the left, and tepid water in the bowl in the middle. Plunge your right arm into the bowl on the right, your left arm into the bowl on the left, and leave them there for a few minutes. When you have become accustomed to the temperature in each bowl, take out your arms and plunge both into the centre bowl. You will now experience the tepid water as hot for your left arm, and as cold for your right arm – by virtue of the contrast with the hot and cold bowls! In other words, the same water can, at the same time and to the same person, feel both hot and cold! Clearly personal sensations cannot be relied upon to give veridical reports.

Similarly with human judgments of intelligence. Most people are somewhat confused by the contrast involved in separating out g_f and g_c, i. e. fluid and crystallized intelligence. Sometimes people talk about intelligence as pure ability to learn cognitive materials, to solve problems, and to think and reason; at others they use the same term to refer to acquired knowledge, calling the person who is knowledgeable "intelligent". Now as we have seen g_f and g_c are not unrelated in our society, or indeed any society about which we have some knowledge; but they are not the same. I can solve many mathematical problems which would have stumped Newton, Leibnitz, and the greatest minds of the middle ages – not because I have an IQ which could remotely compare with theirs, but because I have learned the solutions worked out by thousands of scientists during the past three centuries. On the whole the more intelligent (g_f) have acquired more knowledge (g_c), and in many circumstances it is possible to use a person's possession of this knowledge (as in a vocabulary test) to assess his fluid intelligence. But we must still make an important distinction between the two; simple knowledge is not intelligence, and for the man in the street this distinction is certainly not always clear – although quite often he seems to recognize it clearly enough. Knowledge can be a very uncertain guide to intelligence, although often it is closely related to it. *Idiots savants* have been known who could acquire highly specialized knowledge (or mental arithmetic, say) to a very high degree, but who were otherwise mentally defective. IQ tests are a good measure of intelligence, but they are not perfect; as we shall see in the next few chapters, the correlation between IQ and intelligence (conceived as innate, general mental ability) is about 0.9 – high but not unity.

It would be impossible to summarize all the available evidence on the external validity of the IQ as a measure of intelligence; we shall consider some outstanding studies, but only if these are typical of the large number of others not considered in detail. Our main purpose will be to give an idea of the many different types of studies done in this area; this is far more convincing, of course, than concentration on just one or two areas of investigation. The first and most obvious line of investigation is that of looking at groups which have always been regarded by the man in the street (and the expert!) as typifying low and high intelligence respectively – mental defectives and successful academics and professional people. Mental defectives are so diagnosed in the first place because of their inability to adjust to normal life by virtue of lack of mental powers; in some countries they may be so diagnosed also by virtue of "moral imbecility", and for other causes of misdemeanour, but such cases are of course quite different, and may have quite high IQs. We shall concentrate on mental defectives diagnosed independently of IQ tests by psychiatrists because of extreme dullness. Officially mental defect of this kind is defined by the American Association on Mental

Deficiency in the following way: "Mental retardation refers to subaverage general intellectual functioning which originates during the developmental period and is associated with impairment in adaptive behaviour." In terms of IQ, the A. A. M. D. suggests the following subclassification: Borderline cases – IQs between 70 and 84 on the Wechsler test; mild retardation – 55 to 69; moderate retardation – 40 to 54; severe retardation – 25 to 39; profound retardation – below 25 IQ.

While the IQ has been found extremely useful in diagnosing mental retardation, and in preventing misdiagnosis in more or less normal individuals whose social adaptation was faulty for reasons other than mental defect, there is no one-to-one correspondence between IQ and faulty social adaptation. Employability, for instance, is highly related to social competence, and this has been found, in some British work, to be related to emotional stability as much as to intelligence in a group of high-grade defectives (*Eysenck,* 1970). But on the whole there is nevertheless a high correlation between social and psychiatric assessments of social competence and adaptability, on the one hand, and IQ on the other. Low and very low IQs almost invariably denote mental retardation as expressed in terms of social criteria universally accepted as indicators of poor intelligence; this fact gives powerful support to the view that IQ measures very largely what the man in the street would regard as "intelligence". More detailed discussions of the voluminous evidence on this point will be found in *Matarazzo* (1972), who also reviews the many definitions of mental defect, and its various causes.

At the other extreme we have successful academics and professionals, and it can be said right away that these practically always have IQs well above the average. Fig. 4.1 shows as an example the distribution of IQ for 148 faculty members in various disciplines at the University of Cambridge (*Gibson* and *Light,* 1967). A very similar picture is given by a study of 80 medical students published by *Kole* and *Matarazzo* (1965), and depicted in Fig. 4.2; the two means are almost identical. There is quite a spread of IQ in both groups, but very few members have IQs below the 120 mark. It should be noted that both studies used the Wechsler test, and although this is an excellent test for the majority of the population, it is not particularly well suited to the demands of scientists, such as those examined in Cambridge, or of bright medical students. The testing (particularly the differential testing) of high-grade academics demands specially constructed tests; ordinary tests have a "ceiling" which compresses the scores of such high-grade groups and makes it difficult for them to do themselves justice. Even so the results are in line with expectation, in showing mean scores almost two S. D. s above the mean. *Matarazzo* (1972) gives a table showing that quite generally people receiving advanced academic degrees have an average IQ of around 125; the mean of college graduates in the U. S. A. is 115 (it would be rather higher in European countries, because of the greater selectivity of Universities over here). These figures indicate that persons who do well in academic life are well above average in IQ.

During the first World War, large numbers of recruits were tested by the American Army psychologists on an early group test of intelligence, the Army Alpha; data have been published which show the relative performance of dif-

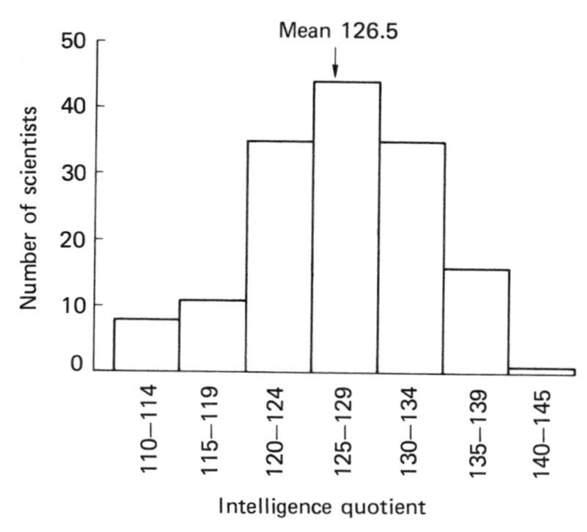

Fig. 4.1. Full-scale Wechsler IQs for 148 faculty members in various disciplines at the University of Cambridge. Adapted from *Gibson* and *Light* (1967)

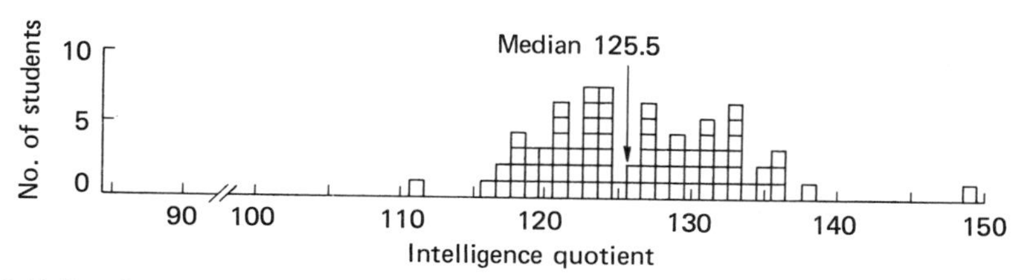

Fig. 4.2. Full-scale Wechsler IQs for 80 medical students. Adapted from *Kole* and *Matarazzo* (1965)

ferent occupations on this test.(The scores are reported in terms of points gained, and have not been transformed into IQs.) Figure 4.3 shows some of the results, giving both the mean score and the *range* found for each occupation; it will be found that the groups decline in mean as would be expected in terms of common assumptions regarding the intelligence required for the different occupations. It will also be seen that there is much overlap. These figures from *Yerkes* (1921) were obtained 60 years ago, but more recent studies have given identical results.

It should not be assumed that in academic life IQ is the only requirement; there is a minimum below which success is unlikely or even impossible, but a high IQ does not of course guarantee success. Personality, luck and hard work all play their part. Thus *Wankowski* (1973) has demonstrated on large samples of students at Birmingham University that students who are extraverted do conspicuously less well than do students who are introverted; similarly, students with neurotic tendencies do much less well than do more stable students. Worst of all is the prediction of success for students who are both extraverted and neurotic; they produce far more failures, and far fewer outstanding successes, than do students who are stable and introverted – in spite of the fact that both groups have similar IQs. This is an important consideration; IQ is a vital ingre-

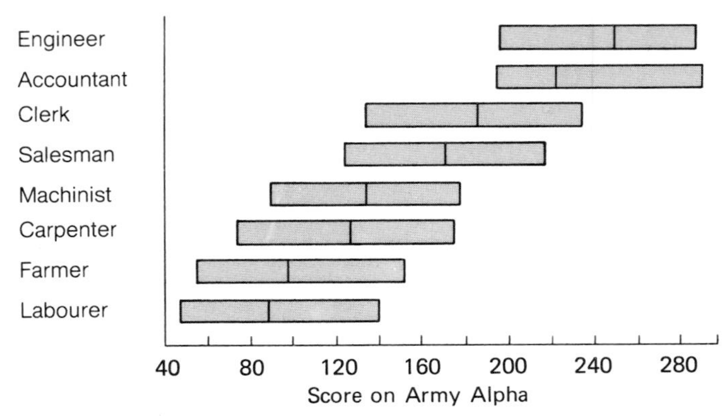

Fig. 4.3. Scores on the Army Alpha test obtained by soldiers in World War I, entering service from various pre service occupations. Adapted from *Yerkes* (1921)

dient in the recipe for academic success, and for success in professional life, but it is not the only ingredient, and if other ingredients are missing the gifted individual may still end up a failure. Psychologists who claim that IQ measures intelligence, and that intelligence is important, are often criticized because some very bright individuals fail, and some dull ones succeed. This would only amount to reasonable criticism if IQ had been suggested to be the *only* relevant variable; this has never been maintained by any responsible psychologist. We have seen that emotional stability can be of great importance in making a mental defective employable; similarly emotional instability can render a bright academic unsuccessful. Success is never unidimensional, i. e. depending on only one quality; correlations can never be expected to be perfect between success and any one quality or characteristic.

Results from a more recent investigation into the mean IQ levels of members of middle class, skilled working class and semi-skilled working class have been published by *Harrel* and *Harrel* (1945), using scores on the American Army General Classification Test; a selection of these results is given below in Table 4.1. It will be seen that those in middle class occupations tend to score above the 120 level; those in semi-skilled occupations below 100. Note also that the S. D. s of these groups go up as the mean IQ goes down; in other words, there is much greater variability in the lower social grades than in the upper ones. This is a phenomenon known technically as *heteroscedasticity;* it is presumably due to the fact, already noted, that higher class occupations require IQ *but also other traits*; where these other traits are missing the individual will become a member of a lower social group, and thus increase the IQ variability within that group. (The terms "lower" and "higher" are here used because they are in common usage, and easily understood; it is not suggested that the work done by a miner or a lumberjack is less socially useful in any was than that done by an accountant or a lawyer. Cynics might feel that it was considerably more useful.)

IQ tests were used in the American Army originally in order to allow some

Table 4.1.[a]

	Mean:	S.D.	
Accountant	128	11.7	
Lawyer	128	10.9	
Auditor	125	11.2	
Reporter	124	11.7	
Chief clerk	124	11.7	Middle class
Teacher	122	12.8	Occupations
Draughtsman	122	12.8	
Pharmacist	120	15.2	
Book-keeper	120	13.1	
Toolmaker	112	12.5	
Machinist	110	16.1	
Foreman	110	16.7	
Airplane mechanic	109	14.9	
Electrician	109	15.2	Skilled working
Lathe operator	108	15.5	class Occupations
Sheet metal worker	108	15.3	
Mechanic	106	16.0	
Riveter	104	15.1	
Painter, general	98	18.7	
Cook & baker	97	20.8	
Truckdriver	96	19.7	
Labourer	96	20.1	Semi-skilled
Barber	95	20.5	Working class
Lumberjack	95	19.8	Occupations
Farmhand	91	20.7	
Miner	91	20.1	
Teamster	88	19.6	

[a] Adapted from *Harrel* and *Harrel* (1945)

estimate of intelligence to be made for the purpose of officer selection. The great and universally agreed success of these tests caused many other countries to adopt them in later years, and presents another external validation criterion for IQ tests as measures of intelligence. Figure 4.4 shows the Army Alpha test scores of officers, sergeants, corporals, and literate and illiterate enlisted men. (Illiterate men were more usually tested with the Army Beta test, a test specially constructed to obviate the use of language.) It will again be seen that variability of scores is greater for the duller groups, as expected; officers require to be intelligent, but they also require to have other attributes not measured by an IQ test.

Can mental tests be used as selection criteria? Figure 4.5 shows results from testing large numbers of recruits by means of a selection battery designed to measure likely proficiency in primary pilot training. These future pilots were only studied, i. e. their scores were not used to eliminate any of them from the

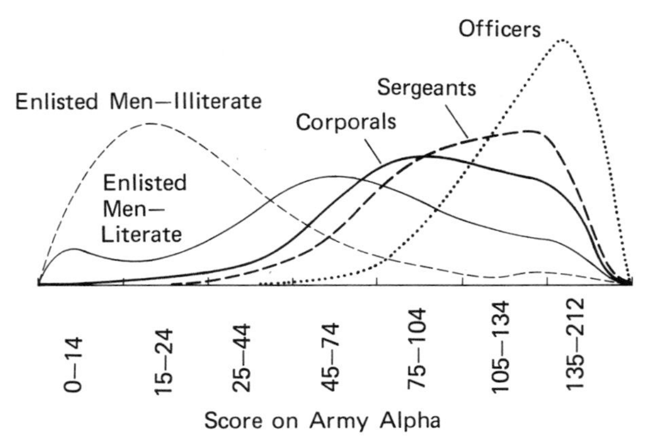

Fig. 4.4. Distribution of intelligence test scores in various Army groups during World War I. Adapted from *Yoakum* and *Yerkes* (1920)

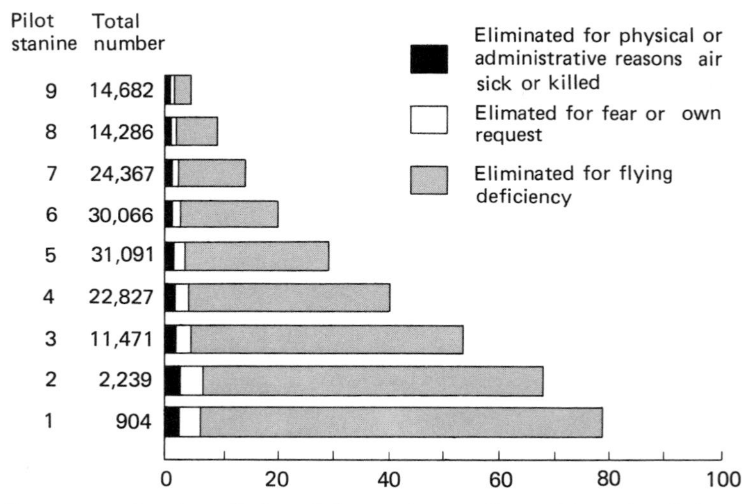

Fig. 4.5. Percentage of cadets eliminated from primary pilot training, classified according to "stanine" scores on selection battery. Adapted from article in Psychol. Bull. *42,* 46 (1945)

course. It will be seen that there is a considerable degree of agreement between score on the test battery, and success in pilot training. The battery was later used for selection, with considerable success. It too has since been adopted by many different nations for the same purpose, in view of its great success. (This study is only partly relevant to a discussion of intelligence because more specific tests of the components of flying ability were also used, but these all correlate with intelligence, although not always very highly.) The study illustrates the use of primary ability tests, for special purposes.

Particularly well known has become the work of the War Office Selection

Boards (W. O. S. B. s) in Great Britain during the War. In the early years of the Second World War, the Army had found its officers from among men who had taken a school certificate, or some higher examination, and who had, at the same time, attended one of the schools providing an Officer Training Course. Selection was carried out by Interview Boards attached to Army Commands, the technique being that of a simple interview lasting for about twenty minutes. Halfway through the war, however, this traditional method of officer selection was braking down, and the failure rate at Officer Cadet Training Units (O. C. T. U. s) was rising to quite alarming proportions. This state of affairs was not only wasteful, but it had a very bad effect on the morale of the ranks, who as a consequence did not apply for commissions in anything like the number required. In addition, it was found through psychiatric examination of officers who had suffered a breakdown in service that many of these men should never have been commisioned at all. As a consequence there was growing public concern about this state of affairs, and questions were being asked in Parliament.

Reasons for this failure were many, but possibly the most important was the fact that until that time, officers had come almost entirely from one social class, and methods of selection were based on this fact, in the sense that they implied the existence of a social background common to selectors and candidates. Reliance on intuitive judgments based on resemblance of candidates and interviewers probably worked reasonably well as long as this fundamental condition was fulfilled, but as the war progressed the reservoir of candidates of this type became exhausted, and selection boards were very soon faced with candidates whose personality and background were quite alien to the officers who had the task of selection. Under these conditions, traditional methods were inadequate and judgments became based on irrelevant factors.

W. O. S. B. s were set up in the summer of 1942 in order to remedy these deficiencies, using psychological tests, of which the intelligence test turned out to be the most prognostic. For a short while W. O. S. B. s and old procedure boards were working side by side, and it was possible to follow up the men whom they had recommended for commission. Of those recommended by W. O. S. B. s, 35% were found to be above average, while of those recommended by the old procedures only 22% were above average. Of those rated below average at O. C. T. U., candidates came from W. O. S. B. s only in 25% of the cases, and from old procedure boards in 37% of the cases. There appears to be very little doubt that the War Office Selection Boards were substantially better than the old procedure boards, and that this success was due largely to the introduction of tests of intelligence. The Army soon abandoned the use of the old fashioned selection board and went over wholehartedly to the new W. O. S. B. s. Intelligence tests have played an important part in selection procedures in the British Army ever since.

What we have said so far can be put in terms of a certain logical chain. Intelligence, as measured by IQ tests, determines a person's socio-economic status to a considerable extent; through this, it determines his earning capacity and his general position in society. (This point is documented in a later chapter more thoroughly.) How is this relevant to our major question, i. e. whether IQ measures what most people would consider "intelligence"? For an answer, consider again Table 4.1. It will be clear that most people would think that the middle class jobs require more intelligence than the skilled working class jobs, and that those in turn require more intelligence than the semi-skilled (or a fortiori the unskilled) working class jobs. The results in Figure 4.3 bear this out – accountants and engineers would commonly be thought to be more brainy than labourers and carpenters. But we can put this on a more precise and objective basis. First, we may have recourse to the Barr scale of occupations; this was drawn up by a number of psychologists who rated 120 representative occupations with respect to the grade of intelligence required in each one for ordinary success – basing themselves of course on studies of the kind reviewed above. Second, there are the results of a large-scale public opinion poll, undertaken by the National Opinion Research Centre (NORC), in which the prestige ratings of a great number of occupations were established. Last, we have ratings of socio-economic status (SES) as assigned officially in the Census of Population of 1960 to each of hundreds of listed occupations on the basis of average income and educational level prevailing in the occupations. Prestige ratings and intellectual requirements (NORC and Barr) correlate 0.91; prestige and income correlate 0.90; intellectual requirements and income correlate 0.81. There is thus a close relation between the intelligence needed in an occupation, its social prestige, and the income and education of the people in it. If we regard income and prestige as having social importance, then it is clear that intelligence precedes occupational choice, and is thus clearly implicated in the other two variables.

It is clear that intelligence, social status and income are fairly closely related when we look at distinct groups of occupations; would it be true to say that within a given occupation there was also a close correspondence between IQ and achievement? The answer must be that there is far less evidence on this point, it being much easier to grade occupations (membership of which is a very objective criterion) than to grade people in given occupations (which would require us to have some criterion of excellence). Such a criterion is usually very difficult to provide, and often impossible. Is Smith a better teacher, or doctor, or scientist than Brown? Judgements can be made using a multiplicity of criteria, and none could be said to be indisputably superior to the others. It might be thought that among scientists at least it would be obvious and agreed who was better than who, but this is true only in retrospect (i. e. when the person in question is dead, and his true contribution can be properly assessed), and with regard to the most eminent – who would now dispute the superiority of Newton, Einstein, or Galileo? But for the great mass of scientists there is confusion, rather than agreement. Readers who are not personally involved with scientific work and research may like to consult for evidence *Mitsoff*s (1974) book on The Subjective Side of Science, in which he interviewed in depth more than forty of the most eminent scientists who studied the moon rocks. These interviews make crystal clear the difficulty of ranking these scientists in order of "goodness" or success; there is total disagreement with respect to the majority, with very strong feelings attached to the value judgements made about each.

Even if there were some agreement on a given person's quality in his chosen field, this would not necessarily be expressed in financial terms. There are no doubt considerable differences in IQ and quality among the professors of psychology (or any other science!) teaching at British Universities, yet by Government decree they all receive the same salary (graded only by age!) This is not so in the United States, where there is competion among Universities for the more prestigious professors; thus a correlation might be found there between IQ and income, but not in the U. K. Even in the U. S. A., but of course much more in the U. K., do we find strong forces which press for the elimination of inequalities in reward (and even in achievement); thus trade unions have been known to expel members who worked too hard, or achieved too much, thus "showing up" their less able or hard-working brothers. Such pressures need not always be formally categorized; often the general feeling among one's co-workers is enough to discourage the brighter, more adventurous, more hard-working from using their abilities to the full. Thus pressures of this kind may eliminate the advantages which would rightly go to the person with the higher IQ, and lead to a dead egalitarianism geared to the dullest, the least proficient, the slowest. The Stakhanovite movement in the U. S. S. R. was a propaganda move directed against this general malaise; little comparable can be found in the Western democracies, other than vague exhortations.

Last, but not least, there is the problem of irrelevance of criteria for advancement which can be very serious. At the risk of seeming frivolous I shall illustrate this risk through a joke which has powerful sociological and psychological implications. A high-ranking businessman is looking for a secretary, and his industrial psychologist has narrowed the field of applicants for this much sought-after job down to three women. He gives them a series of aptitude and intelligence tests, and presents the results to the boss. "The test I used," he says, "was a simple one – what is two and two? Miss Smith said four. Miss Brown said twenty-two. Miss Jones said it could either be four or twenty-two, depending how you put the two figures together. Now you will know whom to pick." "Yes," said the boss, "of course I know. I'll have the one with the big boobs!" Beauty, charm, sexual availability only too often play a prominent part in selection and advancement of female workers, and similar personal factors quite irrelevant to the job can often be found in the working lives of men too. (Simple size correlates with earnings in men!) Intelligence can more easily be overlooked, and can be a positive handicap; many bosses claim to look for men of independence, originality, and integrity when a job is advertised, but prefer to settle for dull and mediocre yes-men. Even scientists may suffer through being too intelligent and original; recognition after death is little recompense for neglect during their working lives, and the same is true of artists, inventors, and others.

In view of all these problems we would not expect much of a correlation between IQ and success within a given job, and this expectation is indeed borne out in the few studies which have been done in this connection[5]. None show a

---

5 It is important in this connection to realize that different jobs have different IQ requirements, even though these jobs may have no scholastic or academic content whatever; it is their complexity (as already suggested on an earlier page) that determine their *g* content. Thus it has been shown in on-the-job work sample tests given to U. S. Army cooks, equated for months of

negative correlation; most show a small positive correlation, with one or two showing a more positive outcome. If social impediments to truly competitive within-occupation behaviour could be removed; if more objective and reliable criteria could be devised; and if irrelevant personal preferences on the part of employers could be ostracized, then and only then would we expect to find high positive correlations between IQ and job success. We are perhaps fortunate that in our type of society there is little evidence of political and ideological interference with employment and promotion (except perhaps through union activity); in countries like the U. S. S. R. political considerations can be much more powerful than any others, thus probably reducing even more the correspondence between IQ and success in a given occupation.

Ghiselli (1966), who has made a detailed study of this whole problem, summarizes the literature by saying that the correlation between IQ and job success in a given occupation is only about 0.20; this should be compared with the correlation of 0.50 typically found between IQ and occupational attainment, i. e. taking into account different occupations. This latter correlation may at first sight seem entirely different from that presented above, between intellectual requirements of different occupations, on the one hand, and prestige ratings and income of the occupations, on the other. The answer, of course, is that the latter correlations are derived from *average* figures for different occupations, the former form *individual* people entering these occupations; thus the latter figure takes into account the variability within each occupation which we have noted. Mention of the variability of IQ within given occupations may serve to remind us of one last and perhaps even more powerful reason than those already given as to why the correlation between IQ and success within a given occupation is so low. Within an occupation there is a considerable restriction of range of ability; thus we have seen from Figs. 4.1 and 4.2 that in the professions of scientists and doctors the range was not from 70 to 150, as it would be in a random sample of the population, but from 110 or 120 to 150 or less. Thus the range was reduced by more than half, and we would accordingly expect any correlation between IQ and success to be reduced correspondingly. (There are statistical formulae which compensate for this restriction of range, but there would be little point in going into detail here.)

Restriction of range is apparent not only in the higher professions, but equally in other occupations. Figure 4.6 shows the Wechsler IQs for 243 police and firemen applicants; the results are quoted from a study by *Matarazzo* et al., (1964). Essentially the range only covers 30 points of IQ, instead of 80 or so; in other words, the range is only about one-third of that of a random sample! The difference in IQ remaining are not sufficient to be very predictive of success, particularly when we remember that IQ is not the only variable concerned with success as a policeman or a fireman.

It is usually assumed that education plays an important part in fitting a man

---

experience in the kitchen, that the various routine tasks performed by cooks are differentially *g*-loaded. Making jellyrolls, as it happens, is much more *g*-loaded than preparing scrambled eggs! Thus *g* intrudes even into apparently simple, non-academic jobs, whenever performances of any degree of complexity are required, or when any kind of mental manipulation is involved.

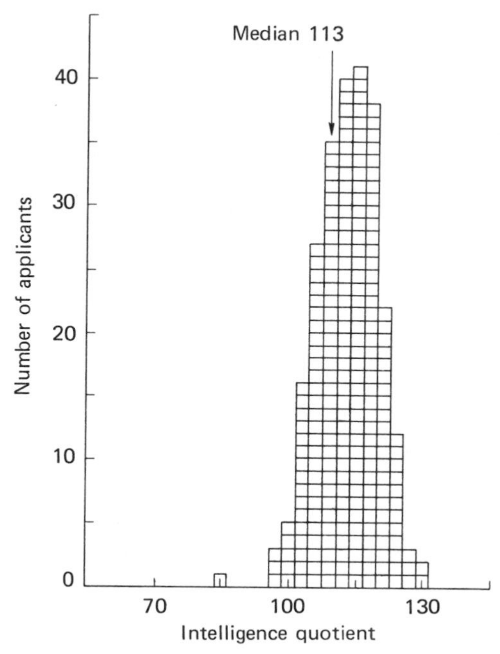

Fig. 4.6. Full-scale Wechsler IQs for 243 police and firemen applicants. Adapted from *Matarazzo* et al. (194)

(or woman) for the more responsible, better paid, higher prestige job, and there is no doubt that this is true in our society, just as much as it is in Communist societies, or in ancient China or any other highly developed society. This suggests that educational attainment would be a reasonable criterion to look at in our search for external validation of IQ tests; success in education, if anything, should be dependent on intelligence, at least in part. We may first state the general finding from thousands of studies in the U. S. A. and elsewhere, namely that there is an average correlation of 0.50 between IQ and success at school (measured by grades, or grade point average, or rank, or leaving age). Much higher correlations have been found, e. g. in Scotland, as well as much lower ones[6]; the actual figures obviously depend on such factors as the degree of

6 It is possible to increase the reliability of both IQ and achievement measures by obtaining repeated measures throughout the course of the child's school career, thus averaging out the fluctuations in performance that often occur between any two single test scores obtained on the same individual tested at different times. Such cumulated IQ and achievement test scores have been found to correlate over 0.90 with each other, suggesting that the *g* factor of any large battery of nonscholastic cognitive tests is the same *g* factor that can be extracted from a comprehensive battery of scholastic achievement tests. It can be shown that it is not scholastic achievement which determines IQ, but IQ which determines achievement; a statistical technique known as cross-lagged correlation analysis (*Crano* et al., 1972) has been used to show that the predominant direction of causality is in the direction going from the more abstract and *g*-loaded tests to the acquisition of the more specific and concrete scholastic skills.

variability in IQ of the school population – restriction of range can often be found in British grammar and so-called public school where selection is very severe, and where accordingly we would expect lower correlations. Similarly we would expect lower correlations due to restriction of range, in some British comprehensive schools where the brighter pupils had been "creamed off" by adjacent independent schools, leaving them with rather dull pupils only. Another factor of course is the reliability of the criterion; some schools use methods of examining and grading which leave much to be desired, and in these the correlation of IQ with the criterion is lowered because of the low validity of the criterion. This can be a very important consideration; it is well known that examinations in school and University are often highly unreliable, particularly in subjects like English, History, Art, and other non-scientific subjects; Mathematics of course is usually highly reliable in the marking, although there are other sources of unreliability.

The whole subject of reliability of criteria is a vital one in considering the data presented in this chapter, and a few words in explanation of the concept may be in order. We have already seen that there are two meanings to the term "validity". This can mean internal validity, as for instance shown in batteries of tests the correlations between which approximate rank one, or it can mean external validity, as for instance when tests of IQ correlate with criteria such as occupational success or school achievement where there are good grounds to believe that the criterion depends to some degree on intelligence, and individual differences in intelligence.

In the same way may it be said that there are two types of reliability. Where validity refers to the question: "Does the test measure what it purports to measure?", so the question of reliability refers to the question: "With what accuracy does the test measure whatever it may measure?" The first type of reliability refers to the consistency of the test items in measuring whatever the test measures; this could be indexed by correlating each item with total score – items which did not correlate with total score, or which correlated negatively, obviously did not belong into the test. Or we might correlate the sum of the odd-numbered items with the sum of the even-numbered items; if all the items measure the same qualtity, then the two halves should correlate together quite highly. This would then be a measure of the consistency of the test. A different type of reliability is the so-called test-retest reliability; it asks the question of consistency over time. If we test 100 children today with the WISC, and test them again next month, when they have forgotten their previous answers, we would expect that each child would gain an IQ the second time of testing which was very similar to that he obtained the first time round; if this were not so the test would be so unreliable as to be practically useless. There would be no consistent, enduring concept of IQ to measure! In fact of course the reliability of the IQ is quite high – in the case of test and retest after a month the correlation for a random group of 100 children of identical age the correlation would be

(There are differences in the results obtained in subsamples of middle and low socioeconomic status children, and in subsamples of bright and dull children, for various types of scholastic achievement, but the overall direction of causality is unmistakeable.)

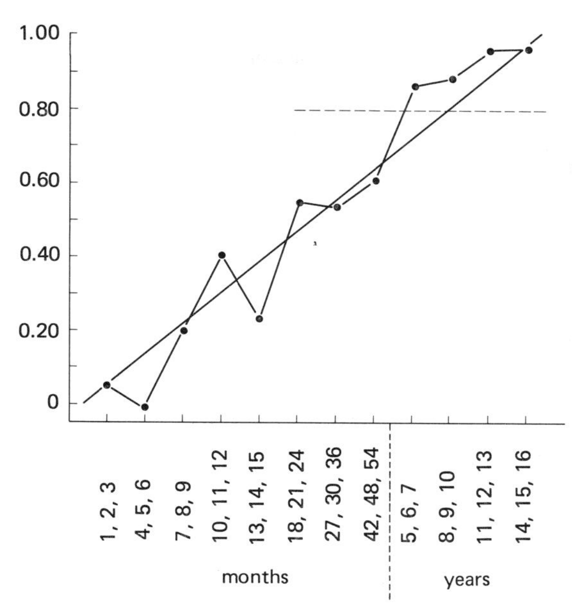

Fig. 4.7. Correlations with terminal IQ of children repeatedly tested from a very early age; each point represents the average of three testings. Drawn from data by *Jones* and *Bayley* (1941)

between 0.90 and 0.95, probably nearer the second figure than the first. This is acceptable for individual measurement. Reliabilities decrease during childhood the longer the duration of the interval between testing and retesting; roughly speaking we may say that from the age of 6 to the age of 16 the reliability of the retest decreases by 0.04 per year. In other words, if the interval is one year, retest reliability is 0.91. After two years, it is 0.87; after three years, 0.83; and after four years, 0.79; and so on.

These figures are of course somewhat idealized; real-life results are never as regular as this! Figure 4.7 shows the results of an actual follow-up study (the Berkeley Growth Study), a longitudinal investigation of 61 children born between 1928 and 1929, and followed up until the age of 36 at the time of the latest publication (*Jones* and *Bayley*, 1941, give a description of the sample.) Individuals were tested repeatedly from infancy to adulthood, and the Fig. gives correlations between terminal IQ scores at ages 17 and 18, and tests scores achieved at various periods during the growth of the children. These test scores are based on the averaged scores of three testing occasions; thus they are more reliable than single administrations of the tests involved. It will be seen immediately that IQ scores below the age of three years are pretty meaningless; in fact, scores do not become useful for prediction in individual cases until the age of between 5 and 7 years, as indicated by the stippled line in the diagram. A straight line can be drawn through the points of the diagram, indicating that the reliabilities follow roughly the rule given above. Note that the line gives a zero reliability roughly at or just before birth; this is another way of locating an absolute zero point for IQ.

The reliability of scholastic examinations unfortunately compares very unfavourably with that of IQ tests (e. g. *Hartog* and *Rhodes*, 1936). It is not only that when two independent examinations are held for the same group of students that the results of the one correlate poorly with those of the other; there are additional sources of unreliability. Different examiners grading identical papers show poor correlation, and even the same examiner, grading the same papers after an interval of a month or so, will not show good agreement with his own first grading! Under such conditions the criterion must be considered to be of doubtful reliability, and it follows directly that correlations with an unreliable criterion cannot themselves be very high. Correction by statistical formula is possible, and assuming for the purpose of the exercise that the correlation between IQ and a given scholastic grade is 0.5, it can be shown that this correlation becomes 0.64 if we assume a reliability of the educational tests of 0.60; it becomes 0.70 if we assume a reliability of 0.50; and it becomes 0.79 if we assume a reliability of 0.40! These calculations should not be taken too seriously (although the range of reliabilities of examinations does lie between the values of 0.40 and 0.60 for many subjects, and may even be lower than 0.40! The figures are mentioned merely because existing and reported correlations always underestimate the true relationship between the variables imperfectly measured by our tests; thus the true validity of IQ tests is always, and sometimes very drastically, underestimated. The high correlations reported from Scotland may bear testimony to the greater care with which traditionally Scottish educationalists conduct their examinations.

These figures are derived from cross-sectional testing in schools; ideally we would like follow-up studies to see what happens to children as they progress through school. Studies by *Bajema* (1968), *Bienstock* (1967), *Dillon* (1949), *Embree* (1948) and *Stice* and *Ekstrom* (1964) provide evidence on this point. Bajema and Embree found correlations of between 0.5 and 0.6 between childhood IQ and later educational achievement; this indicates considerable predictive accuracy in early IQ testing. Dillon started with 2600 youngsters in grade 7 and recorded the number dropping out of school at various grade levels as a function of the youngsters' IQ. Figure 4.8 shows the result for bright and dull pupils respectively; it will be seen that of 400 dull pupils at the time of testing in grade 7, only 14 remained until graduation, while of an equal number of bright pupils, 344 remained. Intermediate degrees of intelligence were related to intermediate degrees of drop out. Proportions of those dropping out from the five IQ groups used by Dillon were, in order, 96% (for the dullest), 46%, 37%, 24% and 14%, respectively. Stice and Ekstrom similarly found in a study of tenth graders that aptitude and proportion dropping out before high school graduation were related as follows: Lowest third in aptitude – drop out 31%; middle third – 20%; top third – 9%. Bienstock, in a study of over a million and a half of American high school students, found a similar decline in rate of graduation with lower IQ; using quartiles to define his IQ ranges, drop-outs made up respectively 20%, 12%, 6% and 5% over a period of one year only! The figures leave no doubt about the close relation between IQ and success at school.

When we turn to University students, we must bear in mind the inevitable restriction of range which makes the discovery of high correlations unlikely;

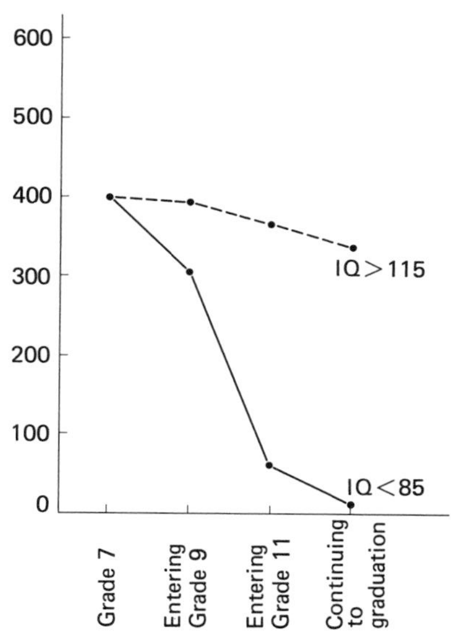

Fig. 4.8. Dropping-out of formal education of bright and dull children respectively. From data by *Dillon* (1949)

undergraduates are already so highly selected that those below average ability never reach University status. In spite of this fact hundreds (indeed thousands) of studies have demonstrated correlations between IQ and success at University varying from small to quite large. *Lavin* (1965) has presented a review of much of this material, and concludes that "on those educational levels for which data are most reliable (high school and college) measures of ability on the average account for 35 to 45 per cent of the variation in academic performance." This, as will be remembered, is equivalent to correlations of 0.60 to 0.67, i. e. the square roots of the percentage figures; these values are somewhat larger than those suggested by us above. At University rather than College level the values are lower, although there is extreme variation between different Universities, Departments, and between males and females – usually correlations are higher for women than for men. These variations are probably due to a great variety of factors, such as range of ability, type of test used, type and reliability of criterion used, and many others. Furthermore, different types of subject matter may demand different tests – English and Mathematics demand different kind of primary abilities, in addition to general IQ. *Eysenck* (1947) in a review of the evidence suggested a value of between 0.50 and 0.60 as being representative of good studies, properly executed, using appropriate IQ tests and reasonably reliable criteria. Instead of discussing the many published studies in detail, it may be better to look at some results from two studies which illustrate the general findings.

Figure 4.9 shows a scatter diagram of the correlation between an IQ test score (abscissa) and the first term grade point average of 589 University of

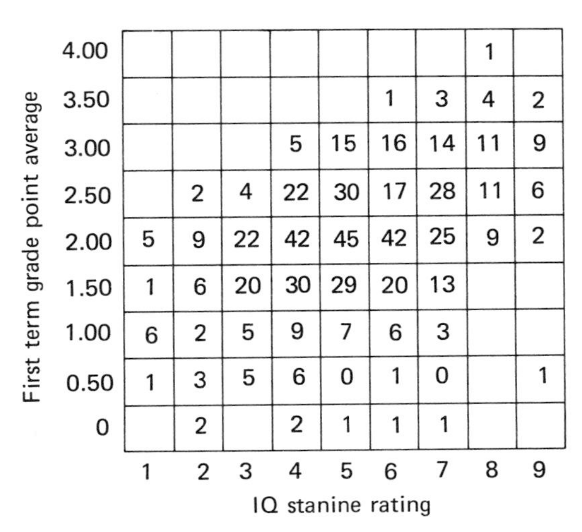

4.00 1
3.50 1 3 4 2
3.00 5 15 16 14 11 9
2.50 2 4 22 30 17 28 11 6
2.00 5 9 22 42 45 42 25 9 2
1.50 1 6 20 30 29 20 13
1.00 6 2 5 9 7 6 3
0.50 1 3 5 6 0 1 0 1
0 2 2 1 1 1
1 2 3 4 5 6 7 8 9
First term grade point average
IQ stanine rating

Fig. 4.9. Scatter diagram showing relationship between IQ test scores, grouped in stanines, and College success for 589 University of Oregon freshmen. Adapted from *Tyler* (1965.)

Oregon freshmen students (*Tyler*, 1965). Grade point averages range from zero (very poor) to 4 (excellent) IQ scores are grouped into nine so-called stanines. The correlation illustrated in the diagram is 0.43, i. e. somewhat less than that suggested as typical above. It will be seen that no student who did really well (grade point average 3.50 or 4.00) had an IQ score that was not above the average (that is to say, the average of his fellow university students; all the students tested would of course have IQ scores above the mean of the population!) Some of the poor students, with very low grade point averages, had quite good IQs; this illustrates again the principle of heteroscedasticity mentioned before – you need more than IQ to succeed, but you need IQ as a foundation for success. IQ is a necessary but not a sufficient cause of academic success, as well as of life success.

This study was carried out in the U. S. A., and it shows to what extent IQ scores can be used to predict academic success. Clearly in this highly selected population this prediction is not very accurate, but it is clearly much better than chance; prediction from high school records would probably be just as good, or even somewhat better. However, a combination of high school record and IQ score, particularly if the IQ were to be derived from a complex combinations of separately scored primary ability measures, would almost certainly be better than either alone. For students who had gone to a poor school, or who for some reason (absence, illness, bad teaching) had done poorly at high school, the IQ would give a better prediction than the high school record. Conversely, for bright students inherently lazy, extraverted, or neurotic the IQ measure might hold out more promise than their high school record, and in these cases the high school record would be a better predictor. IQ tests are a good aid in selection, but a bad master; it would not be reasonable to rely exclusively, in some mechanical fashion, on IQ tests alone. Nevertheless, the addition of IQ tests to the existing machinery of selection would in most cases serve to improve it.

Next we may look at an English example reported by *Himmelweit* (1963); the work was carried out at the London School of Economics (L. S. E.) Eleven tests of ability were given to volunteer students, together with personality tests; the ability tests measured general intelligence, arithmetical reasoning, spatial ability and rote memory. Two main analyses were carried out, the first involving 232 students in economics and commerce, the second 48 social science students. The correlation between psychological tests and final degree class was 0.55 for the first group and 0.60 for the second; note that none of the personality test scores were taken into account in this correlation, but only scores derived from the IQ tests. The correlations found were not significantly different from those between the intermediate examination (held after the first year at the L. S. E.) and the final; i. e. the IQ tests predicted final scores just as well as did the examination held after one year at the University. A third group of 57 medical students was also studied; here the correlation between tests and ratings of the students by two member of staff was 0.63. These are astonishingly high values, considering the high selectivity of University course in England, although it seems likely that on replication these multiple correlations would sag a little.

It is interesting to note that the actual admittance procedure by which the students were selected, did not predict academic success successfully. The multiple correlation between scores obtained from the existing entrance procedure and the Intermediate examination was 0.23, which was not significantly different from zero; in other words, the existing procedure has not predictive value, while the tests do have considerable predictive value. It can be calculated what reduction in the failure rate of the students would have resulted if selection had been based on psychological tests, and if the ratio of candidates to places had been 3:1. Selection by psychological tests would have reduced the failure rate from 15% to 3%; this is a marked improvement. Similarly, selection by tests would have increased the number of 1st class and upper second class degrees from 25% to 48%; this is a tremendous improvement. Finally we may consider that the selection ratio of 3:1 is much lower than would be realistic in most departments at British or continental Universities; ratios of 50:1 or even several hundreds to one are quite common, although the practice of multiple applications makes it difficult to know the exact number. Nevertheless, it is clear that tests of intelligence can improve very significantly the existing practices of selection in European Universities. (Needless to say, the L. S. E. decided after receiving the report of the study to retain its ancient practices, and not supplement them by psychological tests!)

Given that students on the whole would be almost certainly more intelligent than the average, and successful students more so than unsuccessful ones, we would also expect that students who achieve the distinction of obtaining Ph. D. degrees, i. e. the highest honour which the University system has to offer by way of examination, would be even higher in IQ. A study of *Harmon* (1961) used the Army General Classification Test and reported on the results achieved by Ph. D. students in various subjects. This test has a mean of 100 and a S. D. of 20, so that the results are not directly comparable with IQs, but are about 25%

higher. The average level of the successful Ph. D. candidates was 130.8, comparable with an IQ of about 125; physics and mathematics students had rather higher scores (140 and 138, respectively), but students of education rather pulled down the average (their score was only 123!) These results confirm the common belief, not only that Ph. D. students are rather bright, but also that some subjects are much more demanding than others. The social sciences were on a par with arts and the humanities (132 points), just about half-way between physics and education. These figures, taken with those mentioned in previous paragraphs, suggest strongly that one requirement for taking IQ seriously as a measure of intelligence is on the whole fulfilled, namely that Ph. D. students > all students > average run of people > E. S. N. (educationally subnormal pupils) > mental defectives (diagnosed without aid of IQ tests.) In this sentence the sign ">" stands for "having higher IQ scores". This surely is a minimum condition for accepting the IQ as a measure of intelligence; if this condition did not obtain, we would rightly have serious doubts about the value of the IQ in this respect. Data such as these have many applications for higher education; *Price* (1963) has used them in an interesting and provocative manner to draw important social conclusions relevant to many issues ranging from the *numerus clausus* (which is such a debating point in many continental countries) to the possible number of first-rate scientists a country could hope to produce.

Most of the studies quoted so far are cross-sectional, or at most follow up the subjects tested over a period of a few years. What would be more impressive would be a long-term follow-up describing in detail the adult characteristics, successes and failures of a group of children of known IQ. Such a study was planned and carried out by L. M. Terman, in collaboration with M. H. Oden (for a summary, see *Terman* and *Oden*, 1959) Terman originally introduced Binet's test into America, translating, adapting and standardizing it and making it a much better instrument than it had originally been (*Terman*, 1916). The study now to be described, originally somewhat tendentiously labelled "a study of genius", became known later on as a study of "the gifted child"; it was concerned with a large sample of children who scored highly on the Terman-Binet IQ test, all living in California, and all having IQs of 140 or above. Such IQ scores are of course rare, but they do not entitle a child to be considered a genius.

There was a total of 1528 gifted youngsters who probably represented a cross-section of American children of high intelligence. In 1921 these youngsters ranged in age from three to nineteen years, with an average of eleven years; their individual IQ scores ranged from 140 to 200, with a mean of 151. Only a small fraction of 1% of the total population of course would belong into such a group. In the fifty years which have since elapsed, these children were reexamined either in person or by mail on seven occasions, the latest being 1960; full details will be found in the latest report (*Oden*, 1968), which was published after Terman's death in 1956 and gives references to all the previous reports. In 1960, when this last report was inaugurated, 1188 of the children still survived.

In addition to the intelligence test scores, a wealth of data was collected including developmental records, health history and medical examinations; home and family background; school history; trait ratings and personality evaluations by parents and teachers; tests of interest, character and personality; and a battery of school achievement tests. Follow-up surverys have provided further data on subsequent school history; physical health and psychiatric studies; marriage, children and grandchildren; occupation; annual income; the use of alcohol; police records if any; and any distinctions and awards earned in arts, letters, science, the humanities, public and foreign affairs, etc. The successful careers of the men are summarized as follows by *Terman* and *Oden* (1959):

"A number of men have made substantial contributions to the physical, biological, and social sciences. These include members of University faculties as well as scientists in various fields who are engaged in research either in industry or in privately, endowed or government-sponsored research laboratories. Listings in American Men of Science include 70 gifted men, of whom 39 are in the physical sciences, 22 in the biological sciences, and 9 in the social sciences. These listings are several times as numerous as would be found for unselected college graduates. An even greater distinction has been won by the three men who have been elected to the National Academy of Sciences, one of the highest honors accorded American scientists. Not all the notable achievements have been in the sciences; many examples of distinguished accomplishment are found in nearly all fields of endeavour.

Some idea of the distinction and versatility of the group may be found in biographical listings. In addition to the 70 men listed in American Men of Science, 10 others appear in the Directory of American Scholars, a companion volume of biographies of persons with notable accomplishment in the humanities. In both of these volumes, listings depend on the amount of attention the individual's work has attracted from others in his field. Listings in Who's Who in America, on the other hand, are of persons who, by reasons of outstanding achievement, are subjects of extensive and general interest. The 31 men (about 4%) who appear in Who's Who provide striking evidence of the range of talent to be found in this group. Of these, 13 are members of college faculties representing the sciences, arts and humanities; 8 are top-ranking executives in business or industry; and 3 are diplomats. The others in Who's Who include a physicist who heads one of the foremost laboratories for research in nuclear energy; an engineer who is a director of research in an aeronautical laboratory; a landscape architect; and a writer and editor. Still others are a farmer who is also a government official serving in the Department of Agriculture; a brigadier general in the United States Army; and a vice-president and director of one of the largest philanthropic foundations.

Several of the college faculty members listed in Who's Who hold important administrative positions. These include an internationally known scientist who is provost of a leading university, and a distinguished scholar in the field of literature who is vice-chancellor at one of the country's largest universities. Another, holding a doctorate in theology, is president of a small denominational college. Others among the college faculty include one of the world's foremost oceanographers and head of a well-known institute of oceanography; a dean of a leading medical school; and a physiologist who is director of an internationally known laboratory and is himself famous both in this country and abroad for his studies in nutrition and related fields.

The background of the eight businessmen listed in Who's Who is interesting.

Only three prepared for a career in business. These include the president of a food distributing firm of national scope; the controller of one of the leading steel companies in the country; and a vice-president of one of the largest oil companies in the United States. Of the other five business executives, two were trained in the sciences (both hold Ph. D.'s) and one in engineering; the remaining two were both lawyers who specialized in corporation law and are now high-ranking executives. The three men in the diplomatic service are career diplomats in foreign service.

Additional evidence of the productivity and versatility of the men is found in their publications and patents. Nearly 2000 scientific and technical papers and articles and some 60 books and monographs in the sciences, literature, arts, and humanities have been published. Patents granted amount to at least 230. Other writings include 33 novels, about 375 short stories, novelettes, and plays; 60 or more essays, critiques, and sketches; and 265 miscellaneous articles on a variety of subjects" (pp. 146–147).

The women too were successful far above the average. Although the majority of women in the sample were of course housewives and did not choose to pursue a career, the following accomplishments for the 700 women studied are reported by Terman and Oden; seven were listed in *American Men of Science,* two in the *Directory of American Scholars,* and two in *Who's Who in America.* The group had published five novels, five volumes of poetry, 32 technical or scholarly books, 50 short stories, 4 plays, more than 150 essays, and more than 200 scientific papers. The study leaves very little doubt that scores on IQ tests related closely to accomplishments outside of academic success, as well as to academic success. It is very doubtful if the attempt to select children scoring in the top 1% of any other single characteristic would be as predictive of future accomplishment.

Not all the children were successful; roughly 85% in this gifted group might be said to have been successful by our usual standards. The remaining 15% might be counted as failures, and suggests the importance of other, non-cognitive and non-intellectual factors. Some members of the group did not finish high school; others were occupational failures by their own admission, earning incomes below the national standard for the average adult. Others committed suicide, were alcoholics, or homosexuals, or had spent considerable time under psychiatric care. One of the 857 boys in the initial sample served a term of several years in prison for forgery, and two of the gifted women were arrested for vagrancy, with one serving a jail sentence for it. It is interesting to note that many of these failures could have been predicted in terms of the personality ratings made in their childhood; high degrees of emotional instability at that time predicted failure with some degree of precision. It is a pity that better instruments for the measurement of personality were not available at that time; it is the inter-play between intelligence and personality which is so important in making accurate predictions.

It is of course possible to discount these achievements by claiming that other aspects of life may be more important, and such an argument cannot be denied. Let us merely state that the outcomes achieved were successes as defined by people taking part in the investigation themselves, i. e. the men and women who were singled out as children by their extremely high IQs. Values should not be imposed on people; in judging whether the high IQ enables the person to succeed, one must inevitably have regard to the definition he himself, or she herself, gives of "success". Taking this into account there is no doubt that these children in the great majority of instances have succeeded in achieving what they set out to achieve, and that where they failed, to do so the failure lay in personality factors not measured by IQ tests.

These results, and others like them, have often suggested that highly gifted children should receive special education adapted to their needs, rather than being kept to the same slow pace as their less gifted brothers and sisters. This has been suggested particularly with respect to the most highly gifted, i. e. children even more outstanding than the children in the Terman "genius" group. In opposition, it is often said that such *Wunderkinder* may impress as children, but usually fail as adults. This belief is very widespread, but it is not based on fact. The belief seems to be based almost entirely on the career of William James Sidis, who in 1909, as a boy of only 11 years of age, was allowed to enter Harvard College. There, three months before his twelfth birthday, he gave a lecture on higher mathematics. But he never reached the scientific stature that might have been expected of someone possessing his early brilliance, but died alone, obscure and destitute. He left a troublesome legacy which *Montour* (1977) termed the "Sidis fallacy" – that talent like his rarely matures or becomes productive. "Legends and myths about this man whose intellectual grasp as a youth was made to exceed his emotional capacity still exert an adverse influence on the education of intellectually gifted children." As she points out, "Even those who claim to have some knowledge of Sidis probably are aware only of the untruths spread about him after his death."

There can be no doubt about the high level of intelligence of the Sidis boy. He was able to write at the age of 3, type well at the age of 4, and when, at the age of 5, his father gave him several calendars to teach him the idea of time, and to familiarise him with numbers, he was able, by studying these, to devise his own method for predicting on what day of the week a date would fall. "At the same age he had been taught to read Russian, French, and German as well as English." A year later, 6 year old William could also read Hebrew words, and afterwards he learned Latin and Greek.

When the 6 year old boy found a skeleton his father had used as a medical student, he studied the bones and compared them with an anatomy textbook until, as the father said, "He knew so much about the structure of the body that he could pass a medical student's examination at 6 years of age". In his eighth year, William passed the entrance examination for the Massachusetts Institute of Technology, devised a new table of logarithms using a base of 12 instead of 10, and passed the Harvard Medical Schools Anatomy Examination. At the age of 9 he had the knowledge and background for enrolment at Harvard College, but they refused to admit so young a boy. Only at the age of 11 was he permitted to enrol as special student in the Autumn of 1909. It was shortly after that that he delivered his celebrated lecture on the Fourth Dimension before the Harvard Mathematical Club. As Norbert Wiener, another child genius and future father of cybernetics (then a 15 year old Harvard graduate student) wrote of the lecture: "The talk would have done credit to first or second year graduate students of any age . . . Sidis had no access to existing sources (so) that the talk represented a triumph of the unaided effort of a very brilliant child."

William graduated in 1914, but only spent one year doing graduate study at Harvard and did not receive a graduate degree; he entered the Harvard Law School but also failed to take a degree although doing well. He was offered a teaching position at the Rice Institute in Texas, but failed to measure up to the responsibility, probably because of immaturity. He was unable to cope with the reporters who constantly followed him about; was arrested during a May Day demonstration, and although he won an appeal against his conviction, he finally dropped out of sight. He became estranged from his family, who had driven him on throughout his youth, and attempted to lead a solitary, unassuming existence, drifting from one poorly paid and non-demanding job to another. He was always rediscovered by reporters who made his life a misery. "He fled from one low-paying job to another and lived in dismal quarters in the shabbier parts of various cities as he tried to escape his former fame." His case became very widely known through the efforts of reporters and others who used his career as a homily against the intellectual "force-feeding" of children, and in favour of vaguely egalitarian, non-elitist ideas. He finally died in his forties, unmourned and under-achieved.

Montour makes a good case for the belief that the failure of the young man was due to emotional immaturity, produced in large measure by his parents inability to relate to him emotionally and to give him the support he needed. In many ways his parents exploited him as an advertisement for their methods of education. Persecution by the press added an incredible stress to his life with which because of his emotional immaturity he was unable to cope. There is no reason at all to believe that it was his accelerated mental development that was responsible for his failure; rather it was a lack of a proper loving and secure family background that led to his downfall. There certainly are many *Wunderkinder* whose adult achievement does not belie their early promise. Norbert Wiener has already been mentioned; A. A. Berle is another, and so are John Stuart Mill, Edmund Gosse and Samuel Butler. Many others are mentioned in Montour's article. Most of these had difficulties in their parent-child relationships, their homes being usually run, and their education dominated, by a dominant father, who evoked suppressed feelings of revolt in the attitudes of these brilliant sons. There is much to be said for giving the parents of brilliant children guidance on how to avoid the abuses which were suffered by William James Sidis; there is no reason whatsoever to believe that they should not be intellectually advanced well beyond the kind of teaching their years alone might suggest. The USSR has taken this point seriously, and has founded special schools for children showing quite exceptional gifts for mathematics and physics. There is no suggestion among these children that the case of William James Sidis is anything but an exception to the general rule that brilliant children become brilliant adults.

We have now come to the end of a brief glance at the various sources (by no means all the sources) of evidence for the statement that IQ does measure quite well what the man in the street would refer to as "intelligence". External evidence reviewed includes school and university achievement, achievements in later life (scientific, commercial, military, etc.), and the achievement of high social status and a good income. Of course there are many exceptions to the rule that high IQ = success in life. We have seen that neurotic and other personality difficulties can nullify the advantages conferred by a high IQ: we have seen that luck and unfair personal advantages, from good looks to charm, and from nepotism to being born with a silver spoon in one's mouth, can make up for lack of intelligence. In our society, there are various occupations which lead to high income and even adulation, without requiring even average IQ, from being a football or tennis star to earning a living as a prostitute or a pop artist. It is not necessary to list all the exceptions to our rule; the fact that correlations between IQ and criteria are far from perfect indicates that intelligence is only one of many factors which make for success. Nevertheless, it is important to realize that in our (and indeed any complex) society that may exist, intelligence as indexed by IQ is perhaps the most important single quality that makes for success and advancement. This constitutes the social importance of the IQ, and of IQ testing; what political and social deductions we make from this fact, and if how we use IQ tests in school, university, business and elsewhere, are questions which cannot find an answer simply by looking at the facts. Such answers are in part determined by one's social philosophy, political convictions, and even moral and religious beliefs; it cannot be the purpose of a scientific treatise to make any prescriptions in this connection, although we shall discuss some of the possibilities in the final chapter.

This brings us to the end of our discussion of external criteria, but some of the issues raised will be reverted to in later chapters. It should be noted that in this discussion we have purposely omitted any detailed discussion of the question of heredity and environment; we have been concerned only with the question of external validity of IQ measures taken at a particular time, i. e. the correlation of these measures with various criteria. We have not taken up the equally important question as to the causation of these correlations, except in passing. The data quoted, or at least most of them, are equally compatible with a genetic explanation as with an environmental one. It would be equally easy to postulate that IQ differences are caused by environmental events in the lives of the children tested, from intrauterine experiences to post-natal ones, as it would be to postulate that genetic factors were responsible for the major of the observed variance. Clearly the nature-nurture problem is entirely separate from the one considered in this chapter, and deserves extensive discussion. This discussion will also attempt to take further our consideration of the causal chains involving education, IQ, income, social status, and the various other social variables considered in this chapter. The facts here considered establish that IQ is socially important, i. e. is closely related to variables universally regarded as being important; they do not by themselves tell us all we want and need to know about the causal relations obtaining in this field. For that purpose a detailed investigation of the genetic problem is required, and to this we shall turn in the next three chapters.

5 Nature and Nurture: Heredity

D. W. Fulker and H. J. Eysenck

It often happens also that the children may appear like a grandfather and reproduce the looks of a great-grandfather because the parents often conceal in their bodies many primordia mingled in many ways, which fathers hand on to fathers received from their stock; from these Venus brings forth forms with varying lot, and reproduces the countenance, the voice, the hair of their ancestors

Lucretius
On the Nature of Things

The question of the relative importance of nature and nurture in predisposing people to behave differently is a vexed one, having important implications beyond the immediate concerns of psychology. For mental illness, sociopathy or intellectual ability, for example, the broad question of the place of the individual in society is raised. We are forced to consider the nature and extent of the opportunities that face the individual and, in the light of his limitations, what might constitute realistic and humane social policies. These and similar questions naturally generate a great deal of emotion as well as interest, and emotional attitudes have often hindered an objective evaluation of the empirical evidence, resulting in exaggerated claims for the importance of nature or nurture to the complete exclusion of the other.

Of course, such extreme views are quite unfounded in reality, and where they have subsequently been allowed to influence social policy they have been disastrous. Extreme hereditarian views have been used, frequently, to support eugenic arguments both cruel and absurd and to justify the persecution and oppression of minorities. These evils are now, thankfully, less evident, although the world is far from free of them. Less obvious, but hardly less dangerous, is extreme environmentalism which is increasingly used to justify a Procrustean and intolerant treatment of human individuality in the name of equality.

Fortunately, these extreme views have seldom been characteristic of those actively carrying out research into these problems, and we now have a wealth of evidence demonstrating the combined importance of both nature and nurture in determining individual differences in behaviour. Hopefully this knowledge has an important contribution to make to human welfare. It is this evidence in relation to IQ and educational achievement with which we will be concerned in the next three chapters. In the present one we will be concerned mainly with nature, attempting to assess the extent of genetic influences relative to those stemming from the environment and looking, in some detail, at the forms these genetic influences take. In the next chapter we will be concerned more with nurture examining factors such as early environment, the economic quality of the home, its cultural atmosphere and interactions with parents and other children. Finally, in Chapter 7, we will be concerned with how nature and nurture interact during an individual's lifetime and the role they play in influencing social structure.

The theoretical model underlying the partitioning of human variation recognizes that the phenotype or the individuals's level for the trait in question will be determined both by his genetic makeup and his environmental circumstances. In its basic form, the phenotype (P) is expressed quite simply as the sum of the genetic effect (G) and the environmental effect (E).

$$P = G + E$$

This formulation often causes difficulty because it seems to imply that a complex interactive process between genes and the environment in which they develop has been reduced to an unrealistic level of simplicity. It is felt to be a little absurd to claim, for example, that an IQ of twenty points above the average is made up of 15 points from genetic makeup and 5 from the environment, especially since we can only observe a single level of 120 in the individual. However, this is to misunderstand what is really a very straightforward and intuitively sensible model. The genetic effect, G, of an individual is being thought of as the average effect of his genetic makeup assessed across a representative range of environments. In our example we are saying that this individual has the kind of genetic makeup that in general would tend to raise IQ about 15 points, whatever the environment. Similarly, the environmental effect, E, is being defined as the average effect of a particular set of environmental experiences assessed across a range of genotypes. For the individual in our example we are saying that his environmental experiences are of the kind generally beneficial to the extent of about 5 IQ points.

This formulation is therefore no different from that underlying the conventional experimental designs we commonly use to assess the effects of independent variables.

In laboratory animals we can measure the values of G and E without difficulty by rearing animals from a number of strains in a range of environments and observing mean performances. In humans, assessing the effects of G and E is more difficult because we have only limited control over both genetic makeup and the environment. However, the situation is no more difficult than in many other branches of social science where complete experimental control is impossible. Indeed, it is considerably better since the biological mechanisms of Mendelian inheritance guarantee a substantial measure of randomisation of genetic and environmental influences. In practice, the behaviour geneticist adopts approximate or quasi-experimental designs (*Campbell* and *Stanley,* 1963) in which balance and control is achieved not by randomisation, as in true designs, but by exploiting natural situations in a systematic manner. Such designs, of course, require greater caution than truly randomised ones and the use of independent checks on the validity of their underlying assumptions.

In short, then, the definitions of G and E in the model are completely straightforward and operational. The model is, indeed, simple and in its basic form deliberately side-steps the complex problem of how genes and environment have interacted to produce the phenotype. It is the very simplicity of this formulation that provides a firm base from which we can elaborate and take account of a realistic level of complexity, should the situation demand.

What are the quasi-experimental designs that have been used to separate the effects of G from E in IQ variation? There are many, but one of the simplest and certainly the most frequently employed is the twin study.

Approximately one in every hundred births gives rise to a pair of twins. Of these, about one third result from a single conception and are thus genetically identical. These are monozygotic or identical twins (MZ). The remainder are the result of two separate conceptions and so are neither more nor less alike genetically than ordinary siblings. These are dizygotic or fraternal twins (DZ).

A fascination with twins goes back to antiquity, but it was not until the last century that the English scientist, Sir Francis Galton, realised that the two different kinds of twins offered an opportunity to distinguish the effects of nature from nurture. Galton was hampered by the lack of reliable measures of intellectual ability, but with the development of intelligence tests at the turn of the century it became possible to do justice to his approach.

The logic of the twin study is quite straightforward. Twins are divided into monozygotic and dizygotic on the basis of similarity (MZ) or dissimilarity (DZ) of obvious physical characteristics known to be very highly genetically determined. These might be facial appearance, fingerprints or, most reliably of all, a variety of blood group factors. Individuals are then measured on the trait under investigation and the extent to which MZ twins are found to resemble each other more than DZs taken as an indication of the relative importance of genetic influences.

An early, carefully planned study of IQ carried out by *Herrman* and *Hogben* (1932) and involving 65 pairs of MZ twins and 234 pairs of DZs illustrates the approach. Twins were identified in London schools and judged to be MZ or DZ on the basis of finger-printing. They were then given the Otis Advanced Group Intelligence Test, which was standardised to give a mean IQ of 100 and a standard deviation of about 23. In addition to the twins, 103 pairs of ordinary full siblings (FS) were also tested for comparison with the twins.

A number of indices of similarity are available to assess twin resemblance, some like the correlation coefficient, for example, being more useful than others, but the simplest, most obvious index is the average pair difference. These average differences for the twins and siblings in Herrman and Hogben's study are shown in Table 5.1.

The results are quite clear cut. Firstly, there is no difference between like-sexed and unlike sex DZ twins, suggesting that genes and environment operate on both sexes in the same way. Secondly, DZ twins are no more alike than ordinary full siblings, indicating that twins are not treated differently from ordinary brothers and sisters. But, MZ twins are much more alike than DZ twins or siblings, their average difference differing by a factor of almost two. Since MZ pairs are genetically identical, and DZs are not, it is plausible to ascribe their greater IQ resemblance to genetic influences.

Table 5.1. Mean differences in IQ of four groups in *Herrman* and *Hogben's* study (1933)

Groups	N pairs	Mean IQ difference
MZ twins	65	9.2 ± 1.0
DZ twins of like sex	96	17.7 ± 1.5
DZ twins of unlike sex	138	17.9 ± 1.2
Siblings	103	16.8 ± 2.3

This is the basic logic of the twin method and it rests on the critical assumption that relevant environmental influences of MZ twins are shared to the same extent as those of DZs. If the assumption does not hold, then the increased resemblance of MZ twins may simply reflect their greater environmental similarity. The assumption is crucial, and doubts have frequently been raised concerning its validity. At first sight these doubts seem reasonable enough, since they rest on the well established fact that in many respects MZ twins are treated more alike than DZs. For example, a recent study of scholastic achievement by *Loehlin* and *Nichols* (1976), based on over 2000 pairs of twins, obtained parental ratings of the twins for dressing alike, playing together, sharing the same teacher, sleeping in the same room and the extent to which parents consciously tried to treat their twins alike. In all cases, MZ twins were treated more alike than DZs.

However, the important question is whether or not such variables are important determinants of intellectual ability. If they do not influence IQ there can be no possibility of differential treatment causing the surplus MZ resemblance. In Loehlin and Nichols' study it was possible to show that these influences were having absolutely no effect by looking to see if those twins who were treated more alike actually were more alike in intellectual ability. They found that the correlation between differences in similarity of treatment and differences in ability was only -0.05 for MZs, a trivial value and, in any case, opposite in sign to that expected. For DZ twins there was an even smaller correlation of $+0.02$. Clearly these particular treatments are irrelevant, failing to influence intellectual performance. This is not surprising if we recall Herrman and Hogben's finding that neither sharing the same gender nor being a DZ twin rather than an ordinary sibling influenced similarity either. If being treated as a boy rather than a girl does not affect similarity in cognitive performance, it is not surprising that dressing similarly, some parental pressure towards uniformity and the like should also fail to do so. There is not a shred of evidence to suggest any special differential treatment of MZ twins relevant to cognitive development. Indeed, what evidence we have is entirely negative.

We can explore the nature-nurture question in a more thorough manner by developing our simple G and E model and applying it ot other features of twin data. Recall the basic model. The phenotype is expressed as the sum of two components, one due to nature, G, and the other to nuture, E.

$$P = G + E$$

If these two components are independent, then the observed phenotypic variation V (P) can also be expressed as the sum of two components V (G) and V (E), which are the variances of the genetic and environmental effects respectively. That is

$$V(P) = V(G) + V(E)$$

The use of the variance, which is simply the square of the standard deviation, rather than some other summary population statistic, has the advantage of allowing us to move from the individual to the population while still retaining the additive nature of the model. Whereas we cannot separate G and E for any single individual phenotypic score, we can separate V (G) and V (E) from the variances and covariances of groups of individuals such as twins. This fact determines the choice of analysis of variance of twin data to assess the relative effects of G and E.

The analysis of variance of twin pairs partitions total IQ variation into two sources, that Between Pairs and that Within. To the extent that pairs resemble each other, the Mean Square Between (B) will be greater than that Within (W), the ratio (B − W) / (B + W) being a measure of this resemblance known as the intra-class correlation. It is to these Mean Squares or, more simply and sufficient for our purposes, to the correlations derived from them, that we equate our genetic and environmental components V (G) and V (E).

Because people are typically raised in families, we must elaborate the environmental part of the model slightly, replacing E with two components, one reflecting the effects of home background together with shared or common experiences, and the other reflecting experiences that typically differ for children even though they are reared together. We will refer to these as home or common environment (CE) and specific environment (SE) respectively. The expression for the phenotype now becomes

$$P = G + CE + SE$$

and the phenotypic variance

$$V(P) = V(G) + V(CE) + V(SE)$$

Table 5.2. Analysis of Variance of IQ, intraclass correlations and genetic model for MZ and DZ twins

Twin	Source of Variation		MS	r[a]	Model for r
MZ	Between pairs	(B)	850	0.84	V (G) + V (CE)
	Within pairs	(W)	75		
DZ like-sex		B	730	0.47	½V (G) + V (CE)
		W	260		

[a] r = (B − W) / B + W

Analysis of variance of twin data allows us to separate these components. The Mean Squares reconstructed from Herrman and Hogben's data, together with the derived MZ and DZ intra-class correlations and their expectations on this model are shown in Table 5.2.

The genetical and environmental expectations for the intra-class correlations in Table 5.2 are determined by means of the following argument. The correlation reflects the variance of all shared influences. MZ twins share the same home environment (CE) and exactly the same genes (G). Hence their correlation reflects V (G) + V (CE). DZ twins also share the same home environment but only half their genes, the latter following from genetic theory. Hence their correlation will reflect V (CE) + $\frac{1}{2}$V (G). Given this model, straightforward arithmetic gives estimates of the components in the model as follows:

V (G) is twice the difference between the two correlations and
V (CE) the difference between the MZ correlation and our estimate of V (G).

Thus $V(G) = 2\,(0.84 - 0.47) = 0.74$ or 74%
$V(CE) = 0.84 - 0.74 = 0.10$ or 10%

V (SE) is 0.16 or 16%, the amount required to make all three components sum to 100%. The quantity V (G) is often referred to as the broad heritability.

An alternative representation of this model in terms of path coefficients was developed by the geneticist *Wright* (1954). In this approach, the effects G, CE and SE are all assumed to be measured on a scale with a standard deviation of one, a device which puts them on an equal footing as potential influences on the phenotype, P. The phenotype can then be represented by a regression equation in which the beta weights, known as paths, are the correlations between P and G, CE and SE respectively. It follows from this formulation that these correlations are merely the square roots of the associated variance components for G, CE and SE in the previous formulation. In our example

$$V(G) = 0.74, \text{ therefore } R_{G,P} = \sqrt{0.74} = 0.86$$
$$V(CE) = 0.10, \text{ therefore } R_{GE,P} = \sqrt{0.10} = 0.32$$
$$V(SE) = 0.16, \text{ therefore } R_{SE,P} = \sqrt{0.16} = 0.40$$

and the prediction equation for P is

$$P = 0.86G + 0.32CE + 0.40SE$$

Looked at another way, the square of each of these correlations or paths gives the proportion of variance explained or accounted for by the three uncorrelated variables G, CE and SE.

Wright's formulation has two advantages. Firstly, it can be represented in diagrammatic form, as shown in Fig. 5.1. This simple visual representation is extremely useful when we wish to inter-relate variables and consider the more complex multivariate systems in Chapter 9.

Secondly, the values of the paths better indicate the relative importance of the respective influences on individual differences than do the proportions of

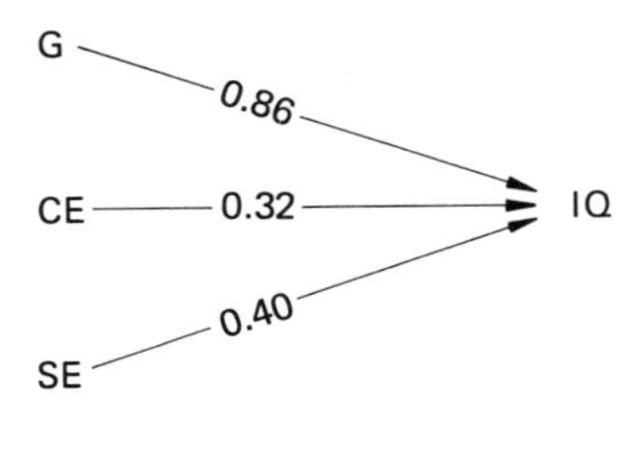

P = 0.86G + 0.32CE + 0.40SE

Fig. 5.1. The simplest realistic path model representation of genetic and environmental influences on IQ

variance. Thus the finding of a heritability of 74% compared with a common environmental variance of only 10% suggests the overwhelming importance of genetic influences. However, their true relative importance in terms of raising or lowering an individual's IQ is in proportion to their paths, 86% to 32%, indicating a sizeable impact of the common environmental influence.

A full discussion of the model underlying the partitioning of IQ variance has been attempted in order to avoid misunderstandings concerning the logic of the approach. The meaning of the component of genetic variation V(G), often referred to as the heritability, has been particularly misunderstood. It is often said, for example, that because it is a population statistic (which it is) it is not in any sense applicable to individuals (which is false). The linear model underlying the partitioning of variation refers to the individual, although we can seldom directly observe the effects involved. The proportions of variance are summary statistics that apply to the population. But they also translate into effects we *expect* to influence individuals, as Wright's formulation clearly shows. This formulation enables us to predict what we would expect an individual's IQ to be in the light of information concerning his environment and genetic makeup. So far as the environment is concerned we can often measure it (*Rao* et al., 1974). In the case of genotype we must rely on information concerning blood relatives. The randomisation of genetic influences makes prediction in the case of any one individual quite inexact, though still better than chance, a fact which is often ignored. However, as the numbers of individuals increases the power of the prediction goes up as can be seen in the case of regression effects, discussed later in the chapter and from recent advances in pedigree analysis (*Lange* et al., 1976) which allow reasonable predictions concerning whole families.

Herrman and Hogben's study (1932) indicates a large genetic influence on IQ. How typical are these results of twin studies in general? Several compilations of the results of twin studies of IQ have appeared in the literature, but probably the best known of these is that of *Erlenmeyer-Kimling* and *Jarvik* (1963) which also includes many other relationships for purposes of comparison. They list 14 studies of MZ twins and 11 of DZs, with median correlations of 0.87 and 0.53, very close to 0.84 and 0.47 found by Herrman and Hogben. These correlations give estimates of components of variance of

V(G) = 68%
V(CE) = 19%
V(SE) = 13%

which are probably the best overall estimates available from twin studies. Roughly speaking, then, twin studies suggest a breakdown of IQ variation of about 70% genetic, at most 20% common environment and about 10% specific environment.

We have dealt at length with twin studies because they are relatively common. How consistent are genetic and environmental estimates from twins with those from other lines of evidence? After all, these estimates depend on an inference from two kinds of twin correlations and rest on the assumptions of equal twin environments and the surplus resemblance of MZ over DZ twins being $^1/_2$ V(G). While these assumptions are quite reasonable, it would obviously be reassuring to have additional evidence and perhaps a more direct indication of the relative importance of genetic and environmental influences.

Adoption studies of various kinds provide such additional and more direct evidence. When children are separated from their natural parents at an early age and brought up in different homes, a variety of relationships are generated that allow a direct separation of nature and nurture, provided there is little selective placement. That is, we require that the children are placed in their foster homes at random with respect to the environmental determinants of the trait in question.

There are two ways of looking at these studies, one from the environmental viewpoint, the other a genetic one. The correlations between an adopted child and its foster sib or foster parents directly reflects the influence of common environment. The correlation between the natural sib or parent, with whom it has had little or no contact directly reflects genetic influences. A special case of great interest but unfortunately (for the behaviour geneticist!) quite rare arises when the foster child has an identical twin who was either reared by the natural mother or fostered elsewhere. For these individuals, separated identical twins, the correlation reflects the total effect of genetic influences, while the extent to which they differ reflects the total effect of the environment.

There are four major studies of IQ in MZ twins reared apart (*Newman et al.*, 1937; *Shields*, 1962; *Juel-Nielsen*, 1965; *Burt*, 1966) comprising a total of 122 pairs[7]. The correlations obtained in these studies are given in Table 5.3. In spite of the relatively small numbers in each the results show a remarkable consis-

7 Recent attempts to discredit Burt's studies of IQ are discussed in Appendix A. The matter is also raised in relation to the discussion of Table 5.9. In relation to Burt's sample of MZ twins reared apart the main criticism concerns the individual test scores which were "corrected" in the light of known factors in the home environment, previous school performance and the like, rather in the manner of an educational psychologist attempting to make a realistic evaluation of a child's intelligence. This procedure, of course, raises the correlation and renders it unsuitable for the approach developed in this chapter. However, as is clear from Table 5.3, the group test correlation which was based on unadjusted scores is entirely comparable with the other studies and its omission would not alter the conclusions.

Table 5.3. IQ Correlations between MZ twins reared apart

	N pairs	Group tests	Individual tests
Newman et al. (1937)	19	0.73	0.67
Shields (1962)	38	0.77	–
Juel-Nielsen (1965)	12	0.77	0.68
Burt (1966)	53	0.77	0.86

tency, particularly as regards the four different group tests. Taken at face value these tests suggest a heritability of about 77%. A figure reasonably close to the 68% obtained from the MZ and DZ twins in Erlenmeyer-Kimling and Jarvik's compilation, while the median individual test correlation suggests 68%, agreeing precisely with earlier twin data.

The main objection raised by critics of foster studies concerns the degree of selective placement. In the case of the studies of MZ twins reared apart, selective placement would raise the correlation and overestimate the heritability. In principle we can detect the presence of selective placement directly by noting a similarity between features of the foster home relevant to the development of IQ and those of the home the child would have had if it had remained with its natural parents. In practice it has proved difficult to measure the relevant variables.

However, some similarity between homes seems likely in the studies of MZ twins reared apart. We know, for example, that in Shields' study a number of the children were reared by aunts or uncles and could not have been as widely separated as one would have expected if foster homes had been chosen unsystematically. However, two factors suggest that this effect exerts only a minor influence on twin resemblance. Firstly, and most importantly, the correlations for MZ reared apart, in all four studies, suggest a heritability only slightly higher than that obtained for MZ and DZ twins reared together. The consistency of evidence from independent sources is an important criterion by which to judge the correctness of a scientific theory. Secondly, even if a number of the twins are reared in related families, by aunts and uncles as in Shields' study, the degree of resemblance produced should be slight. This excess resemblance should not exceed that of ordinary cousins, even assuming zero heritabilities. Studies of cousins typically find a correlation in the region of 0.2. Allowing for some genetic resemblance between cousins and the fact that most twins will be more widely separated than cousins, a placement effect of much less than 10% seems likely. As pointed out comparisons with studies of unseparated twins, which suggest a heritability of about 70% compared with 77% for the separated ones are consistent with this conclusion.

Perhaps the most striking testimony to the importance of genetic factors to come from these studies of 122 pairs of MZ twins reared apart is quite simply the largest recorded IQ difference of 24 points. This difference is for one of Newman, Freeman and Holzinger's twin pairs, 35 year old Gladys and Helen.

Table 5.4. IQ Correlations for siblings reared apart

Study	N pair	Correlation
Hildreth (1925)	78	0.23
Freeman et al. (1928)[a]	125	0.25–0.34
Burt (1966)	151	0.42

[a] The lower figure is intraclass, the higher, product moment calculated for younger and older sibs.

Gladys, who had the lower IQ, had been reared in a remote part of the Canadian Rockies, was of relatively poor health and had missed a great deal of schooling. Helen was reared on a farm, but with encouragement from her foster-mother graduated from a good college and pursued a career in teaching. These environments were different enough, although many other pairs of twins, particularly in Shields' study, were reared under much more diverse conditions. The point to note, however, is that given identical genetic make-up, 24 IQ points is the largest difference typical environmental influences have ever been found to produce. In a comparable sample of 244 individuals drawn at random from the population we would typically expect to find a maximum difference in the region of 80 points, the difference between a subnormal person of IQ 60 and a bright person of 140. Even larger differences, of course, exist. Clearly these studies suggest that the effect of nurture on IQ is much less than that of nature.

Studies of siblings reared apart are even fewer than those of separated MZ twins, there being only three, shown in Table 5.4. Since siblings only share on average half their genes, twice their observed correlation estimates heritability directly. The median figures suggest a value between 50% and 68%, depending on which of the two correlations given by *Freeman et al.*, (1928) is chosen. Thus these studies suggest a somewhat lower heritability than those of twins, but not strikingly so. The difference between these two correlations in Freeman *et al*'s study arises from a negative correlation of IQ with age, an artifact frequently found for older tests, imperfectly standardised. The figure is a product-moment correlation between older and younger siblings and is therefore crudely corrected for this source of bias. Although such artifacts are troublesome when we wish to make precise comparisons, they are of trivial importance in the broad picture.

More numerous are studies of unrelated individuals reared together or foster sibs. Their resemblance, again in the absence of selective placement, will be a pure reflection of shared environment. However, whereas selective placement in studies of twins and siblings reared apart causes an over-estimate of genetic influences, together with an underestimate of environmental effects, the converse is true for studies of foster sibs. A degree of compensation can therefore be expected in the cumulative picture that emerges from considering both kinds of foster studies. Imperfect age standardisation will also have a similar compensatory effect.

The results of seven studies, including two recent ones, are shown in Table 5.5. The median correlation is 0.23, unchanged from Erlenmeyer-Kimling and

Table 5.5. IQ Correlations between unrelated children reared in the same home

Study	N pair	r
Freeman et al. (1928)	140	0.34
Burt (1966)	136	0.25
Scarr[a] and *Weinberg* (1976)	84	−0.03
Scarr and *Weinberg* (1977)	187	0.33
Burks (1928)	21	0.23
Leahy[b] (1935)	35	0.08
Skodak (1950)	63	0.50

[a] In this study most pairs were mixed black and white.
[b] Calculated by *Jencks* (1972).

Jarvik's median of the five studies available in 1963. This direct estimate of 23% for V(CE) (probably a slight overestimate due to selective placement) is only trivially different from the 19% suggested by the MZ and DZ twin data alone. A good broad agreement between the various lines of evidence is beginning to emerge.

The correlations between both foster sibs and sibs reared apart can be compared with the correlation for normal siblings to estimate V(G) and V(CE). For siblings we have a wealth of reliable data. *Jencks* (1972) lists six American studies involving a total of 1951 pairs for the Stanford Binet test alone. From these studies he estimates the sibling correlation to be 0.52. Another American study (*Higgins*, et al., 1962) employing a variety of tests, found exactly the same figure for a sample of just over one thousand pairs. Erlenmeyer-Kimling and Jarvik obtained a median value of 0.49 for 35 studies. There seems little doubt that the sibling correlation is in the region of 0.50. If we accept the estimate of V(CE) of 0.23 from studies of foster sibs and combine this estimate with a sibling correlation of 0.49, we can estimate heritability as twice the difference, or 52%, somewhat lower than the 68% obtained with twins, but not strikingly so. Had we chosen a sibling correlation of 0.52, our estimate of V(G) would have risen to 59%, then only slightly less than our twin estimate of 68%. The precise estimate will be fairly sensitive to very minor variations in the observed correlations. Alternatively, comparing the sibling correlation of 0.49 with that for sibs reared apart of 0.34, we can estimate V(CE) as the difference, or 15%, this time very close to the 19% obtained from twins.

We have used comparisons between correlations for contemporaries such as twins, siblings and foster sibs to estimate V(CE) and V(G). Comparisons between natural and foster parents and their children also allow us to estimate these sources of variation in a similar manner. In this case, however, V(CE) may not have quite the same meaning as it does for contemporaries, since the shared environment of parents and children may not have all its elements in common with the environment shared by siblings.

Correlations between foster parents and adopted children from six major studies, three of them quite recent, are shown separately for mother and fathers

Table 5.6. IQ Correlations between foster parents and their adopted children

	N pair	father	N pair	mother
Burks (1928)	178	0.07	204	0.19
Freeman et al. (1928)	180	0.37	255	0.28
Leahy (1935)	178	0.19	186	0.24
Scarr and *Weinberg* (1977)	111	0.15	109	0.23
Scarr and *Weinberg* (1976)	127	0.18	128	0.17
Horn[a] et al. (1975)	228	0.09	236	0.15

[a] Personal Communication reported by *Munsinger* (1975)

in Table 5.6. These correlations which, in the absence of selective placement, estimate directly the effects of home environment, indicate a median value of 0.17 for foster-fathers and 0.21 for mothers, the overall median value being 0.19. The agreement with estimates of V(CE) for contemporaries from the other lines of evidence so far examined is truly striking. It is of interest that the correlations are very similar for both foster-mothers and foster-fathers, indicating that it is the general quality of the home that influences IQ rather than predominantly the influence of either the mother or the father.

Comparisons between natural parent-child and foster parent-child correlations indicate the influence of genetic factors, just as do comparisons between correlations for natural sibs and foster sibs. In both cases twice the difference estimates the heritability V(G) assuming the very simplest genetical and environmental model. The fosterparent-child correlation is 0.19. Erlenmeyer-Kimling and Jarvik report a median correlation of 0.50 for twelve studies of natural parents and their children. *Jencks* (1972) reports a figure of 0.48 for what he considers to be five of the more reliable US studies. Estimating heritability from Erlenmeyer-Kimling and Jarvik's figure indicates 62%, again only a little different from 68% indicated by the twin date.

The most direct evidence of the genetic component in parent-child resemblance comes from studies of natural parents and their children given up for adoption shortly after birth. Only three such studies exist, for which correlations are shown in Table 5.7. In *Snyggs's* study (1938) threequarters of the children were tested at under 5 years of age, when a reliable measure of IQ is difficult to obtain. However, following the procedure of selecting the median correlation as

Table 5.7. IQ Correlations between mother and child reared apart

	N pair	r
Skodak and *Skeels* (1949)	63	0.40
Horn et al. (1975)[a]	192	0.32
Snygg (1938)	312	0.13

[a] Reported by *Munsinger* (1975)

Table 5.8. IQ Correlations between natural mothers and their children given up for adoption at different ages taken from *Skodak* and *Skeels* (1949)

Age	Correlation	Heritability
2	0.00	0%
4	0.28	56%
7	0.35	70%
14	0.40	80%

typical suggests a heritability of twice 0.32 or 64%. Again, agreement between the various lines of evidence is very good.

The study by *Skodak* and *Skeels* (1949) is particularly interesting since the children were tested at 2, 4, 7 and 14 years of age, allowing us to look at the development of heritable influences. The correlations between the natural mother and the adopted child at these four ages is shown in Table 5.8. The pattern is very clear, heritability being zero when the children are only 2 years old, but rising steadily to 80% by the time they are 14. Finding that a delay between measuring the mother and the child's IQ increases resemblance is strongly suggestive that the cause of this resemblance is genetic in origin.

Unfortunately, these authors did not measure the IQs of the foster parents to allow full comparison of the correlations in Table 5.8 with those from adopted children and their foster parents. However, they did measure years of education of both natural and foster parents, a measure fairly highly correlated with IQ. The correlations between the child's IQ and the educational level of the foster parents and natural parents are shown for both mothers and fathers in Fig. 5.2. Again the pattern is very clear. At no time do adopted children and

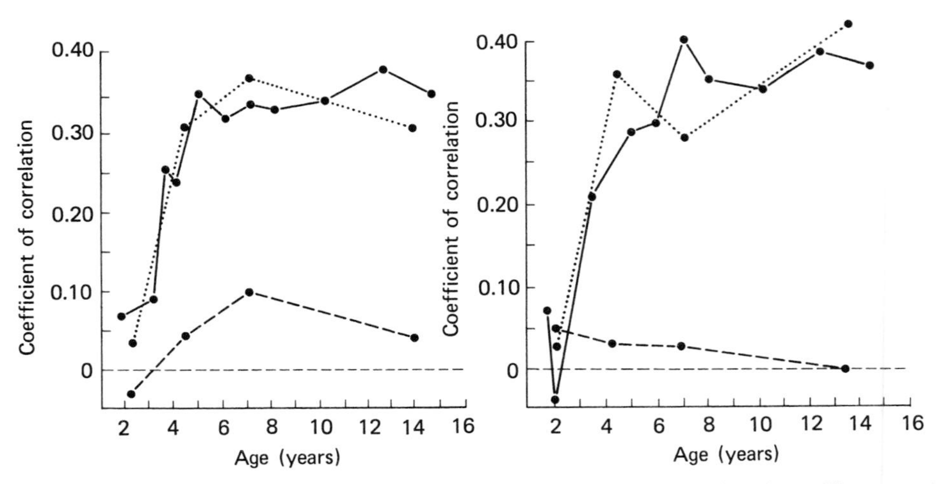

Fig. 5.2. Relation between parents' and child's IQs at different ages. Taken from *Ehrman* and *Parsons* (1976)

Table 5.9. Augmented *Erlenmeyer-Kimling* and *Jarvick* (1963) median Kinship correlations for IQ with simple genetic and environmental model

Relationship	N	Observed Correlation (0)	V(G)	V(CE)	Expected Correlation (E)	O–E
Unrelated pairs apart	4	−0.01	0	0	0.00	−0.01
Unrelated pairs together[a]	7	0.23	0	1	0.18	0.05
Foster parent child[a]	6	0.19	0	1	0.18	0.01
Sibs apart[a]	3	0.34	$^1/_2$	0	0.35	0.01
Parent child apart[a]	3	0.32	$^1/_2$	0	0.35	−0.03
Sibs together	35	0.49	$^1/_2$	1	0.53	−0.04
Parent offspring together	12	0.50	$^1/_2$	1	0.53	−0.03
DZ together	20	0.53	$^1/_2$	1	0.53	0.00
MZ apart	4	0.75	1	0	0.69	0.06
MZ together	14	0.87	1	1	0.88	−0.01

[a] Augmented as indicated in text

Estimated Effects V(G) = 0.69 ± 0.02
V(CE) = 0.18 ± 0.02

By subtraction V(SE) = 0.13

Variation in correlations explained by the model is 98%.

foster parents correlate more than 0.1; for the most part, even less. Adopted children do not grow to resemble their adoptive parents. In contrast, children certainly do grow to resemble their natural parents, whether they are living together or not, and to a substantial degree. The presence of a strong genetic component in parent/child resemblance seems put beyond reasonable doubt.

The overall consistency of the various kinship correlations for IQ when judged against our very simple genetic and environmental model has been remarkable. True, within each category the correlations are quite variable, but the typical median values clearly show the expected patterns. This remarkable consistency can, perhaps, best be demonstrated if we judge our simple model against all these correlations simultaneously. To evaluate the model in this way we have used the median correlation of Erlenmeyer-Kimling and Jarvik, augmented in those cases where numbers were small and critical studies have since been carried out. The assembled median correlations are shown in Table 5.9, together with our simple genetic and environmental model. The additions are indicated by asterisks and are based on Tables 5.4 to 5.8 in the present chapter.

In order to estimate the values of V(G) and V(CE) that best account for the observed correlations, we adopted a simple, unweighted least-squares procedure in which the observed correlations were regressed simultaneously on to the coefficients of V(G) and V(CE). Using this procedure we find the most consistent values of our parameters are a V(G) of 69% and V(CE) of 18%, each with a standard error of only about ± 2%. More sophisticated approaches that take into account the different precision with which each correlation is determined

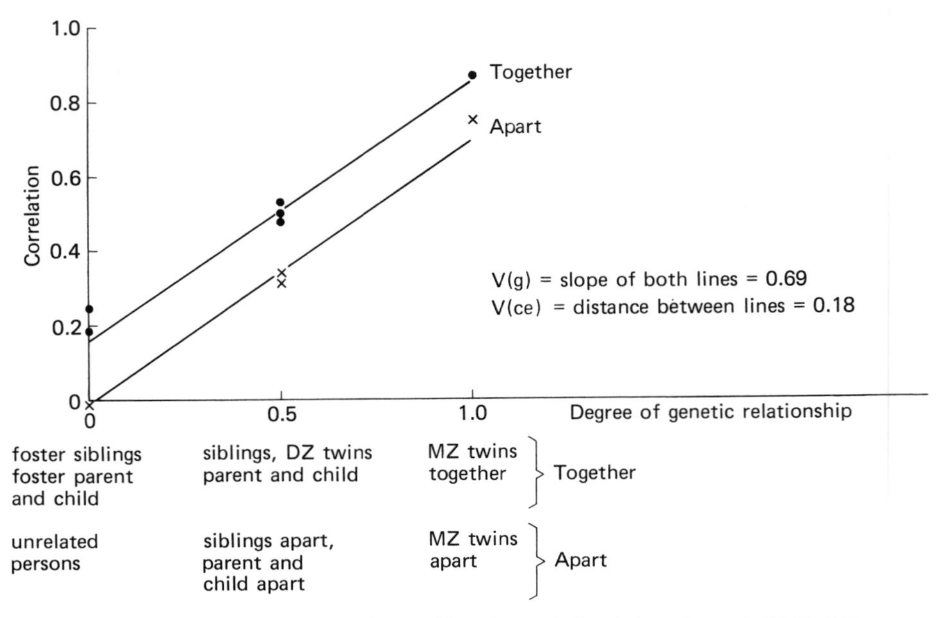

Fig. 5.3. Graphical representation of the model and correlational data shown in Table 5.9

are possible (see *Jinks* and *Fulker*, 1970) but would be out of place in an introductory text. The very simple approach employed here simply judges the model equally against each correlation, has the merit of being intuitively obvious and the adequacy of the model is easily judged by eye.

The model fitting procedure is equivalent to attempting to fit two separate straight lines of equal slope to a plot of the correlations against the degree of genetic relationship, represented by the coefficients for V(G) in Table 5.9, one line to the correlations between individuals reared apart, the other to those between individuals reared together. Figure 5.3 shows these two lines. The slope of the lines estimates the heritability V(G) and the vertical gap between them V(CE). The close fit of the lines in Fig. 5.3 and the similarity of the observed correlations with those expected on the model in Table 5.9 both show how well this simple model explains the various kinship correlations and how consistent the data are when we average across several studies. So well does this model fit, in fact that it explains 98% of the variation in the kinship correlations, a better fit for any model being difficult to imagine. In addition, with only two parameters to explain ten correlations there are 10-2 = 8 independent opportunities for the data to prove the model wrong. There seems little reason, then to doubt that it reflects reality. The remaining 2% for discrepancies between our observed and expected correlations is seen to be mainly due to the correlation for MZA, twins reared apart, and foster sibs, both of which are slightly higher than expected. This slight discrepancy is almost certainly due to a slight degree of selective placement, which cancels out when we evaluate the data as a whole.

The compilation of kinship correlations we have used to estimate the proportion of genetic and environmental variation is open to a number of criticisms. Insofar as we have used the Erlenmeyer-Kimling and Jarvik data it is not quite up to date. In addition it has been criticised for including some very small studies, including studies using poorly standardised tests, confusing some mid-parent offspring correlations with those for single parents and most tellingly, during the last few years, for including the correlations of the late Sir Cyril Burt (1966) whose reporting of data has been shown to be most unreliable (Appendix A).

A number of other compilations have attempted to improve on Erlenmeyer-Kimling and Jarvik's omitting Burt's data and making good some of its more obvious shortcomings. However, these attempts would generally include other arbitrary features and the outcome of the kind of analysis attempted in this chapter was always the same to within one or two percentage points. To illustrate the robustness of the data we refer the reader to one of the most careful recent compilations of kinship correlations by *Roubertoux* and *Carlier* (1977) which attempts to answer all the above criticisms. Whereas we obtained a break-down of V(G) = 69%, V(CE) = 18% and V(SE) = 13%, using the same model their compilation gave 71%, 16% and 13% respectively.

These estimates of V(G) and V(CE) are, in a sense, lower bounds, since part of V(SE) is certainly unreliability variation. Unfortunately, given the variety of tests used we cannot know what their reliabilities might be, but 69% which we found for V(G) sets the lower bound for heritability with 79% the upper bound if we assume all of V(SE) is due to unreliability variation[8]. Few studies have found such a high figure, although one or two of the more careful ones have, such as *Martin's* (1975) small but thorough study of MZ and DZ twins where a heritability of 79% was found for IQ.

The conclusion of a sizeable genetic component is strengthened by the interesting orphanage study of *Lawrence* (1931). Adopted children owe their variance to genetic factors, contributed by their biological parents, and to environmental factors, contributed by their adoptive parents; thus there are two sources of variation. Children admitted to an orphanage at an early age should owe their variance almost entirely to biological factors, i. e. the genetic contribution of their true parents, because an orphanage provides as identical an environment for the children as it is humanly possible to provide. If the contribution of genetic factors were as important as suggested by the studies reviewed so far, there should be little reduction in variance for the orphanage children, as compared with a random sample of ordinary children brought up by their parents; this is precisely what Lawrence found. *Eysenck* (1973) argued that the shrinkage observed was practically identical with that expected if we assumed that $h^2 = 0.80$. The numbers in the study were too small to attribute much importance to the precise values of the shrinkage, but a repetition of the study with larger numbers would be of considerable interest. From the social point of view it is

8 Unreliability variation, which equals one minus the reliability coefficient is confounded with V(SE). To correct the heritability for unreliability we simply subtract the unreliability variation from V(SE), calculate the new total variation, and express V(G) as a fraction of this new total. Many of the tests used in Table 5.9 were relatively unreliable group tests with a reliability

interesting to note that the minute shrinkage in variance found in this study could not be increased in any political regime, however egalitarian, because it is difficult to see how such a regime could provide an environment less varied than that found in an orphange.

The striking adequacy of this very simple genetic and environmental model makes it highly likely that many of the criticisms it has attracted are without foundation. The major criticism most frequently voiced is that a simple additive model in which genetic and environmental influences act independently cannot be realistic. One form of dependency envisaged is an interaction process. For example, it is felt that genes for either very high or very low IQ are quite unlikely to respond to any given environmental experience in exactly the same way. Consider the availability of good library facilities. A favourable genotype might be quite strongly influenced; a poor one not at all. Such possible differential reactions of genotype to environmental experiences are examples of genotype-environmental interaction.

However, even though such effects might be plausible, their presence to any degree would have made it impossible for the simple model to provide such a good account of the available data. We can see this if we consider what effect they would have on the expectations of our kinship correlations. Pairs of individuals sharing both genetic make-up and a common environment would be subject to the same interactive effects and hence show an increased similarity. The effect would be most marked in MZ twins who share all their genes. On the other hand, individuals who were fostered either share no genes if they are foster sibs and foster parents and their adopted children, or share no environmental influences if they are separated pairs of MZ twins, sibs, or parents and offspring and will interact uniquely becoming less alike. Consequently, an interaction between CE and G would result in all the correlations for natural families being higher than the simple model would suggest, and all those for foster families being lower. The correlations in Table 7.9 show no such tendency.

Any interaction between G and specific environment, SE, would in all cases lower the correlations and boost the estimate of V(SE) and this form of interaction would remain undetected. However, since V(SE) is only 13% and includes both genuine SE effects and unreliability variance as well as any G × SE interaction, the amount must be small indeed.

The most likely reason for not finding appreciable genotype-environmental interaction is that it is only expected at extremes of G and E, that is for a relatively small proportion of the population. For the vast majority of individuals within the normal range, who contribute most to our samples, it is probably quite realistic to assume that their more typical G and E effects act more or less independently. We can, perhaps, see the plausibility of this suggestion if we consider schooling. If we ignore very dull or very bright children, it is unlikely that the overall effect of environmental experiences, such as losing a little schooling through illness, benefitting from a particularly considerate or skilled

---

coefficient around 0.80–0.90. Thus the higher figure of 79% for heritability is probably more realistic than the uncorrected, conservative value of 69%.

teacher, or suffering from poor library facilities would affect most of the children in a similar manner. In addition, if the overall effect of these influences were small we would not expect to see marked differences in different genotypic response to them, that is, genotype-environmental interaction.

Animal experiments in behaviour genetics indicate interactive effects operate in this way, only being at all marked either when the environmental experiences or the genotypes are extreme. Most studies of IQ necessarily include relatively few extreme genotypes, IQ being normally distributed. The uniformity of modern industrial society probably excludes really extreme environmental experiences.

We can test directly for some form of genotype-environment interaction in studies of MZ twins reared apart. In these studies the mean score of each pair estimates their genotypic value, pairs in which both IQs are high being high on the genotypic scale and pairs where both have low IQs being low. In contrast, differences between their IQs indicates the effect only of the environment, both CE and SE since they are reared apart. Genotype-environment interaction is indicated if these environmental effects are related systematically to the genotypic ones. For example, if poor genotypes were more at risk environmentally than favourable ones, the twin pairs' means and differences would be negatively correlated. Other forms of interactions might produce a positive correlation or lead to curvilinear relationships between the G and E values. *Jinks* and *Fulker* (1970) looked for such interactive effects for a number of measures of IQ and found them to be of negligible importance.

Another form of dependence between G and E that has given rise to doubts concerning the adequacy of the simple model developed in this chapter is a possible covariance between G and CE. This covariance, it is argued, might arise if favourable genotypes are raised in families with favourable environments. For IQ such covariance seems highly likely, especially if we think of children with gifted parents or, on the other hand, children with mentally handicapped parents. The result would be to reinforce both the genetic and environmental influences and accentuate individual differences. However, as in the case of genotype-environmental interaction, the effects may well be most marked at the extremes which will include relatively few individuals in typical samples. For the vast majority of children the effect may be much less marked, with parental IQ playing a more limited role in the development of IQ differences. That is, although it is almost certain that the differences between parental IQs of 150 and 70 will be important, that due to differences of, say 110 and 90 may not be, factors other than IQ of the parents playing an important part within this range. In addition, if CE is small, as it appears to be for IQ, the effect of this covariance may also be quite small compared with the main effects in the model.

To detect covariance between G and CE directly is possible in principle since it accentuates individual differences in normally reared children. Consequently the total variation of fostered children is expected to be somewhat reduced. In practice it is quite difficult to detect because such groups might be subject to a degree of selection sufficient to reduce the variation slightly and mimic a covariance effect. Differences between tests and inadequate standardisation will often produce differences in overall variation. In fact, though, when available data are pooled, there is no convincing evidence of a reduced variation from fostered individuals (*Jinks* and *Fulker*, 1970; *Fulker*, 1976).

Covariance effects would also show up as a difference in correlation between individuals in two kinds of foster studies, those in which both individuals are fostered and those in which only one is fostered, the other being reared by the natural parents. In the absence of genotype-environmental covariance these two correlations are expected to be the same. In the presence of covariance the adopted-adopted pairs should resemble each other less than the adopted-natural pairs. What evidence we have for these two kinds of fostered children suggests either no effect or, if anything, the reverse (*Jencks*, 1972).

However, the best reason we have for doubting that either genotype-environmental covariance or interaction play any substantial part in defining IQ variation is the very good fit of our simple model. Attempts to incorporate either effect into the model can be shown to greatly worsen the fit.

A heritability of about 70% compared with a common environment effect of, at most, 20% is strikingly consistent with the phenomenon of regression to the mean of the IQs of relations of selected groups of individuals. If we take a group of very high or low IQ parents and assess their children's IQ, we find both groups of children fall nearer to the mean than their parents, the children of bright parents being on average duller, the children of dull parents brighter. Of course, measured across the whole range of parents, the average extent of this regression is simply a reflection of the parent-offspring regression or correlation, which is around 0.5. However, by taking extreme groups the robustness of the genetic and environmental model, which predicts linear effects for extremes, as well as intermediates, is demonstrated.

Terman's famous study of gifted children (see *Oden*, 1968) provides appropriate data for observing regression. In this study, as already explained, 1528 Californian children with IQs of 140 or higher were followed into adulthood in order to assess the importance of IQ in adult success and adjustment. The mean IQ of those that married and had children was 152; that of their spouses, 125. The mean IQ of this whole group of parents was 138.5. The mean IQ of 1571 of their children was 133.2, a little less than the parents and showing some regression to the mean.

Our simple genetic and environmental model can be used to predict what we would expect their IQs to be. The sum of V(G) and V(CE), which was 87%, reflects the total influence of family background, both genetic and environmental. The prediction is very simply that the offspring should fall back 87% towards the mean from their average parental IQ. The parents were 38.5 IQ points above the mean, the children should therefore be 87%, of 38.5 or 33.5 above the mean. In fact they were 33.2 above the mean, the predicted value being very close to that observed. The value of V(G) alone tells us what we might have expected had their children been fostered at random so that only genetic factors would be important. In this situation we would have expected a regression of 69% of 33.2 or 26.6 from the mean, that is an IQ of 126.6, only some 7 points below that found, reflecting the much greater impact of genetic influences compared with those of home environment.

At the other end of the IQ continuum, *Reed* and *Reed* (1965) found for a

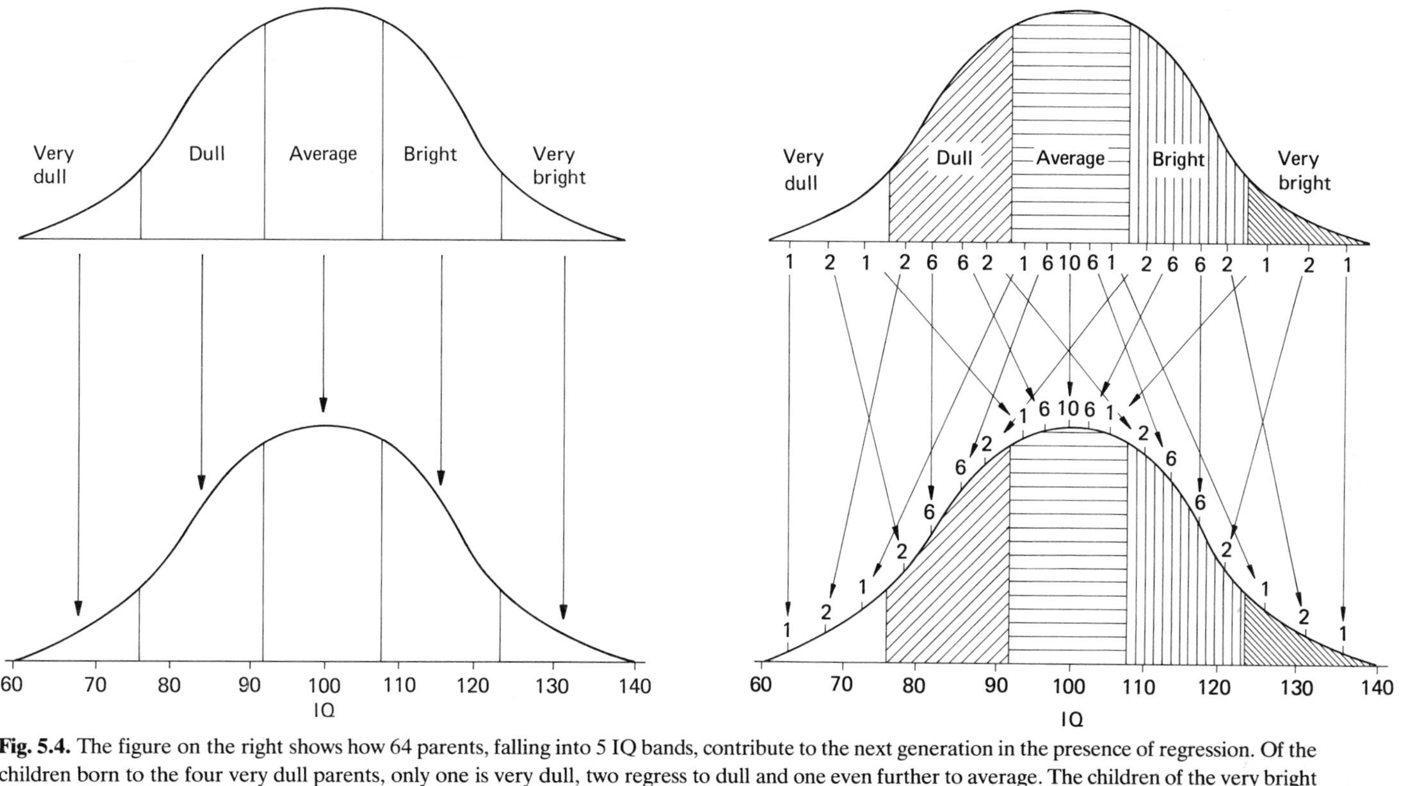

Fig. 5.4. The figure on the right shows how 64 parents, falling into 5 IQ bands, contribute to the next generation in the presence of regression. Of the children born to the four very dull parents, only one is very dull, two regress to dull and one even further to average. The children of the very bright are a mirror image of this pattern. Average parents contribute to all categories of children symmetrically about the mean so that, on average, their children do not regress. The majority of dull children came from dull or average parents; the majority of bright children from bright or average parents. In this manner, the resulting distribution of children's IQ is the same as that of the parents. The figure on the left illustrates the erroneous conception many people have of the inheritance of IQ, which leaves out regression to the mean

small sample of 53 pairs of very low IQ parents, with a mean of only 74, or 26 points below the average, that their 177 children regressed upwards to the mean, having an average IQ of 82. If we take our estimate of all family background factors, both genetic and environmental, again to be 87%, we would expect a regression of 87% of 26 points or 22.6 below average for the children, that is a mean IQ of 77.4, a little lower than the 82 found. In fact, the mean IQ of all the children in their sample was about 106, compared with about 102 for the parents. If it is appropriate to use these norms we predict the children's IQs to be 81.7, again the prediction falling very close to the observed value.

However, with very low IQ subjects both substantial physical defects and recessive genetic ones may contribute appreciably to their low scores introducing a skewness into the distributions of genetic and environmental effects. Then we do not expect complete additivity and strictly linear regression which the prediction equation assumes. Under these conditions children may be expected to regress further back to mean from the low end of the parental scale than from the high end, and Reed and Reed's sample perhaps is, to some extent, reflecting the presence of these extreme genetic and environmental effects.

We have direct evidence of recessive genes for low IQ from studies of inbreeding. There are three major studies, and in each the IQs of children born to parents who are themselves related, usually as cousins, were found to be lower than those of children born to previously unrelated parents.

It is a well-established feature of genetic systems that involve dominant and recessive genes that they also show inbreeding depression, and the cause of this depression is the greatly increased frequency of the double recessive combinations that arise with inbreeding.

We can see how this comes about if we consider the extreme case of a rare recessive gene with a frequency of 1 in 100. Phenylketonuria which, if untreated, results in severe mental retardation, is an example of a disorder caused by such a gene. The frequency of about 1 in 100 implies a population frequency for the double recessive of $(1/100)^2$ or 1 in 10000, which is close to the observed frequency of Phenylketonuria. The probability of being a carrier, however, is close to $2 \times 1/100$, or 1 in 50. Now, should an individual carrying this recessive gene choose a mate at random, the chance that his mate also carries the gene is very remote, again only 1 in 50. When two carriers produce offspring there is a probability of $1/4$ that they will produce a defective child. Consequently, the chances of this individual producing a defective child, given he is a carrier and mating at random, is only $1/4$ of 1 in 50, or 1 in 200.

Now consider the case of this individual mating incestuously with his sister, an extreme form of inbreeding frequently employed in developing inbred strains of animals. If he carries the recessive allele, then there is a probability of $1/2$ that his sister does too. The probability now of producing a defective child is $1/2$ of $1/4$ or 1 in 8. The risk of this individual producing a double recessive defective child is thus increased by a factor of 25 times if he mates with his sister. Should he marry his cousin, one of the closest degrees of blood relationship generally permitted in modern societies, the probability of his cousin also being a carrier is $1/8$ with a consequent risk to their children of $1/8$ of $1/4$, or 1 in 32. Thus, even with cousin marriage the increased risk of producing a double recessive Phenylketonuric individual is increased by a factor of about 6 or 7. Indeed, the commonest way of deciding whether some disorder is controlled by a recessive gene is to look for common ancestry in the family pedigree. Typically, the rest of the pedigree will be clear of the disorder.

The best known inbreeding study of IQ was that carried out in Japan shortly after the second world war by *Schull* and *Neel* (1965) as part of a project designed to detect mutation effects caused by radiation from the atomic explosion at Hiroshima. A Japanese version of the Wechsler intelligence test (WISC) was developed and given to 486 children of parents who were first cousins, 379 children of parents somewhat more distantly related and 989 children whose parents were not related at all. They found a small but highly significant depression of IQ in the partially inbred children corresponding to about 4 IQ points for cousin marriage. This inbreeding depression indicates genes for low IQ are recessive to those for high IQ.

That the effect is small is expected from genetical theory. The degree of inbreeding can be expressed as an index, F, the coefficient of inbreeding which is zero in outbred populations and reaches a maximum of one when all individuals are completely inbred, as in the case of an inbred strain of animals. This coefficient is only $^1/_{16}$ for children born to first cousins and since the inbreeding effect is proportional to F we expect the effect to be quite small.

In Schull and Neel's study there were confounding effects of age and social class which mimicked inbreeding depression unless the IQs were corrected by statistical means. Such statistical corrections are inevitably less convincing than direct control especially when effects are so small. These corrections have caused a certain amount of doubt concerning the outcome of their study. However, a recent Israeli study (*Bashi*, 1977), which is quite free of social class and age biases, completely confirms their findings.

This study was carried out among Arab communities in Israel where consanguineous marriages are strongly encouraged for social and economic reasons. In these communities, cousin marriage reaches the very high figure of 34%, compared with around 6% in Japan and less than 1% in Europe and America. Moreover, the much rarer marriage of double first cousins, which leads to an inbreeding coefficient of $^1/_8$ in their children, was also quite frequent in these Arab communities, being about 4%. Consequently, they were able to see if the children of these marriages, which result from a pair of sibs marrying into the same family, showed greater inbreeding depression than those of first cousins, as genetic theory would predict. The results, involving 970 children of first cousins, 125 of double first cousins and 2108 control children of unrelated parents on a variety of IQ tests and scholastic achievement strikingly confirmed the prediction. In all cases the children of cousin marriages showed inbreeding depression and, in all cases, those of double first cousins showed the larger effect. The depression in IQ corresponding to an inbreeding coefficient of $^1/_{16}$ was about $1^1/_2$ IQ points at age 9 and about 3 IQ points at age 11.

Finally, a small study by *Cohen* (1963) involving 38 children of cousin marriages and employing the WISC found a uniformly depressed response on all the subtests corresponding to about 3 to 4 IQ points.

Taken together these studies of mild inbreeding suggest a depression in IQ of about $3^1/_2$ IQ points from an F of about $^1/_{16}$. We can indicate the importance of this small effect by calculating what would be the effect on IQ of producing completely inbred strains of people as we frequently do with laboratory animals. Their expected mean IQ would be 16 times lower than that of children of first cousins, an appalling value of about 45 IQ points. Inbred strains of people would barely be human.

The finding of mild inbreeding depression for IQ among children of cousin marriages is consistent with the greater frequency of retardation found following inbreeding. *Böök* (1957) found a threefold increase of retardates among the children of cousin marriages, and *Reed* and *Reed* (1965) a fourfold increase, again indicating the presence of recessive genes for low IQ.

These studies involve a mild case of inbreeding. More severe inbreeding, such as would result from incestuous unions between brother and sister, father and daughter or mother and son, should produce much more marked effects, since the inbreeding coefficient would be $^1/_4$. Numerous small studies of incest do, indeed, indicate a high frequency of mental retardation as well as other forms of abnormality among the children resulting from such unions. However, a problem of interpretation arises because individuals who produce children in this way are very often themselves retarded and might therefore be expected to produce a higher than normal frequency of retarded children. A recent Czechoslovakian study (*Seemanova*, 1971) that goes some way towards adequately controlling for this effect provides eloquent, if sad, testimony to the reality of inbreeding depression for intelligence. Of the 161 children born to women who had conceived through sexual intercourse with their fathers or brothers or, in one case, a son, 40 suffered from severe mental retardation, that is 25%, or a 10 fold increase over the population incidence. Of their mothers, 14% were subnormal, of their fathers, only 6%. Clearly inbreeding depression has completely counteracted any expected regression upwards towards the population mean. Most striking, however, was the frequency of mental retardation in the 95 children born later to the same women, but fathered by men to whom they were not related. The frequency of mental retardation was exactly zero.

These studies of inbreeding depression make it quite clear that for many of the genes influencing IQ there is a marked degree of dominance. Combining the information on dominance from inbreeding studies with the information we obtained from the kinship studies allows us to probe further into the nature of the genetical control of IQ.

In constructing our simple G and E model we made the assumption that the degree of genetic resemblance of all first degree relatives, that is of parents and offspring, full siblings and DZ twins, was the same, $^1/_2$V(G). This assumption was clearly justified in the light of the observed correlations. However, a question of interest that arises is, what does this equality of genetic resemblance imply about the genetical system, knowing that there is dominance for genes for high IQ?

Genetic theory predicts that the genetic variation V(G) will be made up of the two independent components V(ADD) and V(DOM). The first of these is the additive genetic variance which reflects mainly increasing or decreasing alleles in homozygous or double combinations. The second, V(DOM), reflects the hybrid or heterozygote combinations made up of one increasing and one decreasing allele insofar as these combinations do not simply fall halfway in their effect between the two homozygotes. If we had just these two effects, additive and dominance variation, they should be reflected in a difference between the genetic resemblance of parents and offspring and full siblings, neither being $^1/_2$V(G). In fact, both would be less than $^1/_2$V(G), but with parent-offspring less than that of full siblings.

Our finding that the genetic resemblance of all first degree relatives was the same, $^1/_2$V(G), clearly suggests some other influence is counteracting the effects of dominance. The only two candidates, for which we also have ample evidence are inbreeding and assortative mating; the tendency for like to marry like. However, inbreeding is relatively uncommon in most of the countries of origin of the kinship studies, these being mainly Europe and the U.S.A., and it is very easy to show from genetical theory that the effects of such modest levels of inbreeding are negligible. Even the exceptionally high level of inbreeding in the Arab population in Israel, observed by Bashi, could not produce anything like the effect necessary to offset the effect of modest dominance variation. This leaves assortative mating as the most likely explanation.

Throughout the world there appears to be a modest but widespread tendency for like to marry like, resulting in a host of positive correlations for all kinds of traits. The most obvious of these correlations is probably indices of size. Height, weight and chest circumference, for example, all show typical correlations of about 0.2 for spouses. Similar correlations have been observed for many, though not all, personality traits (*Vandenberg*, 1972). However, for cognitive traits, and particularly for IQ, the correlations are very high, estimates ranging from 0.3 to 0.6 in available reliable studies (*Jencks*, 1972). With such high heritability for IQ these figures also imply a high degree of genetic resemblance between spouses too, and it is this genetic resemblance that is expected to influence estimates of genetic variation. Unlike the effects of inbreeding, the effects of assortative mating are expected to be quite marked. In its presence, but in the absence of dominance variation, we would expect both the genetic resemblance between siblings and parents and offspring to be greater than $^1/_2$V(G) with parent-offspring resemblance being slightly higher than that for siblings. These effects are exactly opposite to those produced by dominance.

The influence, then, of both dominance and assortative mating together would tend to cancel out, with appropriate levels of each, resulting in $^1/_2$V(G) for all first degree relatives. Given that we have independent evidence for both dominance and assortative mating for IQ and that the presence of both lead us to expect a very simple model of the kind we found for the kinship correlations in Table 5.9 the case for an additive-dominance model with assortative mating for IQ is quite strong. *Sir Ronald Fisher* (1918), in a classical paper, developed a detailed model to explain the kinship correlations in the presence of both assortative mating and dominance. In this model the total genetic variation is made up of three components

$$V(G) = V(ADD) + V(DOM) + V(AS)$$

the additional component V(AS) being that due to assortative mating. The expectations for the genetic resemblance among the kinships we have looked at for IQ are shown in Table 5.10. We can use these relationships and our estimate of V(G) to solve the equations in this table, but to do so we need an estimation of the correlation between spouses, r_{pp}.

Several studies of assortative mating for IQ exist and *Jencks* (1972) gives nine, of which he rejects two as unreliable. One of these is small and the parents were selected on the basis of similarity; another was very large based on *Reed* and *Reed's* (1965) data involving 1016 pairs of parents. They correlated 0.33. Jencks' puts the weighted estimate of r_{pp} at 0.50. Reed and Reed's estimate he rejects because subjects were given a variety of tests which might be expected to lower the correlation. However, their study has one powerful feature the others lack in that all the subjects were assessed as children long before they married and frequently before they even knew each other. As a result, this correlation is

Table 5.10. Genetic model incorporating dominance and assortative mating effects for IQ

Genetic Resemblance	Expectation	Value for IQ
MZ twins	V(ADD) + V(DOM) + VAS	0.690
Siblings	$^1/_2$V(ADD) + $^1/_4$V(DOM) + VAS	0.345
Parent child	{1 + ^{r}pp} {$^1/_2$V(ADD) + $^1/_2$V(AS)}	0.345

Solution for ^{r}pp = 0.47 and for ^{r}pp = 0.33

	^{r}pp = 0.47	^{r}pp = 0.33
V(ADD)	= 0.36	0.44
V(DOM)	= 0.22	0.17
V(AS)	= 0.11	0.08
Total V(G)	= 0.69	0.69

Broad heritability = V(G) = 69%
Narrow heritability = V(ADD) + V(AS) = 47%–52%

free of the effects of husband and wife on each other subsequent to marriage, a problem with many other studies. Since we feel this estimate of r_{pp} is probably a good one we have included it among the eight estimates which, following our usual procedure of choosing the median one, results in an estimate of 0.47. This figure, as well as that of 0.33 is used in Table 7.10 to estimate the effects of V(ADD), V(DOM), and V(AS). The results indicate substantial V(DOM), the estimate being roughly one half that of V(ADD) which indicates on Fisher's model that the level of dominance is very probably complete. That is low IQ alleles appear to be completely recessive to their dominant high IQ counterparts. This finding is completely in accord with studies of major genes known to influence IQ of which Phenylketonuria is an example.

From these analyses we can even gain a rough idea of how many genes might be controlling IQ, or at least how many are showing some degree of dominance. Most methods for estimating the number of genes are very poor and provide gross underestimates, but one quite robust estimate (*Jinks* & *Fulker*, 1970) is given by the square of the ratio of the inbreeding depression and the inbreeding coefficient, F, all divided by the estimate of the dominance variation

$$(\text{Inbreeding depression}/F)^2 \;/\; V(\text{DOM}).$$

If we assume a depression of at least 3 IQ points for the children of cousin marriage who have an F of about $^1/_{16}$ and take as our estimate of V(DOM) the product of IQ variance (225) and the 0.22 we obtained from the correlational data we obtain from the above formula an estimate of the number of genes of about 47. Such estimates are, of course, very gross, but they do serve to emphasise the polygenic nature of IQ.

One of the more interesting features to emerge from a genetic analysis of IQ is this finding of substantial dominance variation which, from the inbreeding studies, is seen to favour high IQ. This kind of genetic control is characteristic of traits intimately concerned with biological fitness and which have probably been

Table 5.11. MZ and DZ correlations for school achievements in *Husén's* (1959) study with corresponding estimates of components of variance

	n pair	Arithmetic	Writing	Reading	History	Mean
MZ	352	0.81	0.76	0.72	0.80	0.773
DZ	668	0.48	0.50	0.57	0.51	0.515
V(G)		0.66	0.52	0.30	0.58	0.51
V(CE)		0.15	0.24	0.42	0.22	0.26
V(SE)		0.19	0.24	0.28	0.20	0.23

under strong directional selection during the evolutionary process. Therefore, in this picture we are probably seeing the result on the genetic architecture of intelligence of man's evolution from his ape-like ancestors. Intelligence, as we would expect, probably played a major role in his evolution.

The evidence relating to a strong heritable component in IQ is overwhelming with several lines of evidence converging on a strikingly consistent picture. As a result there can be little doubt that there is a strong biological basis to individual difference in intelligence as measured in modern industrial societies.

The IQ evidence is particularly strong, but what of the evidence relating to school achievement?

One problem inherent in studying differences in educational attainment is how to choose a measure on which the majority of people will have been assessed but, at the same time, does justice to the full range of intellectual ability. For example, if we choose to look at elementary test results at an age when most people will have been assessed, say attainments before statutory school leaving age, then we will not be discriminating academic ability very well at the top end of the scale. Among those who score high at the lower level will be some who leave school and never take any more examinations, while others may go on to higher education and attain degrees and professional qualifications. However, if we attempt to discriminate at the upper end of the ability levels by studying college examination results, for example, a large proportion of the population will be omitted from assessment altogether. In consequence, the full range of individual differences in cognitive abilities may be grossly under-represented. It is for reasons like these that psychologists favour IQ as a measure of ability, since it covers a wide range of levels and is reasonably constant at different ages. Perhaps the most adequate measure of educational ability we have that gives weight to all levels of ability is years of schooling, although inevitably we lose some discrimination, since people leaving school at the same time will still differ quite considerably in intellectual skills.

In spite of these difficulties, school achievements are of great practical importance and the investigation of their genetic and environmental determinants of some interest. There are three large twin studies of school attainment, each of which falls into one of the three categories of measure described above. At the elementary level is *Husén*'s (1959) involving assessment before statutory

Table 5.12. National Merit Scholarship Qualifying Test correlations and simple genetic and environmental model (Loehlin and Nichols, 1976)

	N pair	English Usage	Mathematics	Social Studies	Natural Science	Vocabulary	Mean
MZ	1300	0.72	0.70	0.69	0.64	0.88	0.726
DZ	864	0.52	0.51	0.52	0.44	0.62	0.522
V(G)		0.40	0.38	0.34	0.40	0.52	0.41
V(CE)		0.32	0.32	0.35	0.24	0.24	0.32
V(SE)		0.28	0.30	0.31	0.36	0.12	0.27

school leaving age in Sweden. In this study twins were obtained from the entire population of males reporting for military service evaluation at age 20, between 1948 and 1952. School records of achievement in Arithmetic, Writing, Reading and History were available for the final year of compulsory education, the children being between 14 and 15 years old. The MZ and DZ correlation for these four school subjects are shown in Table 5.11.

The main feature of the pattern of variation compared with that for IQ is the relatively lower heritability and much greater effect due to common environment. For IQ, the ratio of genetic variation to common environmental is about $3^1/_2$ to 1. Here the ratio is on average only 2 to 1. Specific environmental effects also appear more important than for IQ, but almost certainly reflect the lower reliability of these measures which Husén puts at only about 0.80, compared with 0.95 for IQ.

A large component of variation for common environment was also found by *Loehlin* and *Nichols* (1976) in their large American study of 17 year olds taking the National Merit Qualifying Scholarship Test (NMQST), an examination designed to select students of high academic ability in U.S. high schools. Inevitably this study, while involving some 2000 pairs of twins, suffers from a strong selection bias in that the mean ability level of NMQST examinees is at least one standard deviation above average. However, in spite of this quite marked restriction of ability range, the effects of environmental variation between families, or in our terminology, common environment, is still much more marked than for IQ. Correlations and estimates of components of variance are shown in Table 5.12 for the five NMQST examination subjects. In these data the apparent magnitude of common environment influences is approaching that of the genetic influences.

Perhaps the best overall indicator of scholastic ability is years of schooling, for while the scale must be very coarse, grouping together many people of different intellectual abilities, it does take in the very wide span of educational levels typically found in modern society. Some indication of the discriminatory power of this measure, as well as its social importance, may be judged from its correlations of 0.5 to 0.6 with adult occupational status and earned income.

Taubman (1976) provides the largest body of twin data for this measure on a reasonably widely drawn sample of subjects, although these twins had all served in the US Armed Forces during the second world war so that extremely low ability levels had been excluded. Taubman found for 1019 pairs of MZ and 907 pairs of DZ twins correlations of 0.76 and 0.56 respectively. These correlations provide estimates of

$$V(G) = 44\%$$
$$V(CE) = 32\%$$
$$V(SE) = 24\%$$

Again, heritability is lower than for IQ and the effect of the common environment much greater. Thus in spite of differences between measures and samples the three large studies are in very good agreement concerning the general picture for educational attainments.

With home environment playing almost as important a part as genetic makeup in determining individual differences in educational attainments, the presence of both genotype-environment interaction and covariance seems a distinct possibility. Of the two, covariance seems the more likely, since well educated parents appear to assist their children in school subjects (*Marjoribanks*, 1977) in addition to bestowing upon them favourable genotypes. Unfortunately, there is no very good evidence on this matter, since extensive information on foster sibs, twins reared apart and the like, is lacking. However, some relevant data are available in two studies carried out by *Newman* et al. (1937) and *Burt* (1966). Although Burt's data must be considered unreliable, the two studies are in remarkably good agreement and worth considering together.

The effects of G × E interaction and covariance on our simple G, CE and SE model are shown in Table 5.13, on the assumption that for separated MZ twins only one is fostered, the other being reared by the natural parents, which appears to be the case for most of the twins in Burt's and a number in Newman et al.'s studies.

The two models are quite complicated, involving an additional component of variance, V(G × CE) representing interactions between CE and G and a component of covariance Cov(G, CE), reflecting the covariance between G and CE. V(SE)* represents V(SE) + V(G × SE) which cannot be separated in these data. They lead to rather different results. Using the correlations from these two

Table 5.13. Model for covariance and interaction between genetic and environmental influences

Type of twin	Covariance model	Interaction model
MZT	V(G) + V(CE) + 2Cov(G, CE)	V(G) + V(CE) + V(G × CE)
DZT	$^1/_2$V(G) + V(CE) + 2Cov(G, CE)	$^1/_2$V(G) + V(CE) + $^1/_2$V(G × CE)
MZA	{V(G) + Cov(G, CE)}/{1–Cov(G, CE)}	V(G)
1–MZT	V(SE)	V(SE)[a]

[a] V(SE) in the interaction model includes various interactions with SE.

Table 5.14. Solution to covariance and interaction models for *Burt's* (1966) and *Newman* et al. (1937) studies of educational achievements

	Burt				Newman et al.		
MZT	0.98				0.89		
DZT	0.83				0.70		
MZA	0.62				0.58		
V(G)	= 0.30	V(G)	= 0.62	V(G)	= 0.38	V(G)	= 0.58
V(CE)	= 0.28	V(CE)	= 0.68	V(CE)	= 0.27	V(CE)	= 0.51
2Cov(G, CE)	= 0.40	V(G × CE)	= −0.32	2Cov(G, CE)	= 0.24	V(G × CE)	= −0.20
V(SE)	= 0.02	V(SE)*	= 0.02	V(SE)	= 0.11	V(SE)*	= 0.11
Total	1.00		1.00		1.00		1.00

studies to solve for the parameters gives the results in Table 5.14. Clearly an interaction model is quite inappropriate in both cases, leading firstly to impossible negative estimates of the interaction variance V(G × CE), secondly to estimates of V(SE)* that are too small to allow for other than trivial interactions between G and SE and, thirdly, to estimates of V(CE) that are improbably large, being 0.68 in Burt's study and 0.50 in Newman et al.'s. These estimates of V(CE) imply that unrelated individuals reared together would correlate to an even greater extent, and what evidence we have suggests figures somewhat lower.

The results of fitting a covariance model in Table 5.15, on the other hand, look very sensible. More extensive analysis of Burt's familial correlations for educational attainments also strongly indicated substantial covariance (*Fulker*, 1974; *Jinks* and *Fulker*, 1970). The extent of this covariance between G and CE can be expressed as a correlation coefficient, being Cov(G, CE) / $V(G)^{1/2}$

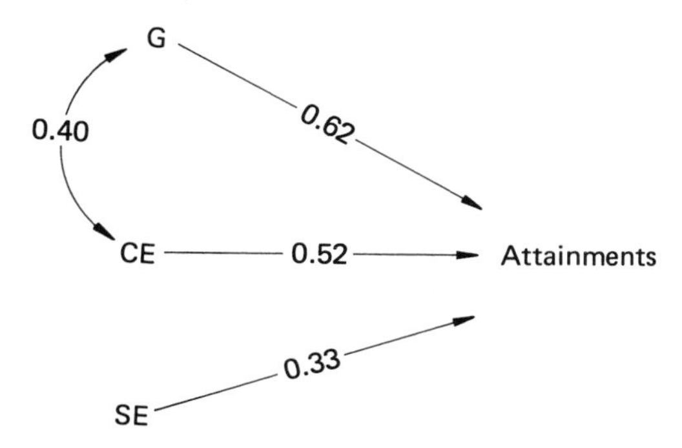

Fig. 5.5. Path diagram of correlated genetic and environmental influences on educational attainment. Based on data in *Newman* et al. (1937)

$V(CE)^{1/2}$. This formula gives 0.7 for Burt's study and 0.4 for Newman et al.'s, and enables us to represent the genetic and environmental determinants for attainments in the form of a path diagram, as shown in Fig. 5.5. When we use only twin data to estimate V(G) and V(CE) this covariance is confounded with our estimates of V(CE).

A correlation between genotype and environment strongly suggests that the parent's own educational level either has a direct influence on that of their children, or at least creates a home environment that perpetuates academic standards. However, the educational level of the parents is in part genetically determined. Therefore, what we see as home environment for the child is in part a genetic influence operating through the phenotype of the parents. That is, genetic determinants of cognitive ability may be exerting an influence on the individual not only through his own genetic make-up, but through the environment his parents and those before them have provided for him. This ancestral influence is often referred to as cultural inheritance, and models have been developed to examine its consequences (*Eaves*, 1976). Many aspects, therefore, of what we consider to be the environment, such as social class differences, cultural quality of the home and the like may well be in part, perhaps a large part, themselves genetic in origin, operating in this way. We will have to take care to distinguish between pseudo-environmental influences and true environmental influences, free of genetic influence, in the next chapter.

In the present chapter we have considered, in some detail, evidence of genetic influences on IQ and educational achievements. The evidence is overwhelmingly in favour of a substantial genetic influence, being particularly high for the former, somewhat less so for the latter. In contrast to IQ, educational achievements reflect a much larger common environmental influences. We have indicated how aspects of population structure may also have their genetic consequences through such processes as inbreeding, assortative mating and cultural inheritance. Clearly, genetic influences are pervasive and subtle, a theme we will take up again in Chapter 7. In the next chapter we turn to the environment.

6 Nature and Nurture: Environment

D. W. Fulker and H. J. Eysenck

> Men who have excessive faith in their theories are not only ill prepared for making discoveries; they also make poor observations
>
> Claude Bernard

In the last chapter we found 69% of variation to be due to genetic influences and only 31% to environmental ones. Clearly, genetic factors outweight environmental factors in causing the wide range of intellectual ability found in human populations.

However, in spite of its greater importance, we are still almost entirely ignorant as to the specific mechanisms that underlie this extensive variation. With so many genes involved, in all probability acting in different ways on a number of underlying neural and biochemical systems, themselves only dimly understood, this ignorance is not really surprising.

Investigating these mechanisms by genetic manipulations currently represents one of the major challenges in behavioural genetics. Meanwhile, the mere fact that so much genetic variation exists should provide a powerful incentive to research workers in psychology and many other related disciplines to search for the physical basis of intelligent behaviour. The existence of this genetic variation guarantees that differences between people do, indeed, have a physical as well as an experiential basis.

As regards the causes of environmental variation, the situation is somewhat different. Although environmental variation is less important than genetic variation, we are better informed about its origins, the reason being that environmental influences are often external to the individual and therefore more easily observed.

The relative ease with which environmental influences can be studied has caused many behavioural and social scientists to forget about genetic factors altogether, an unfortunate mistake, since failure to control for genetic variation has led to a great deal of research claiming to identify strong environmental influences where, in reality, only weak ones may exist.

Schizophrenia research provides a striking example. This illness is known to run in families, the parents of schizophrenics sometimes being schizophrenic themselves, but more often exhibiting a schizoid personality or simply being a little 'odd'. This observation led to a great deal of research focussing on the parent-child relationship in order to discover what might be responsible for the development of schizophrenia in the child. All manner of complex psychodynamic theories were developed. One widely held theory was that of the "double bind" in which the illogical character of much of the conversation taking place between parent and child was said to place intolerable strains on the child's attempts to grasp reality. Another theory holding sway for some time was that of the "schizophrenogenic mother", a cold, unfeeling and puritanical kind of mother said to be associated with schizophrenic patients. These are just two among a number of theories involving the psychodynamics of family life put forward to explain the disorder.

However, we now know that very little, and possibly no general influence attributable to home environment is involved in the aetiology of schizophrenia judging from studies that properly control for common genetic factors in the parent-child relationship (*Gottesman* and *Shields*, 1976; *Fulker*, 1974). In our terminology there is very little evidence of any common environmental variation, V(CE), for susceptibility to schizophrenia, environmental influences being unique or specific to the individual.

Failure to recognise the necessity to control for genetic factors in this instance not only resulted in misleading theories but was very expensive in terms of misplaced research effort. Of even greater concern, however, is the great deal of misery these theories caused to parents of schizophrenic children, who naturally felt that the way they had raised their children was responsible, in some way, for the development of their illness.

In relation to intelligence, our present concern, the extensive literature on social class and intellectual ability is often similarly misleading. It is true that there is a marked relationship between a child's IQ and his parental socio-economic status (SES), the correlation being about 0.3 to 0.4. There is an even larger correlation of about 0.5 between IQ at eleven and a person's own SES as an adult (*Jencks*, 1972). But there are also common underlying genetic factors, and ignoring these factors has led to exaggerated claims for the importance of different aspects of home environment as direct causal agents in determining a child's ability and later socio-economic success as an adult.

In reality, both genetic and environmental factors interact in quite a complex manner to determine adult status, as we will see in the next chapter. However, this complexity need not concern us here. For the purposes of the present chapter, in which we are concerned with identifying environmental influences, we need to recognise the existence of genetic factors mainly in order to control for them properly and not confuse them with the effects of the environment. In addition, keeping genetic influences in mind when thinking about the environment provides us with some idea of how important we can expect particular causal factors to be. The estimate of genetic variation obtained from Chapter 5 was 69%, leaving only 31% attributable to the environment. As we also saw, environmental influences could be subdivided into two parts. One part was environmental influences shared by members of the same family, which we called common environment (CE), and the other was that specific to individuals which we called specific environment (SE). These influences tend to make siblings alike in the case of CE and different in the case of SE. What we found was that the 31% environmental variation could be subdivided into 17% common environmental variance, V(CE), and 13% specific environmental variance,

V(SE). In fact, since the reliability of IQ tests is at most 0.95, V(SE) can account for no more than 8% of reliable IQ variation, compared with 18% for V(CE). With these percentages in mind, both of them small, it is apparent not only that social influences in the environment are likely to outweight other environmental influences by a factor of two, but also that many environmental factors might individually contribute no more than one or two per cent to total variation. In terms of mean effects this will be less than 4 IQ points. Four or five independent influences of this order of magnitude could, for example, completely account for V(SE).

Another way of thinking about the magnitude of environmental influences is in terms of the top and bottom 20% of the distributions of CE and SE, these percentages representing a fairly marked contrast. Since the variance of individual differences in IQ is 225 the variance of environmental effects will be

V(CE) = 18% of 225 = 40.50
V(SE) = 8% of 225 = 18.00

and the corresponding standard deviations the square roots of these variances, 6.36 and 4.24 respectively. Given that the means of the top and bottom 20% of a normal distribution differ by a little under three standard deviations (2.8) even the combined effects of commonly occurring environmental influences can seldom be expected to produce differences of more than about 18 IQ points in the social environment and 12 in that unique to individuals. These effects are large enough and, as we shall see, combinations of environmental factors approaching this order of magnitude can be identified, but they are still rather less than the 35 IQ point differences expected to differentiate the top and bottom 20% with respect to genetic endowment and the 42 points with respect to observed IQ.

Birth order, which has been extensively investigated, is an example of a small, within family, environmental influence affecting IQ. We will consider it in some detail since it is much the best understood influence to contribute to V(SE).

First-born children often show superior intellectual development compared with younger siblings; an observation that dates back at least as far as *Galton* (1869) who discusses the over-representation of first borns among men of eminence in his book *Hereditary Genius.* Furthermore, the more widely spaced the children are, the more pronounced the effect. For IQ, typical findings are about 1 IQ point or less per sibling. However, a problem arises when we attempt to assess the effect accurately, for large families have, on average, lower IQs. Averaging individuals of a given birth order across all families will produce a spuriously large effect, the higher birth orders necessarily coming from large families with lower IQs. Consequently, what appears to be an obvious within family environmental effect may be contaminated with between family genetic and environmental influences unless we are careful.

In order to control effectively for family size, we need to examine birth order effects within families of different sizes. Two recent studies of birth order are sufficiently large to allow this procedure and illustrate the phenomenon.

The first study involves IQ data on almost a quarter of a million nineteen

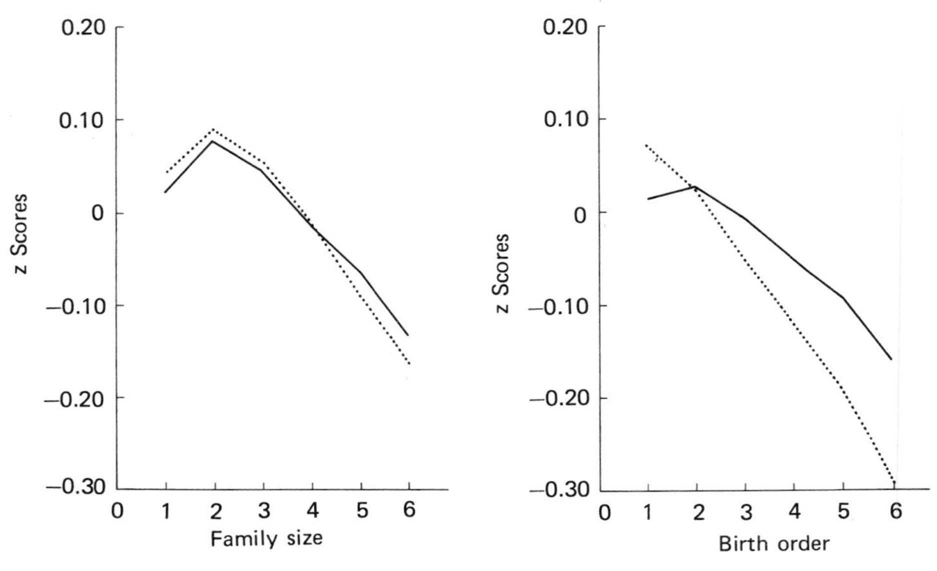

Fig. 6.1 a and b. Family size and birth order effects on height and intelligence averaged across families. Taken from *Belmont* et al. (1975)

year old men assessed during screening for military service (*Belmont* et al., 1975). As a check on the adequacy of their controls, the authors discuss their findings for both height and IQ, for since variation in height for a population of the same sex and age is almost entirely under genetic control, we should find little or no genuine environmental birth order effect once appropriate controls have been employed.

The simple, uncontrolled influence of family size and birth order can be seen in Fig. 6.1. Children in small families and of low birth order are both taller and more intelligent. The effect of an extreme difference, of either family size or birth order one to six, is about 0.3 to 0.4 of a standard deviation, that is about 4 to 6 IQ points and 2 to $2^1/_2$ centimetres in height.

To separate the effects of birth order and family size the authors plot individual birth order curves for five different sized families, the results being shown in Fig. 6.2. The outcome is quite clear cut. For height there is no longer any birth order effect, the five curves being flat and parallel. For IQ, however, there is still quite a marked effect, although somewhat reduced, of about -.7 IQ points per sibling. The curves for height suggest controlling for family size is sufficient to avoid spurious between-family genetic and environmental artifacts, and that the birth order effect for IQ is genuinely specific or within-family in origin.

The size of the birth order effect is what we might expect, given specific environmental influences are only responsible for a total of about 8% of reliable IQ variation. Birth orders 1 through 6 produce a smooth total change of about 4 IQ points. Calculating the variance of these six birth order effects gives a figure of 0.7% or about 10% of V(SE).

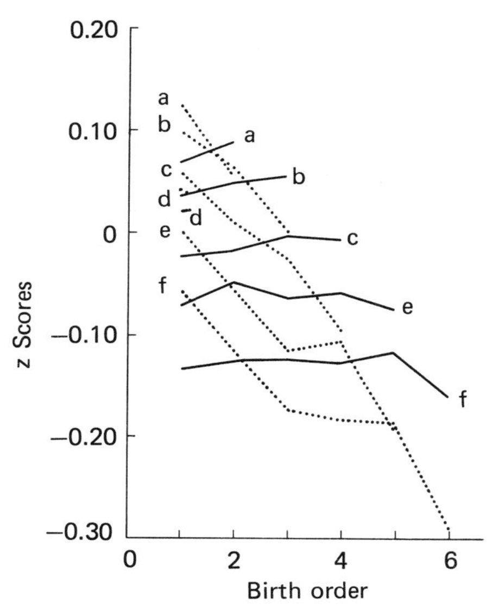

Fig. 6.2. Birth order effects on height and intelligence for families of size 1 to 6. Taken from *Belmont* et al. (1975). Family size 2 = a, 3 = b, 4 = c, 5 = e, 6 = f, singletons = d

The birth order effect is remarkably similar for each size of family, suggesting a common mechanism in all families. What might this mechanism be? The social psychologist Zajonc has put forward an ingenious theory to account for the effect in terms of differential within family socialization (*Zajonc* and *Markus*, 1975). He argues that an important factor in causing IQ differences between siblings is the quality of the attention available to the child when interacting with other members of the family. For the firstborn, the only other members of the family are two fully mature adults. For the second child, however, the parental effect is substantially diluted by the presence of the first-born sibling, necessarily less mature than his parents. That is, the total mental age of the family environment is reduced for the addition of a second sibling. For the third child the dilution effect is even greater, and so on for additional children.

This theoretical model is called the Confluence Model, and explains birth order effects extremely well, not only predicting accurately the gross effects but also the fine detail in respect of spacing and age structure within families. The Confluence Model obtains support from a second, recently published, large study of birth order (*Davis* et al., 1977).

This study involved just over one hundred thousand Israeli students of Asian-African origin and eighty thousand of European-American origin assessed on a test of mathematical ability at age 14. The curves for the two populations are shown in Fig. 6.3. For the children of European-American descent the picture closely follows that of the study by Belmont et al. previously discussed. However, for the children of Asian-African descent, who in general perform somewhat lower, the picture only holds for family sizes two and three. Thereafter, there is a tendency for the curves to rise, not fall, actually suggesting an advantage in being a young sibling in a very large family. Why should this be if

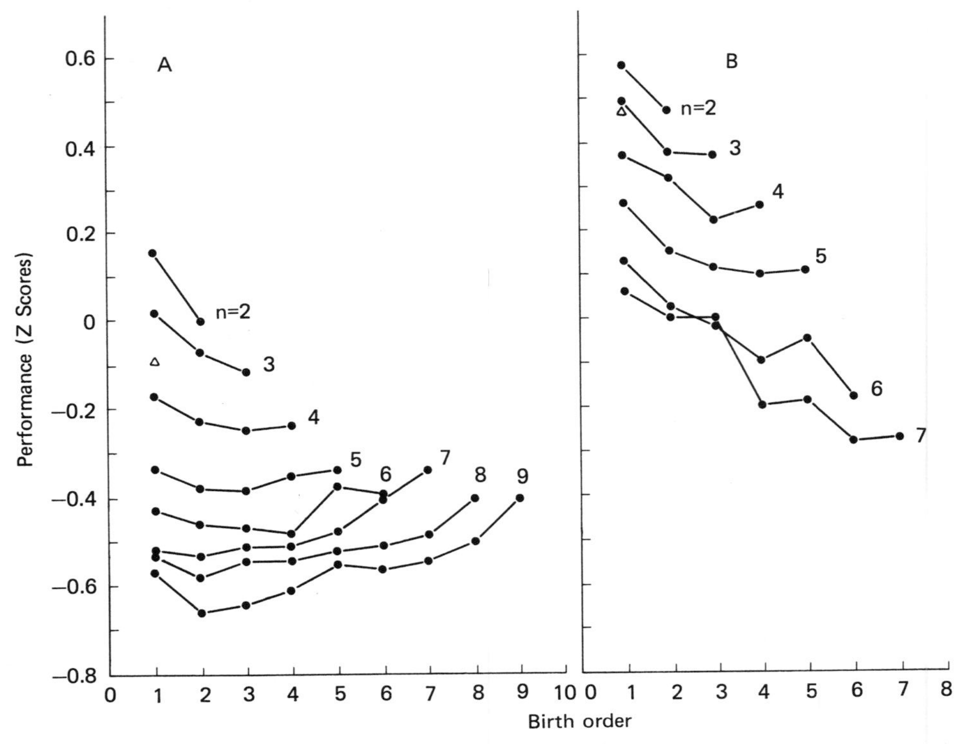

Fig. 6.3. Birth order effects on a test of Mathematical ability for two ethnic groups in Israel. **A)** Afro-Asian descent. **B)** European-American descent. Taken from *Davis* and *Bashi* (1977)

the Confluence Model holds? The authors suggest this rise is precisely what would be expected on the model if the parents were themselves even more poorly educated that their older children, which was apparently the case for this particular ethnic group. Under these conditions, older children, far from diluting the intellectual quality of the home environment provided by the parents, would make a positive contribution. Developing the Confluence Model in this way and carrying out a computer simulation, the author obtained theoretical curves closely matching those in Fig. 6.3

The importance of intra-familial socialization of the kind implied by the Confluence Model is also suggested by a large study of 11 + school examination results carried out in Birmingham (*Record* et al., 1970). In common with very many other twin studies of IQ, it was found that twins averaged less than singletons, about 4.5 IQ points in this case. A unique aspect of this study, however, was that it also looked at twins in which one of the pair had died in early infancy. The mean IQ of the remaining single surviving twin was now only depressed by about half an IQ point. Since the authors were careful only to include pairs where the twin who died had apparently been of normal development at birth, intra-uterine competitive effects resulting in superior develop-

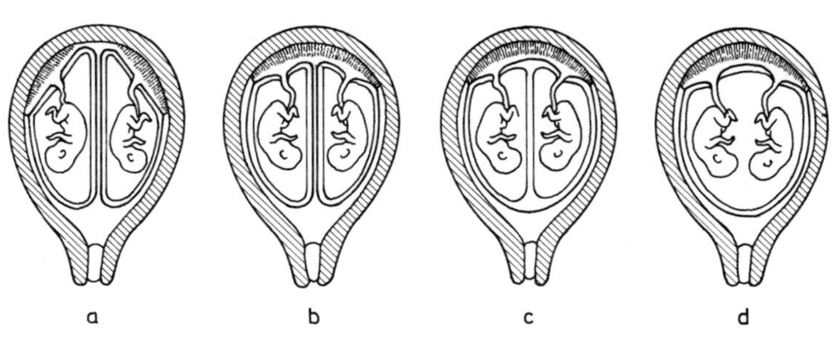

Fig. 6.4. Four different intra-uterine environments experienced by twins. Taken from *Cavalli-Sforza* and *Bodmer* (1971)

ment of the surviving twin were ruled out as a likely explanation of their finding. One is left with the implication that postnatal socialization was probably responsible for the effect. We would expect twins, where both survived, to have markedly reduced parental contact, perhaps even as much as 50%, and they certainly experience the presence of a minimally mature additional sibling in the form of their co-twin. About 4 IQ points, or 2% of variance, does not seem excessive compared with the normal birth-order effect of about 1 IQ point per sibling if twins represent an extreme case for the Confluence Model. Furthermore, Record et al.'s study employed a measure of verbal IQ for which, as we will see later, there is some evidence of greater susceptibility to environmental influences than for other nonverbal measures of IQ.

In principle, monozygotic twins reared together could provide a useful method for studying the nature of specific environmental influences. Confounding effects of genetic factors and home background are completely controlled for in the twins' differences which is a direct estimate of a within family environmental effect. Correlating IQ differences with other differences could identify IQ determinants acting through the specific environment. The use of this technique to study IQ appears to have been largely neglected apart from a few studies of birth weight and adult stature.

The reason for this neglect has probably been a lack of appropriate methodological tools which, as we will see in the next chapter, are now available. Another problem with the technique, however, concerns a peculiarity of monozygotic twin prenatal development. Singletons and dizygotic twins each develop in a single amniotic sac and are sustained through their own separate placenta and chorion. MZ twins may or may not share these features of intra-uterine environment, the four variations that occur being shown in Fig. 6.4. From our point of view the important distinction is whether or not they share the same chorion (A and B compared with C and D in Fig. 6.4). If they do they will share the same blood supply, one twin receiving blood after it has passed through the other. Thus one of the twins will be at a severe competitive disadvantage and develop poorly; a condition known as the 'transfusion syndrome' (*Price*, 1950).

Regarding IQ and birth weight, where the transfusion syndrome may be quite important, it appears that monochorionic pairs may differ by about 4 IQ points in favour of the heavier twin (*Churchill*, 1965). For twins developing with separate chorions the effect may be about half this. Incidentally, since two-thirds of monozygotic twins are monochorionic, the estimate of V(SE) derived from monozygotic twins is probably slightly overestimated, not underestimated as is frequently claimed. Precise information concerning the correlation between birth weight differences and IQ differences required for a reliable quantitative estimate of the effect is not available. But, if we rule out this monochorionic effect, which is peculiar to monozygotic twins in any case, birthweight as a reflection of pre-natal developmental factors influencing IQ appears to explain very little IQ variation. In support of this suggestion, *Shields* (1962) has reported a zero relationship between IQ and birthweight differences in twins and a number of studies suggest the effect is restricted to babies with very large discrepancies in birth weight, implying little or no general effect (*Broadhurst* et al., 1974).

Evidence relating within family differences in IQ to differences in adult stature is provided by *Husén* (1959). Correlational data are presented for height and IQ on just over 500 pairs of MZ male twins aged twenty. A correlation of 0.28 was found between differences in IQ and differences in height, suggesting 0.28^2 or about 8% of V(SE) for IQ may be accounted for by differences in height arising from environmental influences within the family. It is not possible to pursue the origin of this correlation further in this study, but Husén has suggested it may be associated with loss of schooling and other disadvantages relating to illness and poor physical development.

So far we have discussed environmental factors contributing mainly to V(SE). Knowledge is sparse, but a few specific aspects of the within family social environment and some physical factors have been identified and appear capable of accounting for almost half of V(SE). Within family socialization influences seem the most promising candidates for further study and the MZ twin difference method would be useful for investigating them.

However, the most powerful environmental influences on IQ appear to stem not from factors within the family but from the social environment at large. In our conceptual scheme these contribute to V(CE). The literature attempting to identify these factors is vast; nutrition and other physical factors, maternal factors, parental attitudes, schooling and various aspects of SES have been extensively investigated. All these factors correlate to some extent with IQ and are possible environmental influences. However, the number of studies that have convincingly controlled for common underlying genetic influences is, unfortunately, quite small and much of this information is, from a quantitative point of view, of doubtful validity.

A number of strategies may be employed to investigate environmental factors that typically vary between families. One is to study the effects when these experiences are imposed on a random sample of the population, so that all other sources of variation become randomised. Studies of this kind are quite rare, but an interesting example is that by *Stein* et al., (1972) concerning the effects of severe undernourishment during pregnancy. This study involved a large Dutch population in the region of Arnheim during the second world war who were subjected to several months of severe famine. The IQs of the children of women

Table 6.1. Correlation of twin differences in height, weight and IQ with estimated differences in three environmental ratings, taken from *Newman* et al., (1937)

	Environmental ratings		
Trait	Educational	Social	Phyical and health
Height	0.02	0.01	0.18
Weight	0.10	0.23	0.60[b]
Binet IQ	0.79[a]	0.51[c]	0.30
Otis IQ	0.55[c]	0.53[c]	0.23

[a] $p<0.001$
[b] $p<0.01$
[c] $p<0.05$

who were pregnant during this period were assessed at age 19. In spite of a small disadvantage in terms of birth weight, these individuals scored no differently on IQ tests than the general population, whose mothers had not experienced the famine. Obviously, poor maternal nutrition during pregnancy, which also varies to a considerable extent among different social strata and is therefore correlated with IQ, is of no direct causal significance.

Numerous studies have attempted to investigate the effects of postnatal undernourishment on IQ, but have seldom been as rigorous as the study above. For example, in a study carried out in Jamaica (*Hertzig* et al., 1972) children who had been so severely malnourished that they required hospitalization had IQs about 4 points below those of their siblings. Malnourishment of the child would appear to have a definite, though not particularly strong, influence on IQ. But, of course, the use of siblings does not really provide an adequate control for genotype in this study, since it is entirely possible that the duller sibling would be at greater risk with respect to parental neglect. Still, studies of this kind are useful when, in spite of possible biases, they none-the-less indicate quite small effects.

Many studies of this kind have made it clear that a variety of physical factors, such as smoking, drinking and drug taking during pregnancy, as well as inadequate pre-and post-natal nutrition, have a negligible effect on IQ except in the most extreme cases (*Rutter* and *Madge*, 1976).

Studies of MZ twins reared apart are also capable of identifying factors in the social environment, that of *Newman* et al., (1937) being the most useful in this context. In addition to measuring IQ, these authors asked independent investigators to read all case histories, rating each pair with respect to differences in general social advantage, educational background and physical health. The correlations between these differences and differences in IQ, together with those for height and weight, for purposes of comparison, are shown in Table 6.1. As we might expect, height is unaffected by all the environmental variables, and weight only appreciably by physical health. IQ differences, however, correlate substantially with differences in educational and social advantage, and very little or not at all with physical health.

The correlation of 0.52 between differences in social advantage and IQ suggests that 0.52^2 or 27% of variation in pair differences is attributable to the general economic and cultural quality of the home. Variation in pair differences for separated MZ twins is equal to V(CE) + V(SE), for which our best estimate is 31%. Therefore 31% × 27%, or about 8% of IQ variation, appears to be attributable to general social advantage in this study. Since a child's IQ cannot reasonably be seen to cause the social advantages of his home, this correlation almost certainly identifies a direct causal influence on IQ. In terms of the top and bottom 20% of the population with respect to this variable (who differ by 2.8 SD) one would expect a mean difference of $2.8 \times 0.08^{1/2} \times 225^{1/2}$ or about 12 IQ points. Significantly, if we take the four pairs most discrepant on the social environment index, who comprise 21% of the 19 pairs of twins, their mean differences in IQ is 11.75 on the Binet test and 14.25 on the Otis, an average of 13 IQ points.

The correlation between differences in education and IQ is more difficult to interpret, since the direction of causation is far from obvious. On the one hand, IQ differences might be responsible for differences in educational achievement. On the other, a good education might facilitate the taking of IQ tests. A third possibility is that both IQ and educational achievement reflect the same underlying environmental influence. We cannot tell from this study which of these is the case, although some effect of education on IQ would seem to be implied by the correlation of 0.26 between differences in social advantage and education. This correlation may well indicate the effect of schooling on IQ deriving indirectly from social advantage. Since the average correlation between schooling and IQ is 0.67, the influence of education on IQ stemming from this source will be $(0.26 \times 0.67)^2$ which equals about 3% of variation in twin differences or about 1% of the total variation.

Some indication of whether educational achievement influences IQ or vice versa can be obtained by looking at correlations across time. *Crano* et al., (1972) attempted such a study using over five thousand American children measured on both IQ and school achievement in Grades 4 and 6. The two relevant correlations are between IQ at Grade 4 and Achievement at Grade 6 and the reciprocal correlation between Achievement at Grade 6 and IQ at Grade 4. Whichever is the larger will indicate the direction of causation. Correlations of 0.75 and 0.73 respectively would appear to favour neither causal theory but rather one of a common underlying factor of general intelligence. In this study, of course, genetic factors were not separated from those in the environment and it is possible that the two operate quite differently, as we will see in the next chapter.

The effects of various aspects of schooling on IQ and educational achievement have been the subject of a large number of studies both in Europe and the United States. So far as quality of schooling goes, both material and academic, very little effect is found either for IQ or achievement. Variation between children in the same school far outweighs variation in average levels between schools. In addition, insofar as brighter children do go to better schools and achieve more than duller children, their IQs, not the quality of the school, would appear to be the major factor (*Jencks*, 1972; *Rutter* and *Madge*, 1976).

So far as amount of education goes, some effect on IQ has been fond in several studies. Typical of these is that carried out by *Husén* (1951) involving a large sample of children with IQs measured at age ten and later at age 20. Holding intial IQ constant, the overall effect of attending or not attending secondary school after 15 years of age was 5 to 7 IQ points. A study of enforced loss of schooling in Holland during the second world war found a drop of about 5 IQ points (*De Groot,* 1951) across the whole population, but of course this group was also subject to many other kinds of disruption.

The effects of additional pre-school education on the less able child has been extensively studied in the United Staates following the massive government sponsored "Head-start" scheme initiated during the 1960s. This scheme involved voluntary enrolment in specially organised nurseries, together with a certain amount of supportive health care. Something like a million children, mainly black, took part at a cost of nearly 400 million dollars per annum at the peak of the programme. The effects on later educational achievement and IQ appear to have been negligible, largely, it has been suggested, because the programme was so poorly structured and lacked any well defined aims (*Clarke* and *Clarke,* 1974).

More intensive and sharply focussed pre-school projects have raised infant IQ by as much as 15 points compared with control groups. However, these gains were generally lost after a year or two in school when controls frequently caught up and the children with pre-school experience dropped back (*Bronfenbrenner,* 1974). This finding may simply reflect the beneficial effect on IQ of entering the structured environment of a school. The pre-school groups start school earlier but then settle down to their appropriate age norms about the same time to controls receive their boost. In addition, the regression effect is almost certainly reflecting the low validity of infant tests of intelligence, a test given at three years old correlating at most .7 with one given three years later. Indeed, in view of the very poor ability of IQ tests at five years old to predict IQ or, more importantly, educational achievement during adolescence, it is questionable whether it is worth while investing so much effort in the pre-school period. As *Jensen* (1973) has suggested, it might make more sense to try and make sure adolescents leave school with the most useful skills they are capable of acquiring rather than being overly concerned with their IQs as infants.

Nonetheless, one project does appear to have been particularly effective. This is the ambitious pre-school project carried out by Heber (*Heber* and *Garber,* 1970) in Milwaukee, involving 40 black children born to mothers of IQ less than 75 and divided into experimental and control groups. A unique feature of this study was the intensive maternal support given to the family as well as the intensive pre-school coaching of the children. Some idea of just how intensive this study was may be appreciated from its cost of $ 10000 per annum for each pre-school child. A claim of gains of 30 IQ points at age 6 has been made pre-school children averaging 111 compared with 81 for controls. Undeniably, part of this gain was due to the children actually being trained in tasks almost identical to those used as IQ test material, a procedure generally considered to invalidate mental tests. Additional problems that make the interpretation of the findings of this study difficult are inaccessibilty of reliable research reports, lack of detail concerning procedures and doubts about the adequacy of the random allocation of children to experimental and control groups. *Page* (1972), a psychologist with considerable experience of educational intervention schemes considers these shortcomings probably invalidate the study. But still the gains are impressive. On joining school at six the project was discontinued. However, *Vernon* (1976) reports that although a regression has occurred, as one might expect, the mean IQs at around 8 years old are still in the region of 88 and 107, a much more reasonable difference of 19 points. This project is extremely interesting in indicating, perhaps, what the limits of really intensive help, both educational and social, might be in raising the IQs of young children. The long term results, of course, remain to be seen. Unfortunately, the cost involved seems prohibitive for all practical purposes, and the degree of intrusion into the lives of the families likely to be unacceptable to a great many parents.

The pre-school studies show there may be considerable scope for raising the IQ of the severely disadvantaged child, although it is much too soon to judge how effective these efforts might be in the long term. A recent study by *Jensen* (1977) with black and white children in Georgia, one of the most economically depressed areas of the United States, suggests there might also be considerable scope with older children. The study examines the idea that black children fall progressively further behind white as they grow up, due to the cumulative effects of social disadvantage. The method used by Jensen to test this hypothesis was that of sib comparisons in order to control for family background. In this method, sibs of increasing age differences are tested and support for the

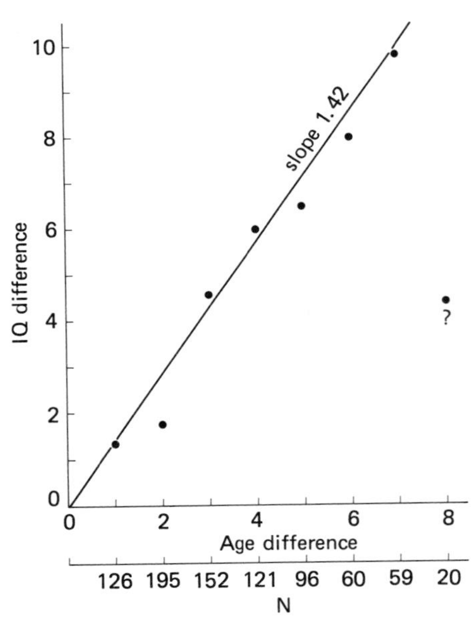

Fig. 6.5. Cumulative deficit in IQ for American blacks in Georgia from age 6 to 16 years. Based on data in *Jensen* (1977). Total predicted deficit is 14 IQ points

hypothesis obtained if the larger age differences are associated with greater decreases in IQ. *Jensen* (1974) had used this method in an earlier study of black children in California, finding only a very slight effect on verbal IQ and little or none on non-verbal measures. However, California is a very prosperous part of the United States and its black population does not appear to suffer anything like the social deprivation typical of Georgia, where the mean IQ level of blacks is a full standard deviation below that of black Californians.

In all, some 653 white and 826 black children were tested. Mean IQs were 102 and 71 respectively. Support for the cumulative deficit hypothesis was striking. No cumulative deficit was found for the white children, but a marked deficit for both verbal and non-verbal IQ was found for the black. The graph of total IQ differences is shown in Fig. 6.5. The points in this graph fall in an almost perfectly straight line, apart from the final one. Since this is a very poorly determined point, being based on only 20 comparisons, Jensen felt it should be discounted. He concludes that the likely deficit for age 6 to 16 years is a massive 14 IQ points, or about one standard deviation. Improved social conditions could be expected to help prevent this deterioration in IQ.

In order to evaluate the effects of a large range of social factors, under reasonably natural conditions, while controlling to a large extent for genetic variation, adoption is probably the best available strategy. These studies provide information of two kinds, firstly that involving gross effects reflected in mean differences between the IQs of adopted children and a suitable comparison group and, secondly, more detailed correlational information relating variation in environmental influences to variation in IQ.

The adoption study of *Skodak* and *Skeels* (1949) provides information concerning the gross mean effects of an enriched, compared with a poor, home environment. The mean IQ of the adopted children in this study was 107 on the test that was used to assess their natural mothers. Their mothers, however, only averaged 86. That of the fathers is unknown, but from information provided in the report it appears to have been quite low too. If we guess the assortative marriage correlation to be at most 0.5, we would expect the fathers to have an average IQ of no more than $100 + 0.5\ (86–100) = 93$. Mean parental IQ, therefore, would appear to have been somewhere in the region of 89. Had the children been reared by these parents we would have expected their IQs to have been $100 + 0.87\ (89–100)$ or about 91, the regression constant 0.87 being the

Table 6.2. Adoptive families with both natural and early adopted children in a transracial adoption study, taken from *Scarr-Salapatek* and *Weinberg* (1976)

IQ	N	Mean	Range
Adoptive mother's	50	118.7	98–134
Adoptive father's	51	121.5	98–140
Early adopted child's	67	109.8	86–144
Natural child's	102	118.5	81–150

sum of V(G) and V(CE). Using this estimate, therefore, the children appear to have gained about 16 IQ points as a result of being reared by foster parents rather than by their natural parents. Given V(CE) is 18%, the two kinds of homes should differ by about 2.5 standard deviations, or represent the top and bottom 25% of home environments, probably an underestimate of the mean SES difference of the home backgrounds in question.

The transracial adoption study of *Scarr-Salapatek* and *Weinberg* (1976) found a very similar effect. This study involved highly educated white adoptive parents, above average in occupational status and income. The adopted children had, for the most part, one white and one black parent. Information on IQ for the natural parents was not available, but information concerning years of schooling indicated an average ability level typical of blacks and whites in the population. The authors estimate that had the children been reared by their natural parents the mean IQ would have been unlikely to exceed 95.

Table 6.2 shows IQ data for those families who both adopted early and also had a natural child of their own. Both from the means and the ranges it is clear that the adoptive parents are of superior IQ. Income and socio-economic status were also much above average. The natural children, as expected, are well above average too, reflecting the effects of both family environment and genetic endowment, although the much greater range indicates the increased variation expected from genetic segregation. The IQs of the black children are somewhat lower, also as expected, since they only share family environment. The mean difference between the value the children's IQ were expected to be on a conservative estimate and what they were is about 15 IQ points, very similar to that found by Skodak and Skeels, and consistent with Newman et al.'s study (1937) of monozygotic twins reared apart.

These adoption studies demonstrate quite dramatically the extent to which a high status family environment, compared with a low status one, can raise IQ by about 15 IQ points; interesting and important information. However, for more specific information about particular factors in the home environment we turn to the correlations between foster parents and their adopted children.

Perhaps the most thorough and detailed foster study from the point of view of measuring environmental factors is that by *Burks* (1928). In this study a great deal of trouble was taken to match almost 200 foster families with 100 natural families for a number of potentially important variables such as parental mental age and occupational status. Binet IQs were measured on 214 foster children and 105 natural children, on average eight years old.

The home environment of all the families was assessed in some detail. Parental IQ and level of education, cultural and economic features of the home, and the extent to which parents took an interest in their children's welfare and education were all assessed. Cultural aspects of the home were assessed in terms of parental education, how articulate the parents were, their spare time interests, the quality of available reading material and evidence of artistic taste, all these being combined into a single Cultural Index. An index of the material adequacy of the home, the Whittier scale, was also employed, combining information on income, quality of food and home comforts, neatness, size of home and adequacy of parental supervision. Correlations between these and other

Table 6.3. Correlations between children's IQ and characteristics of the parents and home background taken from *Burks* (1928)

Measures	Correlations		Estimated mean IQ effect of being in Top vs. bottom 20% with respect to measures	
	Foster	Natural	Foster	Natural
Father's Education	0.01	0.27	0.4	11.3
IQ	0.07	0.45	2.9	18.9
Vocabulary	0.13	0.47	5.5	19.7
Mother's Education	0.17	0.27	7.1	11.3
IQ	0.19	0.46	8.0	19.3
Vocabulary	0.23	0.43	9.7	18.1
Midparent IQ	0.20	0.52	8.4	21.8
Culture index	0.25	0.44	10.5	18.5
Whittier index	0.21	0.42	8.8	17.6
Income	0.23	0.24	9.7	10.1
House ownership	0.25	0.32	10.5	13.4
No. books in home library	0.16	0.34	6.7	14.3
Parental supervision rating	0.12	0.40	5.04	16.8
[a]Estimated multiple correlation	0.35	0.53	14.7	22.3
Estimated multiple correlation corrected for attenuation	0.42	0.61	17.6	25.6

[a] Due to the labour involved in computing multiple Rs in 1928, *Burks* used variables 2, 3, 6 and 10 to calculate for the foster group correlations and 2, 3, 4 and 9 to calculate for the natural group. She argues convincingly that these multiple correlations are close to what would have been obtained using all variables.

Ns are 206–173 for foster children, 105–99 for natural ones. Age range 5–14 years.

measures of the home environment and the adopted children's IQs are shown in Table 6.3, together with the predicted mean effects on IQ of homes falling in the top and bottom 20% with respect to these features. In terms of occupational status this contrast corresponds to professionals, teachers and above on the one hand, and skilled labour and below on the other. It therefore provides a contrast corresponding roughly to that between the upper-middle and the working class. These estimates are simply 2.8 times the correlation further multiplied by the standard deviation of IQ. Providing the various measures are distributed in a roughly normal fashion these estimates should be close to those that could be obtained directly from the raw data.

The pattern of correlations in Table 6.3 is informative concerning IQ determinants of young children. Correlations for foster parents indicate the direct effect of the home environment created by the parents on the IQ of their children. The correlations for natural parents, which in general are much higher, indicate the additional importance of underlying inherited genetic factors unrelated in any direct way to the effects of the environment. The difference between corresponding correlations indicates the relative importance of these common underlying genetic factors compared with the direct effects of the environment. This contrast is most marked in the case of parental IQ, indicating a strong genetic influence, and least marked for the economic factors, income and home ownership, which appear to exert their influence almost entirely through the environment. The cultural quality of the home falls midway. Of course, to say that economic factors operate entirely through the environment is not to say that there is no genetic component in income, only that insofar as there is it is not controlled to any appreciable extent by the same genes that control IQ in young children. The same may not be true if IQ is measured at a later age.

Comparing foster parent correlations only, it appears that mothers influence the child's IQ more than fathers, insofar as the effect is mediated by parental IQ, verbal facility and level of education. Since the children in this study are young, half being between 5 and 7 years old, the greater maternal influence is, perhaps, not surprising. Its apparent absence among the natural children is more surprising and may indicate that foster mothers pay more attention to their children than natural mothers.

Although the impact of the father's educational level and IQ appears less important than that of mother, his influence through the level of economic support he provides is at least as powerful as the maternal influences. Although the data are not available to explore the situation more thoroughly, the picture that emerges for a home environment likely to develop a high IQ for young children is one of a well educated, cultured mother supported by a capable, high income man.

The overall effect of home background is indicated by the estimated multiple correlation between adopted child's IQ and home background characteristics. The raw estimate of 0.35, implying a mean difference between the top and bottom 20% of about 15 IQ points, by now a familiar figure, also implies a value of V(CE) of 0.35^2 or 12%. The estimated multiple correlation, corrected for unreliability, of 0.42 implies a V(CE) of 18%, the exact figure suggested by our simple model in the last chapter.

Burks' foster study is, perhaps, the most complete available. However, other early studies of young children provide a similar picture (*Freeman* et al., 1928; *Leahy,* 1935). In particular, that by Leahy, which was designed in a similar manner to Burks', gave very similar correlation patterns. More recently, the trans-racial adoption study of *Scarr-Salapatek* and *Weinberg* (1976) found slightly weaker but broadly similar effects for black children of a similar age. In studies by Leahy and Freeman et al., no multiple correlations were computed, but in the transracial study the multiple correlation for features of the home background was 0.39, implying a V(CE) of 16%. All four studies suggest the mother's influence is a little greater than that of the father.

Scarr-Salapatek and *Weinberg's* (1977) study of adopted adolescent children shows a much weaker environmental effect, the multiple correlation squared being only 8%, and the effect of father's IQ in this study exceeding that of the mother. Possibly these differences indicate a changing pattern of environmental influences with age of child, although much more extensive data would be required to be sure.

Since in Burks' study parental verbal skills appeared to be more potent in raising IQ itself, the possibility arises that the main impact on the child is verbal too. With a test like the Stanford-Binet, which relies heavily on verbal material, this possibility seems quite likely. Some support for this notion is to be found in the study, since for foster children between 8 and 12 years old, for whom it was possible to assess vocabulary, correlations between mother's and father's vocabulary were 0.34 and 0.28. respectively, compared with 0.23 and 0.13 for parental vocabulary and child's IQ based on the whole sample. However, better evidence of the impact of parental verbal skills on foster chilren's verbal IQ is to be found in *Scarr-Salapatek* and *Weinberg's* (1977) study of adopted adolescents, in spite of the rather small general effect of home environment. They used the WAIS, and calculated correlations between parents and both adopted and natural children on the four subscales. For natural children, total score IQ correlations are larger than those for subscales, as we would expect from the greater unreliability of the subscales. For the adopted children, however, the vocabulary subscale correlations are larger than those for the full scale IQ as well as all the other subscales. In this study, then, as in Burk's, the largest home environmental influence on IQ appears to be the verbal ability of the parents acting directly on the verbal ability of the children.

The effects of environmental influences on educational achievement have not been nearly as well investigated as those on IQ, most foster studies only having been concerned with IQ. However, at a phenotypic level the broad influences seem much the same, involving both direct and indirect effects of SES and quality of home environment (*Marjoribanks,* 1977). However, since a much larger V(CE) is associated with educational attainments, the scope for environmental influences would appear to be much greater than for IQ. In addition, the probable existence of some gene-environmental covariance, discussed in the last chapter, suggests direct parental factors may also be more powerful, although without good, detailed evidence there seems little point in speculating further.

We have so far discussed evidence on the genetic and environmental influences which cause differences in IQ; how would one actually set about changing a person's IQ? Intensive individual training, improvements in home and school conditions, fostering and other methods have been tried, and we have noted the kinds of effects which can be expected. There are two types of approach which have curiously enough not been investigated in anything like the detail that has been lavished on educational methods of the orthodox kind. One of these methods uses the *biological* approach, the other the *psychological.* Both hold out much promise, although at present we do not know enough about either to be more than cautiously optimistic.

Along biological lines, the use of pharmacological aids aroused a certain amount of interest some 30 years ago when glutamic acid was shown to boost the intelligence of children (and rats!) of below average ability; the evidence is surveyed in *Hughes* and *Zubeck* (1956). Interest was quickly lost when negative findings were published, but these were due in part to the fact that investigators chose samples of average ability; the drug seems to work only on below-average individuals.

What may the effects be due to? The most likely hypothesis seems to be that glutamic acid acts upon certain metabolic processes underlying neural activity.

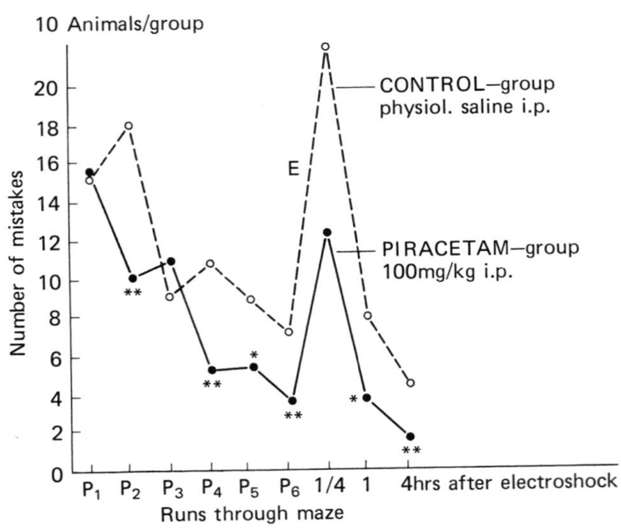

Fig. 6.6. Number of errors made by rats in water maze under drug and control (placebo) conditions, before and after electroshock. Asterisks denote statistical significance ($p<0.05$, $p<0.01$) of comparisons

Thus it has been shown that glutamic acid is important in the synthesis of acetylcholine, a chemical substance necessary for the production of various electrical changes occurring during neural transmission. It is known, for instance, that glutamic acid exerts its main action on the cerebral cortex, lowering the threshold of excitability; that the rate of acetylcholine formation could be increased four to five times by adding glutamic acid to dialysed extracts of rat brain, and that the concentration of this acid is disproportionately high in the brain, as compared with the concentration of other amino acids, or with its concentration in other body tissues; furthermore, of all the amino acids, glutamic acid alone is capable of serving as the respiratory substrate of the brain in lieu of glucose. If we assume that the cerebral metabolism of the dull organism is defective in some way, as compared with the bright or average, then glutamic acid might facilitate or improve the defective cerebral metabolism of the dull organism, while having no effect on that of the bright; there is evidence for a relationship between cerebral metabolism and mental functioning. It seems unfortunate that further intensive work has not been done to establish, more clearly the specific drug-person interaction which mediates the results, to discover more specifically the chemical properties in the drug which are responsible for any effects, and to try to improve the effectiveness of the active principle. One would have imagined that such a drug (if indeed it performed as suggested by the literature) would be the egalitarian's dream, seeing that it only benefits the dull; nevertheless, no work seems to have been done on this drug in recent years.

Glutamic acid is not the only drug which has been shown to have an effect on mental efficiency; piracetam is another. A summary of work on this drug is

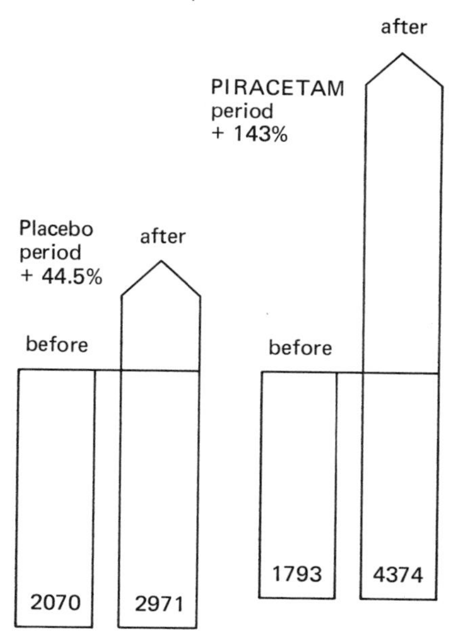

Fig. 6.7. Improvement of Kraepelin's Additions test of groups of mental defective children given a placebo (left) or piracetam (right)

given by *Cassella-Riedel* (1976); only three experiments will be mentioned here. The first compares rats learning a water-maze under piracetam and placebo injection conditions; after 6 trials the animals are administered an electroshock which temporarily confuses them. It will be seen form Fig.6.6 that animals under piracetam learn significantly better, and suffer less from the shock. The score in this test is the number of errors, i. e. wrong alleys entered.

Piracetam was administered to 44 children whose average IQ was below 75; they were tested before and after on the Kraepelin additions test, which for these children would be a reasonable IQ measure. Compared with a placebo, the drug produced a highly significant improvement (Fig.6.7). In school performance also an effect was observed; the subjects were two groups of 50 deaf-and-dumb children, one receiving a placebo, the other the drug. The children were of average IQ; their school performance, expressed as percent of initial performance, are plotted in Fig. 6.8 over six two-weekly periods. It will be seen that the drug group improves considerably more than the placebo group. These and other similar studies are somewhat indirect, in that they have not so far used IQ tests to monitor intellectual improvement, but the possibility of affecting mental performance by pharmacological means is clearly there.

School performance, and performance on tests such as those mentioned, is of course affected by factors other than changes in IQ; thus a drug acting as a minor tranquillizer might improve performance in anxious subjects. However, it

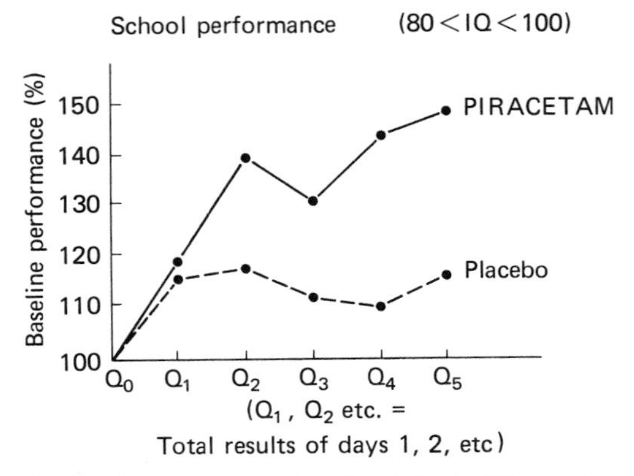

Fig. 6.8. Improvement in verbal performance of deaf and dumb children given piracetam or placebo

has also been shown that minor tranquillizers worsen the performance of non-anxious subjects, so that this does not seem a likely hypothesis. Much further work is required, using IQ tests proper and adding many control conditions, before we can be confident about the conclusions that can be drawn from this type of drug work.

On the psychological side, it is perhaps surprising to find that very little work has been done on the problem in any systematic sort of fashion; one would have thought that psychologists would have regarded it as a primary scientific duty to see to what extent the application of psychological (as contrasted with educational) methods could produce changes in measured IQ. The only point on which there is much evidence is the effect of multiple testing and the emergence of "test sophistication"; repeated IQ testing has a measurable effect on IQ, but only for the first three or at most five repetitions; after this no further testing or coaching seems to have any positive results. (It is of course assumed that different tests are used each time.) This finding has led to the recommendation that when results of IQ testing are important for selection or other applied purposes, several pre-tests should be given before the crucial test, so as to eliminate this effect.

As an example of a proper experimental approach to this problem we would like to describe briefly the work of *Merz* (1969; *Franzen and Merz,* 1976) based on some earlier studies by *Gagné* and *Smith* (1962). Merz was concerned with the influence of "verbalization" on thinking; using non-verbal tests, and getting his subjects to verbalize their procedures of solution, he found that increases in IQ of up to 10 points could be produced by this method. Improvement was achieved in tasks in which the soultion could be reached either by analyses of the task, or by comparison of the different offered solutions to the task (multiple choice format). The improvement in performance was maintained to some extent even when similar tasks were solved without verbalization. By registering eye movements, Merz demonstrated that verbalization leads to a change in problem solving behaviour, in the direction of a more analytic approach, leading to a decrease in individual differences in test performance.

Merz looked carefully at different explanations of the effect, using the experimental method; it would take us too far afield here to go into details of his ingenious investigations. We strongly believe that a more experimental approach to the investigation of IQ testing as an example of problem solving would pay a rich dividend; the point will be made again in connection with the Eysenck-Furneaux-White model. An application to the problem of increasing IQ is urgently needed.

We have examined some of the environmental influences that affect IQ, finding that social factors both within and between families exert the greatest effect, physical factors being quite difficult to find. Most of these factors were fairly small in effect; for example, birth order, typical variations in schooling and various aspects of home environment. However, a most striking and consistent finding has been the powerful effect of combined features of the home background and general social advantage. Time and again these combined factors appeared to be capable of producing mean differences of around 15 IQ points and to account for the whole of our 18% estimate of V(CE). In no instance did we find evidence that either V(CE) or V(SE) might be greater than the estimates we obtained from the analysis of genetic and environmental variation in the previous chapter, although the evidence reviewed was of a very different kind. This consistency of the empirical evidence supporting the quantitative genetic and environmental model suggested to underlie variation in IQ is truly striking. This model therefore provides a reliable basis for considering some of the social consequences of this variation.

7 Nature, Nurture and Socio-economic Status

D. W. Fulker and H. J. Eysenck

> We are too much accustomed to attribute to a single cause that which is the product of several, and the majority of our controversies come from that
>
> Von Liebig

In the previous chapter we examined the nature of the genetic and environmental influences that cause individual differences in IQ and school achievement. In the present one we attempt to carry the discussion a step further and look at how these influences affect the individual's social and economic status when he has left school and taken his place in adult society.

Socio-economic status (SES) is generally defined in terms of social class or occupational status, there being considerable overlap between the two definitions. When people are classified according to social class, the major distinction is between whether they carry out professional and white collar work on the one hand, or skilled and unskilled manual work on the other. This distinction corresponds broadly to that between the middle class and the working class; a distinction that implies marked differences in life style, aspirations, economic security and political affiliations. These two broad categories are usually further subdivided to provide a rough five or six point scale. In spite of its simplicity, the scale provides a valid index of many aspects of SES.

Classification according to occupational status is based on a concensus of opinion regarding the perceived status of various jobs. One widely used scale is that developed by *Duncan* (1961) based on a survey carried out in the United States by the National Opinion Research Center (NORC) in 1947. In this

Table 7.1. Ratings of five occupations in the 1947 NORC Survey (taken from *Jencks*, 1972)

Occupation	% Responses					
	Excellent	Good	Average	Below Average	Poor	Don't know
Physician	67	30	3	0	0	0
Novelist	32	44	19	3	2	9
Undertaker	14	43	36	5	2	2
Mail Carrier	8	26	54	10	2	0
Bar tender	1	6	35	36	31	2

survey, people were asked to rate a list of job titles in terms of "general standing" in the community and the responses were used to determine a consensus ranking. Typical results for five occupations according to the six categories of response permitted are shown in Table 7.1. The consensus view is obvious, the occupations falling in the order shown, although it is also evident that there is considerable variation in individual opinion. Another problem with occupational status scales is their failure to make any distinction between the individual who is good or bad at his particular job, and for this reason income is a useful additional index of SES.

In spite of these disadvantages, the consensus approach to the measurement of occupational status produces a very stable measure. The order of rankings obtained in the NORC survey hardly changed at all between 1925 and 1947, a period of considerable upheaval; all sections of society, men or women, black or white, high or low status, agree in their ratings and the picture is very similar in other industrial societies (*Jencks,* 1972).

A very striking feature of SES, whether it is measured using scales of occupational status or quite simply in terms of social class, is the extent to which it changes between successive generations, the correlation between father and son being not much more than 0.4 (*Blau* and *Duncan,* 1967). Thus many children born to either low or high status parents will move into quite a different social status when they leave the environment provided by their school and family to make their own way as adults.

Just how dramatic this movement is can be seen from the transition percentages set out in Table 7.2. SES is measured on a simple four point scale and the rows give the distribution of sons finishing up in each category for any given category of origin. The table refers to American white males surveyed in the 1960s. Looking at the extremes, 21% of children born into the lower manual worker category moved right up the SES scale to reach the status of higher white collar workers. Of those born into the high status category, only 54% remained in it. In terms of numbers the two groups of sons eventually making up Category I are almost the same, the smaller percentage from lower origins coming from a larger pool. For children born into high white collar families, 12% drop right down to the level of lower manual worker, while only 36% remain in that category. The two intermediate categories show movements both up and down

Table 7.2. % Social mobility of 36000 white American sons aged 25–46 in 1962 (taken from *Blau* and *Duncan,* 1967)

Father's status	Sons' status					
	1	2	3	4	5	None
Higher White Collar (1)	*54*	15	12	12	1	6
Lower White Collar (2)	45	*18*	14	15	2	6
Higher Manual (3)	28	12	*28*	24	1	7
Lower Manual (4)	21	12	23	*36*	2	7
Farm worker (5)	17	7	20	29	*20*	8

the social scale and again no marked tendency to remain in the status to which they were born. In all, roughly 30% of sons rise in status compared with their fathers, while somewhat less fall.

The table also shows two interesting changes that have taken place in the United States and many other industrial societies during the first half of the century. That is, the dramatic move away from work on the land into urban occupations and the greater degree of mobility upwards compared with that downwards resulting from an increasing demand for skilled labour during a period of increasingly complex industrialisation.

This dramatic picture of social mobility in the highly industrialised United States is in accord with the popular view of a land of opportunity in which the individual rises or falls in status according to his own merit, rather than that of his father or family background. Is it true that American society is more open and meritocratic than others? Apparently not. Using the simple measure of mobility of movement across the manual/non-manual boundary, upward mobility in the United States is 31–35%, in France 35%, in Sweden 29% and in Japan 33%. Downward mobility shows a similar but more variable picture (*Lipset* and *Bendix,* 1960). Social mobility therefore appears to follow a similar pattern in what are in many ways rather different cultures. This pattern suggests, therefore, that minor differences in social organization play a relatively small part in generating social mobility, compared with the broad constraints imposed by industrialisation. What factors do influence this social process?

At the observed phenotypic level the mechanisms are reasonably clear. First, educational achievement is important, as we might expect, since most high status occupations require educational credentials before entry is permitted. IQ plays an important part in whether or not an individual is capable of obtaining these credentials. In addition, family background, as measured by the SES of the father, appears to play an important conservative role, tending to maintain the *status quo.*

The matrix of correlations among these variables can be used to formalise this picture in terms of a quantitative model. A typical set of correlations, including those for income, is shown in Table 7.3.

The most ineresting feature of this matrix, besides the positive correlations which the above picture of the determinants of SES implies, is the general

Table 7.3. Typical correlations between factors involved in social mobility (taken from *Jencks,* 1972)

		1	2	3	4	5	6
Father's schooling	(1)	1.00					
Father's occupation	(2)	0.51	1.00				
IQ	(3)	0.30	0.30	1.00			
Schooling	(4)	0.38	0.42	0.55	1.00		
Occupation	(5)	0.30	0.37	0.46	0.61	1.00	
Income	(6)	0.18	0.24	a	0.33	0.40	1.00

[a] Not available but estimated to be between 0.2 and 0.3.

tendency for the correlations to decrease as we move forwards in time down through the columns or back through the rows, a pattern typically generated by a set of variables in which the first is the main cause of the second, the second of the third, and so on along a causal chain.

A simplified version of this model developed by *Blau* and *Duncan* (1967) relating the measures in Table 7.3 is presented in two stages in Figs. 7.1 and 7.2, both for the sake of simplicity and in order to demonstrate the causal structure outlined above. First, Fig. 7.1 shows the segment of the model relating to IQ, schooling, accupation and income. The form of the model is a path diagram, the conventions of which were discussed in Chapter 5. The arrows, which are called paths, denote causal relationships, while the strengths of the relationships are denoted by the partial regression weights, or path coefficients, written alongside the arrows. The path coefficients give the predicted change in the variable at the head of the arrow following a change of one standard deviation in the variable at the tail, assuming all other variables are held constant. The short arrows coming in from outside the model denote residual factors unexplained by the specified variables.

The strong chain of causal influences implied by the structure of the correlation matrix can be seen in the path diagram, the largest influences being those linking variables adjacent in time, that is IQ, schooling, occupation and income. The remaining specified influences in the model are all much weaker than the main causal links. Finally, the unexplained influences denoted by the short arrows indicate that considerable variation still remains unexplained by the model.

The explanatory power of the model is indicated by the multiple correlation between a predicted variable and those antecedent to it. For income the multiple correlation is 0.4, indicating 0.4^2 or 16% of variation is explained by the combined effects of IQ, schooling and occupational status. For occupational status the multiple correlation is much larger, being 0.68 and indicating that 46% of variation is accounted for by IQ and schooling. Obviously the model explains occupational status much more effectively than income.

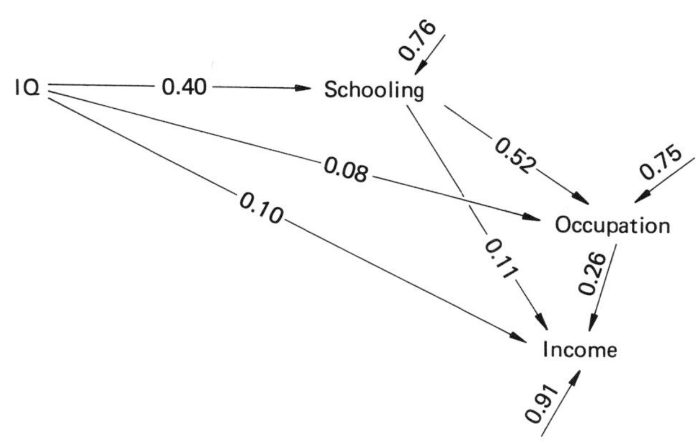

Fig. 7.1. Causal model relating IQ, schooling, occupation and income (taken from *Duncan*, 1967)

In its present form the model is incomplete, since we have yet to add the background variables of father's schooling and occupational status. The more complete model is shown in Fig. 7.2 which now becomes quite complex. In addition to paths indicating causal links, we have to add curved arrows between variables to denote simple associations where no clear cut causal links can be specified.

As in the case of IQ, the additional background variables, father's schooling and occupational status, appear to exert their main effects early in the causal chain, having most impact on schooling, less on occupational status and still less in income.

So far as it goes, the model provides an adequate account of the major influences known to determine an individual's SES. IQ and schooling play the major role along with the status of the nuclear family into which the child is born. The model is also able to make quantitative predictions given specified changes in the causal variables. However, the rules for operating the model in a predictive manner are quite complex and can be left aside for the time being. What the model does not do is to distinguish very well between those factors which promote social mobility, causing the individual to rise or fall in status and those that inhibit mobility and conserve status causing the individual to remain at his social origin.

In order to draw out this aspect of the model we can look at the correlational data in another way. Suppose we pose the following question. Given SES and some causal variable, say schooling, to what extent are *differences* in schooling between father and son responsible for the son's SES, compared with *similarities?* The differences will be associated with the social mobility that derives from schooling, while the similarities will be associated with the conser-

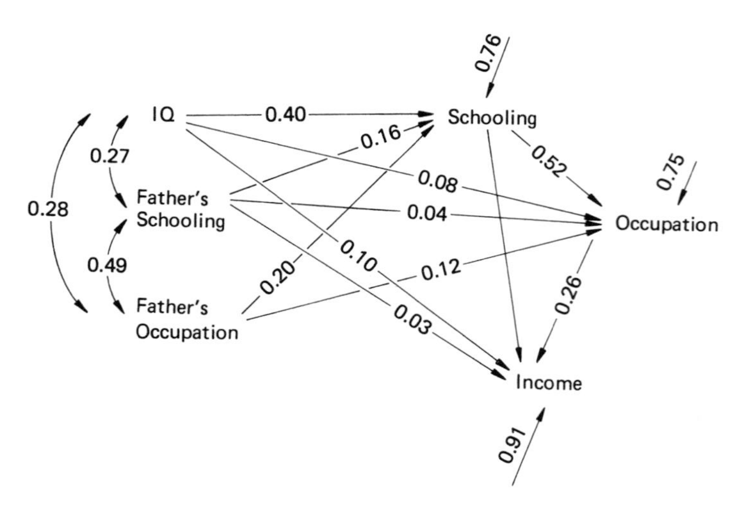

Fig. 7.2. Path model of ability and achievement including parental variables based on *Duncan* (1967)

vative element tending to maintain the individual in the same social position as his father.

In order to look at the question in this way we need information on both fathers and sons for all the variables, in order to generate all possible pair-wise correlations. In the case of schooling and occupational status we have all the correlations we need to illustrate the approach in Table 7.3, namely those between variables 1, 2, 4 and 5. These correlations are grouped together into two kinds in Table 7.4. The first are the straightforward phenotypic correlations for fathers and for sons. The second are the so-called cross-correlations which are the correlations between one variable in the father and another in the son. If we average the two cross-correlations, schooling in fathers, occupation in sons, and its reciprocal schooling in sons and occupation in fathers, we obtain the part of the phenotypic correlation between schooling and occupation due to similarities between father and son, that is the conservative element in Duncan's model of SES. The difference between this average cross-correlation and the mean phenotypic one for fathers and sons gives the part of the correlation that contributes to social mobility. Thus the mean phenotypic correlation of 0.56 between schooling and occupation is divided as follows:

$$0.56 = 0.36 + 0.20$$

That is, the correlation is made up largely of conservative influences tending to perpetuate the social status of the family (0.36) and to a lesser extent to influences tending to produce mobility (0.20). Thus, so far as schooling is concerned,

Table 7.4. 2 × 2 correlation matrices for schooling and occupational status for both fathers and sons (taken from Table 7.3)

	Phenotypic correlations					
	Fathers		Sons		Mean (A)	
	1	2	1	2		
Schooling (1)	1.00	0.51	1.00	0.61	1.00	0.56
Occupation (2)		1.00		1.00		1.00
	Cross Correlations					
Fathers	Sons				Mean (B)	
	1	2				
Schooling (1)	0.38	0.30			0.38	0.36
Occupation (2)	0.42	0.37				0.37
	Estimated Correlations between father son differences (A–B)					
Schooling	0.62	0.20				
Occupation		0.63				

its influence is largely conservative, tending to maintain status rather than redistributing it.

Two further points arise form Table 7.4 that are of some interest. Firstly, there is a slightly larger phenotypic correlation between schooling and occupation for sons than for fathers. This difference suggests education is playing a more powerful role in determining occupational status for sons than it previously did for fathers which, in turn, probably reflects an increasing insistence on appropriate educational credentials on the part of employers and employee associations. Secondly, the mean cross correlations in matrix B are almost identical, implying very similar mechanisms cause fathers and sons to resemble each other with respect to schooling and status. These cross correlations can be thought of as standardised variances and covariances of shared family influences and can consequently be combined with a single correlation coefficient

$$0.36/(0.38 \times 0.37)^{1/2} \text{ or } 0.96$$

almost unity. The numerator in this formula is the standardised covariance between shared influences on schooling and occupation of fathers and sons and the denominator is composed of the variances of their shared effects for the two variables separately. Thus the covariance is restandardised about unit variance of its two constituent variables following the usual definition of a correlation coefficient. The unity of conservative family background influences determining SES is a theme to which we will return.

A small study by *Waller* (1971) demonstrates the importance of differences in both IQ and schooling between fathers and sons in determining social mobility. Waller's study involved 131 fathers and 173 sons taken from a large body of data collected by *Reed* and *Reed* (1965) to which we have referred in previous chapters. The individuals were representative of white males in the State of Minnesota, being selected for the study solely on the basis of availability of IQ scores. These IQs were obtained while both sons and fathers were at school, using group tests and the comparability of IQs between the two generations,

Table 7.5. Relationship between IQ and social class in two generations (taken from *Waller*, 1971)

Social Class of fathers	Fathers		Sons by SES of fathers		Sons by own SES	
	N	mean IQ	N	mean IQ	N	mean IQ
I	1	(140)	1	(127)	7	114.4
II	19	113.5	26	109.0	29	112.1
III	43	105.6	54	104.8	67	106.0
IV	53	93.6	66	101.2	58	96.9
V	15	81.0	26	90.9	12	88.0
Total	131	99.3	173	103.1	173	103.1

both with respect to age and tests, represents the main strength of this study. Details of schooling and occupation were obtained by questionnaire.

The distributions of IQs for fathers and sons are shown in Table 7.5. Comparison of the first two columns of means reflects the regression of son's IQ toward the population mean disussed in Chapter 7. This regression reflects the incomplete correlation between father and son, which is 0.36 in this sample; a rather low figure, since in the larger sample from which this sample was drawn, the correlation was 0.50 (*Higgins* et al., 1962). This discrepancy is well within the fluctuations expected for this sample size. Comparison of the means in columns 1 and 3 demonstrates the stability of the SES IQ distribution between the two generations after mobility has taken place. This similarity is quite striking if we omit category I for which there is only one case in the parental distribution. Apparently, sons have become rearranged with respect to SES on the basis of IQ. The role played by IQ in this reassortment was demonstrated more directly by Waller by correlating father/son differences in IQ with those for occupational status, obtaining 0.29 ± 0.08, a highly significant correlation. He represented this finding by means of the diagram shown in Fig. 7.3. On the horizontal axis, IQ discrepancies between father and sons are grouped into five categories ranging from $+30$ to -30 IQ points. On the vertical axis is shown the percentage of these sons that rose or fell in status compared with their fathers. Clearly IQ differences play an important part in the processes of occupational mobility.

Waller's approach is similar to that just outlined. However, we can carry the analysis further and partition all the phenotypic correlations between IQ,

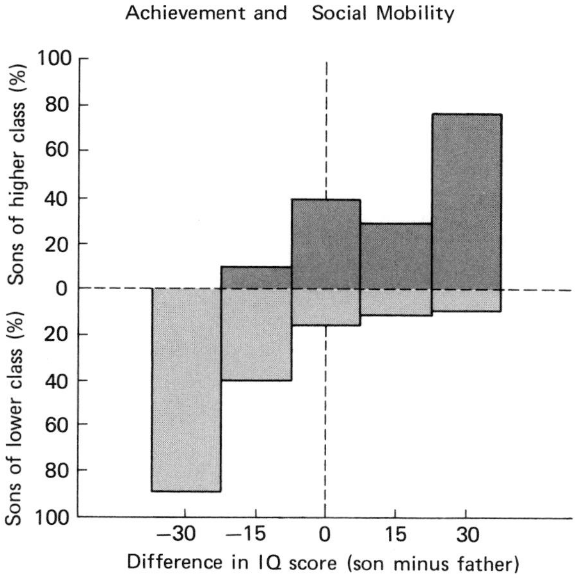

Fig. 7.3. Percentage of sons moving up or down from their father's social class by differences in IQ (taken from *Waller*, 1971)

schooling and occupational status into family background factors which conserve status and father/son differences that promote mobility. The appropriate correlations are schown in Table 7.6, together with the simple calculations necessary to estimate the between and within family correlation matrices. So far as the results for schooling and occupation are concerned, they are almost identical to those obtained before and shown in Table 7.4. The addition of IQ is interesting, however, because we can now see more clearly what a consistent effect family background is exerting, the correlations in the 3 × 3 matrix derived from the average cross-correlations in B all approaching unity. The phenotypic correlations between IQ, schooling and occupational status have been partitioned into this family background influence and that due to differences between father and son. The three phenotypic correlations and their respective constituent parts are

Table 7.6. Correlations between IQ, schooling and occupation for fathers, sons together with father son cross-correlations and difference correlations (taken from *Waller*, 1971)

	Phenotypic correlations								
	Fathers			Sons			Mean (A)		
	1	2	3	1	2	3	1	2	3
IQ (1)	1.00	0.71	0.57	1.00	0.52	0.50	1.00	0.61	0.53
Schooling (2)		1.00	0.58		1.00	0.72		1.00	0.65
Occupation (3)			1.00			1.00			1.00

	Cross-correlations								
Fathers	Sons			Mean (B)			Family background correlation matrix derived from B		
	1	2	3	1	2	3	1	2	3
IQ (1)	0.36	0.34	0.32	0.36	0.40	0.37	1.00	0.99	0.91
Schooling (2)	0.47	0.46	0.53		0.46	0.45		1.00	0.96
Occupation (3)	0.43	0.37	0.48			0.48			1.00

	Estimated covariances between differences (A–B)			Within family correlation matrix of differences derived from (A–B)		
	1	2	3	1	2	3
IQ (1)	0.64	0.21	0.16	1.00	0.36	0.27
Schooling (2)		0.54	0.20		1.00	0.38
Occupation (3)			0.52			1.00

0.61 = 0.40 + 0.21 for IQ and schooling
0.53 = 0.37 + 0.16 for IQ and occupation
and 0.65 = 0.45 + 0.20 for schooling and occupation.

Thus the phenotypic correlation between IQ and schooling of 0.61 is made up of 0.40 due to influences shared by fathers and sons and only 0.21 by influences they do not share, that is, influences unique to the individual. The phenotypic correlations for IQ and occupation of 0.53 and for schooling and occupation of 0.65 follow a very similar pattern. Again, conservative influences appear to outweigh those that promote intergenerational mobility so far as cognitive factors are concerned.

We have looked at the determinants of SES at the phenotypic level and subsequently in terms of family influences tending to conserve status and father/son differences that promote social mobility. What we have not done so far, however, is partition these influences and the residual differences as yet unexplained in the model into the genetic and environmental components which we know exist, at least for IQ and schooling, from the evidence presented in the previous two chapters. In order to carry out this more complete analysis fully we need information not only on IQ, schooling and the measures of SES from fathers and sons but from siblings, twins, adopted children and the like. That is, we need to combine the strategies of the present chapter with those of the previous two and carry out a multivariate genetic analysis.

Unfortunately, very little effort has been put into this kind of research until quite recently. This is a pity, for it would in many cases have been relatively straightforward to follow-up subjects in twin and adoption studies into adulthood in order to assess the later consequences of genetic and environmental influences on childhood IQ and schooling.

In 1972, *Jencks* published his book, *Inequality*, in which he attempted to synthesise the kinship data on IQ with Duncan's path model of SES with a view to solving this problem. The details of his approach are quite complex. However, in principle, what he attempted was to extend Duncan's model of SES one step backwards to include genetic and environmental influences on IQ along the lines indicated in Fig. 7.4.[9]

In this model, genetic and environmental influences are seen to affect IQ which, in turn, affects schooling and eventually occupational status. The effect

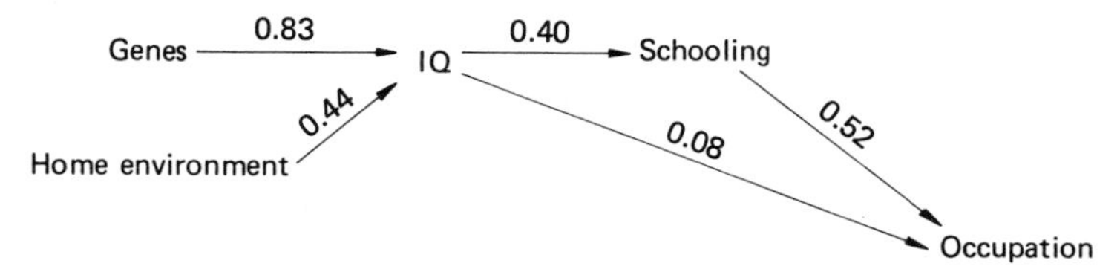

Fig. 7.4. Very simple path model of SES including genetic and environmental influences

---

9 Value of path coefficients are taken from Duncan's model in Figure 7.2 and the heritability values obtained in Chapter 5.

of IQ on occupation is made up of the direct path of value 0.08 and the indirect path via schooling of $0.40 \times 0.52 = 0.21$, giving a combined effect of 0.29. The model, in the form shown, simply divides this influence between genetic and environmental influences in the ratio 0.83 to 0.44, that is, in proportion to the paths for G and E. The effect of IQ genes on occupational status is therefore $0.83 \times 0.29 = 0.24$, somewhat less than the IQ phenotypic effect of 0.29. Using a model of this kind, family effects can be explored by representing brothers, for example, by two such path diagrams and allowing their genetic and environmental contributions to be correlated.

Jencks' model was much more complex than that shown in Fig. 7.4. He introduced additional home environmental influences on schooling as well as on IQ, introduced adult IQ as an intervening variable and allowed his background genetic and environmental variables to be correlated which, as we have seen in Chapters 5 and 6, is probably more appropriate for schooling than for IQ. In addition, he used a much lower heritability of about 50% compared with the figure of 70% we obtained in Chapter 5. Jencks' actual estimate of the effect of genes influencing IQ on occupational status was between 0.14 and 0.21, depending on assumptions, a figure somewhat lower than that implied by the simplified model in Fig. 7.4, but consistent with it if we adopt a heritability of 50%. Their effect on income was estimated to be between 0.14 and 0.18. Using this model, Jencks then concluded that IQ genes had a fairly modest effect on components of SES such as schooling, occupational status and income and that chance factors or luck played the more important role.

Jencks' model was important because it drew attention to the complexity of the problem of separating genetic and environmental components of SES. However, it is now apparent that it suffers from a number of limitations. In the first place, it almost certainly underestimates the heritability of IQ which inevitably weakens the apparent impact of genetic influences throughout the rest of the model. Secondly, the model only considers genetic influences that affect IQ so that any additional genetic and environmental influences involving specific skills and personality factors, which Jencks felt were important, are ignored. The importance of these limitations can be appreciated if we consider, for example, Jencks' estimate of the income correlation for siblings, at most 0.13 when estimated on the basis of his model. As we will shortly see, this correlation is much larger, being about 0.30. The main problem with Jencks' approach is the number of assumptions he is forced to make in the absence of emperical data on the heritability of the components of SES which, as we have indicated, requires familial data or, at the very least, data on twins. A recent large twin study of schooling, occupational status and income carried out by the American economist, *Taubman* (1976) provides empirical evidence of this kind and indicates the true complexity of the genetic and environmental determinants of SES.

Taubman's study involved 1019 pairs of male MZ twins and 907 pairs of DZ twins with average age around 51 years. In addition to years of schooling, information on occupational status after leaving school, current occupational status and income was available. The subjects were Military Service second world war veterans and reasonably representative of employed White males of their age group, although the very low end of the SES scale was, to some extent,

Table 7.7. Individual and cross-sib correlations between four SES measures for MZ and DZ (taken from *Taubman*, 1976)

	MZ twins							
	phenotypic correlation matrix				cross-sib correlation matrix			
Schooling (S)	1.00	0.53	0.54	0.44	0.76	0.47	0.44	0.40
Initial Occupation (OC_1)		1.00	0.45	0.35		0.53	0.35	0.32
Adult Occupation (OC_2)			1.00	0.35			0.43	0.27
Income (I)				1.00				0.54
	DZ twins							
S	1.00	0.53	0.51	0.44	0.54	0.37	0.29	0.29
OC_1		1.00	0.43	0.36		0.33	0.22	0.22
OC_2			1.00	0.35			0.20	0.19
I				1.00				0.30

S is years of education.
OC_1 and OC_2 Measured on Duncan's scale.
I is the natural logarithm of income in dollars.

under-represented. The phenotypic and cross-sib correlation matrices for both MZ and DZ twins are shown in Table 7.7.

With these data we are in a position to separate genetic and environmental influences that determine SES. The values on the leading diagonals of the cross-sib correlation matrices are the MZ and DZ intra-class correlations for each of the four SES variables. Using the approach outlined in Chapter 5 we can use these correlations to estimate V(G), the genetic variance, V(CE), the common family environmental variance and V(SE), that environmental variance specific to individuals, partitioning the phenotypic variation for each of the SES variables into its components. V(G) is estimated as $2(r_{MZ}-r_{DZ})$, V(CE) as $2r_D-r_{MZ}$ and V(SE) as $1-r_{MZ}$.

The results are shown in Table 7.8 and indicate a substantial genetic component, between 40% and 50%, for all the variables, establishing that genetic factors are quite potent throughout the entire process of acquiring adult status, contrary to the conclusion reached by Jencks. In contrast, home environmental influences appear to become progressively weaker as the individuals moves on from school to make his way in the adult world. As home environmental influences weaken, those specific to the individual show a corresponding increase so that the combined impact of the environment remains relatively constant. Referring back to Duncan's model, we can now see that the weakening impact of background factors as we move forward in time is to a large extent a function of the weakening of the home environment rather than any decreasing impact of inherited genetic influences. The strength of Taubman's study, however, is that it allows us to go beyond this univariate form of analysis and see how these separate factors interact and change during the individual's lifetime.

Table 7.8. Proportions of variance in univariate analysis of the cross-sib correlations in Table 7.7

	Schooling	Initial Occupation	Adult Occupation	Income
V(G)	0.44	0.40	0.46	0.48
V(CE)	0.32	0.13	0.06	0.06
V(SE)	0.24	0.47	0.57	0.46

To analyse these interactions is quite straightforward in principle, although awkward technical problems may be encountered in practice. The starting point of the analysis is to estimate genetic and environmental components of variance and covariance in the place of the components of variance estimated in the univariate analysis. Just as we used $2(r_{MZ}-r_{DZ})$ to estimate the gentic variances for the separate variables, so we can use twice the difference between each of the correlations in the MZ and DZ cross-sib correlation matrices in Table 7.7 to estimate the genetic covariances between all pairs of variables. Thus the genetic covariance between schooling and income is 2(0.40–0.29) = 0.22, while the genetic variances of schooling and income are 2(0.76–0.54) = 0.44 and 2(0.54–0.20) =0.48 respectively. The genetic correlation, therefore, between schooling and income is $0.22/(0.44 \times 0.48)^{1/2}$ or 0.48.These calculations, carried out for all the ten corresponding elements of the MZ and DZ cross-sib correlation matrices generate the genetic variance-covariance matrix and its associated genetic correlation matrix. This correlation matrix indicates the extent to which the same genes underlie individual differences for any given pair of variables.

A similar multivariate analogue defines the common and specific environmental variance-covariance matrices. That for the environment common to sibs can be estimated by $2r_{DZ}-r_{MZ}$ again element for element, and for specific environment it is the phenotypic correlation matrix less the cross-sib correlation matrix for MZ twins. In practice a more elaborate statistical procedure is often necessary to keep the component correlations within the limits of ± 1 (*Fulker,* 1978). This procedure was used in the present case giving the genetic and environmental correlations together with proportions of variation for each measure shown in Table 7.9.

Several points arise from the results of this analysis. The presence of genetic variation for all variables is confirmed, although the constraining procedure ensuring sensible correlations appears to have resulted in more variable estimates than those given in Table 7.8. From the similar but intermediate values of the genetic correlations it is clear that genetic variation is comprised of both common and specific components. The common or shared genetic influences, which account for about half the genetic variation, if a simple factor model is fitted to these correlations, identifies the genes that are common to all the SES variables. This common genetic factor, representing a general tendency to success or failure, very likely relates to general ability or IQ. The specific genetic variation, which is just as powerful, probably relates more to individual differ-

Table 7.9. Components of variance and associated component correlation matrices for Taubman's study of schooling, occupational status and income (taken from *Fulker*, 1978)

Genetic	Correlations S	OC_1	OC_2	I	Proportions of Variance
Schooling (S)	1.00	0.60	0.62	0.55	0.46
Initial Occupation (OC_1)		1.00	0.63	0.52	0.33
Adult Occupation (OC_2)			1.00	0.44	0.28
Income (I)				1.00	0.48
Common Environment					
S	1.00	1.00	1.00	1.00	0.30
OC_1		1.00	1.00	1.00	0.19
OC_2			1.00	1.00	0.08
I				1.00	0.08
Specific Environment					
S	1.00	0.17	0.24	0.10	0.23
OC_1		1.00	0.17	0.07	0.48
OC_2			1.00	0.14	0.64
I				1.00	0.45

ences in skills, personality factors such as perseverance and personal taste influencing facets of SES over and above the influence of the general factor.

Terman in his study of gifted children to which we have referred elsewhere (see *Oden*, 1968) was able to identify some of these determinants of socio-economic success that are independent of IQ. Among individuals in this groups, all of whom were very bright, those who were successful as adults tended to be of better physical and mental health, to have much more ambition and drive and to have a more relaxed friendly and attractive personality. So far as extremes of mental illhealth are concerned we know that psychoticism results in quite marked downward mobility (*Hollingshead* and *Redlich*, 1958). It is well established, of course, that most aspects of personality, normal and abnormal, have a substantial genetic component (*Eysenck*, 1976).

The home or shared environmental influences are particularly interesting. Decreasing impact is indicated as the individual gets older, just as in the univariate analyses. However, all the component correlations have converged on a value of unity, indicating that whatever the source of this environmental influence, it is exactly the same for all variables. That is, all common environmental variation is due to a general factor with no specific variation whatsoever. This powerful environmental factor appears to be in large part responsible for the persistence of family background influences noted throughout the SES data and most probably represents the influence of parental SES which emerged as a powerful unitary influence in the last chapter.

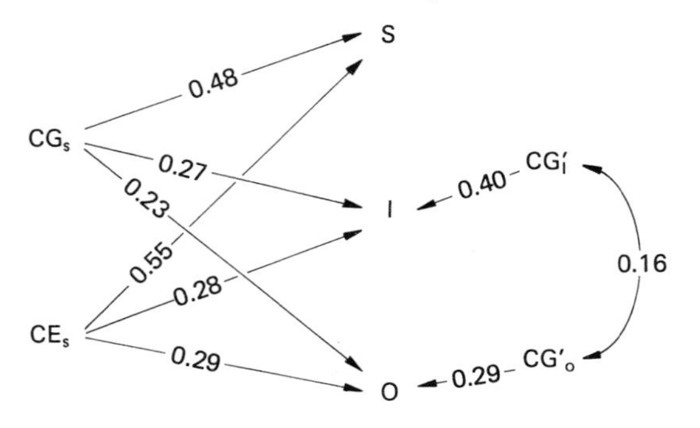

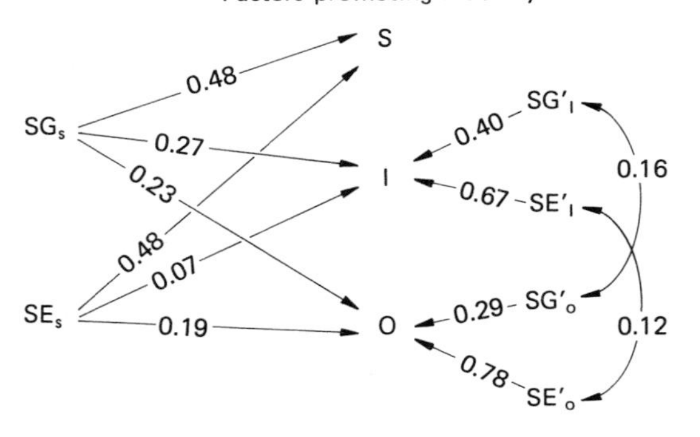

Complete specification equations

Factors conserving family status | Factors promoting social mobility

$$O = \overbrace{0.23CG_s + 0.29CE_s + 0.29CG'_O}^{} + \overbrace{0.23SG_s + 0.29SG'_O + 0.05SG'_I + 0.78SE'_O + 0.09SE'_I + 0.19SE_s}^{}$$

$$I = 0.27CG_s + 0.28CE_s + 0.40CG'_I + 0.27SG_s + 0.40SG'_I + 0.06SG'_O + 0.67SE'_I + 0.07SE_s + 0.08SE'_O$$

Fig. 7.5. A model of genetic and environmental determinants of adult SES (based on *Taubman,* 1977, and *Fulker,* 1978)

The specific environmental influences, in contrast to those which are common to siblings, are hardly correlated at all. These low correlations reflect unpredictable influences on SES including important effects such as illness, good and bad fortune and also the development of specific tastes and interests together with market imperfections so far as occupation and income are concerned. In addition, they reflect more trivial effects such as unreliability of measurement and the supplying of false information by subjects. However, unreliability and falsification are unlikely to play a large part in the present study, and the low intercorrelations probably indicate, for the most part, the highly specific nature of chance factors in the environment.

The correlations and variances in Table 7.9 can be used to construct a model of the influence of schooling on adult SES that distinguishes the conservative influences that maintain family status from those that promote mobility, as shown in Fig. 7.5. The initial occupational status of the twins on leaving school or college has been omitted from the model for the sake of simplicity.

In this model, genetic influences are subdivided into those common to siblings and tending therefore to conserve family status, denoted CG, and those specific to individuals tending to promote mobility, denoted SG. These genetic influences are further subdivided into those that directly affect schooling, subscripted S, and those independent of schooling that affect adult occupation and income, subscripted O and I respectively. These latter influences are also marked with a dash to indicate that they are independent of the genetic influences affecting schooling. Although these residual genetic influences are independent of genetic influences on schooling they are not independent of each other, their correlation being indicated by a curved arrow. In addition to genetic effects there is a single common environmental influence on schooling, occupation and income, denoted by CE_s, that tends to conserve family status. The remaining environmental influences, specific to the individual, denoted SE, all serve to promote mobility.

The paths indicate the relative importance of each causal factor, and may be combined to give a specification for both occupation and income. These equations are given at the foot of the figure and completely specify these two measures of adult status. This specification is complete since, following the rules of path analysis, the sum of squares of the coefficients in the equations sum to unity, the standardised value of the total variance of the two measures in question. The figure is drawn in two parts in order to separate shared from specific influences, and for the sake of clarity. However the variables S, I and O refer to a single individual in the two halves of the daigram. The two values are brought together in the specification equations at the foot of the figure.

All genetic influences, to a first approximation, will contribute equally to both maintaining and redistributing status, since both sibs and parents and offspring share, on average, 50% of their genes. Thus the values of the genetic paths in the top and bottom halves of the figure are the same. The genetic influences that affect schooling also affect occupation and income, although to a lessser extent. Independent genetic influences, marked with a dash, play an equal part in determining occupation and a somewhat greater one in determining income. These genetic influences, independent of those affecting schooling, are also largely independent of each other, only correlating .16. That is, once we take account of the genetic influences on schooling, large independent genetic influences unrelated to school performance and to each other remain. In all probability, these independent genetic influences are related to special skills and abilities, personality factors and personal preferences that also determine status as well as academic ability. These influences correspond to the general and specific genetic factors in the genetic correlation matrix discussed earlier. The importance of these additional specific genetic factors in status suggest that models such as Duncan's fail to include a number of important aspects of individual differences affecting adult status.

In contrast to genetic influences, environmental ones act either to conserve status or promote mobility. Common environmental influences, which act to preserve status, apparently play a simple role, the same influences that affect schooling also much later affecting occupation and income, albeit with reduced impact. Obviously the advantages or disadvantages of an individual's home environment persist throughout his lifetime.

Specific environmental influences that promote mobility are more complex. Surprisingly, those that affect schooling have little effect later on adult status, the paths being .19 to occupation and .07 to income. Thus, if an individual loses schooling through illness or some other chance factor, these being the kind of influences that contribute to the specific environment, the deficit is apparently fairly easily made good, unlike the more persistent effects of the shared home environment. The residual specific environmental influences that act on occupation and income, independent of schooling are, however, very powerful. Like the residual genetic influences they are also largely independent of each other, correlating only .12. These influences are, in all probability, largely chance factors, relating to job opportunities, health and economic factors outside the control of the individual; what Jencks called 'luck'. Referring to the equations at the foot of Fig. 7.5 for occupation, the total effect of specific environmental influences from all sources is about half as powerful again as the total effect of genetic factors in promoting social mobility, while for income it is about equally important compared with genetic factors.

The model can also be used to evaluate the relative importance of its causal variables in terms of probabilities and risks to the individual. For example, the model estimates that the path from home environment to adult income is .28. What implication does this have, say for the probability of ending up in any particular income bracket? Individuals in the top and bottom 20% of the distribution of home environments differ, on average, $\pm$ 1.4 standard deviation units. With the path from home environment to income being .28, the effect on income will be $\pm .28 \times 1.4$ or $\pm .39$ standard deviation units of income. If we take as our reference point the 1968 distribution of income in the United States $\pm .39$ standard deviations corresponds to incomes of \$10588 and \$6292, quite a large difference. More interesting, however, is the probability of earning above or below a certain limit, say more than \$15000. For the lower group their mean is 1.58 standard deviation units below the threshold, for the higher group only .80 units below. In terms of probabilities, which are simply the areas under the two normal curves cut off by the threshold, it is .056 for the lower income group and .212 for the higher one. Therefore, the probability is about 4 times greater of earning more than \$15000 if one is born in the upper 20% of homes compared with the lower 20% purely in terms of environmental influences. Thus, in spite of so little variation in income being attributable to the effects of home environment, its influence on income expectation can be considerable.

The information that can be obtained from even a relatively simple multivariate twin study like *Taubman*'s (1976) is prodigious and should provide a stimulus to further research. Of course, as it stands, the study suffers from all the potential problems of twin studies when unsupported by evidence from other kinds of kinship studies. What we have labelled 'common environment', for example, may well include effects due to genetic and environmental covariance, which, as we saw in Chapter 5, is simply genotype in disguise, stemming from the genetic makeup of the parents influencing the home environment they provide for their children. Also, the study is restricted to men. The social mobility of women is controlled by many different factors and would provide a fascinating subject for a similar behaviour genetic analysis. Multivariate studies involving important real life variables, of which Taubman's is at present a solitary example, have the potential to answer an astonishing variety of important questions concerning the nature of human individuality and its social significance. We confidently predict, therefore, many more such studies in future.

We have seen how a large genetic component in intellectual ability has important consequences for socio-economic status and the way in which status changes between successive generations. We now consider the consequences of this genetic component for long term changes in population structure through the action of natural selction.

Natural selection was originally suggested by the great naturalist Charles Darwin as the principal mechanism of evolutionary change. In any population individuals will differ and those possessing certain characteristics will be better adapted to their environment than others. These individuals will therefore contribute more offspring to future generations and, if their characteristics have a genetic basis, the composition of the population will gradually change.

Natural selection operates mainly through survival and differential fertility. Obviously survival is important if an individual is to make any contribution at all to subsequent generations, but, given survival, differences in fertility or reproductive rate will then be the main factor determining who will contribute more than another.

Survival is thought to play the major role in many animal populations and primitive human societies. However, in modern societies, where many of the hazards present in primitive ones no longer exist, differential fertility has taken over as the main agent of evolutionary change (*Cavalli-Sforza* and *Bodmer,* 1971).

For the purpose of discussing natural selection, fertility is simply the number of children an individual produces, and lower SES parents have, on average, more than those higher up the social scale. As we have seen in the previous chapter they also have lower IQs. This negative relationship between SES and fertility has been evident as far back as the seventeenth century (*United Nations,* 1955) and if, as we have good reason to believe from the studies discussed in the earlier part of this chapter, there is a genetic component in SES related to intellectual ability, then this differential fertility might be expected to result in a gradual change in the genetic make-up of the population with a corresponding decline in IQ.

At first sight it may seem paradoxical that natural selection should favour low IQ, the implication being that high IQ is maladaptive. However, insofar as the low fertility of the upper classes results from social and psychological factors causing them to reproduce far below their natural capacity, it is far from clear that in any biological sense they are better adapted to their environment than the apparently less inhibited lower classes.

The case for a decline in IQ was put dramatically over forty years ago by

Cattell (1937) in his book *The Fight for our National Intelligence,* in which he calculated that a correlation of -.3 between an individual's IQ and the number of siblings in his family should result in a decline of a little over 3 IQ points per generation.

Subsequent studies failed to find any such effect. *Thomson* et al., (1953) in a massive study carried out in Scotland, found a small increase in children aged 11 between 1932 and 1947. *Cattell* (1950), in a smaller study, also found a small increase, around one IQ point, between 1936 and 1949. Many other larger increases have been found, whereas the expected decline has not (*Hunt,* 1961).

Cattell suggested that the increase was due to the environmental effects of improved education masking genetic deterioration. This explanation may well be, in part, correct, for many reported gains are much too large to have other than an environmental explanation. However, the problem is more complex than originally envisaged. Cattell's argument was based on the classical plant and animal breeding model of artificial selection. In this model, individuals are selected as parents, usually on the basis of some trait of economic importance, in order that their offspring might show an improvement over the parental generation. Over many generations considerable improvement can often be achieved.

The formula predicting the response (R) involves the narrow heritability (h^2) of the trait, that is the proportion of variance due to additive genes, and the selection differential (S). S is the difference between the weighted average of the individuals chosen as parents and the mean of the group from which they were drawn, the weights being the relative number of offspring produced by each individual. The predicted response is then given by the expression used in Chapter 5 to explore the phenomenon of filial regression.

$$R = h^2S$$

There are a number of problems with this formulation. In the first place, it is difficult to calculate exactly the selection differential, S, for any given population. Many early studies, such as Cattell's, used the correlation between the IQ of a child and the size of family into which he was born in order to estimate S. However, what we really need to know is the IQ of parents and the size of their completed families. Moreover, as the geneticist *Penrose* (1948) pointed out, it is important to take into account individuals who do not reproduce at all, that is 'parents' with zero family size. Allowing for these individuals is often quite difficult since most studies of parents and children use the children as a starting point in the investigation. People without children are consequently often not included in such studies.

The omission of childless individuals has been shown to be important in at least two American studies. In one (*Higgins* et al., 1961) almost 2000 parents of known IQ were involved. Their IQs and the number of children they had are shown in columns one and three in Table 7.10.

Unlike the relationship between IQ of child and number of siblings, which varies inversely in a fairly steady fashion, we can see that IQ of parent and number of children has a U-shaped distribution with the largest families falling in the two extremes. Both the very bright and the very dull have the largest

Table 7.10. Differential fertility of parents of differing IQs. Based on *Higgins* et al. 1962

IQ of parents	number of parents	Average number of children	Number of childless siblings of parents	Average number of children of parents and childless sibs	Total number of parents and childless sibs
0–55	11	3.64	18	1.38	29
56–70	64	2.84	10	2.46	74
71–85	202	2.47	6	2.39	208
86–100	572	2.20	11	2.16	583
101–115	763	2.30	15	2.26	778
116–130	263	2.50	6	2.45	269
131 and above	25	2.96	0	2.96	25
Total	1900				1966

mean family sizes, with the smallest belonging to parents around average IQ. The selection differential based on these figures is negative overall, implying a declining IQ. What is striking, however, is the relatively large number of very low IQ individuals who remain childless, shown in column four. Thus very low IQ individuals, when they do reproduce, appear to have large families, but many fail to reproduce at all, presumably finding it difficult to attract mates. When these individuals are taken into account the bimodal relationship between family size and IQ is much less marked and the selection differential hardly differs from zero being, in fact, very slightly positive.

A similar picture was found in another American study carried out by *Bajema* (1963) in which the relationship between fertility and IQ was bimodal, but less so when childless individuals were taken into account. Again, the selection differential was positive. In these two studies the selection differentials are very small, being in the region of +1.0 IQ point. Consequently, applying our formula

$$R = h^2 S$$

gives a trivial predicted change of about $+1/2$ an IQ point per generation.

Even the small change implied by the calculation above is an over-estimate, since it assumes we are selecting on the basis of the trait of interest, in this case, IQ. In fact, the selection is not directly on IQ but on fertility, the only trait natural selection can act directly upon. We are only observing the correlated response of IQ. In this case the formula is more complex, the response in IQ to natural selection on the basis of fertility being

$$R_{IQ} = rg_{IQ,F} h_{IQ}\ h_F\ S_F$$

if IQ and relative fertility are measured in standard units. The correlation $rg_{IQ,F}$ is the genetic correlation between IQ and fertility, h_F and h_{IQ} being the square roots of the heritabilities of fertility and IQ respectively and S_F the selection differential of fertility. In effect, $rg_{IQ,F}\ h_{IQ}\ h_F$ replaces h^2_{IQ} in the simple formula previously assumed. The formula takes account of the following limitations when selection is not directly on IQ but indirectly through fertility. Firstly, only genes common both to IQ and fertility can cause any permanent change in IQ, since changes in IQ must always follow those in fertility. Secondly, the rate of change in IQ will depend on the heritability of fertility, the primary trait of natural selection. Should fertility have a low heritability, very little effect on IQ could be expected.

Although h_F and $rg_{IQ,F}$ are unknown, h_F is almost certainly much less than h_{IQ} and $rg_{IQ,F}$ is probably little more than about 0.5, the phenotypic correlation (*Falconer,* 1966). Thus, in place of a narrow heritability of about 0.5 in the earlier formula, we have an effective heritability of about 0.2 to 0.3 at most, perhaps much less. This figure implies large negative selection differentials in the region of 4 and 5 IQ points would be required to shift the population mean by as little as 1 IQ point per generation. Since what evidence we have suggests selection differentials are smaller and perhaps even positive in some populations, a rapid decline in mean IQ is not to be expected.

This is not to say, of course, that we should be complacent about dysgenic trends where they exist. The relatively high fertility of the 50–70 IQ group, which although counterbalanced by increased fertility of those well above average, is still dysgenic and could probably be avoided. There is evidence that a proportion of these children are unwanted and that their parents, given adequate contraceptive advice and support would be both willing and able to limit their families (*Morgan,* 1965). There seems a case to be made for considering such eugenic measures both from the long term point of view and in the short term in order to reduce the social and economic cost of unwanted children. At the same time it makes good sense to encourage higher fertility at the high end of the IQ scale as well as to reduce it at the low end, perhaps by means of increased grants to married students or some other economic means. Of course, there are dangers. We cannot be sure, for example, that some future generation may not require quite different individuals for its survival, particularly if a dramatic environmental change were to take place, perhaps through a natural or man-made disaster. The truth is we cannot be certain in such matters since our knowledge is currently far from perfect. There is need of a great deal more empirical information concerning the causes of human individuality and its short and long term consequences. We have tried to indicate in these three chapters on nature and nurture the kinds of research that would provide this information.

8 Structure of Intellect Models: Guilford and Eysenck

It has been suggested in the Introduction that the modern theory of intelligence, as here presented, constitutes a good example of a scientific paradigm. As we have seen, the conception of intelligence as general, innate cognitive ability is strongly supported by a great variety of researches. This does not mean that alternative theories have not been offered, or that improvements in the model are impossible. In this Chapter we shall be dealing with two alternative models which attempt to change the picture of the structure of the intellect; in the next Chapter we shall be dealing with attempts to put on the map developmental models of one kind or another which have sometimes been suggested to supplant, but which in reality only supplement, the paradigmatic theory. The authors considered in this Chapter are Guilford, whose structure-of-intellect theory suggested the title, and Eysenck, whose work falls into the same category, although quite different in intent and design from Guilford's. In the next Chapter we shall be concerned with Piaget and Jensen; again two quite dissimilar authors attempting to approach similar goals along quite different paths. These are of couse not the only, but they are perhaps the major efforts at theoretical reconstruction of the Spearman-Thurstone model, and we must note most carefully to what extent they require a change in the paradigm outlined so far.

J. P. Guilford and the structure of intellect

> I science the word criticism is not a synonym for disparagement; criticizing means looking for truth
>
> Claude Bernard

Guilford (1967) has called his theory the Structure-of-Intellect (SI) Theory, in order to demonstrate his departure from the Spearman-Thurstone tradition. His theory completely denies the existence of general intelligence, even as a higher order factor, and insists rather on the existence of a large number of independent abilities. His model is based on the view that there are a number of dimensions whose combinations determine different types of intellectual abilities. The first of these dimensions refers to the kind of *mental operation* involved in the ability. Guilford distinguishes five types of mental operations, namely cognition (knowing), memory, divergent production (i. e. the generation

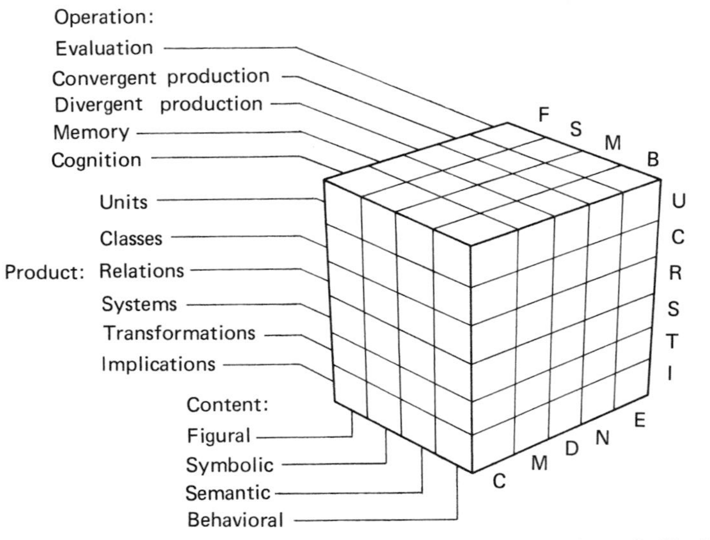

Fig. 8.1. Guilford's structure-of-intellect model of intelligence. Adapted from *Guilford* (1967)

of logical alternatives), convergent production (generation of logic-type conclusions), and evaluation. We shall in a later section deal specifically with the difference between divergent and convergent production; here let us merely note that most of the traditional problems in IQ tests are convergent, i. e. the relations obtaining between the individual parts of the problems point to one single correct conclusion. Divergent Production is concerned with a problem which has an infinite number of solutions, all of which may be correct; thus we might ask the question "How many uses can you think of for a brick?" This distinction, first made by *Woodworth* in 1918, has given rise to a great deal of research that will be considered later.

The second dimension of classification relates to the *content* or area of information in which the operations are performed. Guilford suggests the existence of four such types of content – figural, symbolic, semantic, and behavioural. His third dimension is concerned with the *product* that results from a particular kind of mental operation applied to a particular type of content; he distinguishes six types of products. These are units, classes, relations, systems, transformations, and implications. Figure 8.1 shows a diagrammatic picture of intelligence; it includes all possible combinations of operations, contents, and products, and therefore results in 120 different abilities that may be defined by his SI model.

Guilford does not assume that these three dimensions are comparable to what would be higher-order factors in Thurstone's sense. Each ability is defined by its particular position on each of the three dimensions, and it is not assumed that abilities sharing position with respect to two dimensions, but differing in a third, are necessarily more closely related than abilities sharing only a single dimension. Guilford's model presupposes that it should be possible to construct tests measuring a single ability, and consequently it should be possible to construct a battery of tests each of which would load substantially on only of the many different factors that can be extracted.

It may be easier to follow this discussion if we were to illustrate it by certain combinations of dimensions giving rise to certain tests. Let us begin with a combination of D, N and R, i. e. the divergent production of semantic relations. An example here would be a test presenting a pair of words, such as FATHER-DAUGHTER, the subject being instructed to list all of the ways in which the two are related, e. g. parent-child, old young, male-female, etc. The test would be scored in terms of the number of acceptable answers provided. The test is obviously divergent, there being a large number of possible answers; the content of the test item is clearly semantic; and the product or outcome deals with the relation between the contents.

Entirely different would be a test combining C, B and I, i. e. the cognition of behavioural implications. Guilford has published a test called "reflections" which is assumed to measure this ability. The subject is given a statement of the kind that a patient might make during psychotherapy. The subject is then required to pick out the best justified psychological implications of the statement. Such a statement might be for instance "I'm just wondering how I'll act; I mean how things will turn out." Does this mean that the patient is looking forward to it, that she is worried about it, or that she is just interested how things will turn out? The second of these answers is supposed to be the correct one, and would be scored a point in the test. Clearly, the test deals with behavioural content, and the product is equally clearly an implication; consequently the test falls in that part of the cube in Fig. 8.1 which is located on the meeting point of demension C, B and I. (It might be said that the test deals with semantic analysis, rather than with behavioural content; this might be a valid criticism.)

As a last example let us consider a test measuring the cognition of figural units (CFV.) A test labelled "Hidden Print" by Guilford would illustrate this combination. The subject is presented with pictures of digits and letters formed by patterns of dots; in addition, a variety of dots are scattered at random about the dots forming the digits and letters, thus serving to obscure the stimuli and make correct recognition difficult. The subject is required to recognise and name the stimuli presented to him. Cognition is involved because the subject is asked to become aware or discover something; stimuli are present in the visual mode and are therefore figural. Finally, the product of the operation is the unit, in this case a particular digit or letter.

This wide ranging theory was presented by *Guilford* (1967) in an important book on The Nature of Human Intelligence, and in a later publication *Guilford* and *Hoepfner* (1971) claim that out of a possible 120 different factors, and tests defining them, 98 had in fact been identified in the various studies undertaken by Guilford and his students. These two books give descriptions of the tests measuring the various factors, and should be consulted by anyone interested in this model. Harking back to our discussion of factor analysis, and the rotation of factors, we must note here that the factors discovered by Guilford in his empirical work are found with orthogonal rotations, and hence are independent of one another; Guilford rejects Thurstone's development of oblique rotation, i. e. of correlated factors, and thus we cannot derive from his factors any higher order concept of "general intelligence". The arguments about factor analysis are necessarily a little technical, but the main areas of debate between Guilfort on the one hand and most other modern theorists, on the other, are fairly obvious on simple common sense terms.

We may, with advantage, begin with the observation, to which attention has been drawn before, that the correlations between cognitive tests tend to fall into a "positive manifold", i. e. that they tend to be uniformly positive. Guilford has pointed out that out of 48 140 correlation coefficients between tests observed in his own work, 8.677 fell in the interval between −.10 and +.10, and that for 24% of the correlations found in his numerous studies the null hypothesis could not be rejected, i. e. they were compatible with the view that the true correlation was zero. He goes on to argue that data such as these do not support the view of the existence of a single pervasive general factor of intellectual ability.

There are two ways of meeting this particular argument. The first one is to point out that even in his own work, 76% of the time correlations are found between these tests of allegedly independent abilities which are high enough to reject the null hypothesis; in other words, in 76% of all the cases there are statistically significant relationships between variables, a finding certainly not compatible with Guilford's view that measures of intellectual ability are unrelated except insofar as they are measures of the same ability. On his theory we would expect measures selected at random from his studies to show significant positive correlations only infrequently; the fact that the great majority do correlate positively, and often quite highly, is, if anything, a death blow to his theoretical conceptions. We would have to postulate factors more general than those extracted by Guilford to account for the facts. In other words, it is clear that Guilford has not succeeded in getting away from the problems that caused Thurstone originally to introduce the notion of correlated (oblique) factors. These cannot be argued out of existence by an arbitrary fiat.

Thus even if we accept the figure of 24% we can see that it does not invalidate the Spearman-Thurstone hypothesis of general ability. But there are many reasons why this figure is of very doubtful value. There are three reasons for this doubt. In the first place, many of the populations studied by Guilford were highly selected for intelligence, e. g. Airforce Cadets in an officers' training programme. This inevitably reduces the range of ability in the sample, and consequently also the correlations to be found. For the purpose for which Guilford uses his data, it is absolutely essential that the correlations should be calculated for a random sample, or at least a sample not differing too widely in range of ability from the average of the whole population. Restriction of range is a very powerful factor in reducing correlations that are significant and positive in the general population to a level of insignificance in samples showing this restriction of range.

In the second place, many of the tests used by Guilford have had relatively low reliabilities, occasionally with values of below 0.50. This means of course that a large proportion of the total variance in these tests is error variance, and consequently that these tests cannot correlate highly with other tests, as they measure whatever it is they measure so unreliably. The unreliability may be due to the shortness of the tests, or to poor construction, or to other causes, but to use a test for the purpose intended by Guilford in his comparison, minimum reliabilities of 0.80 or above would be required.

The third criticism would be that some at least of the tests Guilford has used are of doubtful relavance to the concept of intelligence as general *cognitive* ability. The tests involving divergent thought for instance are, as we shall see, considerably determined not by intellectual factors but by personality ones; *Spearman* (1927) already pointed out that high divergent ability was likely to be related to extraverted personality, and the data seem to bear this out. If divergent thought production is essentially a measure of personality, then we would not expect it to correlate with cognitive abilities. This is not the only one of Guilford's test functions which make one doubtful about its relevance; those involving behavioural content are also questionable. Areas covered by behavioural content deal with sensitivity to psychological states and feelings, and in our work these have been found to be related again to personality, particularly neuroticism. So some at least of the low or zero correlations found by Guilford may be due to the inappropriate choice of tests.

It is possible to look at some of the correlation matrices reported by Guilford and his associates, and to remove all those tests with reliabilities lower than 0.6 (removing all those with reliabilities below 0.8, as would otherwise be reasonable, would exclude too many tests to make our examination worthwhile.) When this is done the number of correlations not statistically significant goes down to below 2%, and sometimes below 1%. Thus the true number of apparently insignificant correlations is vanishingly small even in Guilford's own work. Furthermore, it can be shown that when tests of general intelligence have been used, they correlate positively and significantly with all the other variables in the batteries in question. In one study reported by Dunham et al. (1966), results including 43 different tests were reported, and 15 different orthogonal factors derived by the authors. When variables with low reliabilities are excluded, less than 1% of the correlations fail to be significantly different from zero, and a simple multiple choice vocabulary test correlates with the remaining variables (excluding those with reliabilities below 0.50) between 0.27 and 0.60, with a medium value of 0.5. This indicates that a substantial part of the total variance in all of the measures used in this study is identical with the variance included in a multiple choice vocabulary test, i. e. a good measure of g_c. Guilford's "proof" of the failure of the Spearman-Thurstone model involving a strong general factor of intelligence breaks down completely, and can be shown to be due to a variety of statistical and psychological errors.

Are the factors in Guilford's research replicable? This question is difficult to answer because Guilford has seldom used the same battery of tests in two different investigations. Mostly he has used "marker" variables for the factor discovered in one analysis for inclusion in another; this makes for subjectivity in interpretation of factors. However, a few cases made it possible to use numerical indices of invariance of factors, and where this was done, "the uses lead to unimpressive results". (*Guilford* and *Hoepfner,* 1971, p. 42). Repeatability of factor structures, therefore, which is an important part of the evidence one would need in order to accept Giolford's SI, is therefore almost wholly missing.

The major objection however to Guilford's claim of having discovered a large number of the postulated factors in his system is based on his use of "targeted rotations" or Procrustes methods of rotation (*Humphreys,* 1962; *Horn* and *Knapp,* 1973; *Undheim* and *Horn,* in press; see also *Guilford's,* 1974, reply to Horn and Knapp.) Procrustes, it will be remembered, was the famous robber who adjusted the length of his guests by chopping off their feet if they were too long for sleeping in his bed, or thoughtfully extended their length on the rack if they were too short! The Procrustes system of rotation does the same enforced adjustment for a factorial solution. Thurstone had introduced a method of rotation which gave an objective criterion, namely that of simple structure; the Procrustes method, on the other hand, enables the investigator to state beforehand the kind of solution which he would like to see, or which his theory specifies, and the programme then instructs the computer to rotate axes in such a way as to bring the final structure into as close correspondence with that specified as possible. It will be seen that this method of "targeted" rotation involves serious problems of subjectivity; any arbitrary collections of correlations can be factored and rotated into some degree of conformity with an *a priori* scheme, and we must beware of accepting such conformity as necessarily providing evidence for the correctness of the theory. Several investigators have used random variables generated by computer procedure; these were then arbitrarily labelled, correlated and factored, and Procrustes rotational procedures were used to force the factors into position that would give the best support for the set of "hypotheses" states in advance of the analysis. In each case the results suggested that unless careful precautions are taken, an investigator can conclude that a factor analytic study based upon Procrustes rotational procedures provides support for his theory even when this "support" simply consists of random numbers!

An interesting analysis was done by *Horn* and *Knapp* (1973), using data from three Guilford studies. Horn and Knapp compared the factor solutions achieved with a target matrix representing SI theory, and a target determined arbitrarily, i. e. on a random basis, each solution being determined by the same Procrustes programme of rotation. A "hit" was defined as a factor loading on the predicted factor which was larger than 0.30; "misses" were defined as the number of failures to achieve this conformity, and the number of factor coefficients larger than 0.30 for which there was in fact a zero correlation with the factors hypothesised was identified as "extras". The proportion of hits was 0.84 for the random hypothesis, averaged over the three studies; for hypotheses based upon SI theory alone (i. e. excluding factors established prior to the origins of the theory) the proportion of hits was 0.84! Thus on this showing the SI theory did not predict factor structure any better than a completely randomly derived theory which had no psychological meaning whatsoever. It may be unfair to look at hits alone, but this has been characteristic in past research interpreted as supporting SI theory; when misses and extras are taken into account the story becomes more complicated, but, as *Undheim* and *Horn* (in press) point out, it does not give any greater support to the Guilford hypothesis.

The truth of the matter is simply that Procrustes rotations enable any theory to be "verified", provided that the number of factors involved is large; it is difficult to fit data to an incorrect hypothesis when you only have two or three factors, but it becomes quite easy when the number of factors goes above 10, or even 20. When objective criteria are used, such as simple structure, it is found that the factors extracted pretty well resemble the Thurstone primary ability factors, leaving very little variance to be accounted for in terms of the many other factors postulated by Guilford. Thus it is very doubtful if Guilford's tests really measure anything additional to Thurstone's factors, other than relatively specific content.

Cronbach (1970) has suggested another, related criticism. He has shown that the correlations between tests defining one and the same factor are not so very different from tests defining different factors. In other words, if we conceive of a factor as producing correlations between certain tests, and derived in turn from these observed correlations, then we would expect that if a factor is defined by, say, six tests, these tests would correlate together more highly than six tests each of which was part of an entirely different factor! This was not so in Guilford's work. Cronbach also noted that similarities in content between tests produced correlations much more reliably than similarity of products.

These findings suggested to Cronbach that there were probably broad general factors contained in the matrices analysed by Guilford, but that these factors were obscured by his analyses. This is pretty much the same conclusion to which Horn and his associates have also come, namely that essentially there are broad factors analogous to Thurstone's primary abilities underlying the correlations of those postulated by Guilford, and that these in turn give rise to a factor of general intelligence equivalent in large measure to Spearman's g.

Can we conclude that Guilford's contribution is on the whole worthless, not worthy of being considered? Such a conclusion would be entirely mistaken. In the first place, Guilford has certainly alerted everyone to the dimensionality of the test contents of tests of mental ability, to a degree that is quite unprecedented. He has constructed large numbers of interesting and intriguing tests which would not have been thought of but for his adventurous tendency to investigate new and untrodden paths. These are important new contributions, and they should not be underestimated. Where he has gone wrong perhaps is in identifying dimensionality of *test content* with the dimensionality of *human ability*. There may of course be a direct relationship between the two, but this cannot be assumed. Because we can construct tests lying along certain continua, it does not follow that the mind works along these same continua. This remains to be proved, and the factors of the mind may not be isomorphic with the dimensions of test construction.

Even when this is said, we cannot conclude that Guilford's theory is erroneous; we can only say that he has failed entirely to give satisfactory empirical support for it. In other words the verdict must be "not proven" rather than disproved. It is not always realised just what demands for satisfactory proof for Guilford's system would imply by way of test construction and administration. Such a test would involve that each of the 120 abilities postulated should be separable empirically from the other 119; this means that all factors would have to be investigated in one single investigation, and that tests should be available for all of them. It is known among factor analysts that at least four tests are needed to determine each factor sufficiently for a suitable identification and separation, so that on the whole 480 tests as a minimum would be needed in a satisfactory study. (We are assuming here that each of the four tests would be so constructed and selected that it did in fact measure what it was meant to measure; this cannot be assumed of course, and consequently many more tests would in reality be required.) If we assume that each test required ten minutes for both instruction and administration (and this is a gross underestimate for the length of time required by a reliable test), then 80 hours of testing, or two full weeks of work would be required. Furthermore if the sample of subjects were to be five times the size of the sample of tests, a requirement advocated by factor analysts, then a sample of at least 2.400 subjects would be needed, making a total amount of subject-hours of 192000! It is of course not impossible to conduct such an investigation, but it has never been done, and it is unlikely that many subjects would be found to give the time and energy required to such a project. Furthermore, it cannot be assumed that working for two weeks non-stop on intelligence tests would not have effects which change the mental habits and work practices of the subjects so that early and late tests might not be comparable. There are of course other ways of carrying out the tests of Guilford's hypothesis, but these would require even larger numbers of subject-hours.

In conclusion therefore we may say that Guilford's important attempt to construct a structure-of-intellect model has not been successful, and cannot at the moment dethrone the paradigm originally set up by Spearman and Thurstone. It may add important new primary factors to the model, and it will certainly lead to an innovative search for new and different directions in which mental testing may proceed to add to the orthodox types of tests used over the last 30 to 50 years. Guilford has added to the paradigm; he has certainly not replaced it.

The structure-of-intellect model of Guilford, which we have discussed so far, has also given rise to a good deal of controversy and empirical work with respect to just one of the distinctions made by him, namely that between convergent and divergent types of test. These terms have already been explained, and although they are neither new (Woodworth already used them in 1918), and although similar tests were already used by Spearman and Cattell to define a factor of "fluency" before the war, it is only since Guilford's advocacy that interest has begun to center on tests of divergent ability. The hope has been that here we might be dealing with something new and rather different from typical IQ tests, and might even be tapping some such complex abilities as "creativity" or "originality".

The work of *Getzels* and *Jackson* (1962) has often been quoted in this connection, and their argument has become widely known and accepted. They explain their point of view as follows: "Our argument then is this. Giftedness in children has most frequently been defined as a score on an intelligence test, and typically the study of the so-called gifted child has been equated with the study of the single IQ variable. Involved in this definition of giftedness are several types of confusion, if not of outright error. First, there is the limitation of the single metric itself, which not only restricts our perspective of the more general phenomenon, but places on the one concept a greater theoretical and predictive burden than it was intended to carry. For all practical purposes, the term 'gifted child' has become synonymous with the expression 'child with a high IQ', thus blinding us to other forms of excellence. And second, within the universe of intellectual functions themselves, we have most often behaved as if the intelligence test represented an adequate sampling of all mental abilities and cognitive processes. Despite the already substantial and increasing literature regarding the intellectual functions closely allied to creativity, we still treat the latter concept as applicable only to performance in one or more of the arts to the exclusion of other types of achievement requiring inventiveness, originality, and perfection. The term 'creative child', in becoming synonymous with the expression 'child with artistic talents', has limited our attempts to identify and foster cognitive abilities related to creative functioning in areas other than the arts.

Despite its longevity there is after all nothing inevitable about the use of IQ in defining giftedness. Indeed we might argue that in many ways this definition is only a historical accident – a consequence of the fact that early inquiries in the field has as their context the classroom and its attendant concern with academic abilities and achievement. If we were to move the focus of inquiry from the classroom setting, we might identify cognitive qualities defining giftedness for other situations just as the IQ did in the classroom. Should we change only the original criteria of learning, we might change the cognitive qualities defining giftedness even in the classroom. For example, if we recognize that learning involves the production of novelty as well as the remembrance of course content – *discovering* as well as *recalling* – measures of creativity as well as IQ become appropriate defining characteristics of giftedness.

The issues we have raised are, of course, not new or unique to us. The American Association for Gifted Children some time ago argued that qualities other than IQ be included in the conception of giftedness, and defined the gifted individual as 'a person whose performance in any line of socially useful endeavor is consistently superior. This definition includes those talented in art, music, drama, and mathematics, as well as those who possess mechanical and social skills and those with high abstract verbal intelligence.' Despite such calls for freeing the concept of giftedness from its one-sided attachment to the IQ metric and for broadening the base for examining intellectual and social excellence in children, the essential point remains: in research as in educational practice, the IQ metric has continued to be the predominant and often exclusive criterion of giftedness. Accordingly, we undertook to examine empirically the consequences of applying other conceptions as giftedness as well as 'high IQ' to the study of children."

Getzels and Jackson used five tests of divergent ability:

1. *Word association.* Meanings and uses required of common words with multiple meanings e. g. 'bolt', 'sack'. Scored both for number of definitions, and number of radically different meanings.

2. *Uses for things.* As many different uses as possible to be given for objects such as 'brick', 'paper-clip'. Scored for number of uses and originality of uses.

3. *Hidden shapes* (part of Cattell's Objective-Analytic Test Battery). 18

simple geometrical figures, each followed by four complex figures. Subject required to find the geometric figure hidden in the more complex pattern.

4. *Fables*. Four fables were presented in which the last lines were missing. The subject was required to provide three different endings to each story, one moralistic, one humorous and one sad.

5. *Make-up Problems*. Four complex paragraphs containing many numerical statements were presented. Subject required to make up as many mathematical problems as possible from them (but no need to solve them). Scored on number, complexity, appropriateness and originality of problems.

The five separate measures were then combined into one composite measure of creativity, and contrasting groups were formed, one high creativity group but below the top scoring 20% in IQ, and one high IQ group which was below the top scoring creativity group. Out of 533 original subjects studied, the high creativity group contained 26 and the high IQ group 28 children. It was found that the high creativity group equalled the high IQ group in scholastic achievement, in spite of having an average IQ 23 points lower (127 against 150). Teachers however approved more strongly of the high IQ group than of the high creativity group. Another difference was attitudes to success in adult life. In the high IQ group there was quite good correspondence between the qualities they valued for themselves, and the qualities which they thought would be conducive to success in adult life; similarly there was quite a close correspondence between qualities they said they would like to possess themselves and qualities they thought teachers tended to approve of. For the high creativity group, neither of these correspondence held to nearly the same extent. One of the qualities the creative group valued considerably more highly than did the high IQ group was a sense of humour!

Getzels and Jackson have deservedly attracted a good deal of criticism (e. g. *De Mille* and *Merryfield,* 1962). Children selected for the study were quite atypical, the mean IQ being 132. The way the test scores were combined, and the way the contrasting groups formed, are not made clear in the book. Getzels and Jackson seem only to be reporting what favours their own view point and to be omitting crucial information, such as the characteristics of the children who scored highly in both intelligence and creativity. The statistical treatment used is sketchy and often misleading. Last, and most important, the creativity tests in this research did not correlate with each other to a much higher degree than they correlated with IQ, and this indicates that the so-called creativity tests may simply measure general intelligence for the most part, and in addition perhaps a primary factor of fluency, as Spearman had already suggested (*Thorndike,* 1963.)

Replications of this work have given mixed results (*Torrance,* 1965; *Yamamoto,* 1965), but on the whole support this view. *Hasan* and *Butcher* (1966) carried out a fairly precise repetition of the Getzels and Jackson study, using 175 Scottish children who were unselected for ability. As expected, they found very much more over-lap between the measure of intelligence and those of creativity than had been found in the Chicago studies. They also found that IQ correlated more highly with total "creativity" score than did nine out of ten of the separate "creativity" tests!

One of the most unsatisfactory aspects of all the research that has been carried out along these lines has been the failure to provide good evidence for the validity of the tests. To call children "creative" or "original" simply because they give more alternative answers on simple tests such as those used seems premature, in the absence of an outside criterion of creativity or originality. *Datta* (1964a, 1964b), who uses as his criterion scientific output in terms of patents, published papers and so forth among 1.300 scientists (both academic and industrial), failed to find any marked positive relations, and indeed there is a dearth of positive results along these lines in the literature. Before taking too seriously the claim that these divergent tests actually measure something called "creativity", one would want to have evidence that there was a general factor of creativity which was not just specific to one particular line of work; that such creativity could indeed be tapped by simple tests of the divergent type; and that this alleged ability was indeed independent of IQ. The evidence on any of these points is far from reassuring. In England, the concept of divergent tests as measures of creativity has been championed particularly by *Hudson* (1966) whose interesting work suggests a relationship between divergent thinking and preference for the arts, and convergent thinking and a preference for science. It seems likely that these, as well as most of the other relationships discovered, are due to personality factors. Spearman already suggested that fluency was related more to extraverted personalities than to any cognitive ability, and the recent work of *Di Scipio* (1971) and *Eysenck* and *Eysenck* (1976) suggests that this is indeed so, although other personality factors also play a part. The work of *Wankowski* (1973) has shown a definite relationship between personality and choice of subject studied at university, roughly agreeing with Hudson's findings, and this hypothesis would seem to give us the best explanation of the findings on "creativity" to date. It certainly cannot be concluded that the data support the massive claims and assertions made by Getzels and Jackson in their inaugural statement. Divergent tests tap an interesting ability which is very much a part of general intelligence, highly correlates with other tests of general intelligence, but is also to some extent influenced by personality factors which may link it with certain academic preferences, and possibly even with "creativity" (*Eysenck* and *Eysenck*, 1976). To claim that it presents an alternative to classical IQ testing is going altogether beyond the evidence[10].

---

10 More detailed treatment of the whole topic of creativity, which is only incidental to the theme of this book can be found in *Butcher* (1968), *Lytton* (1971), *Taylor* and *Barron* (1963), and *Wallach* and *Kogan* (1965).

Eysenck and the Splitting of the IQ

> In science one must search for ideas; if there are no ideas then there is no science. A knowledge of facts is only valuable in so far as facts conceal ideas; facts without ideas clutter up the mind and the memory
>
> V. G. Belinskii

One unresolved problem in IQ testing has always been the question of speed vs. power. People differ with respect to the speed with which they can solve those problems which they can solve, and they differ with respect to the difficulty level of the problems which they succeed in solving. Do these two aspects of problem solving refer to the same ability, or not? It is conceivable that some people have a more profound type of intelligence which enables them to solve difficult problems, while others have a more facile superficial type of intelligence which enables them to solve easy problems more quickly than the more profound thinker, but which fails them when difficult problems are requiring a solution[11]. Intelligence tests are sometimes given with a time limit, sometimes without; some tests, such as Raven's Matrices, has norms both for a 20 minute time limit version and an unlimited time version. Usually timed and untimed versions of the same test correlate together quite highly, but as the two versions have much material in common such a correlation is almost meaningless. This problem formed the starting point of a series of studies in which *Eysenck, Furneaux* and *White* (1973) attempted to look at the fundamental psychological processes involved in IQ testing (*Eysenck,* 1973).

This problem is only soluble if looked at in a wider context, namely that of the unit of analysis in IQ testing. All the classical writers in this field have confined themselves to the analysis of intercorrelations between test scores; yet it is by no means clear why test scores should be regarded as in any sense fundamental. Psychologists familiar with the test responses of children and adults know that identical scores can often be achieved along quite different routes. Fundamentally, a person can solve a given IQ test problem correctly (R), incorrectly (W), abandon the problem because he thinks that it is too difficult (A), or fail to attempt it altogether – either for lack of time, or because he does not think that he will be able to solve it (F). Consider now five children who have been given a test containing 10 items, and all of whom obtain an identical score of 6. Table 8.1 shows an hypothetical set of solutions.

It will be seen that although all five children obtain the same score, they all obtain it along different routes. John works up through the easy to the more difficult problems, until he reaches problem 7 which he believes (rightly or

11 *Spearman* (1927) argued that "it is unnecessary to distinguish between speed and quality of thinking on the assumption that these two characteristics correlate almost perfectly." The assumption seems rather daring, in the absence of any evidence, and *Porebski* (1954, 1960) has thrown much doubt on it at the empirical level (but see *Vincent,* 1955).

Table 8.1. Imaginary responses of five subjects to 10 IQ problems, in terms of right (R), wrong (W), abandoned (A), and failure to attempt (F)

Item	1	2	3	4	5	6	7	8	9	10	Score
John	R	R	R	R	R	R	F	F	F	F	6
Mary	R	W	R	W	R	W	R	R	R	A	6
Joe	R	R	A	R	A	A	R	A	R	R	6
Susie	R	W	A	R	R	A	R	R	W	R	6
Phil	R	R	W	W	F	R	R	R	R	F	6

wrongly) that he cannot solve. Mary gets some difficult problems right, and some easy ones wrong, and finally abandons the most difficult one. Where John is a plodder, she is clearly careless. Joe does not get any answers wrong, but he is easily discouraged, abandoning easy problems when the solution does not come at once, although the fact that he succeeds with more difficult ones shows that he could have solved the abandoned ones. Susie and Phil show a mixture of carelessness and discouragement, with Phil possibly also demonstrating a lack of motivation, seeing that he does not even try some problems he could have solved. It is not at all obvious that the simple score of 6 right, a score which would be produced by all these children, does justice to the observed differences in their problem-solving behaviour. The differences illustrated may seem exaggerated, but each could be duplicated from our records of the behaviour of normal children on typical IQ tests.

Allied to this is another problem. In an untimed test we do not obtain any record of the child's working time, by definition. Even in a timed test we only obtain a total time – all children, for instance, are given 20 minutes for the Raven's Matrices, and consequently all work to this time limit (although some may give up earlier.) But it would seem that we are throwing away an important item of information by neglecting to time each item for each child; clearly it is possible that the brighter child solves a given problem more speedily than a dull one, even though both solve it eventually. Such information of speed of item solution should be available to the investigator if he is to make the most of the information supplied by the child's efforts to solve the battery of IQ problems constituting the test. There are obvious difficulties in making use of such information (how can we compare different children's speed of solution of a given problem when some get the answer right, others get it wrong, others still abandon it, and some in fact never try it at all?) Nevertheless, the existence of such difficulties does not justify us in neglecting possible vital information. Eysenck, Furneaux and White have therefore taken as the starting-out point of their analyses the individual problem solution time, separately tabled for problems correctly done, incorrectly done, or abandoned; this means of course individual testing, and in practice had meant machine testing – the problem is presented on slides, projected on to a screen, and the subject responds by pressing a numbered button which corresponds with the number of the answer he considers correct. An X'' button is also supplied, to be pressed in case of abandonment of the problem, and the time from exposure of the problem to solution or abandonment is automatically recorded by the computer which govern the process.

After each exposure and attempted solution, there is a short breathing space during which the subject is asked to rank the certainty of being right in his answer on a five-point scale. This makes possible analysis of risk-taking and guessing behaviour, and also makes it less likely that the subject will get tired and take involuntary (or voluntary) rest pauses during problem solving time. Problems have known difficulty levels, following the prescription of the Rasch model already discussed in an earlier chapter, and analysis takes these difficulty levels into account. Before looking briefly at the methods of analysis, we may perhaps state the major outcome of the work so far done. It turns out that there are three major, independent aspects of the IQ, as usually measured: (1) mental speed, (2) persistence, and (3) error-checking. Probably the most fundamental cognitive attribute is mental speed, or the speed with which solutions are furnished. Persistence refers to the degree to which a person perseveres with a difficult problem, or conversely the ease with which he gives up. Error-checking refers to the tendency on the part of a person to make errors without checking to see that his solution was in fact correct. *Furneaux* (1973) has shown that in certain circumstances, and for certain populations, these three aspects of the IQ are uncorrelated or independent; it is to be expected that the amount of correlation found will depend on type of test, motivation, instructions, and many other factors, so that we cannot expect independence to occur under all circumstances.

These results suggest that the concept of the IQ has been "split", rather like the atom has been split in physics; we no longer have an indestructible atom, such as was posited by physicists at the beginning of the century, but rather a congeries of elementary particles, baryons, bosons and leptons; we have neutrons, protons, photons, electrons, neutrinos – both in particle and anti-particle form. All of these differ in electric charge, in mass, spin, strangeness, "charm", mean lifetime, and distintegration products. Yet the atom continues to play an important and useful role in physics, and clearly still represents something very real and meaningful, even though no longer conceived as indestructible. In the same way, it may be suggested, can we say that the IQ has been split into component parts, each of which is separately measurable, but without thereby destroying the utility of the concept of the IQ. It may of course be necessary for many practical and theoretical purposes to relate concepts and achievements to these constituent parts separately, and to discover which of them are most closely related to other concepts; it will also be necessary to discover the heritability of the separate aspects of the IQ, and the genetic model which best describes them. But these are tasks for the future; at the moment the work of splitting up the IQ into its component parts has only begun.

Against the background of this theoretical model, we can now try and answer the question put at the beginning of this section. Let us assume that we have administered, without time limit, a battery of IQ test items to a large group of subjects, and that we have timed each solution accurately. Let us discard for our present purpose all the incorrect and abandoned items, and concern ourselves only with the correctly solved items. Let us furthermore look at them from the point of view of the difficulty level of the items in question. When this is done we

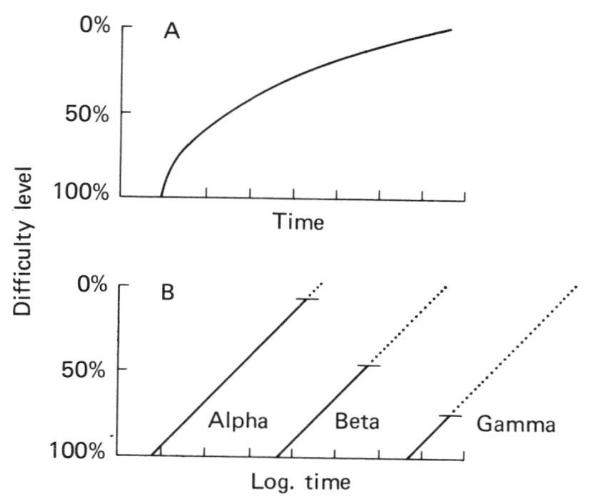

Fig. 8.2. Relation between difficulty level of test items and time (A) and log time (B) needed for completion. Alpha, beta, and gamma are three imaginary subjects of high, medium and low mental speed, respectively. Adapted from *Eysenck* (1953)

find a rather interesting and important general law which suggests that these data, and the way in which they were derived and plotted, are meaningful and scientifically worthwhile. In order to understand this law, let us consider Fig. 8.2. In part A of this Figure we have plotted the time taken by one particular imaginary subject to solve problems of varying levels of difficulty; it will be seen that as difficulty increases, as shown on the ordinate, the time taken to solve the respective items increases disproportionately – hence the curved nature of the line linking up the points representing individual problems. (Difficulty level is here plotted simply in terms of the proportion of random sample of the population which succeeds in solving the various problems, from the easiest, which are solved by 100% of respondents, to the most difficult, which is solved by 0%.)

It is usual, when dealing with time relations, to take the logarithm of the time variable; this can be done with data like those represented in our Figure, and the result is a very startling one, as is shown in Fig. 8.2 B. Let us call the line drawn in Fig. 8.2 A a trace line; when we plot the logarithms of the times taken to solution against the difficulty levels of the problems, then we find that all the trace lines become straight lines; furthermore, lines of different subjects (alpha, beta, gamma in the diagram) are all parallel to each other! This means that the angle they form with the abscissa is a natural constant, and that mental speed is completely represented by the intercept on the abscissa of these trace lines! This may be a very fundamental natural law, and as the original work has since been replicated it seems that we may have to take these relationships seriously. Much further work will have to be done, however, in order to extend the observed relationships from one kind of IQ test to another, and to demonstrate the predictability of one from the other. However that may be, clearly alpha is in a very meaningful way the quickest of our subjects, while gamma is the slowest.

We further see that the measurement here implied is of a more fundamental kind than that usual in IQ testing, partaking of the natural physical system in which we usually express the measurable properties of physical objects.

The Figure also allows us to incorporate persistence. Each trace line has been cut off at some point, and continued by a stippled line; this indicates that the persistence of each subject has caused him to fail on, or abandon, items of a higher degree of difficulty. It is conceivable (and indeed found in actual practice) that a person who is relatively slow nevertheless can do better (in terms of total number of problems correctly solved) than does another who is quicker in terms of item solution times. This is possible where the former gives up prematurely on items he could have solved successfully, whereas the second continues to try for a solution for a much longer time. Fortunately this persistence difference does not interfere in any way with the measurement of our mental speed variable, as it does not alter the position of the intercept of the trace line on the abscissa. Neither does error checking influence the position of the intercept, in so far as our analysis takes into account only correct solutions; the number or duration of incorrect solutions is irrelevant. (Time used for checking is of course part of the measurement taken.)

On the theoretical side, *Furneaux* (1973) has suggested that what may be involved in problem solving activity may be some kind of scanning mechanism the speed of which determines the probability of a right solution being brought into focus more or less quickly. If we join this notion with that of information processing, to be discussed presently, we may have here not only the suggestion of a useful theory of intellectual functioning, but also an argument against those who abandoned the whole theory of "speed" as underlying intelligence because of the failure of reaction time experiments to correlate with intelligence tests. We have already seen in our first chapter that while simple reaction times do not correlate with intelligence, increasing the amount of information having to be processed (e. g. by having several lamps the flashing of any of which has to be responded to by pressing a button positioned underneath that lamp) produces significant correlations with intelligence. As the number of combinations increases, to the amount of information conveyed increases logarithmically; this very simple test therefore seems to require a scanning process which sorts out the required signal-response coordination, and produces the correlation with IQ as a function of the amount of scanning required. Scanning may be the physiological basis underlying Spearman's laws of neogenesis.

A statistical model, corresponding to our verbal description, has been presented by *White* (1973); this is based in part on Furneaux's conceptual model, and in part on the logistic latent trait model for test scores suggested by *Birnbaum* (1968). It would not be appropriate to discuss this rather technical model here[12], but we may note a typical result from testing the model against some empirical data. Table 8.2 shows speed, accuracy, and persistence scores and number of abandonments for each of 4 subjects, all having the same total score, all having correctly solved 10 out of 20 problems.

A test of conventional design would not have differentiated between these

12 Appendix C gives a brief summary of the algorithms used in the analysis.

Table 8.2. Scores on speed, accuracy, and persistence components of IQ by four subjects having identical total scores on 20-item test. Adapted from *White* (1973)

Subject	Abandonments	Speed	Accuracy	Persistence
A	3	0.99	0.40	0.84
B	2	0.99	0.39	1.07
C	1	0.99	0.08	1.35
D	1	0.97	0.79	1.47

four subjects, as all have the same total score. However, the model discussed here responds vigorously and apparently with good sense to individual differences. The four subjects here illustrated had very similar mean times to correct response, and this is indicated in the model by giving them very similar speed scores (in the total sample the speed scores ranged from 0.01 to 0.99!) Subjects A and B have virtually identical scores on speed and accuracy. Subject B has 1 less abandonment and this is reflected in a higher persistence score. Subjects C and D not only have identical total scores and similar mean times to correct response; they also have the same number of abandonments, and the model correctly gives them very similar persistence scores.

Perhaps the most striking feature in Table 8.2 is the difference in accuracy scores for these same two subjects. We have noted that these two individuals have identical total scores and the same number of abandonments, as well as quite similar mean times to correct response and quite similar mean times to abandonment. Why then do they show such a striking difference in accuracy scores? Things seem even more striking when we note that of the 10 problems correctly solved, 7 were the same for both subjects. The reason for the apparent discrepancy becomes quite apparent when we note that the mean difficulty level of the remaining 3 correctly solved problems was considerably higher for subject D than for subject C. It is gratifying that the model is sensitive to such small but quite important differences among response patterns. Note that the model goes well beyond a simple counting of R, W, A and F items, and their latencies; it also takes into account, e. g. the difficulty levels of the respective items. The model is still undergoing changes and improvements, but on the whole it seems to fit empirical data surprisingly well.

It might be thought that the persistence and error factors might be more in the nature of personality (non-cognitive) factors, as opposed to mental speed, which is more likely to be a cognitive factor. Little evidence exists on this point, and future work will naturally seek to answer this quite clear-cut question. There is no doubt, however, that personality factors can produce quite significant differences in performance characteristics on this model, as shown for instance by *Brierley* (1961.) Brierley tested forty neurotic subjects, subdivided into hysterics (extraverted) and dysthymics (introverted), and twenty normal subjects, all of average or above-average intelligence. The groups were matched on age and score on a Vocabulary test, and were administered the Nufferno Speed Test, which consists of eighteen scored items, all of similar difficulty level

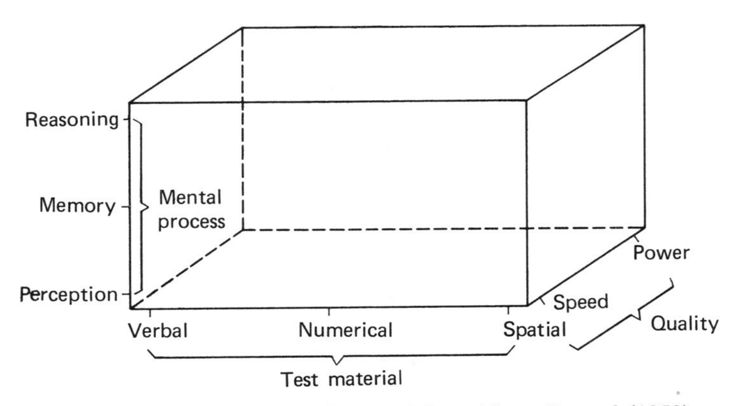

Fig. 8.3. Structure-of-intellect model of intelligence. Adapted from *Eysenck* (1953)

and all of the Thurstone letter-series type. It was found that the dysthymics were significantly slower than the control group, with the hysterics intermediate. Hysterics were the least accurate, with dysthymics intermediate. Thus hysterics, as would be predicted in terms of personality theory (*Eysenck,* 1967) were characterized by low accuracy, and dysthymics by low speed, with both groups tending to be both slower and less accurate than the control group. This experiment suggests the possibilities opened up by the more detailed analysis of IQ test results for diagnostic and other clinical purposes; hitherto little use has been made of such analyses for the testing of psychotic and neurotic subjects, or for mental deficiencies occurring in drug addicts, senile patients, and other psychiatric groups.

Eysenck (1953) suggested a model-of-intellect which while it predicted some of the elements of Guilford's model differed strikingly from it in one respect at least. The model is reproduced in Fig. 8.3, and it will be seen that like Guilford's later model it also defined a cube made up by the intersection of different modalities. In our case these are mental processes (like reasoning, memory, perception, etc.), test material (verbal, numerical, spatial, etc.), and a variable called "quality", by which was meant the constituents of our present model, i. e. mental speed, error-checking, and persistence. It was thought then that the term "power" probably represented a combination of persistence and error-checking, so that a person who persisted in his mental efforts until a solution was reached, and who checked his operations so that no errors slipped through, would be appearing, as compared with another person lacking in these qualities, but equal in mental speed, to possess the attribute of power". Clearly Eysenck's concept of mental processes" closely resembles Guilford's operations"; Eysenck's test materials" corresponds to Guilford's contents". However, Guilford's products" are replaced by the concept of quality", and as we have seen, there is little evidence for Guilford's suggestion, but a great deal for Eysenck's.

If we can derive a model of the intellect, therefore, from the existing literature, it may be suggested that a combination of Spearman's *g,* Thurstone's primary abilities (grouped under mental processes and test material), and the break-down of the IQ into speed, persistence and error-checking, may be the best available at the moment. Much remains to be done, of course, but to date no better model seems to be in sight.

One last point may be mentioned in connection with the splitting of the IQ into its component processes. We have stated, in criticism of Guilford, that he may have mistaken an analysis of test material into factors for an analysis of the intellect into cognitive operations. This indeed is an obvious difficulty with the method of factor analysis; it tells us nothing about the derivation and causal meaning of the factors discovered. The situation is rather different in the case of such variables as mental speed, error-checking and persistence. These are mental processes by definition; they are not deduced from complex statistical calculations using methods which are of doubtful relevance to a psychological analysis of mental processes; and they have direct meaning and relevance in a demonstrable manner. These are important advantages. It has often been suggested by opponents of factor analysis (or even of statistical analysis altogether) that these methods cannot deal with mental processes, because they are confined to dealing with certain results of these processes which may bear no direct relation to the processes themselves. Factors have to be interpreted in order to be psychologically meaningful, and such interpretations are subjective and may easily be mistaken; it is difficult to see how they could be objectified, or how we could test their relevance experimentally. Such objections cannot lie against the three factors into which the IQ has been broken down; the analysis may be erroneous, and better analyses may be possible, but whatever it is, it is a psychological analysis first and foremost, with recognizable psychological content. Furthermore, the hypotheses embodied in the concepts involved are empirically testable; there is direct evidence for a factor of persistence (*Eysenck,* 1970), for instance, and the relation of this factor to results from an analysis of IQ tests along the lines here described can easily be ascertained. We may conclude that the causal analysis of the components of the IQ has certain definite advantages over simple factorial studies of total test scores.

9 Developmental Models: Piaget and Jensen

Non que les idées que nous formons ne puissent être just logiquement, mais nous ne savons pas si elles sont vraies

M. Proust

Piaget and the Stages of Development of Intelligence

The work of *Piaget* (1950, 1956, 1958) was at first unjustifiably neglected in the English-speaking countries, and then equally unjustifiably elevated to the status of sacred doctrine (*Phillips,* 1975). Piaget is fundamentally concerned with the stages through which intellectual development passes, and not at all concerned with individual differences, or intelligence as measured by I. Q. tests. This might seen to suggest that this work could not be very relevant to this book, but such a view would be mistaken. If the child, in growing up, passes from stage A, through B and C, to stages D, E, F etc., then clearly these stages fulfil the same function for anyone interested in the measurement of intelligence as did the age-related test items in Binet's work. We might classify a child's mental age in terms of the stage which he had reached, and then obtain something like on I. Q. by relating this stage to his actual chronological age. Piaget himself would not be interested in this and would consider it an abuse of his theoretical work, but the question of whether such a scheme would be workable, and how it would relate to ordinary measures of I. Q., is an important one. Piaget's work is sometimes suggested as an alternative to orthodox psychometric intelligence testing. As we shall see, his tests and test items behave very much in the same way as do those customarily used by psychometrists interested in intelligence testing, and so far as they do they suggest that they belong to the same paradigm. The conclusion would then be that Piaget's system is not in fact an alternative, but at best a supplement to the orthodox system we have been describing throughout this book.

A brief account of the developmental stages which are posited by Piaget will here be given, but his system is a very complex one, and it cannot be said that it is easy to understand. The elephantine opacity of Piaget's style, and his entanglement in philosophical arguments both contribute to an obfuscation which envelops even secondary sources attempting to explain his system. *Flavell* (1963), *Inhelder* (1953), and *Butcher* (1968) give some idea of Piaget's system; his own publications are too numerous to mention in detail, and even in their original French too *embrouillé* to be readily intelligible. Piaget is very much the philosopher rather than the experimentalist, and he has described his field of study correctly as "genetic epistemology", a phrase which suggests his dual interest in biological adaptation and development, and in the study of knowledge. Piaget attempts to explain what this means in the first paragraph in his book on the Psychology of Intelligence:

"Every psychological explanation comes sooner or later to lean either on biology or on logic (or on sociology, but this in turn leads to the same alternatives). For some writers mental phenomena become intelligible only when related to the organism. This view is of course inescapable when we study the elementary functions (perception, motor functions, etc.) in which intelligence originates. But we can hardly see neurology explaining why 2 and 2 make 4, or why the laws of deduction are forced on the mind of necessity. Thus arises the second tendency, which consists in regarding logical and mathematical relations as irreducible, and in making an analysis of the higher intellectual functions depend on an analysis of them. But it is questionable whether logic, regarded as something eluding the attempts of experimental psychology to explain it, can in its turn legitimately explain anything in psychological experience. Formal logic, or logistics, is simply the axiomatics of states of equilibrium of thought, and the positive science corresponding to this axiomatics is none other than the psychology of thought. With the tasks thus allotted, the psychology of intelligence must assuredly continue to take account of logistic discoveries, but these will never go so far as to dictate to psychology its own solutions; they will merely raise problems for it.

So we must start from this dual nature of intelligence as something both biological and logical."

Much of what Piaget has to say is not directly relevant to our purpose; we may begin a consideration of the "structure" or "organisation" of intelligence, which he considers as changing qualitatively in several main periods of development from birth to adolescence. Each of these structures as its succeeds the previous one, develops from and incorporates the preceding structure, giving rise to a kind of hierarchical development. At each stage new kinds of concepts are attained, thus opening up the possibility of many new problem-solving capabilities. Much of Piaget's empirical work has been devoted to the establishment of these successive stages through observation and experiment. He believes that these stages always occur in the same order, although he admits that there is a certain amount of variation in actual chronological age. It is this that has encouraged several American investigators to look at these variations in the hope of aligning Piaget's system with modern intelligence testing.

Piaget's system distinguishes four main periods. The first of these is the period of *sensory-motor operations,* extending from birth to 18 months or 2 years. The second period is one of *preoperational representations,* lasting until the age of about 7. The third period deals with *concrete operations* and extends to between the ages of 11 and 12. Finally, the period of *formal operations* begins and is typically completed at about the age of 15. Piaget also describes sub-periods and sub-sub-periods within these main areas. Actually Piaget says very little about the first period, which he regards rather as the base for the development of intelligence in the adult sense. It is as he sometimes puts it an *intelligence of the limbs,* the coordination of movement and the differentiation of the self from environment; at this level, "penser, c'est opérer". By this Piaget means that the more abstract kinds of cognitive thinking have evolved from simpler manipulations of ideas, and that these in turn evolved from physical manipulations in this early period of development.

Piaget's descriptions of the other three periods are largely based on observations on his own children, perhaps, one might think, a somewhat limited base for the construction of such a very large intellectual edifice. In the second period the child advances from mainly sensory-motor manipulations to the first appearance of inner, symbolic, abstract representation. Here and in the third period, important changes are taking place in the child's conception of causality, time, space, quantity, chance, morality, and various other basic categories and constructs. Piaget has been particularly concerned with the developing ideas of children during the pre-operational period and in the early part of the period of concrete operations, about the nature of the world, and about cause and effect in nature. Pre-causal thinking, i. e. thinking in terms of "animism", "realism", and "artificialism", is superceded by more objective and scientific modes of thought. The final period of development then leads on to adult modes of thinking and conception.

In the course of his work Piaget has devised a large number of very ingenious "tests", although this term may give the wrong idea of what Piaget actually does. His tests are clinically oriented procedures for assessing the child's mental development, and he expressly designates his methods as the "méthode clinique", to contrast it with a proper psychometric or experimental approach. The technique relies a lot on asking the child questions, and delving in detail into the reasons for his answers. That means of course that these "tests" are not in any way standardized, and do not give a quantitative answer to such questions as the age at which the problem is first solved. Most of these "tests" can be objectified and properly scored, and as we shall see English and American psychologists have successfully done so. As an example of the type of test used by Piaget, let us consider the development of the child's capacity to grasp and utilize the concepts of *conservation* of numbers, weight, and volume, in that order, which marks the development of operational thinking. At the age of seven or eight years of age, the child is already advanced in concrete operations and implicitly accepts the notion that volume is conserved, that is, that the quantity of volume of a ball of clay or a jar of liquid is to be conceived as invariant regardless of its changing shape (a round ball of clay, as contrasted with the same ball of clay flattened out like a pancake) or the variety of differently shaped flasks into which the liquid can be put.

At a pre-operational age or state of development, the child does not assume this invariance. To a child in this early stage of development a round ball of clay is flattened out and made to look "bigger", so that he actually believes that the quantity of clay has been increased. Similarly, when he sees liquid poured from a shallow, broad bowl into a tall, slender flask, he believes that a change in quantity has taken place. Piaget has been extremely ingenious in devising means of assessing children's conservation concepts in volume, number, length, area, time, weight, and so on. Similar measures have been made of the development of other conceps in other areas; it would take us much too far to discuss these in this volume.

Have Piaget's notions found empirical support by workers not inside his system? By and large, the answer must be yes. The work of *Laurendeau* and *Pinard* (1962) for instance, concerned in particular with the child's conception of physical causality, shows the kind of advance in conception from an egocentric to an objective view of the world, as postulated by Piaget. Other support has come from the work of *Dennis* and *Russell* (1940) and *Dennis* (1943), and of *Dennis* and *Mallenger* (1949). *Lunzer* (1955) pointed out that there should be a direct and measurable change in the performance of children on certain kinds of test items according to whether they had or had not yet attained a particular stage of Piagetian progression. He constructed various types of analogy items, both verbal and numerical, the hypothesis being that some of these would clearly demand reasoning at the stage of formal operations for correct answers to be given. The hypothesis was well borne out by the results, although the number of cases in each age group was rather small. Other writers have not been so successful, and on the whole it is probably fair to say that while there clearly is considerable development which can be roughly described in terms of Piaget's categories, other descriptions might equally apply, and may be superior to his. Most apparent of all however is the fact that children of a given age differ considerably in the stage of development they may have reached, very much as one would expect if Piaget's "tests" measured something like general intelligence.

There are indeed definite links between development in the sense that Piaget uses the term, and intelligence. Indeed, Piaget uses the term "intelligence" quite frequently, often in the titles of his books and articles. Note further that the age at which, according to Piaget, the major change from concrete to formal operations occurs, i. e. between the ages of 11 and 12, is the age also at which in England and Scotland there is a break between primary and secondary education, a break based largely on traditional educational work and intelligence test results. Also there is good agreement between the psychometric point of view and that of Piaget about the age at which mental development is complete in most individuals, i. e. around the age of 15 or 16. As *Butcher* (1968) points out, it seems very possible that Piaget-type observation and intelligence testing have both independently and almost accidentally hit upon the completion of biological or neurological development. There are other lines of evidence pointing in the same direction. Channel capacity for intake of information (in the technical, information theory" sense of the word) increases rapidly and almost linearly from ages 10 to 14, and then much more slowly, reaching an asymptote value between 14 and 18. What increases after 15, as observed by common sense, is attainment, and perhaps, if one accepts Cattell's distinction, "crystallized intelligence."

What now about the direct comparison between Piaget-type tests and typical psychometric tests? *Vernon* (1965) carried out a factor analysis of the intercorrelations between a large number of Piagetian tests along with conventional psychometric measures of intelligence and found that the Piagetian tests were heavily loaded on *g*. In fact, Piaget's tests measured little else apart from *g*, i. e. the non-*g* variance seemed to be task specific, that is to say it had nothing in common with other Piagetian tests or with other conventional IQ tests. Similarly, *Tuddenham* (1970) gave a battery of Piaget-type tests, along with Raven's Matrices and the Peabody Picture Vocabulary Test, to a large number of elementary schoolchildren and found that the matrices test gave higher correlations, ranging from 0.24 to 0.50, than the Peabody test, which gave values of 0.13 to 0.37 for a similar though not identical set of Piagetian items. Correlations between the matrices and a composite of six or eight items of the Piaget-type amounted to 0.60; this is quite a high correlation considering the relative unreliability of Piaget-type items. We may conclude from these studies that Piaget-type items behave very much as do other good intelligence test items of the psychometric kind, and that they measure the same kind of intelligence as does the usual range of tests described in this book. Piaget's stages of development are an interesting extension of Binet's idea of mental age, and they particularize the changes that take place with age. Piaget's system therefore is not an alternative to the psychometric system described in this book; it merely extends it and makes certain suggestions about the precise nature of the changes that take place as a child's mental age increases.

It is noteworthy that there is also considerable agreement between Piaget-type tests and ordinary mental tests when we look at the performance of different racial groups. *Vernon* (1965) and *MacArthur* (1968, 1969) found that Arctic Eskimos excelled white urban Canadian children on Piaget's tests, although only very slightly; this is in good agreement with what is known about their performance on culture-fair IQ test. *De Lemos* (1969) found the performance of Australian Aborigines markedly retarded as compared with European and American norms, and the same is true of the performance on IQ tests. *Tuddenham* (1970) gave a battery of ten Piaget-type tests to some 500 white, negro and oriental children in three Californian communities. Negroes did less well than whites on every item, which is again similar to their performance on ordinary IQ tests. The average percentage of children passing the concept tested by the particular items was 32.6% for whites and 15.9% for Negroes. Oriental children, on the other hand, were more advanced than white children on seven of the ten items, and as we have seen before the IQ of Orientals tends to be somewhat higher than that of whites. There was also a substantial correlation between the Piaget-type items and socio-economic status, as indexed by father's occupation, even though, as Tuddenham notes, "these items tend to involve reasoning about matters universally available to observation, e. g. the horizontality of water levels. It is hard to see how social advantage could be a very large factor in success on some of these items. The genetic selection implicit in occupational level may have more to do with it." (p. 65). In all these racial and class comparisons, therefore, Piaget-type tests give results essentially similar to, if not identical with, those obtained with IQ tests. Unless future research very much changes the picture, we must conclude that Piaget's work supports, rather than confounds, the traditional paradigm.

Jensen's Two-Level Theory of Mental Ability

Science is willingness to accept facts even when they are opposed to wishes

B. F. Skinner

One of the earliest definitions of intelligence was the capacity to learn, or the ability to acquire ability. This formulation is too general to be of much use, because there are many things which we learn which have little cognitive content, and correlate very little with intelligence. Learning to play tennis, or billiards, or football are examples; so are abilities to learn to drive a motor car, to make love, or to sit on top of a pole for four weeks in order to be mentioned in the Guinness Book of Records. Nevertheless, the general notion has a meaning which can be realised when we recall that mental tests can be ordered along a continuum going from simple to complex, and that the intercorrelations among tests are roughly related to the degree of complexity along this continuum. Such relatively pure tests of *g* as Raven's Progressive Matrices show increasing correlations with other tasks as one moves along the continuum from simple to complex. The factor loadings of psychological tests on the general factor of intelligence are roughly proportional to the psychological judgement of the task degree of complexity.

This notion links up very well with the theory proposed by *Gagné* (1968) in which he tried to construct a generalised learning hierarchy in terms of different levels of complexity. This hierarchy, which has some interesting resemblances to Piaget's levels of development, lists in order: stimulus-response, motor chaining, verbal chaining, multiple discrimination, concepts, principles and problem solving. *Alvord* (1969), in his research on transfer in learning hierarchy, has shown that measures of general intelligence become increasingly predictive of performance at each successively higher level in the learning hierarchy. Similarly, *Fox* and *Taylor* (1967) constructed a battery of training tests to represent different levels of complexity in terms of Gagné's theory. They compared two groups of Army recruits on all these tasks, one having high, the other low scores on an omnibus test of general intelligence. The performance of these two groups diverged increasingly as they went from the lower to the higher tasks in the hierarchy. *Jensen* (1970) reports several other studies all in agreement with this notion that *the more complex the learning task, the greater the IQ required for its accomplishment.*

Jensen has summarized the conditions under which learning does correlate with IQ; complexity of the material to be learned is only one of many.

1. "Learning is more highly correlated with IQ when it is *intentional* and the task calls forth conscious mental effort and is paced in such a way as to permit the subject to think. It is possible to learn passively without thinking, by mere repetition of simple material; such learning is only slightly correlated with IQ. In fact, *negative* correlations between learning speed and IQ have been found in

some simple tasks which could only be learned by simple repetition or rote learning but were disguised to appear more complex so as to evoke thinking". Persons with higher IQs engaged in more complex mental processes (reasoning, hypothesis testing, etc.) which in this specially contrived task only interfered with rote learning. Persons of lower IQ were not hindered by this interference of more complex mental processes and learned the material by simple rote association.

2. Learning is more highly correlated with IQ when the material to be learned is *hierarchical,* in the sense that the learning of later elements depends upon mastery of earlier elements. A task of many elements in which the order of learning the elements has no effect on learning rate or level of final performance is less correlated with IQ than a task in which there is some more or less optimal order in which the elements are learned, and the acquisition of earlier elements in the sequence facilitates the acquisation of later elements.

3. Learning is more highly correlated with IQ when the material to be learned is *meaningful,* in the sense that it is in some way related to other knowledge or experience already possessed by the learner. Rote learning of the serial order of a list of meaningless three-letter nonsense syllables or colored forms, for example, shows little correlation with IQ. In contrast, learning the essential content of a meaningful prose passage is more highly correlated with IQ.

4. Learning is more highly correlated with IQ when the nature of the learning task permits *transfer* from somewhat different but related past learning. Outside the intentionally artifical learning tasks of the experimental psychology laboratory, little that we are called upon to learn beyond infancy is *entirely* new and unrelated to anything we had previously learned. "Making more and better use of elements of past learning in learning something new" – in short, the transfer of learning – is positively correlated with IQ.

5. Learning is more highly correlated with IQ when it is *insightful,* that is to say, when the learning involves "catching on" or "getting the idea." Learning to name the capital cities of the 50 States, for example, does not permit this aspect of learning to come into play and would therefore be less correlated with IQ than, say, learning to prove the Pythagorean Theorem.

6. Learning is more highly correlated with IQ when the material to be learned is of *moderate difficulty and complexity.* If a learning task is too complex, everyone, regardless of his IQ, flounders and falls back on simpler processes such as trial and error and rote association. Complexity, as contrasted with sheer difficulty due to the amount of material to be learned, refers to the number of elements that must be integrated simultaneously for the learning to progress.

7. Learning is more highly correlated with IQ when the *amount of time* for learning is fixed for all students. This condition becomes increasingly important to the extent that the other conditions listed above are brought into play.

8. Learning is more highly correlated with IQ the more the learning material is *age-related.* Some things can be learned almost as easily by a 9-year-old child as by an 18-year-old. Such learning shows relatively little correlation with IQ. Other forms of learning, on the other hand, are facilitated by maturation and

show a substantial correlation with age. The concept of "learning readiness" is based on this fact. Tests of readiness which predict rate of progress in certain kinds of learning, particularly reading and mathematics, are highly correlated with IQ.

9. Learning is more highly correlated with IQ at an *early stage* of "learning something new" than is performance or gains later in the course of practice. That is, IQ is related more to rate of acquisition of new skills or knowledge rather than to rate of improvement or degree of proficiency at later stages of learning, assuming that new material and concepts have not been introduced at the intermediate stages. Practice makes a task less cognitively demanding and decreases its correlation with IQ. With practice the learner's performance becomes more or less automatic and hence less demanding of conscious effort and attention. For example, learning to read music is an intellectually demanding task for the beginner. But for an experienced musician it is an almost automatic process which makes little conscious demand on the higher mental processes. Individual differences in proficiency at this stage are scarcely related to IQ. Much the same thing is true of other skills such as typing, stenography, and Morse code sending and receiving.

It can be seen that all of the above listed conditions which influence the correlation between learning and IQ are highly characteristic of much of school learning. Hence the impression of teachers that IQ is an index of learning aptitude is quite justifiable. Under the above listed conditions of learning, the low IQ child is indeed a "slow learner" as compared with children of high IQ.

Very similar conditions pertain to the relation between memory or retention and IQ. When persons are equated in degree of original learning of simple material, their retention measured at a later time is only slightly if at all correlated with IQ. The retention of more complex learning, however, involves meaningfulness and the way in which the learner has transformed or encoded the material. This is related to the degree of the learner's understanding, the extent to which the learned material is linked into the learner's preexisting associative and conceptual network, and the learner's capacity for conceptual reconstruction of the whole material from a few recollected principles. The more that these aspects of memory can play a part in the material to be learned and later recalled, the more that retention measures are correlated with IQ.

These developments, whether along the lines described by Piaget or by Gagné, reflect the transition from one main level of mental development to another; these have been categorised by *White* (1965) as the *associative* and the *cognitive*. The associative level is most in evidence during the pre-school years, and the emergence of the cognitive level becomes manifest between the ages of five and seven in the majority of children. The associative layer, laid down early in development, consists of the capacity for basic aspects of associative learning, discrimination and primary stimulus generalization. The cognitive layer is built on this associative layer but introduces a number of changes, improvements and advances which make performance more like that of human adults. There is for instance a change from narrow to broad transposition; the onset of resistance to classical conditioning; a growth of inference in a problem solving task; a shift from "near receptors" (tactual, kinesthetic, etc.,) to "distance receptors" (visual and auditory) in attending to environmental events; a shift from colour to form dominance in classifying objects; an ability to hold spatial information in spite of disorientation; the internalization of speech; an increased disruptive influence of delayed auditory feedback; a transition from social to abstract reinforcement; a shift of verbalization towards the planning function in the child's activity; and a number of transitions involving conservation of number, length, space, volume, etc., as demonstrated by Piaget. Altogether the shift from the associative level to a predominantly cognitive level of mental functioning can best be summarized in terms of four general transitions: (1) From direct responses to stimuli to responses produced by mediated stimuli; (2) The emergence of the ability to induce invariance on the welter of phenomenal variability; (3) The capacity to organize past experience to permit inference and prediction; and (4) Increased sensitivity to information yielded by distance as against near receptors.

Jensen has used these elemental theories of Piaget, Gagné, White and others to arrive at a formulation of a two-level theory of mental abilities which has far-reaching educational effects. This theory is closely related to the dimensionality of social class differences, and his own account begins with a summary of some work on this topic. As he says, "the research literature on social class differences in intelligence makes it apparent to me that evidence for social class differences in intelligence cannot be readily systematized or comprehended without positing at least two dimensions along which the differences range." The work of *Eells* et al. (1951) pointed out, on the basis of a large volume of data in which individual test items were analysed in terms of the percentage of children in different socio-economic status groups (abbreviated SES) who could answer the items correctly, that the SES differences were related to (a) the cultural content of the test items and (b) the complexity of the items, that is, the degree of abstractness and problem solving involved in the test items. Thus one dimension along which test items can range would be that of cultural loading or, in Cattell's terms, g_c versus g_f. Thus test items involving knowledge of musical instruments, exotic zoo animals, and fairy tales, for examples could be said to have a high cultural loading.

However, the largest social class differences did not show up on the most culturally loaded items, but were observed rather on those items which involved the highest degree of abstraction, conceptual thinking, and problem solving ability. Quite frequently these items had no particular cultural content, in the sense of differential exposure to item content in different social classes. These and other findings lead Jensen to suggest a two-dimensional space required for integrating the facts of SES differences, and the performance on tests of intelligence and learning ability outlined at the beginning of this section. Fig. 9.1 represents this two – dimensional space and includes rather speculatively the positions which certain tests might have within that space; the figure is adapted from one given by *Jensen* (1970).

The ordinates in Fig. 9.1 represent, according to Jensen, the relative predominance in various tests of two fundamental genotypes of ability, which he calls level one (associative learning ability) and level two (conceptual learning and problem solving). By "genotype" he simply means the physiological substrate of the ability, regardless of whether it is genetically or experientially con-

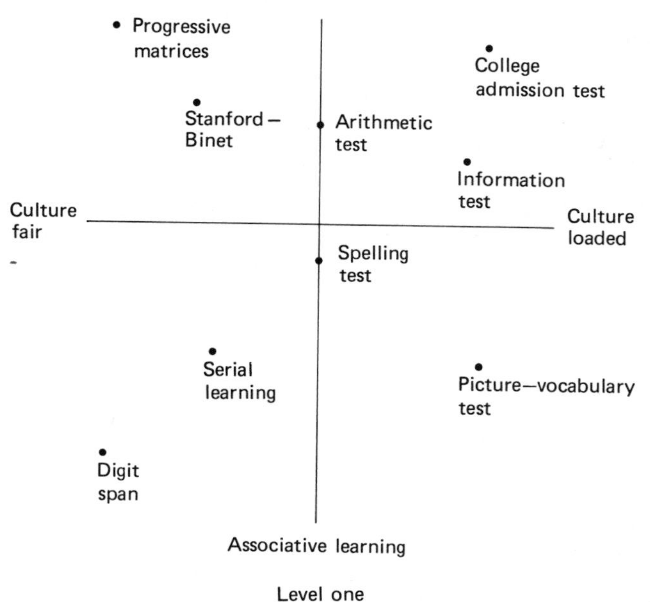

Fig. 9.1 The position of some mental tests in the two-dimensional space provided by Cattell's culture fair – culture loaded dimension, and Jensen's Level I – Level II dimension. Adapted from *Jensen* (1970)

ditioned. "Level I ability is essentially the capacity to receive or register stimuli, to store them, and to later recognize or recall the material with a high degree of fidelity . . . . It is characterised especially by the lack of any need of elaboration, transformation or manipulation of the input in order to arrive at the output. The input need not be referred to other past learning in order to issue effective output. A tape recorder exemplifies level one ability. In human performance digit span is one of the clearest examples of level one ability." Originally Jensen called this "the basic learning ability". Digit span, i. e. the simple repetition of a series of digits pronounced by the experimenter, immediately afterwards, is a most elementary demonstration that such basic learning ability is present. Reverse digit span, i. e. the repetition of the digits pronounced by the experimenter in reverse order by the subject, already involves an admixture of level two ability, and so do serial rote learning and paired associate rote learning. "Level one is the source of most individual differences variance and performance on rote learning task, digit span, and other types of learning and recall which do not depend upon much transformation of the input."

Level II, on the other hand, is at the "high complexity" end of the Gagné

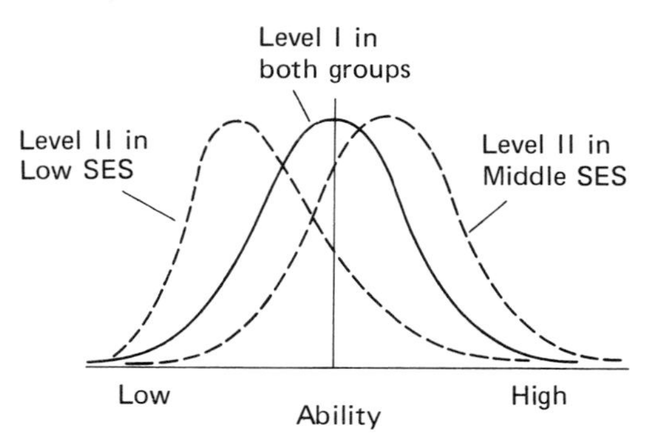

Fig 9.2. Hyothetical distribution of Level I (solid line) and Level II (dashed line) abilities in middle-class and working-class populations. Adapted from *Jensen* (1970)

scale of learning. "Level II ability . . . is characterised by transformation and manipulation of the stimulus prior to making the response. It is the set of mechanisms which make generalization beyond primary stimulus generalization possible. Semantic generalization and concept formation depend upon level two ability; then coding and decoding of stimuli in terms of past experience, relating new learning to old learning, transfer in terms of concepts and principles, are all examples of level two. *Spearman*'s (1927) characterization of *g* as the "deduction of relations and correlates" corresponds to level two." Most standard intelligence tests, and especially culture-fair tests, depend heavily on level two rather than upon level one ability. Jensen maintains that level II processes are functionally dependent upon level one processes. He states that this hypothesis was formulated as part of the theory to account for some of his earlier observations that some children with quite low IQs (i. e. 50 to 75) had quite average or even superior scores on level one type tests (simple stimulus-response, trial and error learning, serial and paired-associate rote learning, and digit span), while the reverse relationship did not seem to exist; children who were very poor on the level one test never had high IQs! "It also seems to make sense psychologically to suppose that basic learning and short term memory processes are involved in performance on a complex level two task, such as the Progressive Matrices, although the complex inductive reasoning strategy called for by the matrices would not be called upon for success in level one tests such as digit span and serial rote learning."

Jensen's theory postulated that level one ability is about equally distributed in all SES groups, and that therefore little if any correlation between level I ability and SES will be discovered. Level II ability is distributed quite differently as a function of SES, showing a strong positive correlation between performance level and SES. Figure 9.2 shows the hypothetical distribution of level I and II in lower-class and middle-class populations, as postulated by Jensen. Jensen gives a genetic interpretation of the reasons for the middle-class and working-class differentiation on level II tasks, but as we have discussed the whole question of heredity and environment in an earlier chapter we shall pass over this point here.

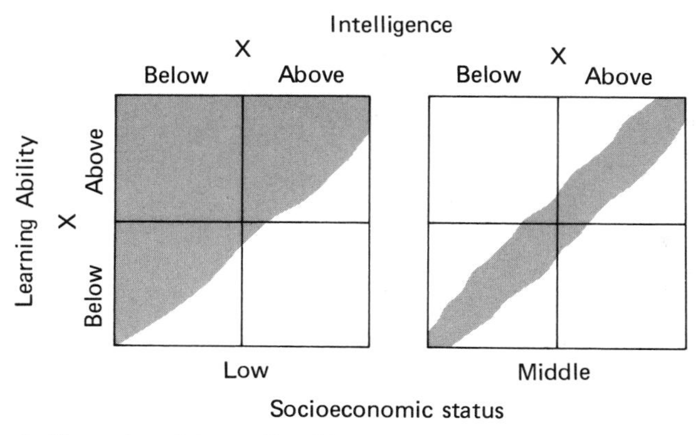

Fig. 9.3. Schematic illustration of the predicted form of the correlation scatter-diagram according to the Jensen model, for the relationship between Level I and Level II abilities in low and middle SES groups. Adapted from *Jensen* (1970)

From his theory Jensen predicts that the correlation scatter diagrams between level I and level II tests would appear somewhat as is shown in exaggerated form in Fig. 9.3. It is here assumed that the correlations are run between typical level I tests (e. g. digit span) and level II tests (e. g. IQ) in low and middle SES groups. It can be seen that the correlations should be positive and high for the middle SES group, and quite low for the low SES group. Clearly, in the low SES group there are many subjects in quadrant two, i. e. above average in level I and below average in level II. There are very few such in the middle SES group. Now the interesting point is that it is an empirical fact that these correlations differ in the way depicted by the model, which was indeed devised to account for the differences in correlations between level I and level II tests in lower and middle-class groups. "The difference in correlations cannot be accounted for by restriction of range in the low SES group or by differences in test reliability. The theory of intelligence must be able to account for the well-established difference in correlations. The present model does so and is also consistent with much other evidence. At present, however, the model can only be regarded at best as a rather crude first approximation to the model that will hopefully evolve as the result of empirical investigations directed at obtaining kinds of information needed for refining the model and rigorously testing its basic assumptions."

Jensen also postulated that level I and level II have quite different growth curves, as shown in Fig. 9.4. "The curves were merely intended to convey the hypothesis that level I rises rapidly with age, approaches asymptotic level relatively early, and shows little SES difference, as contrasted with level II, which does not begin to show a rapid rise until four or five years of age, beyond which the SES groups increasingly diverge and approach quite different asymptotes. The forms of the level I and level II curves express some of the developmental characteristics that *White* (1965) called associative ability (level I) and cognitive ability (level II)." *Jensen* (1970) has reviewed the empirical evidence to demonstrate that level I and level II abilities are largely independent, particularly in

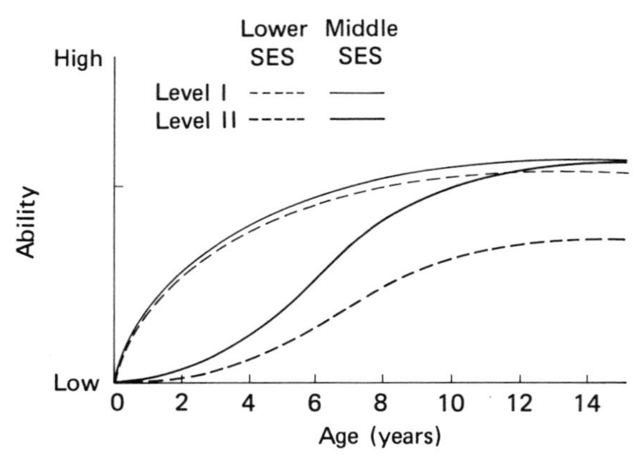

Fig. 9.4. Hypothetical growth curves for Level I and Level II abilities in middle-SES and low-SES populations

lower SES populations. It will be remembered that in our Table 2.6 rote memory tests had a relatively low saturation on Thurstone's general ability factor; this saturation would be even lower had the test been done largely or entirely on children of lower socio-economic status. As *Zeaman* and *House* (1967) have shown, in general *as the learning task becomes more rote, it* correlates less with IQ. Pure rote learning would be an extrapolation of existing data because no really pure rote memory tests exist, but the data suggest that the correlation with IQ would be very low or effectively zero.

Jensen's major research effort has centered on the triple interaction of IQ, learning ability and SES. The essential features of the results are shown in Fig. 9.5. This figure shows a marked interaction between the three variables in question, where learning ability was measured by tasks such as free recall, serial learning, paired associates learning and memory for digits. Low SES children in the IQ range from 60 to 80 perform significantly better in these learning tasks than do middle-class children in the same range of IQ. Low SES children who are above average in IQ, on the other hand, do not show learning performance that is significantly different from that of middle-class children of similar IQ. Other relationships predicted on Jensen's theory have also been verified and lend some support to his views.

What emerged as possibly the most important results of Jensen's work is that in every single study that has been performed by him low SES and middle SES groups differ much less on level I test than on level II. For instance, *Jensen* (1963) found some low SES children with Sandford-Binet IQs that range from 50 to 75, who on level I tests (trial and error selective learning) exceeded the mean performance of children of the same age classed as "gifted" (IQs above 135). This finding is the basis of some practical proposals for education which Jensen has made on the basis of his work, and which concern the interaction between the pupils aptitudes and the instruction which he receives. "The fact that we have discovered a class of mental abilities (level I) on which social class

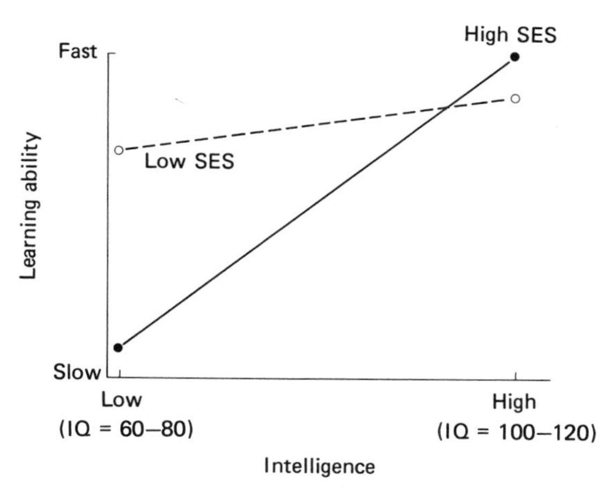

Fig. 9.5. Summary graph of a number of studies showing relationship between learning ability (free recall, serial and paired-associate learning) and IQ as a function of socio-economic status (SES.) Adapted from *Jensen* (1970)

differences are much less than those found on IQ tests raises a question of whether it is possible to devise instruction on basic scholastic skills in such a way as to be less dependent upon level II abilities and more fully utilize the level I abilities which children called disadvantaged possess to a relatively greater degree. Can instruction geared to level I ability improve the scholastic performance of the majority of low SES children who now perform relatively poorly in school?"

Jensen suggests that school succes is highly predictable from standard IQ tests precisely because instruction is mainly aimed at level II abilities. If this is so then it is simply not true to say that a child who is low on level II ability, but high on level I, must fail to acquire the basic skills in school. "Children who are above the general average on level I abilities, but below the average on level II performance, usually appear bright and capable of normal learning and achievement in many situations, although they invariably have inordinate difficulties in school work under the traditional methods of classroom instruction. Many such children who are classed as mentally retarded in school later become socially and economically adequate persons when they leave the academic situation. On the other hand, children who are much below average on level I, and consequently on level II as well, appear to be much more handicapped in the world of work. One shortcoming of traditional IQ tests is that they make both types of children look much alike."

Jensen is asking for tests that will reliably assess *both* level I and level II separately. Even more important, he considers, there is a need for research on more effect utilization on level I abilities in scholastic instruction. "It seems sensible that instruction should be based upon a pupil's strengths rather than upon his weaknesses, and we have found that many children lacking strength in level II possess strength in level I. At present we do not know how to teach to level I ability. Although level I is manifested in rote learning, it is not advocated that simple notions of rote learning be the model for instruction. Instructional techniques that can utilize the abilities that are manifested in rote learning are needed, but this does not necessarily imply that instruction consists of rote learning *per se*. . . . The theory presented here provides a broad base for the discovery of Alls (aptitudes x instruction interaction) that will possibly prove fruitful for improving the education of many children who under present methods of instruction seem to derive little educational benefit from schooling. Present day schooling is highly geared to conceptual modes of learning, and this is suitable for children of average and superior levels of ability. But many children whose weakness is in conceptual ability are frustrated by schooling and therefore learn far less than would seem to be warranted by their good level I learning ability. A certainly important avenue of exploration is the extent to which school subjects can be taught by techniques which depend mostly on level I ability and very little upon level II. After all, much of the work of the world depends largely on level I ability, and it seems reasonable to believe that many persons can acquire basic scholastic and occupational skills and become employable and productive members of society by making the most of level I ability."

So much for a broad account of Jensen's hypothesis. In rough outline it fits in very well with Piaget's developmental theory, and with the other developmental theories mentioned briefly in this section. Could it be said that Jensen's theory is in opposition to the hierarchical model presented by the classical Spearman-Thurstone theory? My own view would be that it is not. The Spearman-Thurstone model posits a hierarchy corresponding to the vertical line in Jensen's theory as shown in Fig. 9.1. It is essentially a theory of abstract problem solving ability and conceptual learning, and that is after all what to the man in the street and to professional psychologists alike the term "intelligence" denotes. At the bottom of this scale, as shown in Table 2.6, we have associative learning tasks representative of Jensen's level I, requiring little in the way of intelligence as so defined. Nevertheless, associative learning also can be of considerable importance in coping with many of the problems presented to the child and the adult in real life terms. The gas fitter may not have the abstract ability to work out new methods of dealing with the problems presented by gas cookers that go wrong, or gas-fired central heating that does not function, but if he possesses a strong degree of associative learning ability he should be able to learn the correct methods of testing for faults and remedying these faults. As Jensen said in the quotation immediately preceding this paragraph, "much of the work of the world depends largely on level I ability", and possibly one of the faults in our educational system has been to apply methods of instruction of an academic and abstract-conceptual type to pupils who would benefit from an associative type of instruction. These are wide ranging consequences of Jensen's theory to which we shall briefly return in a later chapter. Here let us merely note that his work, just like that of Guilford and Piaget, serves to extend the range of the paradigm, but does not in efffect disprove it or render it out of date. We may note further that in gerneral outline, though not necessarily in specific detail, the various theories of development associated with Piaget, Jensen, White, Gagné and others stress very similar stages of development, and integrate in a very similar manner changes in mental age and IQ. The fact that all these theories are dressed up in different clothing, use different nomenclatures, and try to go their own way does not detract from the fact that overall agreement between them on factual issues is quite high. They all make an important contribution to our better understanding of the concept of "intelligence".

A topic closely related to the development of intelligence is the question of the constancy of the IQ (*Thorndike*, 1933). Clearly, if the IQ of a given child varied widely from year to year so that no prediction was possible, then the notion of IQ would lose any practical or theoretical meaning. Equally, we should not expect, for many reasons, that the IQ would remain identical from year to year. There are many causes of slight or even not-so-slight changes. There is first of all the unreliability of the test; like all scientific measurements, IQ testing is not perfectly accurate, and chance errors can raise or lower the IQ by a few points. This can be largely eliminated by giving much longer tests; the reliability of a test is mainly dependent on the number of problems contained in it, and hence on the length of the test. However, using the normal and rather short type of test reliability is fairly high but not perfect, and hence deviations of a few points occur even if the two occasions of testing are separated only by a week or so – i. e. much less time than would cause us to assume that the IQ had actually changed.

Another important reason for discrepancies is the fact that the composition of the tests used at different stages is often different. Thus the so-called "baby tests" used before the age of 2 are usually tests of muscular coordination and perceptual adequacy; gradually tests begin to incorporate verbal elements after that, and finally inductive and deductive reasoning assume a prominent part (*Maurer*, 1946; *Hofstaetter*, 1954). Piaget-type tests also clearly change in composition with age, so that we are actually in part testing different things at different ages. Even where the same test is used, the method adopted for the solution of the problems in the test may change with age, i. e. using language at one stage, simple perceptual mechanisms at another. This would lead us to expect some change in IQ from year to year although not perhaps going beyond a few points.

Critics of IQ testing have drawn attention to the lack of complete constancy of the IQ, and the (admittedly rare) cases where quite sizeable changes have occurred in the IQ of children followed up over many years. We have already considered the test-retest reliabilities of IQ scores, showing that when correlated with terminal IQ at the end of adolescence, earlier measures correlate more and more highly with this terminal measure the closer they are to it in point of time – with scores obtained before the age of 4 or thereabouts correlating only very imperfectly with terminal IQ. How can we account for the development underlying this change? *Anderson* (1939) has proposed an "overlap" theory which has been widely accepted, although it has also been criticized (e. g. *Thorndike*, 1966). The hypothesis deals with the relationship between the first measurement in point of time of a given variable (IQ in our case); the second measurement of the same variable on the same sample of subjects after a lapse of time t; and the difference, or gain, from the first to the second measurement. Anderson hypothesized that the correlations in longitudinal studies are a

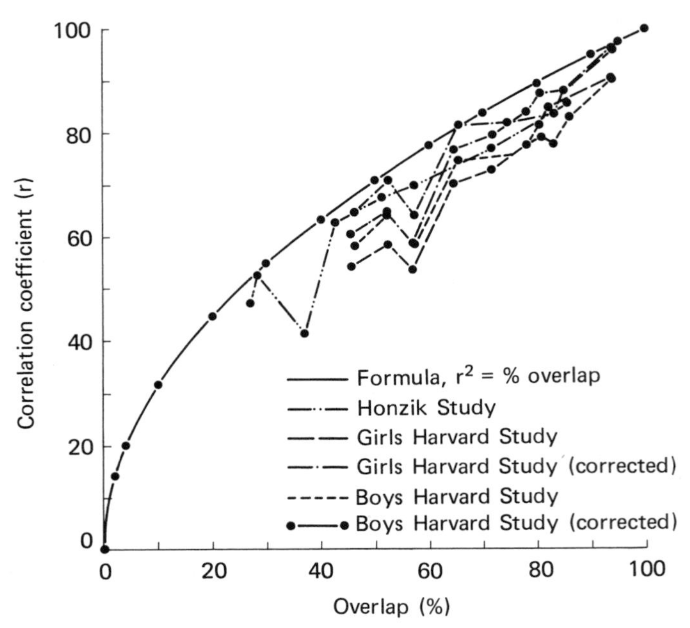

Fig. 9.6. Correlation coefficient between test and retest on IQ tests plotted against percent of overlap for five empirical studies. Adapted from *Anderson* (1939)

direct function of the percent of the development at one age which has been attained at an earlier age. His formulation of the "overlap" hypothesis assumes an absolute scale with equal units and a definite zero; it presents an obvious development of Thurstone's pioneering approach to scaling, and his definition of an absolute zero of intelligence which we have already discussed in an earlier chapter.

What Anderson proposes, put quite simply, is this. At a given age the child has a certain quantity of *g*; let us call it x. At a later stage he has added another quantity, let us call this y, so that his *g* now amounts to x + y. This now constitutes his intellectual capital to which he adds another increment, z, during the next interval of time, making the total x + y + z. Anderson now states that in his theory the size of the increments is uncorrelated with the size of the capital; in other words, x does not correlate in the sample of children tested with y or z, and x + y does not correlate with z. This formulation explains the increment in correlation between different measurements of the IQ the closer these are together in point of time, and also the fact that early measures of IQ are less revealing about terminal IQ than later ones. Early measures are taken at a time when the "capital" available to the child is only a small proportion of terminal intelligence; hence the correlation is small. Later on the "capital" portion is relatively large, and the increments small; hence prediction of terminal status is good. Figure 9.6 shows agreement between theoretical formulation and the actual results of five follow-up studies; it will be seen that the shape of the curve is accurately predicted by Anderson's formulation.

It may be useful to state an alternative hypothesis recently put forward by *Jensen* (1973). Starting from the usual pattern of correlation coefficients between individuals tested at different ages in a longitudinal study, in which the size of the correlations is largest near the leading diagonal and decreases more or less regularly the further away they are from the diagonal, he points out that this corresponds to Guttman's *simplex* model. The theory of the simplex is rather well understood, and Jensen asks what kind of model will produce a simplex in this situation. As points out, "only two basic elements are required: (1) a *rate of consolidation* factor, C, on which individuals maintain their relative positions in the population over the course of development, and (2) a random increment or gain, G, from time x to time x + 1 (t_x to t_{x+1}). An individual's status, S, at any given time consists of the sum of C × G over all previous time plus the G of the immediate past. In effect, the consolidation factor C is a positive constant for a given individual; the gain factor G is a positive random variable in each time interval $t_x - t_{x+1}$. An individual's growth curve can then be presented as follows:

$t_1 : G_1$ (Gain since t_0)
$t_2 : CG_1 = S_2$ (Consolidated gain from time 1 to time 2 plus unconsolidated gain at time 2 = status at time 2.)
$t_3 : CG_1 + CG_2 + G_3 = S_3$
$t_4 : CG_1 + CG_2 + CG_3 + G_4 = S_4$
$T_n : C\,(G_1 + G_2 + G_3 + G_4 + \ldots + G_{n\text{-}1}) + G_n = S_n$

Actually, only one element is needed for a simplex, the random G element in the following model (as would be the case if C = 1 or was the same constant value for every member of the population). But this one-element model, consisting of cumulating random increments, as we shall see, would be too simple to reproduce all the essential characteristics of the growth curves and intercorrelations actually found in such characteristics as intelligence, stature, and achievement, e. g., the predictability of predetermination of the individual growth curves' asymptotic values implied by the substantial heritability of these characteristics.

Can we make a reasonable psychological interpretation of this model? The S values, of course, are no problem; they are simply the achievement measurements taken at different times. They are composed of consolidated gains, CG, plus unconsolidated gains, G, plus random errors of measurement, e.

The consolidation factor, C, is a variable which is more or less intrinsic to the individual; it is that aspect of individual differences in S values in the population at any cross section of development which may be attributed to genetic and constitutional factors (which are not distinguishable in this model per se). The term consolidation as used here does not refer to the consolidation of short-term memory traces into long-term storage, but to the assimilation of experience (e. g., learning) into cognitive structures which organize what has been learned in easy stages that subsequently permit quick and adequate retrieval and broad transfer of the learning in new relevant situations. Stated in simplest terms, C is the process of understanding what one has learned. It is "getting the idea," "catching on," having the "'Aha'!" experience that may accompany or follow experiencing or learning something, and the relating of new learning to past learning and vice versa. When learning takes place without C acting upon it, it is less retrievable and much less transferable for use in solving problems that are more or less remote from the original learning situation. C is what is generally meant by the term *intelligence*, but it can be manifested, observed, and measured only through its interaction with experience or learning. There can be learning without intelligence (i. e. without C) but intelligence cannot be manifested without learning. In our simple model we have represented the capacity for consolidation as a constant value for each individual; this is not an essential feature, although a more or less constant rank order of individuals' C values is essential. On the average, over the life span the C value probably increases up to maturity, levels off at maturity, and gradually declines in old age. Our concept of C comes very close to R. B. Cattel's concept of *fluid intelligence.* All intelligence tests measure S, but some tests reflect more of the C component (which Cattell would call tests of fluid intelligence) and some reflect more of the G component (which Cattell would call tests of crystallized intelligence).

The gain factor, G, consists of experience or learning and unconsolidated (or rote) memory of such learning. But is G properly represented as a random variable in our model? Consider the following quite well established empirical findings. Learning abilities (which do not involve problem solving) have been found to show quite low often negligible correlations with intelligence. (For an excellent review, see *Zeaman* and *House*, 1967). Moreover, a general factor of learning ability has not been found. There is a great deal of situation specific or task specific variance in learning, making for very low or even zero correlations among various kinds of learning. Therefore, learning *per se* in the vast variety of conditions under which it occurs in real life, cannot show much correlation, if any, with relatively stable individual difference variables such as intelligence.

Furthermore, consider the relative unpredictability or randomness of the individual's day-to-day experiences or opportunities for learning this or that, and the poorly correlated other variables, such as attention, motivation, and persistence, that can affect learning at any given moment, All these factors within a given interval of time, add up in effect to a more or less random variable. It should be understood that random does not mean uncaused. A child may come down with measles and have to stay out of school for 10 days and so miss out on a good many school learning experiences. Another child may miss out for a few weeks because his family moves to another city. Another child may learn a great deal for a period when the teacher is presenting something that especially interests him. And so on. The gains (or lack of gains) in any short period, though caused by a multitude of factors, appear in effect to be more or less random in the school population."

On Jensen's model, then, intelligence can be thought of psychologically as that aspect of mental ability which *consolidates* learning and experience in an integrated, organized way, relating it to past learning and encoding it in ways that permit its retrieval in relevant new situations. The products of learning become an aspect of intelligence (or are correlates of intelligence) only when they are organized and retrievable, generalizable and transferable to new problem situations. The G component is on this account largely a function of environmental influences, interests, motivation, and the like, acting at any given time; C, on the other hand, is genetically and constitutionally determined. The evidence that G is more related to environmental factors while C is genetically determined, has been well reviewed by *Bloom* (1964). This accounts for the fact that accelerated achievement gains brought about by an enriched and intensified instructional program generally "fade out" in a few months to a year; without a strong C factor, accelerated gains are not maintained without constant rehearsal of the acquired knowledge or skill. Other deductions from his hypothesis are made by Jensen, and the largely confirmatory evidence reviewed. It seems to fit the facts better than the overlap hypothesis, and is likely to take its place in the near future[13].

The models here discussed seem to assume a rather regular growth of mental age as the child develops, but this seems unlikely. Just as height develops in spurts and starts, rather than in a regular fashion, so also intelligence. This fact must contribute to the apparent inconstancy in IQ sometimes reported. Let us assume that a child's intelligence grows by having a "spurt" every year; before and after the spurt his mental age remains on a fairly level plateau. Let us assume that this child has a "true" IQ of 100, so that if he is measured at the age of 5 he has a mental age of 5. Let us also assume that this measurement is taken just after a "spurt", and that during the next six months no change takes place in his MA. This would give him an IQ at the age of 5.5 of 91, and of 83 just before turning 6, and experiencing his next spurt! After this spurt he resumes his IQ of 100. The example is of course quite artificial and purposely exaggerated, but it will illustrate the point. The importance of the spurts diminishes as the child grows older because his "capital" makes up a much larger portion of his later IQ than does any increment affected by these spurts, but in early youth the changes in IQ thus produced can be quite sizeable. This is of course a good argument for not trusting a single IQ measurement in young children for making any important decision concerning their educational future, but rather testing them regu-

---

13 At the same time as Jensen's alternative model to the Anderson-Bloom overlap one was published, there appeared another critique of the overlap model (*Merz* and *Stelzl,* 1973). These authors also put forward a model of the development of intelligence during childhood which agreed quite well with empirical data. This new model makes certain assumptions, starting with the axiom that measured IQ is the result of experience; it goes on to argue that intraindividually the amount of consolidated experience tends to remain constant – similar amounts are learned by a given person during succeeding months or years. These amounts differ from one individual to another. The model also assumes a forgetting parameter; memory losses are differentiated interindividually, and are proportional to the amount of material in the memory store. The model is developed in a very interesting manner, resulting in a formula which can replicate empirical data quite well. It is to be hoped that the Jensen and the Merz/Stelzl models will be subjected to a more detailed empirical comparison than has been done so far; they both seem to present a distinct advance on the older models. On a priori grounds the assumptions made by the Jensen model seem more acceptable than those made by Merz and Stelzl, but the argument can only be resolved by a special experiment designed to exploit the differential predictions of the two models.

larly through the years to obtain some more clear-cut idea about their intellectual development.

It is interesting that not only the occurrence of the spurts and lags, but also their size and timing is influenced powerfully by genetic factors. *Wilson* (1972) explicitly designed an experiment to study the mental development of infant twins during the first and second years of their lives. This is a particularly important period because spurts are much more noticeable than later on in life when a good deal of "capital" has been accumulated. Twins showed high concordance for level of mental development and, what is of particular interest, they also showed concordance for the spurts and lags in development during this peroid – MZ twins more so than DZ twins. "From these results it was inferred that infant mental development was primarily determined by the twins' genetic blueprint and that, except in unusual cases, other factors served mainly a supportive function." The families in this study ranged from the welfare case to the wealthy professional family, but there was very little relationship between the socio-economic status of the family and the overall level of development during the second year (the correlation was only 0.2)

These various factors – chance errors of measurement, changes in test composition, spurts and lags – together with some form of "overlap" hypothesis (although probably not in the oversimplified form given to it by Anderson) probably account for such lack of constancy in the IQ as has been observed. Similar inconstancy can of course be observed in the measurement of height; here too we find changes in the position of a given child among his peers over time, and here too there is evidence of sometimes quite marked spurts and lags. This has not caused anyone to doubt the existence of differences in stature, or to imagine that height is not a real variable. Similarly the facts as detailed do not suggest that differences in IQ are not real, or that the notion of IQ should be given up. What we must give up is an oversimplified idea of a fixed IQ which remains absolutely constant as the child grows up, and which can be measured at any age. Such a notion has of course never been put forward by any serious psychologist, but teachers and others have often made unwarranted assumptions of this kind, only to be disappointed when reality was found to be more complex. Such complexities must be taken into account in measuring intelligence; the development of the child, and in particular his mental development, presents us with a difficult and compound problem which is unduly reduced for practical convenience by the single administration of an IQ test. Repeated testing, continued over many years, using many-faceted test to investigate not only *g* but also many of the primary abilities so far isolated should be the minimum requirement before the psychologist is willing to make serious recommendations in educational or clinical work.

10 Intelligence and Society

Science without conscience is but death of the soul

M. E. Montaigne

A chapter under this title would have been looked upon as unusual even a dozen or so years ago. However, in recent years there has been a tendency to look upon the social consequences and the "relevance" of scientific discoveries and theories, and to raise questions concerning these; as a consequence, it may be useful in this brief terminal chapter to consider some of the queries raised. There are three major reasons for raising problems of this kind. The first is the growing feeling that scientific discoveries have an important effect on society, and that society must watch and monitor these discoveries and their applications lest they lead to harmful and undesirable consequences. This feeling became particularly strong in the aftermath of the dropping of the first atomic bomb, and has been gaining strength ever since. The motives underlying this particular source of anxiety are undoubtedly wholly desirable, and in line with modern conceptions of a democratic society. There is no reason why scientists should be exempted from public scrutiny, and why they should not be asked to account in popular terms for their work and the results of this work. *Salus publicae summum bonum.* It used to be taken for granted that IQ testing had a small but on the whole beneficial influence on social conditions; this has been questioned, and it has been suggested that instead the influence of IQ testing has been to further disadvantage children already disadvantaged for reasons of class or race. If true this would be a serious indictment, and it should certainly not be passed over in silence.

The second reason why questions are being raised concerning modern developments in science is related to the first (*MacRae*, 1976). Scientists have begun to realize that they have special social responsibilities, and these responsibilities may not be discharged entirely by virtue of their actions as citizens; more may be required. This feeling has led to the formation of societies devoted to the study of the social responsibilities of scientists, and although these have tended to be overly political, and one-sidedly propagandist in their pronouncements, nevertheless the point made is a sound one. Scientists do have special responsibilities for their creations, and they should be expected to discharge these responsibilities in a fashion that clearly indicated their awareness of social needs.

A third reason, probably less sound, lies in the attention recently given to what has become known as the sociology of knowledge, or of science. This is an outgrowth of Marxian thinking, applying Marxian theories to science, and suggesting that scientific theories and experiments cannot in the nature of things lead to objective knowledge, but will always mirror simply the social conditions and the methods of production and distribution of material goods current at the time. Thus "human thought or the superstructure of a society is recognized to be, in part, conditioned by or based upon the social substructure of human relationships. The sociology of knowledge attempts to explore and understand the relationship between cognitive structure (broadly speaking) and social structure." (*Buss*, 1975). Or as *Mannheim* (1936) put it, "with the emergence of the general formulation of the total conception of ideology, the simple theory of ideology develops into the sociology of knowledge . . . the thought of every group is seen as arising out of its life conditions." *Stark* (1958) and *Berger* and *Luckmann* (1966) have written extensively on this topic, and many other sources are quoted by Buss. Many more have attempted to apply this approach specifically to psychology, or social science in general (*Vallance*, 1972; *Beit-Hallahmi*, 1974; *Bryan*, 1972; *Tyler*, 1970; *Lasswell*, 1970; *Levine*, 1974.) Thus Vallance writes: "All science is increasingly embedded in value systems, and most clearly in the values that relate to the output side of the science progress . . . science is not value free, and . . . social science, whether "purely theoretical" or "applied", is in its every phase entwined in the values of the society in which or on which it would operate. The choosing of *what* to investigate in any field is culturally relevant and represents value judgements present in the culture and manifested in the scientist."

What is alleged here is undoubtedly true in part, but only in part. As a general law, the sociology of knowledge partakes of the paradox of the Cretan liar. It will be recalled that Greek philosophy, which placed much store on paradoxes, puzzled endlessly about the Cretan who said: "All Cretans always lie." But if his statement was untrue, and as a Cretan who always lied he could hardly speak the truth on this occasion, then Cretans did not always lie, and consequently he might have spoken the truth. But if he had spoken the truth, then Cretans do always lie, and consequently he could not have spoken the truth! But if his statement could be neither a true statement nor a lie, what was it? We need not struggle with this paradox, which has a simple solution (no real, live Cretan, given that Cretans always lie, could have made such a statement), but will instead indicate how it applies to the sociology of knowledge. If in the social sciences (and according to some in the physical sciences also) scientific truth and objectivity are impossible because aims and methods are determined by social factors, such as the class structure obtaining in a given country, then clearly this general law itself cannot be true and determined objectively; it too must be value-laden and the product of the class structure of the society which originated it! But if the law itself is merely subjective and socially determined, there is no reason for taking it seriously or believing that it has any scientific importance. If it is true, it cannot be true; if it is untrue, it must be unimportant.

Marx, of course, put a caveat on the reasoning underlying this law which is disregarded by many of his followers; as he pointed out, "the materialistic doctrine that men are products of other circumstances and upbringing and that, therefore, changed men are products of other circumstances and changed upbringing, forgets that circumstances are changed precisely by men." Another disclaimer relates to the circumstances under which the law would operate; as

Salamini (1974) has pointed out, "for Marx, the social factor conditioning knowledge can determine the deformation of reality only in historical conditions where the proletarian classes have not attained political hegemony (the proletariat is the bearer of objectivity!)" Even if this were true (and clearly there is no evidence available to even suggest any such thing), nevertheless in the Western world this condition certainly does not obtain (and even behind the Iron Curtain one may be sceptical about its realization). Consequently this does not provide a way out for the sociologist of knowledge; he would still have to take each particular scientific theory or fact and demonstrate, if he can, that the theory or fact contradicts scientific objectivity in some way. But this reduces to precisely the method of criticism which has obtained traditionally in the social and the natural sciences; the sociology of knowledge cannot be conceded to make any novel or important contribution.

It has been suggested, following the dictates of this new sociology, that advocates of the importance of genetic factors in intelligence are motivated to do so by the prevailing right-wing political beliefs characteristic of a capitalistic society (and the advocates of the importance of environmental factors presumably by the prevailing left-wing political beliefs of countries governed by socialist parties like England and Germany!) *Pastore*, (1949). Such simplistic views disregard the empirical evidence, and they fail to explain why a famous geneticist like J. B. S. Haldane, one of the leaders of the British Communist Party for many years, should strongly advocate belief in *genetic* causes of differences in IQ, while a prominent conservative psychologist like J. B. Watson, the founder of behaviourism, should equally strongly advocate belief in 100% *environmentalism*! The point is discussed by *Eysenck* (1973), who quotes some of the original sources; sociologists of knowledge restrict their discussion to argumenta ad hominem, a method of argumentation rightly condemned by all philosophers of science. They neglect the possibility that a person's political beliefs may be altered by factual evidence, such as that contained in this book; this is a more likely explanation of any correlation that may be found between political and scientific beliefs than the determination of the latter by the former. Whichever way we look at the matter, we must always return to the factual evidence; this alone determines the degree to which our theories are acceptable or not. It is not of course intended here to deny the possibility, or even the probability, that personal biases and prejudices may colour a person's judgements on scientific matters, as much as on political and social matters; the history of Lysenko's crimes alone would show that such a belief was untenable. Nor is it denied that the social conditions prevailing at the time scientific work is being done might influence the scientist's mental frame work, his aims, his choice of subject matter, and occasionally even his conclusions. What is being denied is that social conditions determine the scientist's work so completely that no objective criteria are available in terms of which to judge the outcome of his studies. Once this is granted, sociological conditions can be seen as just some of the sources of possible error scientists have to guard against.

Given that the conclusions of psychological research into intelligence, as detailed in this book, have objective backing, and support a general theory of the kind outlined, can it be said that IQ testing, i. e. the practical application of the knowledge gained, is ethically defensible, has on the whole a beneficial influence on those fields where it is being used, and is indicative of social responsiblility on the part of those advocating it? In its origins, IQ testing was seen by those psychologists who introduced it as having an important function in two major, socially useful ways. In the first place, it would help in recognizing those children whose school progress was hindered by low intelligence or mental defect, in contradistinction to those where other causes (social deprivation, laziness, neurosis, etc.) were responsible; this would lead to a much more appropriate categorization and disposal (e. g. to E. S. N. schools) of the children in question. This was the social problem which originated Binet's work, as already noted. In the second place, English psychologists like Godfrey Thomson and Cyril Burt in particular were concerned with the loss of talent which was caused by the division of English schools into academic (grammar) and non-academic types; admission to the prestigious grammar schools was in terms of school achievement, and this was clearly dependent in part on the equality of primary school teaching, leading to many working-class children of high ability being excluded because of defects in their teaching for which they were clearly not responsible. The introduction of IQ tests into the 11+ examination, which was used to decide on a child's future schooling, had the effect of increasing the proportion of working class children who went to the better type of school, and conversely it has been extensively documented that when the 11+ was abolished, the proportion of working class children admitted to grammar schools dropped sharply (*Eysenck*, 1970). Both these functions of the IQ test, which is much less dependent on social and class factors than achievement tests, are probably socially desirable and useful, although some critics have argued that this use of the IQ test merely serves to improve and shore up a system of social organization of which they disapprove in principle.

As an example of the salutary function which IQ tests can play in this connection, we may consider a report by *Floud & Halsey* (1957). The Hertfordshire Education Authority dropped the use of the IQ test, in response to attacks, and these investigators compared the social composition of the local grammar schools in 1952 and 1954 – i. e., before and after the IQ test had been dropped. The categorizing of children by parental occupation was less reliable in the later year, and they allocated "all doubtful and unclassifiable cases" to the working class group; yet the proportion of working class children fell from 14.9% to 11.5%! At the same time the percentage of children of professional and managerial parents rose from 40% to 64%. These figures indicate the degree to which social injustice can be ameliorated by the use (even though somewhat half-hearted!) of IQ tests, and the odd reluctance of left-wing critics to consider the effects of their attacks on the use of such tests. Given that such critics favour the greater equalization of the benefits of grammar-type education, the effect of removing IQ testing is to promote greater inequality. The introduction of comprehensive schools does not alter this judgement; if anything, the effect to date has been that of making the grammar-type school even more middle class than before.

It is perhaps odd that in spite of these important contributions which IQ testing has made to the better allocation of social resources in education, both at the school and the university level, and to a more just treatment of working class and other underprivileged children, there should now be such a strong reaction to it in the U. S. A. particularly (where IQ testing for selection purposes has been banned in several states), but also in Europe, while at the same time the U. S. S. R., where IQ testing was banned by Stalin in 1935, has somewhat clandestinely reintroduced it, and is widely using it, though under different names! The whole discussion in educational circles about IQ testing is somewhat unreal, and tied to ideological rather than scientific considerations, linked as it is to such concepts as the abolition of selection, the mixed ability class, and the virtues or otherwise of the comprehensive school. What is known about the nature of intelligence, its relation to learning, and its responsiveness to environmental influences must surely be basic to any intelligent and meaningful discussion of these issues, but this book is clearly not the place for such a debate.

The tendency in the U. S. A. for ethical problems, such as those here considered, to lead to legal battles, has highlighted two particular questions, respectively concerned with "reverse discrimination" and the selection of EMR children (educable mentally retarded pupils – comparable to what in G. B. is called E. S. N. or educationally subnormal pupils.) Taking these two cases in order, we must first of all note that many leading Universities in the U. S. A., used to selecting students on the basis of objective tests (partly IQ, partly academic achievement), have found that black students passed these admission tests in much smaller numbers than would be reasonable in terms of the proportions of blacks in the total pupulation. (In fact, the number is close to what would be expected if we accepted the well-known finding that blacks score about one standard deviation (15 points) below the white mean on IQ tests.) In order to fulfil the demands of "affirmative action" legislation (legislation passed to ensure equal representation of minority groups, such as blacks, Chicanos, and women (!),) some Universities instituted quotas giving preference for employment to members of minority groups, and others similarly argued that if reliance on traditional standards, including grades and test scores, resulted in the admission of few minority students because of the highly competitive nature of the process, then the University was justified in setting aside a number of openings for special minority groups regardless of the presence of much better qualified members of majority groups who would thus be refused admission.

The Regents of the University of California adopted this practice, in relation to admission to their medical school, and refused admission to a well-qualified white student, Allan Bakke, giving preference to a number of less well qualified black students. Bakke sued the University, and two lower court decisions in California found in his favour on the grounds that racial selection was involved in this process, and was unconstitutional. (The case was appealed, and may go to the Supreme Court.) Bakke's high grade point average of 3.51 and aptitude test scores gave him traditional credentials greatly superior to those students admitted under the special admissions procedures, who on the average scored below the average on all aptitude subtests; in addition, the combined numerical ranking by the special admissions committee showed that these students had scores some 20 to 30 points below Bakke's.

In the legal case, the Regents sought to convince the courts that their procedure did not go counter to the Fourteenth Amendment, on the grounds that this was written to prohibit *invidious* discrimination *against* minorities but did not apply to their *benign* special admissions programme, the intent of which was to be *beneficial.* The California Supreme Court did not agree. "We cannot agree with the proposition that deprivation based upon race is subject to a less demanding standard of review under the Fourteenth Amendment if the race discriminated against is the majority rather than the minority. We have found no cases so holding, and we do not hesitate to reject the notion that racial discrimination may be more easily justified against one race than another, nor can we permit the validity of such discrimination to be determined by a mere census count of the races." Clearly what is benign and what is invidious discrimination must vary according to the point of view of the person viewing the case; the discrimination practiced by the Regents might appear benign to the poorly qualified black students, but might appear invidious to the well qualified white students rejected.

The case discussed above concerned admission to medical school; a similar case was brought by Marco DeFunis, a white graduate of the University of Washington, against the university's law school when it rejected him but admitted 37 minority students whose college grades and law school test scores were lower than his. Such admission practices, common in law and medical school all over the U. S. A., have consequences which inexorably follow from the premises adopted; one of these is that the minority students selected in spite of low admission qualifications tend to fail their courses in unusually high numbers. At the University of California Law School at Los Angeles, where a quota system of admission operates (as admitted by the Dean of the School), just two of the 14 minority students admitted in 1967 passed the bar examination; of the 39 members of the 1971 class, only 12 went on to be admitted to the bar. Of the 64 minority students admitted in 1973, nine passed the bar examination. These failure rates far surpass anything ever found with candidates admitted following the normal procedures. It is difficult to see that the majority of failed minority candidates were in fact done a kindness in admitting them to courses they were almost bound to fail. Consider these figures. Some 823 graduates nationally took the bar examinations in 1973, including approximately 200 blacks; 551 passed, of whom fewer than 20 were black! Thus some 85% whites passed, but only some 10% of blacks. These are not encouraging figures for "affirmative action" or quota systems.

Harvard College raised the standards in its admissions policies after a number of black youths, chosen on the basis of their political and social involvement, encountered severe emotional and academic problems and had to leave. Other universities have had similar experiences. Some universities, instead, were led to a relaxation of their examination standards for minority groups; this "double standard" has been much criticized, because it leads to a devaluation of the achievements of those blacks who succeed on an equal level with whites. Clearly the situation is a complex one, in which ethical imperatives are not as clear as they ought perhaps to be, and in which men of good will may be found on opposing sides of what is becoming an impassable divide.

The case of the mental testing of children to determine placement in EMR classes raises similar complex issues. On February 5, 1975, the California Board of Education imposed a moratorium on the use of intelligence tests in the placement of students in special programmes for mentally retarded pupils; this had a considerable impact on the delivery of adequate service to academically retarded children referred for special educational assistance. As a result of the moratorium, many children are being deprived of the services they need. The judgement is a consequence of a lengthy civil rights suit concerned with the inordinate overrepresentation of minority children in EMR special education programmes. "IQ testing" was considered prejudicial to black children. Deprived of their main objective basis for making recommendations, and having to rely on subjective and inevitably inaccurate observations of classroom behaviour, teacher reports, and achievement test data, psychologists ceased to conduct evaluations and making placement recommendations, with the consequence that many children who stood in need of special educational assistance were not getting it.

An earlier court judgement had required the Board of Education to take steps to reduce the ethnic disparity in special class enrollments and to show cause if it continued. This reevaluation did not appreciably alter the ethnic minority imbalance, but it drastically reduced the EMR enrollment in California, which is now only about 30% of what it was in 1969. Thus the final outcome of these concerns with quotas has been to deprive large numbers of children in urgent need of help of the educational programmes most likely to assist them to reach acceptable levels of scholastic achievement, and to leave them stranded in no man's land, incapable of following ordinary classes, and not allowed to enter special EMR classes. Similar problems of ethnic disparity have arisen in Great Britain, where black children also figure disproportionately in ESN classes, and where protests against this imbalance have also been widespread. The argument seems to disregard the fact that these classes are meant to help, not to penalize, those in them, and that there is good evidence to show that the alternative is not successful school attendance in ordinary classes, but failure, truanting, vandalism, and dislike of things academic. Again we see ethical problems raised, not so much by IQ testing, but by the simple facts of the situation; tests do not create the problems, they merely quantify them.

The uses of IQ and ability testing in general in other directions, such as army selection, vocational guidance, and industry have already been discussed; nobody nowadays would be willing to dispute their practical utility in preventing round pegs from being put into square holes. It is sometimes objected that testing of this kind may prevent a person from obtaining a job, and that this is socially undesirable; it should always be borne in mind that this is true of any selection method whatever, and that psychological tests have been shown to make fewer mistakes than any other techniques available. Mistakes there will always be, but the crucial question to ask of course is precisely this: which system minimizes the number of mistakes? Here there can now be no question that the use of psychological tests can drastically reduce this number to a reasonable figure. Of course this method of selection can also be abused; it has been shown that on occasion white trade unionists in the U. S. A. have insisted on the use of irrelevant IQ tests for job selection in order to keep out black applicants, knowing that the mean IQ of blacks in the U. S. A. is something like 15 points lower than that of whites. The use of psychological tests in job selection should always be qualified by demonstrated relevance to the job in question. (*Wallace*, 1976; *Novick* and *Ellis*, 1977)

I will not here discuss any further the practical applications of IQ testing; in part these have already been dealt with in the body of the book (Chapter 4), but in the main we are here concerned with the scientific problem of intelligence, rather than with the applied problem of IQ testing. As a general statement, however, it may be worth while stressing three points which are relevant to the judgement of any scientific advance in its relation to society. Two of these are probably fairly obvious, while the third may require some discussion. In the first place, then it must be said that judgements about the ethical problems posed by scientific advances depend on the value systems of the persons making the judgements; as these differ, so may the judgements made. We cannot expect agreement, and the whole matter is well beyond the competence of scientists to decide. Do the advantages of being able to produce almost unlimited power from nuclear fission and fusion at a time when fossil reserves of energy are running out, more than counteract the disadvantages (uses for military purposes, health risks of radiation, environmental spoliation)? There is no easy answer to questions of this kind, and none should be expected.

In the second place, even the most outstanding scientists cannot predict the possible applications of their discoveries and inventions. Both Einstein and Rutherford, the greatest theoretical and experimental physicists of this century, predicted with absolute confidence that the splitting of the atom would never have any practical, applied consequences – barely a dozen years before the first atom bomb was dropped on Hiroshima! Clearly prediction in even well-understood and developed fields of science is so difficult as to be practically impossible; how much more so is this the case in psychology! Thus we cannot predict what uses may be made of our discoveries, and we cannot easily weigh up the good and the bad consequences even when these are known. Ethics clearly is an uncertain business, as applied to scientific endeavours!

In psychology, however, there is an additional point which muddies the waters and deserves to be treated at some length. Francis Bacon already warned readers against the "idola" which stood in the way of proper understanding in matters scientific; these exist in the hard sciences, but they exist even more in the social sciences. There is a Zeitgeist which welcomes certain results and rejects others, regardless of truth or rigour of investigation; this may lead to the acceptance of erroneous ideas which make proper assessment impossible. One example must suffice to illustrate this point in relation to intelligence testing, and the phenomenon selected is the so-called *Pygmalion Effect.* In 1968, *Rosenthal* and *Jacobson* published a book, Pygmalion in the Classroom, in which they tried to prove that low performance of pupils on IQ tests resulted from teachers' expectations; these in turn would come from considerations of the pupil's race or social class, and other sociological and biological background variables. This hypothesis has achieved wide acceptance, and if true would tend to discredit IQ testing, and with it the whole theory of intelligence supported by so much evidence reviewed in this book. Is the hypothesis true?

What Rosenthal & Jacobson essentially postulated is that a teacher's expectation of what pupils are able to do creates a "self-fulfilling prophecy" which has the effect of actually raising or lowering the childrens' IQs and level of scholastic achievement. Initial differences in test scores, provided they were known to the teachers, would thus become magnified on subsequent testing as a result of teacher expectations, and similarly, such expectations, based on previous experience, preconceptions, etc., concerning the relative abilities of Negro and white children, or of middle class or working class children, should create or magnify performance differences between pupils belonging to these different groups.

Rosenthal and Jacobson had teachers administer a group paper-and-pencil intelligence test to all pupils from kindergarten through sixth grade in a South San Francisco elementary school. The teachers were told that the test was intended "... to predict which youngsters are more likely to show an academic spurt". In September teachers were given lists of such children who were supposedly predicted by the test to be most likely to show an academic spurt during the school year; actually the children were selected by a table of random numbers. Retests of the children were carried out by the teachers in January and May, and the authors' conclusion was that the teachers' expectancies influenced the mental development, as shown by test performance, of the children. This belief has been widely repeated and accepted in educational circles, but the evidence presented in this study itself does not support the conclusion reached. All the major critical reviewers of the study (*Thorndike*, 1968; *Snow*, 1969; *Elashoff* and *Snow*, 1971) have pointed to vital faults and errors in the design and the analysis of the study. The main criticism must be that the data as presented show so many bizarre features that they must be regarded as suspect. For example, in one grade the control group had a mean IQ of 31! Children of such low IQs, i. e. barely at the imbecile level, would never be enrolled in regular classes, and for a whole class to have a mean IQ of that size is simply impossible. Even apart from this, the "prophecy" effects show up in only 19 pupils in two grades, one of which has the control group with the mean IQ of 31. Thorndike commented in his review: "If these present data show anything, they show that the testing was utterly worthless and meaningless". Thorndike's final conclusions are worthy of quotation; he emphasises that the study "... is so defective technically that one can only regret that it ever got beyond the eyes of the original investigators! Though the volume may be an effective addition to educational propagandising, it does nothing to raise the standard of educational research ... in conclusion, then, the indications are that the basic data upon which this structure has been raised are so untrustworthy that any conclusions based upon them must be suspect."

Since the appearance of the book, the expectancy hypothesis has been subjected to proper testing, using appropriate methodology and properly selected controls. The work of *Claiborn* (1969) and *Fleming* and *Anttonen* (1971) may be quoted in this connection. Claiborn found no evidence of the expectancy effect, and Fleming and Anttonen, in what is probably the largest study so far carried out (they used 1087 second-rate pupils in 39 classrooms in 22 schools, representing two socioeconomic levels) came to the following conclusion. "It appears that, in the real world of the teacher using IQ test information, the self-fulfilling prophecy does not operate as Rosenthal hypothesises. We can only conclude that teachers are more sensitive to the functioning levels of students than previously believed, since teachers, in fact, identified the inflated group as less accurate. Recognition of the deception by the teachers suggests that day to day living with the academic performance and behaviour of children, at least for this group of teachers, provides more inputs than the results of an intelligence test administered on one given day." They came to the following conclusion on looking at the total of 9 attempts which had been made to replicate the *Rosenthal* and *Jacobson* (RJ) Pygmalion effect. This is what they say: ". . . it can be seen that of 9 studies (other than RJ) attempting to demonstrate teacher expectancy effects on IQ, none has succeeded. Of 12 expectancy studies including pupil achievement measures as criteria, 6 have succeeded. Of 7 studies including measures of observable pupil behaviour, 3 have succeeded. And of 17 studies including measures of observable teacher behaviour, 14 have succeeded. Thus it seems that teacher expectancy effects are most likely to influence proximal variables (those "closest" in a psychological sense to the source of effect, e. g. teacher behaviour) and progressively less likely to influence distal variables (or variables psychologically remote from the source of expectations). IQ, the most remote of pupil variables, is unlikely to be affected. These results . . . suggest that teacher expectancies may be important and are certainly deserving of study, but they fail utterly to support the celebrated Pygmalion effect on IQ." Readers unconvinced of the worthlessness of the Rosenthal and Jacobson study should consult the evidence quoted; few alleged phenomena in psychology have been so decisively disproved as this. (*Carlier* and *Gottesdiener*, 1935)

It will be clear that a fair judgement of the good and bad effects of IQ testing must be based on sound factual knowledge, and refuse to be influenced by poorly supported if widely known allegations about weaknesses (such as expectancy effects) which are not based on proper research. What is so interesting about the Pygmalion effect is that although it is probably wholly imaginary, yet it is well known to most teachers, and widely believed by them to be an actual fact. Here we have an interesting expectancy effect; teachers expect IQ measures to be affected by their attitudes and beliefs, and hence are prone to believe confirmatory evidence, and disregard contradictory evidence!

In conclusion we may leave behind the applied uses of IQ testing and look rather at some wider issues which face society as a consequence of the accumulating knowledge concerning intelligence. These wider implications were already adumbrated by Plato, in his fable of the different metals quoted in the first chapter. As Plato's discussion in the Republic makes clear, his ideas are based on two major hypotheses or assumptions. The first is that the efficiency, and indeed the ultimate survival, of any civilized society depends on the acceptance of the principle of division of labour – different social functions demand different individual qualities – physical, mental, and moral. The second is that the differences which are so apparent between individuals are to a large extent inborn, although environmental effects are of course also recognized. The first of these assumptions is now almost universally accepted; the second still encounters much opposition, particularly from egalitarian writers who take their cue from Rousseau, Locke, and other philosophers who wrote long before the birth of modern genetics.

The debate about equality, and the mix-up between equality of opportunity (which is desirable) and equality of achievement (which is biologically impossible), have both been documented elsewhere (*Eysenck*, 1973). It is unfortunate that a single word, *equality*, is being used in many different senses; this only confounds an already confused situation. The Greeks, as always, had a word for each of the different meanings of equality; thus they talked about *isonomia* (equality before the law), *isotimia* (equality of human value), *isopolitia* (equality of political rights), *isokratia* (equality of political influence), *isopsephia* (equality of voting rights), *isoteleia* (equality of taxes and duties), *isokleria* (equality of ownerhip), *isodaimonia* (equality of income), and many more. Some of these are possible and desirable, others possible and undesirable; some are impossible and desirable, others impossible and undesirable. Individuals differ profoundly in what they regard as desirable, and no scientific consensus is likely on these points. But such consensus is possible on the problem of possibility, i. e. the influence of biological and genetic factors on equality of abilities, personality, health, etc. It is with these questions that this book has been concerned, and it is suggested that all meaningful discussion of equality must be based on firm scientific knowledge concerning these issues. We have a limited freedom to select from among a variety of courses that which comes closest to our desires; we do not have freedom to select courses which in the nature of things cannot be pursued. Nature sets limits to our endeavours, and in emphasising this point Plato was indubitably right. The exact working out of these limitations is the task of science; the application of this knowledge to society, in line with social values, is the task of every citizen in a democratic country.

One last word must be said concerning the belief held by many people, including some psychologists, that no further research should be done into socially sensitive issues such as the inheritance of intelligence, racial and social class differences in IQ, or educational inequality. Some even go further than that and maintain that such issues are so socially divisive that a curtain of silence should be drawn across all that is known about them, and that psychologists should pretend that nothing was in fact known about them. Unfortunately we cannot make problems go away by refusing to study them, or to discuss such knowledge as may have been acquired already. Victorians refused to discuss sex, or permit scientific studies of it; this did not prevent sex from playing an important part in their lives. Many people refuse to discuss death, but death comes to us all. We will not eliminate the threat of cancer by refusing to talk about it, or study it; quite the opposite. In the same way, psychologists have not *created* the problems posed by the inheritance of intelligence, or the observed differences between races and classes; they have merely given them a quantitative dimension. Problems of differential ability in the classroom were recognized long before modern psychology or mental testing were thought of; witness this moving quotation from the great Swiss educationalist Pestalozzi: "Er ist es, Gott ist es selber, der die Ungleichheit der Menschen durch die Ungleichheit der Gaben, die er einem jeden von uns von innen verliehen, gegründet; aber er hat sie mit väterlicher Liebe und Weisheit unter seine Kinder verteilt, und wir sollen darin mit menschlicher Liebe und Weisheit benützen und leisten, was er mit göttlicher Liebe und Weisheit also gegründet." (Pestalozzi, Rede über die Idee der Elementarbildung.) (It is God himself who gave rise to the inequality of men through the inequality of the talents which He hath bestowed on them; with fatherly love and wisdom He hath distributed them among His children, and we must with human love and wisdom use and accomplish what with divine love and wisdom He hath founded.)

Undoubtedly the facts are somber enough when regarded from the point of view of the high hopes held by egalitarians from Rousseau and Locke onwards; this is no good reason for dissimulating, or burying them in silence. As Rabbie Burns once said: "Facts are chiels that winna ding, an' downa be disputed." (Facts are things that cannot be manipulated or disputed.) On the other hand, from the biological point of view human diversity is an unqualified blessing; it is our safeguard and standby in times of change. How boring and deadly would human life be if we were indeed all alike! I think we must take our stand with Thomas Jefferson, the great democrat, when he said: "There is no truth existing which I fear, or would wish unknown to the whole world."

Epilogue

> Not to be absolutely certain is, I think, one of the essential things about rationality
>
> Bertrand Russell

It is possible, and may be useful, to pull together the major conclusions to which the research summarized and surveyed in this book may lead us. These conclusions are of course not final verities, never to be challenged; they are simply points of view, concepts and generalizations which are supported by the existing evidence, but which might be disproved by experiments in the future. Taking into account this uncertain status (which of course is shared to a greater or lesser degree by all scientific findings), we may list our major conclusions as follows:

1. Cognitive, intellectual performance can be described objectively in terms of concepts like abilities, intelligence, etc.
2. It is possible to measure these concepts empirically, through the use of tests, problems, and questions, and indirectly through psychophysiological measures.
3. The intercorrelations between special types of tests define certain primary mental factors, usually referred to as primary or group factors.
4. Primary abilities correlate together to form higher order concepts, such as fluid and crystallized intelligence; these concepts are defined in terms of observed correlations.
5. Underlying such higher order concepts as "intelligence" there are physiological structures, such as those giving rise to individual differences in evoked potentials.
6. Among major primary factors or abilities thus far demonstrated by research are verbal ability, numerical ability, memory, perceptual ability, divergent ability, reasoning, visuo-spatial ability, and several others.
7. The IQ, as measured by standard tests, can be shown to be the product of three major independent factors; mental speed, persistence, and error checking mechanisms. This "splitting" of the IQ suggests more analytical research designs than have been customary hitherto.
8. Intelligence as measured by IQ tests has a strong genetic basis; genetic factors account for an estimated 80% of the total variance, although this estimate has a standard error of some 5% to 10% attached to it.
9. Intelligence as measured by IQ tests is markedly affected by environmental factors; such factors account for an estimated 20% of the total variance, but this estimate too is of course subject to a sizeable standard error.
10. Genetic factors in intelligence are largely additive, but with a demon-

strable contribution from assortative mating and dominance. This accounts for the fact that the broad heritability is some 10 points higher than the narrow heritability.

11. Primary abilities, when the influence of general intelligence is removed, also show evidence of genetic determination, sometimes with sex linkage (visuo-spatial ability) suspected.

12. Intelligence, as measured by IQ tests, is related to social behaviours, especially as evidenced in educational achievement, determination of social class, and income (earnings). These in turn show evidence of genetic determination, mediated in part through differences in intelligence.

13. The facts summarized above lead to a definition of general intelligence as general, inherited mental ability; IQ tests measure this ability only with a certain degree of inaccuracy, being influenced to a variable extent by environmental factors.

14. The paradigm here outlined is entirely quantitative and scientific; there has been no attempt to deal with so-called humanistic and other idiographic (subjective) ways of attacking the problem. Approaches such as that of Piaget can easily be accommodated within the present scheme.

15. The concepts used in this book are human inventions, like all scientific concepts; they are abstractions which cannot be said to exist or not to exist. Concepts are useful or useless; they cannot be true or false. It is only by this criterion that the theories here discussed should be judged.

Appendix A
The Case of Sir Cyril Burt

Verily, it is easier for a camel to pass through the eye of a needle than for a scientific man to pass through a door

A. S. Eddington

In 1972 Professor Arthur Jensen began to reanalyse data relevant to the controversy concerning the inheritance of intelligence, and among others reanalyse data published by *Sir Cyril Burt* (1966). He discovered (and later published) twenty cases where Sir Cyril had reanalysed twin data and other data several times, adding new cases each time; thus the number of cases included in the analyses differed. However, some of the results (e. g. the correlations between twins) were identical from analysis to analysis, even to the third decimal. This is so unlikely as to be practically impossible. As Jensen says: "Any particular instance of an invariant r despite a changed N can be rationalised as being not too improbable. But 20 such instances unduly strain the laws of chance and can only mean error, at least in some cases. But error there surely must be." (*Jensen,* 1974.) Jensen concluded that for further analysis and theory-testing, Burt's data could no longer be relied upon. They had to be rejected as useless, a conclusion which it is diffult to fault. Jensen did not suggest that Burt's data were in any sense faked or fraudulently obtained; he simply suggested error or possible carelessness.

What were the reasons for these errors? Jensen writes as follows: "The reporting of kinship correlations at times with and at times without noting the sample size, the rather inconsistent reporting of sample sizes, the higher than ordinary rate of misprints in Burt's published tables . . . and the quite casual description of the tests and the exact procedures and methods of data analysis all stand in quite strange and marked contrast to the theoretical aspects of Burt's writings in this field, which were elegantly and meticulously composed, with profound erudition and impressive technical sophistication. It is almost as if Burt regarded the actual data as merely and incidental backdrop for the illustration of the theoretical issues in quantitative genetics, which, to him, seemed always to hold the centre of the stage."

This is well said, and probably suggests the right explanation. One must bear in mind that at the time of data collection and calculation, standards of evidence were less strict than today. Furthermore, Sir Cyril did not regard his data so much as proving a case which most psychologists at the time would have considered as proven already, but rather as being used to illustrate new methods of analysis which he was putting forward, and which marked a great improvement on methods previously used. He was thus more concerned with the didactic elements in his papers rather than with the substantive ones. This may in part explain, although it does not excuse, his apparent carelessness in the treatment of data.

The question of whether, in addition to treating his data with almost criminal carelessness, Burt actually faked at least some of these data is still unresolved. Some eminent experts, like Jensen, have concluded that the evidence is insufficient; others, equally eminent (e. g. A. D. B. Clarke, Anne Clarke, and J. Tizard) believe that the case is proven. Professor L. Hearnshaw is preparing a biography of Burt, and is in possession of all the written and verbal evidence; until the appearance of his book it is probably best to avoid further speculation on this point. Perhaps it is best to remember the first principle of English justice, namely that the accused should be presumed innocent until *proven* guilty. Such proof is obviously difficult, particularly when the accused is no longer with us; nevertheless the possibility cannot be ruled out that circumstantial evidence may in due course be sufficiently strong to require us to return a different verdict. Investigations currently going on suggest that Burt was certainly guilty of same depree of deception; whether this amounts to actual "faking" of data is another question (*Dorfman,* 1978).

What is important to consider is the degree to which the exclusion of Burt's data makes any difference to the conclusions which we may draw from the remaining evidence on the genetic contribution of phenotypic IQ differences. In this book we have looked at the evidence that remains, and find that the conclusions to be drawn are not materially affected by this exclusion of Burt's data. The same conclusion was drawn by *Rimland* and *Munsinger* (1977), when they plotted the position of Burt's averaged results in a diagram made up from the results of almost 100 studies of twins, family relations, and adoption results. It is clear that Burt's results are very similar to those reported by numerous other workers, and that while in their time they were of considerable importance, at the moment they are not needed to buttress the case for heredity as a major determinant of IQ differences.

Appendix B

The Mathematical Basis of Factor Analysis

Et harum scientarum porta et clavis est Mathematica.
(Mathematics is the door and the key to the sciences.)

Roger Bacon

The basic equation of factor analysis may be stated as follows:

$$X = AF + A_u F_u \tag{1}$$

where X is an m x n data (score) matrix having m variables and n subjects, A is the m x k factor pattern matrix having k common factors, and F denotes the k x n common factor score matrix. A_u is the m x m unique factor matrix, F_u the m x n unique factor score matrix. The factor analytic model states that a given data matrix X can be analyzed according to equation 1, with $k < m$, the rows of the supermatrix

$$F \equiv \left(F_u^F \right) \tag{2}$$

being linearly independent (i. e. F being of rank $k + m$), and A_u being a diagonal matrix. This being the case, the Gramian matrix of the row vectors of X is solely a function of the k common factors. If we now normalize the row vectors of Equation 2, assigning to them length n, then we obtain the generalized Garnett equation for the case of orthogonal unique factors:

$$\frac{1}{n} XX' = AC_f A' + A_u^2 \tag{3}$$

where $C_f \equiv \frac{1}{n} FF'$. The way data are scaled does not affect the application of this model to data matrices, and if the scores are in standard form, the left-hand side of Equation 3 becomes the matrix of test intercorrelations, C_f, the matrix of common factor intercorrelations, and $I - A_u^2 = H^2$ denotes the diagonal matrix of test communalities.

In determining the number of factors to be extracted the Guttman criterion is widely used. According to this, the number s of eigenvalues of the correlation matrix (with unities in the principal diagonal) equal to or greater than one is the lower bound to the number k of common factors

$$s \leqslant k \tag{4}$$

if s is the number of eigenvalues δ of R fulfilling

$$\delta \geqslant 1. \tag{5}$$

Other criteria are available, and the Guttman criterion is not universally used by factor analysts nowadays.

The model assumes that a set of m variables can be decomposed into k common factors and m unique factors, all $k + m$ factors being linearly independent vectors, and the k common factors being in addition orthogonal to the m unique factors. (In Thurstone's model we actually need, in addition to the k common factors, m error factors and m specific factors, making a total of $k + 2m$ linearly independent factors.) These restrictions make the common factors uncontaminated by errors of measurement, but unfortunately this property of the common factors is lost when the restrictions are violated as they may be (and often are), e. g. when the row vectors of X cease to be linearly independent, or when unique variance components are correlated between variables.

Appendix C

Algorithm for Speed – Persistence – Error Theory of Intelligence (SPET)

After *White* (1973b)

> I often say that when you can measure what you are speaking about, and express it in numbers, you know something about it; but when you cannot measure it, when you cannot express it in numbers, your knowledge is of a meagre and unsatisfactory kind
>
> William Thomson (Lord Kelvin)

A set of n problems has been administered to each of N subjects, problems being indexed by the subscript j and subjects by the subscript i. Having been presented with problem j, subject i responds after some time $T_{ji} = t_{ji}$, either by putting forward an attempt at solution, which may be either correct or incorrect, or by abandoning it. We define the observed data in terms of the following relationships; these define the data to which a model requires to be fitted.

$$X_{ji} = x_{ji} = \begin{cases} 1, \text{ correct response} \\ 0, \text{ otherwise} \end{cases} \quad (1)$$

$$Y_{ji} = y_{jl} = \begin{cases} 1, \text{ abandoned} \\ 0, \text{ otherwise} \end{cases} \quad (2)$$

$$T_{ji} = t_{ji} = \quad \text{response time} \quad (3)$$

We next list the unobserved quantities of the model, and state some constraints imposed on them. For each subject, we assume three unobservable random variables: s_i (speed), p_i (persistence), and a_i (accuracy.) For each problem, we assume two unknown parameters: d_j (difficulty level) and D_j (discriminating power.) It is assumed that speed, accuracy, persistence, and discriminating power are all positive quantities, and that speed has an upper limit of unity. These constraints are stated formally in equations (4) to (7)

$$\left.\begin{matrix} a_i, p_i > 0 \quad (4) \\ 0 < s_i < 1 \quad (5) \end{matrix}\right\} \quad i = 1, 2, \ldots, \text{N}$$

$$\left.\begin{matrix} D_j > 0 \quad (6) \\ -\infty < d_j < +\infty \quad (7) \end{matrix}\right\} \quad j = 1, 2, \ldots, \text{n}$$

The aim is to develop a mathematical function which will express the probability of observed X_{ji}, Y_{ji} combinations (given the observed response time) as a function of the speed, persistence and accuracy of the subject, and of the difficulty level and discriminating power of the problems. In order to do this, we next introduce the concept of effective ability, θ_{ji}. This is defined in equation (8):

$$\theta_{ji} = a_i[1 - \exp(-s_i t_{ji})] \tag{8}$$

The role played by speed in equation (8) can be seen more clearly if we look at the rate of change of θ_{ji} with respect to t_{ji}. To do this we take the derivative with respect to t_{ji} of equation (8). In differential equation (9), the numerator is the rate of change with respect to time, and the denominator is the amount of change still possible. Thus θ_{ji} grows towards a_i at "rate" s_i, but the "rate" is a relative growth rate. The speed parameter in equation (8) is the growth rate relative to the amount of growth still possible

$$s_i = \frac{d\theta_{ji}/dt_{ji}}{(a_i - \theta_{ji})} \tag{9}$$

We next introduce the cumulative logistic function, defined in equation (10). We shall use the cumulative logistic function rather than the cumulative normal because the former is computationally more convenient, and because its use tends in general to lead to more simple mathematical relationships.

$$\Phi[z] = \frac{1}{1 + e^{-z}} = \frac{e^z}{1 + e^z}. \tag{10}$$

Equations (11) and (12) now follow; these are the two main equations of the model (*White,* 1973a, 1973b.) (In these equations, we use the symbol ω_i; for a vector of subject variables for subject i. Thus, $\omega_i = \{a_i, s_i, p_i\}$.).

$$\Pr[X_{ji} = 1 \mid Y_{ji} = 0, T_{ji} = t_{ji}; \omega_i] = \Phi[D_j(\theta_{ji} - d_j)] = \alpha_{ji} \tag{11}$$

$$\Pr[Y_{ji} = l \mid T_{ji} = t_{ji}; \omega_i] = \Phi[c(t_{ji} - p_i)] = \beta_{ji} \tag{12}$$

These equations may be taken with the well-known "law of compound probabilities", and the assumption of "local independence", to give equations (13–15).

$$\Pr[X_{ji} = 0, Y_{ji} = 0 \mid T_{ji} = t_{ji}, \omega_i] = (1 - \alpha_{ji})(1 - \beta_{ji}) \tag{13}$$

$$\Pr[X_{ji} = 0, Y_{ji} = 1 \mid T_{ji} = t_{ji}; \omega_i] = \beta_{ji} \tag{14}$$

$$\Pr[X_{ji} = 1, Y_{ji} = 0 \mid T_{ji} = t_{ji}; \omega_i] = \alpha_{ji}(1 - \beta_{ji}) \tag{15}$$

As indicated above, if the subject abandons the problem he cannot give a correct response. Tus the event $X_{ji} = 1$, Y_{ji} cannot occur. Mathematically we say that the event occurs with probability zero.

These equations can be combined to form equation (16), which highlights the relationships between this model and the two-parameter logistic model of *Birnbaum* (1968).

$$\Pr[X_{ji} = x_{ji}, Y_{ji} = y_{ji} \mid T_{ji} = t_{ji}; \omega_i]$$
$$= \alpha_{ji}^{x_{ji}}(1-\alpha_{ji})^{1-x_{ji}-y_{ji}}\beta_{ji}^{y_{ji}}(1-\beta_{ji})^{1-y_{ji}}(1-x_{ji}y_{ji}) = L_{ji} \quad (16)$$

For each subject we have observed x_{ji}, y_{ji}, t_{ji} for each of the n problems, and in equation (16) we have given the probability for the event $\{X_{ji} = x_{ji}, Y_{ji} = y_{ji}\}$ given that $T_{ji} = t_{ji}$. Formula (17) now gives the probability for the simultaneous occurrence of the n events $(\{X_{ji} = x_{ji}, Y_{ji} = y_{ji}\}, j = 1,n)$ given that $\{T_{ji} = t_{ji}, j = 1, 2, \ldots n\}$.

$$\Pr[X_{1i} = x_{1i}\, Y_{1i} = y_{1i}, X_{2i} = x_{2i}, Y_{2i} = Y_{2i} \ldots,$$
$$\ldots, X_{ni} = x_{ni}, Y_{ni} = y_{ni} \doteq T_{1i} = t_{1i}, T_{2i}, \ldots, T_{ni} = t_{ni}; \omega_i]$$
$$= \prod_{j=1}^{n} \mathrm{L}_{\mathrm{ji}} = \mathrm{L}_{\mathrm{i}} \quad (17)$$

We may interpret equation (17) in either of two ways. We may say "making the usual assumption of local independence, equation (17) follows directly." Alternatively, we may just state equation (17) and regard it as a definition of local independence. In either event, equation (17) stands as the joint probability of the n response-pairs $\{x_{ji}, y_{ji}\}$ for subject i.

Finally, if we assume independent sampling across subjects we may write equation (18).

$$L = \prod_{j=1}^{n} \prod_{i=1}^{N} L_{ji} = \prod_{i=1}^{N} L_i \quad (18)$$

L is the likelihood of the set of response patterns of N different subjects to the same set of n items, expressed as a function of the $3nN$ observed quantities $\{x_{ji}, y_{ji}, t_{ji}\}$: $j = 1, 2, \ldots, n$; $i = 1, 2, \ldots, N$; of the $3N$ unobservable subject variables $\{s_i, p_i, a_i\}$, $i = 1, 2, \ldots, N$; and of the $2n$ unobservable problem parameters $\{d_j, D_j\}$, $j = 1, 2, \ldots, n$.

The likelihood function defined in equation (18) provides a basis for the computation of joint maximum likelihood estimates of the unobservable subject variables and of the unobservable problem parameters.

References

Introduction

Aleksander, I.: The Human Machin. London: Georgi Publishing Company 1977
Baker, J. R.: Race. London: Oxford University Press 1974
Bashi, J.: Effects of inbreeding on cognitive performance. Nature *226,* 440–442 (1977)
Butcher, H. J.: Human Intelligence: Its nature and assessment. London: Methuen 1968
Cattell, R. B.: The multiple abstract variance analysis equations and solutions for nature-nuture research on continuous variables. Psychol. Rev. *67,* 353–372 (1960)
Cattell, R. B.: Abilities, Their Structure, Growth, and Action. Boston: Houghton Mifflin 1971
Elcock, E. W. & Michie, D. (Eds.): Machine Intelligence. London: Johan Wiley & Sons 1977
Elliott, C., Pearson, L., Murray, D.: The British Intelligence Scale: Final Report before Standardization, 1975–1976. Occasional Papers of the Division of Educational and Child Psychology of the British Psychological Society *10,* (1976)
Eysenck, H. J. The measurement of intelligence. Lancaster: Medical and Technical Publishing Co. 1973a
Eysenck, H. J. The Inequality of Man. London: Temple Smith 1973b
Eysenck, H. J. The Measurement of Personality. Lancaster: Medical and Technical Publishing Co. 1976
Eysenck, H. J.: The case of Sir Cyril Burt. Encounter *48,* 19–24 (1977)
Fisher, R. A.: The correlation between relatives on the supposition of Mendelian inheritance. Trans. R. Soc. [Gotinburgh] *52,* 339–433 (1918)
Franzen, U., Merz, F.: Einfluss des Verbalisierens auf die Leistung bei Intelligenzprüfungen: Gene Untersuchungen. Z. Entwicklungspsychol. Pädagog. Psychol. *8,* 117–134 (1976)
Fulker, D.: The science and politics of I.Q. Am. J. Psychol. *88,* 505–519 (1975)
Hebert, J-P.: Race et Intelligence. Paris: Copernic 1977
Horn, J. L., Knapp, J. R.: On the subjective character of the empirical base of Guiford's structure-of-intellect model. Psychol. Bull. 33–43 (1973)
Jensen, A. R.: Genetics and Education. London: Harper and Row 1972
Jensen, A. R.: Genetics and Education. New York: Harper and Row 1972
Jensen, A. R.: Kinship correlations reported by Sir Cyril Burt. Behav. Genet. *4,* 1–28 (1974)
Jerison, H. J.: Evolution of the Brain and Intelligence. London: Academic Press 1973
Jinks, J. L., Fulker, D. W.: Comparison of the biometrical genetical, MAVA, and classical approaches to the analysis of human behavior. Psychol. Bull. *73,* 311–349 (1970)
Kamin, L. J.: The Science and Politics of IQ. New York: John Wiley 1974
Kuhn, T. S. Second thoughts on paradigms. In: F. Suppe, op. cit., 1974
Lloyd-Still, J. D. (Ed.): Malnutrition and Intellectual Development. Lancaster: Medical & Techn. Publications 1976
Loehlin, J. C., Lindzey, G & Spuhler, J. N.: Race differences in Intelligence. San Francisco: W. H. Freeman, 1975.
Mcaskie, M. & Clarke, A. M.: Parent-offspring resemblance in intelligence: theories and evidence. Br. J. Psychol. *67,* 243–273 (1976)
Matarazzo, J. D.: Wechsler's Measurement and Appraisal of Adult Intelligence (5th Ed.). Baltimore: Williams and Wilkins 1972
Mather, K., Jinks, J. L. Biometrical Genetics. London: Chapman & Hall 1971
Medvedev, Z. A. The Rise and Fall of T. D. Lysenko. London: Columbia University Press 1969
Merz, F.: Der Einfluss des Verbalisierens auf die Leistung bei Intelligenzaufgaben. Z. Exp. Angew. Psychol. *16,* 114–137 (1969)

Merz, F. & Stelzl, I.: Modellvorstellungen über die Entwicklung der Intelligenz in Kindheit und Jugend. Z. Entwicklungspsychologie und Pädagogische Psychol. *5*, 153–166 (1973)
Munsinger, H.: Children's resemblances to their biological and adopting parents in two ethnic groups. Behav. Genetics *5*, 239–254 (1975)
Oliverio, A. (Ed.): Genetics, Environment and Intelligence. North Holland: Elsevier 1977
Perry, N. V., McCoy, J. G., Cunningham, W. R., Falgout, J. C. & Street, J.: Multivariate visual evoked response correlates of intelligence. *Psychophysiology 13*, 323–329 (1976)
Resnick, L. B. (Ed.): The Nature of Intelligence. Hillside, N. J.: Lawrence Erlbaum Assoc. 1976
Rutter, M. & Madge, N.: Cycles of Disadvantage. London: Heinemann 1976
Sanderson, A., Laycock, P. J., MacCulloch, H. & Girling, A.: Morphological jaw differences in mentally subnormal and normal adult males. J. Biosoc. Sci. *7*, 393–410 (1975
Shucard, D., Horn, J. L.: Evoked potential amplitude change related to intelligence and arousal. *Psychophysiology 10*, 445–452 (1973)
Stenhouse, D.: The Evolution of Intelligence. London: George Allen & Unwin 1973
Sternberg, R. J.: Intelligence, Information Processing, and Analogical Reasoning. Hillsdale, N. J.: Lawrence Erlbaum Associates 1977
Suppé, F. (Ed.): *The Structure of Scientific Theories*. London: University of Illinois Press 1974
Taubman, P. The determinants of earnings: genetics family and other environments, a study of white male twins. Am. Economic Rev. *66*, 858–870 (1976)
Thorndike, E. L. et al.: The Measurement of Intelligence. New York: Columbia University 1927
Undheim, J. O., Horn, J. L.: Critical evaluation of Guiford's structure-of-intellect theory. *Intelligence: a multidisciplinary Journal* (in press)

Chapter 1

Berry, J. W.: Temne and Eskimo perceptual skills. Int. J. Psychol. *1*, 207–222 (1966)
Bridgman, P. V.: The Logic of Modern Science. London: Macmillan 1927
Cattell, R. B.: Abilities, Their Structure, Growth and Action. Boston: Houghton Mifflin 1971
Eysenck, H. J.: The Measurement of Intelligence. Lancaster: Medical, Technical Publishers 1973
Jensen, A. R.: The nature of intelligence and its relation to learning. University of Melbourne Studies in Education (1978, 107–133)
Lynn, R.: The intelligence of the Japanese. Bull. Br. Psychol. Soc. (in press)
MacArthur, R. S.: Some differential abilities of northern Canadian native youth. Int. J. Psychol. *3*, 43–51 (1968)
Middleton, W. E.: A History of the Thermometer. Baltimore: Johns Hopkins Press 1966
Nelkon, M., Parker, P.: Advanced Level Physics. London: Heinemann 1968
Roth, E.: Die Geschwindigkeit der Verarbeitung von Information und ihr Zusammenhang mit Intelligenz. Z. Exp. Angew. Psychol. *11*, 616–622 (1964)
Spearman, C.: The Abilities of Man. London: Macmillan 1927
Sternberg, R. J.: Intelligence, Information Processing, and Analogical Reasoning: The Componential Analysis of Human Ability. London: John Wiley & Son 1977
Thorndike, E. L., Bregman, E. O., Cobb, M. V. & Woodyard, E. I.: The Measurement of Intelligence. New York: Teachers College 1928
Thurstone, L. L.: The absolute zero in intelligence measurement. Psychol. Rev. *35*, 175–197 (1928)
Valen, L. van: Brain size and intelligence in man. Am. J. Phys. Anthropol. *40*, 417–424 (1976)
Vernon, P. E.: Ability factors and environmental influences. American Psychologist *20*, 723–733 (1965)

Chapter 2

Bashi, J.: Effects of inbreeding on cognitive performance of Israeli-Arab Children Nature, 206, 440–442 (1977)
Bastendorf, W. L.: Activation level, as measured by palmar conductance, and intelligence in children. Ph. D. thesis, Claremont Graduate School 1960
Bignum, H. B., Dustman, R. E., Beck, E.: Visual and somato-sensory evoked responses from mongoloid and normal children. Electroencephalogr. Clin. Neurophysiol. *28,* 576–585 (1970)
Bogan, J. E. and Gazzaniga, M. S.: Cerebral communissurotomy in man. J. Neurosurg. *23,* 394–399 (1965)
Burt, C. L.: The Factors of the Mind. London: University of London Press. 1940
Ertl, J.: Evoked potentials, neral efficiency and I.Q. Paper presented at the International Symposium for Biocybernetics, Washington, D. C., 1968.
Ertl, J. P. and Schafer, E. W. P.: Brain Response Correlates of Psychometric Intelligence Nature, 223, 421–422 (1969)
Eysenck, H. J.: Dimensions of Personality. London: Routledge & Kegan Paul 1947
Eysenck, H. J.: Primary mental abilities. Br. J. Educ. Psychol. *9,* 260–265 (1937)
Eysenck, H. J.: The Measurement of Intelligence. Lancaster: Medical and Technical Publishing Co. 1973
Gatt, P. S., Rossiter, U. S., Galbraith, G. C. & Saul, R. E.: Visual evoked response correlates of cerebral specializations after human commissurotomy. Biol. Psychol. *5,* 245–255 (1977)
Harman, H. H.: Modern Factor Analysis. Chicago: University of Chicago Press. 1967
Humphreys, L. G.: The organization of human abilities. Am. Psychol. *17,* 475–483 (1962)
Lawley, D. N., Maxwell, A. E.: Factor Analysis as a Statistical Method. London: Butterworth 1971
Levi-Agresti, J. and Sperry, R. W.: Differential perceptual capacities in major and minor hemispheres. Proc. Nat. Acad. Sci. (USA) *61,* (1968) 1151
McNemar, Q. Lost: Our intelligence? Why? Am. Psychol. *19,* 871–882 (1964)
Pawlik, K.,: Dimensionen des Verhaltens. Bern: Hans Huber 1971
Schull, W. J., Neel, J. V.: The Effects of Inbreeding on Japanese Children. New York: Harper & Row 1965
Shucard, D. W., Horn, J. L.: Evoked cortical potentials and measurement of human abilities. J. Comp. Physiol. Psychol. *78,* 59–68 (1972)
Shucard, D. W., Horn, J. L.: Evoked potential amplitude change related to intelligence and arousal. Psychophysiology *10,* 445–452 (1973)
Street, W. J., Perry, N. W., Cunningham, W. R.: A factor analysis of visual evoked responses. Psychophysiology *13,* 352–356 (1976)
Thomson, G. H.: The Factorial Analysis of Human Ability. London: University of London Press 1939
Thurstone, L. L.: *Primary mental abilities.* Chicago: University of Chicago Press 1938
Thurstone, L. L.: Multiple-factor analysis. Chicage: University of Chicago Press 1950
Thurstone, L. L. and Thurstone, T. G.: Factorial Studies of Intelligence. Chicago: University of Chicago Press 1941
Vernon, P. E.: Ability factors and environmental influences. Am. Psychol. *20,* 723–733 (1965)
Wechsler, D.: The non-intellective factors in general intelligence. J. Abnorm. Psychol. *38,* 100–104 (1943)

Chapter 3

Bayley, N.: Development of mental abilities. In: Carmichael's Manual of Child Psychology, Vol. 1, P. Mussen (Ed.), New York: Wiley 1970 pp. 1163–1209
Berger, L., Bernstein, A. Klein, E., Eohen, J. & Lucas, G.: Effects of aging and pathology on the factorial structure of intelligence. J. Consult. Psychol. *28,* 201–203 (1969)

Bloom, B. S.: Stability and Change in Human Characteristics. London: Wiley 1965
Burt, C.: Is intelligence distributed normally? Br. J. Statistical Psychology *16,* 175–190 (1963)
Cattell, R. B.: Abilities, Their Structure, Growth, and Action. Boston: Houghton Mifflin 1971
Eysenck, H. J.: Race, Intelligence and Education. London: Maurice Temple Smith 1971 American title: The IQ Argument. New York: The Library Press 1971
Gutjahr, W.: Die Bestimmung von Messwerten durch "Logits". In: Die Messung psychischer Eigenschaften, Berlin: Deutscher Verlag der Wissenschaften 1974 pp. 221–256
Jensen, A. R.: Genetics and Education. New York: Harper & Row 1972
Lynn, R.: The intelligence of the Japanes. Bull. Br. Psychol. Soc. *30.* 69–72 (1977)
Lynn, R.: Selective emigration and the decline of intelligence in Scotland. Soc. Biol. *24,* 173–182 (1977)
Maccoby, E. E., Jacklin, C. N.: The Psychological Sex Differences. London: Oxford University Press 1975
Matarazzo, J. D.: Wechsler's Measurement and Appraisal of Adult Intelligence (5 th Ed.). Baltimore: Williams & Wilkins 1972
Rasch, G.: Probabilistic models for some intelligence and attainment tests. Kopenhagen: The Danish Institute for Educational Research 1960
Rasch, G.: An item analysis which takes individual differences into account. British Journal of Mathematical and Statistical Psychology *19,* 49–57 (1966)
Roberts, J. A. F.: The genetics of mental deficiency. Eugenics Review *44,* 71–83 (1952)
Schaie, K. W.: Translations in gerontology – from lab to life: intellectual functioning. Am. Psychol. p. 133 (1976)
Schaie, K. W., Storther, C. R.: A cross-sequential study of age changes in cognitive behavior. Psychol. Bull. *70,* 671–680 (1968)
Shuey, A. M.: The Testing of Negro Intelligence. New York: Social Science Press 1966
Thurstone, L. L. The absolute zero in intelligence measurement. Psychol. Rev. *35,* 175–197 (1928)
Thurstone, L. L.: *The differential growth of mental abilities.* Chapel Hill, N. C.: University of North Carolina Psychometric Laboratory No. 14, 1955
Tuddenham, R. D.: The nature and measurement of intelligence. In: Psychology in the Making, L. Postman (ed.). New York: Knopf 1962

Chapter 4

Bajema, C. J.: A note on the interrelations among intellectual ability, educational attainment and occupational achievement: A follow-up study of a male Kalamazoo Public School population. Sociology of Education *41,* 317–319 (1968)
Bienstock, H.: Realities of the job market for the high school dropout. In: Profile of the School Dropout, D. Schreiber (ed.). New York: Vintage Books (Random House) 1967
Crano, W. D., Kenny, D. A. & Campbell, D. T. Does intelligence cause achievement? A cross-lagged panel analysis. J. Educ. Psychol. *63,* 258–275 (1972)
Dillon, H. J.: Early School Leavers: A Major Educational Problem. New York: National Child Labor Committee 1949
Embree, R. B.: The status of college students in terms of IQs determined during childhood. Am. Psychol. *3,* 259 (1948)
Eysenck, H. J.: Student selection by means of psychological test – A critical survey. Br. J. Educ. Psychol. *17,* 20–39 (1947)
Eysenck, H. J.: The Structure of Human Personality (3rd Ed.). London: Methuen 1970
Ghiselli, E. E.: The Validity of Occupational Aptitude Tests. New York: Wiley 1966
Gibson, J., Light, P.: Intelligence among university scientists. Nature *213,* 441–443 (1967)

Harmon, L. R.: The higt school background of science doctorates. Science, *133,* 679–688 (1961)
Harrell, T. W., Harrell, M. S.: Group classification test scores for civilian occupations. Educational and psychological measurement *5,* 231–239 (1945)
Hartog, P., Rhodes, E. C.: An Examination of Examinations. London: Macmillan 1936
Himmelweit, H. T.: What to do about student selection – some implications from the results of two selection enquiries. Soc. Rev. [Monogr.] *7,* 1–30 (1963)
Horn, J. L. Donaldson, G. On the myth of intellectual decline in adulthood. *American American Psychologist, 31,* 701–719 (1976)
Jensen, A. R.: Educability and Group Differences. London: Methuen 1973
Jones, H. E., Bayley, N.: The Berkeley growth study. Child Dev. *12,* 167–173 (1941)
Kole, D. M., Matarazzo, J. D.: Intellectual and personality characteristics of two classes of medical students. J. Med. Educ. *40,* 1130–1143 (1965)
Lavin, D. E.: The Prediction of Academic Performance. New York: Russell Sage Foundation 1965
Matarazzo, J. D.: Wechsler's Measurement and Appraisal of Adult Intelligence (5th Ed.). Baltimore: Williams and Wilkins 1972
Matarazzo, J. D., Allen, B. V., Saslow, C. & Wiens, A. N.: Characteristics of successful policemen and firemen applicants J. Appl. Psychol. *48,* 123–133 (1964)
Mitsoff, J.: The Subjective Side of Science. Amsterdam: Elsevier 1974
Montour, K.: William James Sidis, the broken twig. Am. Psychol. 2. *32,* 265–279 (1977)
Oden, M. H.: The fulfillment of promise: 40-year follow-up of the Therman gifted groups. Genet. Psychol. Monogr. *77,* 3–93 (1968)
Price, D. de Solla: Little Science, Big Science. London: Columbia University Press 1963
Staff, Psychological Section, Office of the Surgeons, Headquarters A. A. F. Training Command, Fort Worth, Texas: Psychological activities in the training command, Army Air Forces. Psychol. Bull. *42,* 37–54 (1945)
Stice, G., Ekstrom, R. B.: High School attrition. Res. Bull. *64/53.* Princeton: Educational Testing Service 1964
Terman, L. M.: The Measurement of Intelligence. Boston: Houghton Mifflin 1916
Terman, L. M., Oden, M. H.: The Gifted Group of Mid-Life. Stanford: Stanford University Press 1959
Tyler, L. E.: The Psychology of Human Differences. New York: Appleton-Century-Crofts 1965
Wankowski, J. A.: Temperament, Motivation and Academic Achievement. University of Birmingham: Educational Survey 1973
Yerkes, D. M.: Psychological examining in the U. S. Army. Memoirs of the National Academy of Science *15,* 890 (1971)
Yoakum, C. S., Yerkes, R. M. (eds.): Army Mental Tests. New York: Henry Holt 1970

Chapter 5

Bashi, J.: Effects of inbreeding on cognitive performance of Israeli Arab children. Nature 266, 440–442 1977
Böök, J. A.:Genetical investigations in a North Swedish population: the offspring of first-cousin marriages. Ann. Hum. Genet. *21,* 191–221 (1957)
Burks, B. S.: The relative influence of nature and nurture upon mental development: a comparative study of foster parent-foster child resemblance and true parent-true child resemblance. Twenty-seventh Yearbook of the National Society for the Study of Education *27,* 9–38 (1928)
Burt, C.: The genetic determination of differences in intelligence. Br. J. Psychol. *57,* 137–153 (1966)
Campbell, D. T., Stanley, J. C.: Experimental and quasi-experimental designs for research. Chicago: Rand McNally & Company 1963

Cohen, R., Bloch, N., Flum, Y., Kadar, M. and Goldschmidt, E.: School Attainment in an immigrant village. In: E. Goldschmidt (ed.), The Genetics of Migrant and Isolate Populations. Baltimore: Williams & Wilkins, 350–351 (1963)
Eaves, L. J.: The effect of cultural transmission on continuous variation. Heredity *37*, 69–81 (1976)
Ehrman, L., Parsons, P. A.: The Genetics of Behaviour. New York: Sinauer 1976
Erlenmeyer-Kimling, L., Jarvik, L. F.: Genetics and intelligence: a review. Science *142*, 1477–1479 (1963)
Eysenck, H. J.: The Measurement of Intelligence. Lancaster: Medical and Technical Publishers 1973
Fisher, R. A.: The correlation between relatives on the supposition of Mendelian inheritance. Trans. R. Soc. [Edinburgh] *52*, 399–433 (1918)
Freeman, F. N., Holzinger, K. J. & Mitchell, B. C.: The influence of environment on the intelligence, school achievement and conduct of foster children. Twenty-Seventh Yearbook of the National Society for the Study of Education *27*, 103–205 (1928)
Fulker, D. W.: Applications of Biometrical Genetics to Human Behaviour. In: The Genetics of Behaviour, J. H. F. van Abeelen (ed.). Amsterdam: North-Holland 1974
Herrman, L., Hogben, L.: The intellectual resemblance of twins. Proc. R. Soc. Edinb. *53*, 105–129 (1932)
Higgins, J. V., Reed, Elizabeth W., Reed, S. C.: Intelligence and family size: a paradox resolved. Eugenics Quart. *9*, 84–90 (1962)
Horn et al.: Personal communication reported by Munsinger 1975
Hildreth, G.: The Resemblance of Siblings in Intelligence and Achievement. New York: Teachers College, Colombia University 1925
Honzik, M. P.: Developmental studies of parent-child resemblance in intelligence. Child Development, *28*, 215–228 (1957)
Husén, T.: Psychological twin research: a methodological study. Stockholm: Almquist & Wiksell 1959
Jencks, C.: Inequality: A Reassessment of the Effect of Family and Schooling in America. London & New York: Basic Books 1972
Jinks, J. L., Fulker, D. W.: Comparison of the biometrical genetical, MAVA, and classical approaches to the analysis of human behaviour. Psychol. Bull. *73*, 311–349 (1970)
Juel-Nielsen, N.: Individual and environment: a psychiatric-psychological investigation of monozygous twins reared apart. Acta Psychiatr. Scand. [Suppl.] *183*, 1965
Lange, K. L., Westlake, J., Spence, M. A.: Extensions to pedigree analysis. III. Variance components by the scoring method. Ann. Hum. Genet. *39*, 485–491 (1976)
Lawrence, E. M.: An investigation into the relation between intelligence and inheritance. Br. J. Psychol. [Suppl.] *5*, (1931)
Leahy, Alice M.: Nature-nurture and intelligence. Genet. Psychol. Monogr. XVII, *4*, (1935)
Loehlin, J. C., Nichols, R. C.: Heredity, Environment and Personality. Austin and London: University of Texas Press 1976
Marjoribanks, K.: Socioeconomic status and its relation to cognitive performance as mediated through the family environment. In: Genetics, Environment and Intelligence, A. Oliverio (ed.). Amsterdam: Elsevier/North Holland 1977
Martin, N. G.: The inheritance of scholastic abilities in a sample of twins. II. Genetical analysis of examination results. Ann. Hum. Genet. *39*, 219 (1975)
Munsinger, H.: The adopted child's IQ: A critical review. Psychol. Bull. *82*, 623–659 (1975)
Newman, H. H., Freeman, F. N., Holzinger, K. J.: Twins: A Study of Heredity and Environment. Chicago: University of Chicago Press 1937
Oden, M. H.: The fulfillment of promise: 40-year follow-up of the Terman gifted group. Genet. Psychol. Monogr. *77*, 3–93 (1968)
Price, B.: Primary biases in twin studies. American Journal of Human Genetics, *2*, 293–355 (1950)

Rao, D. C., Morton, N. E., Yee, S.: Analysis of family resemblance. II. A linear model for familial correlation. Am. J. Hum. Genet. *26,* 331–359 (1974)

Reed, T. E., Reed, S. C.: Mental Retardation. Philadelphia and London: Saunders 1965

Roubertoux, P., Carlier, M.: Intelligence: differences individuelles, facteurs genetiques, facteurs d'environnement et interaction entre genotype et environnement. Annales de Biologie Médicales in press. (1978)

Scarr-Salapatek, S. & Weinberg, R. A.: IQ test performance of black children adopted by white families. Am. Psychol. *31,* 726–739 (1976)

Scarr-Salapatek, S. & Weinberg, R. A.: Intellectual similarities within families of both adopted and biological children. Intelligence, (1978) in press.

Schull, W. J., Neel, J. V.: The Effects of Inbreeding on Japanese Children. New York: Harper & Row 1965

Seemanova, E.: A study of children of incestuous matings. Hum. Hered. *21,* 108–128 (1971)

Shields, J.: Monozygotic twins. Oxford: Oxford University Press 1962

Skodak, M.: Mental Growth of adopted children in the same family. The Pedagogical Seminary and Journal of Genetic Psychology *77,* 3–9 (1950)

Skodak, M., Skeels, H. M.: A final follow-up study of one hundred adopted children. J. Genet. Psychol. *75,* 85–125 (1949)

Snygg, D.: The relation between the intelligence of mothers and their children living in foster homes. J. Genet. Psychol. *52,* 401–406 (1938)

Taubman, P.: The determinants of earnings: Genetics, Family and other environments: a study of white male twins. Am. Econ. Rev. *66,* 858–870 (1976)

Vandenberg, S. G.: Assortative mating, or Who marries Whom? Behav. Genet. *2,* 127–157 (1972)

Wright, S.: The interpretation of Multivariate systems. In: Statistics and Mathematics in Biology, O. Kempthorne, T. A. Bancroft, J. W. Gowen & J. L. Lush, (eds.). Iowa State College Press 1954, pp. 11–33

Chapter 6

Belmont, L., Stein, Z. A., Susser, M. W.: Comparisons of associations of birth order with intelligence test score and height. Nature *255,* No. 5503, 54–56 (1975)

Broadhurst, P. L., Fulker, D. W., Wilcock, J.: Behavioral genetics. Ann. Rev. Psychol. *25,* 398–415 (1974)

Bronfenbrenner, U.: Is early intervention effective? A report on the longitudinal evaluations of preschool programs. Office of Child Development, U. S. Dept. of Health, Education and Welfare 1974

Burks, B. S.: The relative influence of nature and nurture upon mental development: a comparative study of foster-parent-foster-child resemblance and true parent-true child resemblance. Twenty-seventh Yearbook of the National Society for the Study of Education *27,* 9–38 (1928)

Cassella-Riedel.: Dokumentation Piracetam. Frankfurt: Casella Riedel 1976

Cavalli-Sforza, L. L., Bodmer, W. F.: The Genetics of Human Populations. San Francisco: W. H. Freeman 1971

Churchill, J. A.: The relation between intelligence and birth weight in twins. Neurology *15,* 341–347 (1965)

Clarke, A. M., Clarke, A. D. B.: Genetic environmental interactions in cognitive development. In: Mental Deficiency: the Changing Outlook, A. M. Clarke, A. D. B. Clarke (eds.). 3rd edition. London: Methuen 1974

Crano, W. D., Kenny, D. A., Campbell, D. T.: Does intelligence cause achievement?: A cross lagged panel analysis. J. Educ. Psychol. *66,* 258–275 (1972)

Davis, D., Cahan, S., Bashi, J.: Birth order and intellectual development: the confluence model in the light of cross-cultural evidence. Science *196,* 1470–1472 (1977)

De Groot, A. D.: War and the intelligence of youth. J. Abnorm. Psychol. *46,* 596–597 (1951)

Eysenck, H. J. (Ed.): The measurement of intelligence. Lancaster: Medical and Technical Publishers, 1973.

Franzen, U., Merz, F.: Einfluss das Verbalisierens auf die Leistung bei Intelligenz & Prüfungen: Neue Untersuchungen. Z. Entwicklungspsychol. Pädagog. Psychol. *8,* 117–134 (1976)

Freeman, F. N., Holzinger, K. J., Mitchell, B. C.: The influence of environment on the intelligence, school achievement and conduct of foster children. Twenty-seventh yearbook of the National Society for the Study of Education *27,* 103–205 (1928)

Fulker, D. W. Applications of Biometrical genetics to human behaviour. In: The Genetics of Behaviour, J. H. F. van Abeelen (ed.) Amsterdam: North-Holland 1974

Gagné, R., Smith, E. C.: A study of the effects of verbalization on problem solving. J. Exp. Psychol. *63,* 12–18 (1962)

Galton, F.: Hereditary Genius: An enquiry into its laws and consequences. London: MacMillan 1869

Gottesman, I. I., Shields, J.: A critical review of recent adoption, twin and family studies of schizophrenia: Behavioral Genetics Perspectives. Schizophrenia Bull. *2,* 260–400 (1976)

Heber, R., Garber, H.: An experiment in the prevention of cultural-familial retardation. Proc. 2nd Congr. Int. Assoc. Sci. Study Mental Deficiency 1970

Hertzig, M. E., Birch, H. G., Richardson, S. A., Tizard, J.: Intellectual levels of school children severely malnourished during the first two years of life. Pediatrics *49,* 814–824 (1972)

Hughes, K. R., Zubeck, J. P.: Effects of glutamic acid on the learning ability of bright and dull rats: 1. Administration during infancy. Can. J. Psychol. *10,* 132–138 (1956)

Husén, T.: The influence of schooling on IQ. Theoria *17,* 61–68 (1951)

Jencks, C.: Inequality: A Reassessment of the Effect of Family and Schooling in America. London & New York: Basic Books 1972

Jensen, A. R.: Educability and Group Differences. London: Methuen 1973

Jensen, A. R.: Cumulative deficit: A testable hypothesis? Dev. Psychol. *10,* 996–1019 (1974)

Jensen, A. R.: Cumulative deficit in IQ of blacks in the rural south. Dev. Psychol. *13,* 184–191 (1977)

Leahy, A. M.: Nature-nurture and intelligence. Genet. Psychol. Monogr. *17,* 241–305 (1935)

Marjoribanks, K.: Socioeconomic status and its relation to cognitive performance as mediated through the family environment. In: Genetics, Environment and Intelligence, A. Oliverio (ed.). Amsterdam: Elsevier/North Holland 1977

Merz, F.: Der Einfluss des Vernalisierens auf die Leistung bei Intelligenzaufgaben. Z. Exp. Angew. Psychol. *16,* 114–137 (1969)

Newman, H. H., Freeman, F. N., Holzinger, K. J.: Twins: A Study of Heredity and Environment. Chicago: University of Chicago Press 1937

Page, E. B.: Miracle in Milwaukee: Raising the IQ. Educ. Res. *1,* 8–16 (1972)

Potter, E. L. Fundamentals of human reproduction. New York: McGraw-Hill, 1948.

Record, R. G., McKeown, T., Edwards, J. H.: An investigation of the difference in measured intelligence between twins and singletons. Ann. Hum. Genet. *34,* 11–20 (1970)

Rutter, M., Madge, N.: Cycles of Disadvantage. London: Heineman 1976

Scarr-Salapatek, S., Weinberg, R. A.: IQ test performance of black children adopted by white families. Am. Psychol. *31,* 726–739 (1976)

Scarr-Salapatek, S., Weinberg, R. A. Intellectual similarities within families of both adopted and biological children. Intelligence, (1978) in press.

Shields, J.: Monozygotic twins. Oxford: Oxford University Press 1962

Skodak, M., Skeels, H. M.: A final follow-up study of one hundred adopted children. J. Genet. Psychol. *75,* 85–125 (1949)

Stein, Z., Susser, M., Saenger, G., Marolla, F.: Intelligence test results of individuals exposed during gestation to the World War II famine in the Netherlands. T. Soc. Geneesk. *50,* 766–774 (1972)
Stern, C. Principles of Human Genetics (2 nd ed.). San Francisco: W. H. Freeman, 1960
Vernon, P. E.: IQ, heredity and environment. Distinguished Lecture Series, University of Calgary (mimeograph), September 1976
Zajonc, R. B., Marcus, G. B.: Birth order and intellectual development. Psychol. Rev. *82,* 74–88 (1975)

Chapter 7

Bajema, C. J.: Estimation of the direction and intensity of natural selection in relation to human intelligence by means of the intrinsic rate of natural increase. Eugenics Quarterly *10,* 175–187 (1963)
Blau, P., Duncan, O. D.: The American Occupational Structure. New York: John Wiley 1967
Cattell, R. B.: The fight for our national intelligence. London: King 1937
Cattell, R. B.: The fate of national intelligence: test of a thirteen-year prediction. Eugenics Rev. *42,* 136–148 (1950)
Cavalli-Sforza, L. L., Bodmer, W. F.: The Genetics of Human Populations. San Francisco: W. H. Freeman 1971
Duncan, O. D.: A socioeconomic index for all occupations. In: Occupations and Social Status, A. J. Reiss (ed.). New York: Free Press 1961
Eysenck, H. J.: Genetic factors in personality development. In: Human Behavior Gentics, A. R. Kaplin (ed.). Springfield, Illinois: C. C. Thomas 1976, pp. 198–229
Falconer, D. S.: Genetic consequences of selection pressure. In: Genetic and Environmental Factors in Human Ability, J. E. Meade, A. S. Parkes (eds.). Edinburgh and London: Oliver and Boyd 1966
Fulker, D. W.: Multivariate Extensions of a Biometrical Model of Twin data. In Twin Research W. E. Nance (ed.) New York: Alan R. Liss 1978
Higgins, J. V., Reed, Elizabeth W., Reed, S. C.: Intelligence and family size: a paradox resolved. Eugenics Quarterly *9,* 84–90 (1962)
Hollingshead, A. B., Redlich, F. C: Social Class and Mental Illness: A Community Study. New York: Wiley 1958
Hunt, J. McV.: Intelligence and Experience. New York: Ronald Press 1961
Jencks, C.: Inequality: A Reassessment of the Effect of Family and Schooling in America. London and New York: Basic Books 1972
Lipset, S. M., Bendix, R.: Social Mobility in Industrial Society. Berkeley: University of California Press 1959
Morgan, D.: The acceptance by problem parents in Southampton of a domiciliary birth control service. In: Biological Aspects of Social Problems. J. E. Meade, A. S. Parkes (eds.). Edinburgh and London: Oliver and Boyd 1965
Oden, M. H.: The fulfillment of promise: 40-year follow-up of the Terman gifted group. Genet. Psychol. Monogr. *77,* 3–93 (1968)
Penrose, L. S.: The supposed threat of declining intelligence. Am. J. Ment. Defic. *53,* 114–118 (1948)
Reed, T. E., Reed, S. C.: Mental Retardation. Philadelphia and London: Saunders 1965
Taubman, P.: The determinants of earnings: Genetics, family, and other environments; a study of white male twins. Am. Econ. Rev. *66,* 858–870 (1976)
Thomson, G. H. et al. of the Scottish Council for Research in Education, 1953: Social Implications of the 1947 Mental Survey. London: University of London Press 1953

United Nations.: Proc. World Population Conf., Rome, 1954. New York: United Nations, Dept. of Social Affairs, 1955

Waller, J. H.: Achievement and social mobility: Relationships among IQ score, education, and occupation in two generations. Soc. Biol. *18,* 252–259 (1971)

Chapter 8

Birnbaum, A.: Some latent trait models and their use in improving an examiner's ability. In: Statistical Theories of Mental Test Scoring, F. M. Lord & M. R. Novick (Eds.) Reading, Mass: Addison-Wesley 1960

Brierley, H.: The speed and accuracy characteristics of neurosis. Br. J. Psychol. *52,* 273–280 (1961)

Cronbach, L. J.: Essentials of Psychological Testing, (3rd. Ed). New York: Harper & Row 1970

Di Scipio, W. J.: Divergent thinking: a complex function of interacting dimensions of extraversion-introversion and neuroticismstability. Br. J. Psychol. *62,* 545–550 (1971)

Datta, L.: The remote associates test as a predictor of creativity in engineers. J. Appl. Psychol. *48,* 183 (1964a)

Datta, L.: A note on the remote associates test, U. S. culture and creativity. J. Appl. Psychol. *48,* 184 (1964)

De Mille R, Merrifield, P. R.: Review of 'Creativity and Intelligence' by Getzels and Jackson. Educ. Psychol. Measurement *22,* 803–808 (1962)

Dunham, J. L., Guilford, J. P., Hoepfner, R.: Abilities related to classes and the learning of concepts. Reports from the Psychological Laboratory, University of Southern California, No. 39, 1966

Eysenck, H. J.: Uses and Abuses of Psychology. London: Pelican Books 1953

Eysenck, H. J.: The Biological Basis of Personality. Springfield: C. C. Thomas 1967

Eysenck, H. J.: The Structure of Human Personality. London: Methuen, (3rd ed.) 1970

Eysenck, H. J: The Measurement of Intelligence. Lancaster: Medical and Technical Publishing Co. 1973

Eysenck, H. J., Eysenck, S. B. G.: Psychoticism as a Dimension of Personality. London: Hodder & Stoughton 1976

Furneaux, W. D.: Intellectual abilities and problem-solving behaviour. In: The Measurement of Intelligence, H. J. Eysenck (ed.) Lancaster: Medical and Technical Publishing Co. 1973

Getzels, J. V., Jackson, P. W.: Creativity and Intelligence. New York: Wiley 1962

Guilford, J. P.: The Nature of Human Intelligence. New York: McGraw-Hill 1967

Guilford, J. P.: Rotation problems in factor analysis. Psychol. Bull. *81,* 498–501 (1974)

Guilford, J. P., Hoepfner, R.: The Analysis of Intelligence. New York: McGraw-Hill 1971

Hasan, P., Butcher, H. J.: Creativity and intelligence: a partial replication with Scottish children of Getzels and Jackson's study. Br. J. Psychol. *57,* 129–135 (1966)

Horn, J. L., Knapp, J. R.: On the subjective character of the empirical base of Guilford's structure-of-intellect model. Psychol. Bull. *80,* 33–43 (1973)

Hudson, L.: Contrary Imaginations. London: Methuen 1966

Humphreys, L. G.: The organization of human abilities. Am. Psychol. *17,* 475–483 (1962)

Lytton, H.: Creativity and education. London: Routledge & Kegan Paul 1971

Porebski, O.: Speed and power in intelligence. Occup. Psychol. *34,* 184–194 (1960)

Spearman, C.: The Abilities of Man. London: Macmillan 1927

Taylor, C. W., Barron, F. (eds.): Scientific Creativity: Its Recognition and Development. New York: Wiley 1963

Thorndike, R. L.: Some methodological issues in the study of creativity. Proceedings 1962 Invitational Conference on Testing Problems, 40–54. Princeton: Educational Testing Service 1963

Torrance, E. P.: Rewarding Creative Behavior. Englewood Cliffs. N. J.: Prentice-Hall 1965
Undheim, J. O., Horn, J. L.: Critical evaluation of Guilford's structure of intellect theory. Intelligence: a multidisciplinary Journal (in press)
Vernon, P. E. Environmental handicaps and intellectual development. British Journal of educational Psychology, *35,* 1–22 (1965)
Vincent, D. F.: Porebski's theory of speed and power. Occup. Psychol. *29,* 193–200 (1955)
Wallach, M. A., Kogan, N.: Modes of Thinking In Young Children. New York: Holt, Rinehart and Winston 1965
Wankowski, J. A.: Temperament, Motivation and Academic Achievement. Birmingham: University of Birmingham Educational Survey 1973
White, P. O.: Individual differences in speed accuracy and persistence: a mathematical model for problem solving. In: The Measurement of Intelligence H. J. Eysenck (ed.). Lancaster: Medical and Technical Publishing Co., 1973
Yamamoto, K.: Effects of restriction of range and test unreliability on correlations between measures of intelligence and creative thinking. Br. J. Educ. Psychol. *35,* 300–305 (1965)

Chapter 9

Alvord, R. W.: Learning and transfer in a concept-attainment task: A study of individual differences. Technical Report No. 4. Project on individual differences in learning ability as a function of instructional variables. Stanford: School of Education Stanford University, 1969
Anderson, J. E.: The limitations of infant and preschool tests in the measurement of intelligence. J. Psychol. *8,* 351–379 (1939)
Bloom, B. S.: Stability and Change in Human Characteristics. London: Wiley 1965, pp. 113–119
Butcher, H. J.: Human Intelligence. London: Methuen 1968
DeLemos, M. M.: The development of conservation in aboriginal children. Int. J. Psychol. *4,* 255–269 (1969)
Dennis, W.: Animism and related tendencies in Hopi children. J. Abnorm. Soc. Psychol. *38,* 21–36 (1943)
Dennis, W., Mallenger, B.: Animism and related tendencies in senescence. J. Gerontol. *4,* 218–221 (1949)
Dennis, W., Russell, R. W.: Piaget's questions applied to Zuni children. Child Dev. *11,* 181–187 (1940)
Eells, K., David, A., Harighunt, R.: Intelligence and Cultural Differences. Chicago: University of Chicago Press 1951
Flavell, J. H.: The Developmental Psychology of Jean Piaget. Princeton, N. J.: Van Nostrand 1963
Fox, W. L., Taylor, J. E.: Adaptation of training to individual differences. Quoted by Jensen, 1970
Gagné, R. M.: Contributions of learning to human development. Psychol. Rev. *75,* 177–191 (1968)
Hofstaetter, P. R.: The changing composition of "intelligence": a study in T-technique. J. Genet. Psychol. *85,* 159–164 (1954)
Inhelder, B.: Criteria of the stages of mental development. In: Discussions on Child Development, Vol. I, J. M. Tanner, B. Inhelder (eds.) London: Tavistock 1953
Jensen, A. R.: Hierarchical theories of mental ability. In: On Intelligence, W. B. Dockrell, (ed.) London: Methuen 1970
Jensen, A. R.: Educability and Group Differences. London: Methuen 1973
Laurendeau, M., Pinard, A.: Causal thinking in the child: A genetic and experimental approach. New York: International Universities Press 1962
Lunzer, E. A.: Problems of formal reasoning in test situations. Monogr. Soc. Res. Child Dev. *100,* 19–46 (1965)

MacArthur, R. S.: Some differential abilities of northern Canadian native youth. Int. J. Psychol. *3,* 43–51 (1968)
MaoArthur, R. S.: Some cognitive abilities of Eskimo, white and Indian-Metis pupils aged 9–12 years. Can. J. Behav. Sci. *1,* 50–59 (1969)
Maurer, K. M.: Intellectual Status of Maturity as a Criterion for Selecting Items in Pre-School Tests. Minneapolis: University of Minnesota Press 1946
Merz, F. and Stelzl, I.: Modellvorstellung über die Entwicklung der Intelligenz in Kindheit und Jugend. Z. Entwicklungspsychol. Pädagog. Psychol. *5,* 153–166 (1973)
Phillips, J. L.: The Origins of Intellect, (2nd ed.). New York: Freeman 1975
Piaget, J.: The Psychology of Intelligence. London: Routledge 1950
Piaget, J.: Les relations entre la perception et l'intelligence dans le dévelopement de l'enfant. Bull. Psychol. [Paris] *10,* 376–381, 751–760 (1956)
Piaget, J.: The Crowth of Logical Thinking. London: Routledge & Kegan Paul 1958
Spearman, C.: The Abilities of Man. London: Macmillan 1927
Thorndike, R. L.: The effect of the interval between test and retest on the constancy of the I.Q. J. Educ. Psychol. *24,* 543–549 (1933)
Thorndike, R. L.: Intellectual status and intellectual growth. J. Educ. Psychol. *57,* 121–127 (1966)
Tuddenham, R. D.: A 'Piagetian' test of cognitive development. In: On Intelligence, B. Dockrell (ed.). Toronto: Ontario Institute for Studies in Education. London: Methuen, 1970, pp. 49–70
White, S. H.: Evidence for a hierarchical arrangement of learning processes. In: Advances in Child Development and Behaviour, L. P. Lipsitt, C. C. Spiker (eds.). New York: Academic Press 1965
Wilson, R. S.: Twins: Early Mental Development. Science *175,* 914–917 (1972)
Zeaman, D., House, B.: The relation of IQ and learning. In: Learning and individual differences, R. M. Gagné (ed.). Columbus, Ohio: Merrill 1967, pp. 192–217

Chapter 10

Beit-Hallahmi, B.: Salvation and its vicissitudes: clinical psychology and political values. Am Psychol. *29,* 124–129 (1974)
Berger, P. L., Luckman, T.: The Social Construction of Reality: A Treatise in the Sociology of Knowledge. New York: Doubleday 1966
Bryan, G. L.: Evaluation of basic research in the context of mission orientation. Am. Psychol. *27,* 947–950 (1972)
Buss, A. R.: The emerging field of the sociology of psychological knowledge. Am. Psychol. *30,* 988–1002 (1975)
Carlier, M., Gottesdiener, H.: Effet de l'expérimentateur, effet du maître, réalité ou illusion? Enfance *2,* 219–241 (1975)
Claiborn, W. L.: Expectancy effects in the classroom: a failure to replicate. J. Educ. Psychol. *60,* 377–383 (1969)
Elashoff, J., Snow, R. E.: "Pygmalian" Reconsidered. Worthington, Ohio: C. A. Jones Publishing Co. 1971
Eysenck, H. J.: The rise of the mediocracy In: Black Paper Two: The Crisis in Education, C. B. Cox, A. E. Dyson (eds.). London: The Critical Quarterly Society 1970
Eysenck, H. J.: The Inequality of Man. London: Temple Smith 1973
Fleming, E., Attonen, R. G.: Teacher expectancy or my fair lady. Am. Educ. Res. J. *8,* 241–252 (1971)
Floud, J., Halsey, A. H.: Intelligence tests, social class and selection for secondary schools. Br. J. Sociol. *8,* 33–39 (1957)
Lasswell, H. D.: Must science serve political power? Am. Psychol. *25,* 117–123 (1970)

Levine, M.: Scientific method and the adversary model: some preliminary thoughts. Am. Psychol. *29,* 661–677 (1974)
MacRae, D.: The Social Function of Social Science. New Haven: Yale University Press 1976
Mannheim, K.: Ideology and Utopia. New York: Harcourt, Brace & World 1936
Novick, M. R., Ellis, D.: Equal opportunity in education and employment selection. Am. Psychol. *32,* 306–320 (1977)
Pastore, N.: The Nature-Nurture Controversy. New York: King's Crown Press 1949
Rosenthal, R., Jacobson, L.: Pygmalian in the classroom. New York: Holt, Rinehart & Winston 1968
Salamini, L.: Gramsci and Marxist sociology of knowledge: An analysis of hegemony-ideology-knowledge. Sociolog. Quart. *15,* 359–380 (1974)
Snow, R.: Unfinished Pygmalian. Contemp. Psychol. *14,* 197–199 (1969)
Stark, W.: The Sociology of Knowledge. London: Routledge & Kegan Paul 1958
Thorndike, R. L.: Review of R. Rosenthal and L. Jacobson, "Pygmalianin the Classroom." Am. Educ. Res. J. *5,* 708–711 (1968)
Tyler, F. B.: Shaping of the science. Am. Psychol. *25,* 219–226 (1970)
Vallance, T. R.: Social science and social policy: amoral methodology in a matrix of values. Am. Psychol. *27,* 107–113 (1972)
Wallace, P. A. (ed.): Equal Employment Opportunity and the AT&T Case. Cambridge, Mass: MIT Press 1976

Appendix A

Dorfman, D. D.: The Cyril Burt question: new findings. Schience *201,* 1177–1186 (1978)
Jensen, A. R.: Kinship correlations reported by Sir Cyril Burt. Behav. Genet. *4,* 1–28 (1974)
Rimland, B., Munsinger, H.: Letter. Science 21st Jan., 195 (1977)

Appendix C

Birnbaum, A.: Some latent trait models and their use in inferring an examinee's ability. Statistical theories of mental test scores, (Chapt. 17–20, Lord, F. M., Novick, M. R. Reading, Mass.: Addison-Wesley 1968
White, P. O.: A mathematical model for individual differences in problem solving, In: Artificial and Human thinking. Chapt. 20, Elithorn, A., D. Jones. Amsterdam: Elsevier 1973a
White, P. O.: Individual differences in speed, accuracy and persistence: a mathematical model for problem solving. In: The Measurement of Intelligence, H. J. Eysenck (ed.). Lancaster: Medical and Technical Publishers 1973b

Index